SQL SERVER 2000

SQL Server™ 2000
Administration

About the Authors . . .

Mark A. Linsenbardt is President of KLS Enterprises, a consulting and development firm based in Las Vegas, Nevada. A Microsoft Certified Trainer and Systems Engineer, Mark has taught classes on SQL Server and other Microsoft products throughout the country, and has authored several other books covering both software products and certification.

M. Shane Stigler is an experienced administrator who has owned and operated several computer-related businesses. A Microsoft Certified Trainer and Systems Engineer, Shane is one of the most senior and well-respected consultants on the West Coast, and has authored numerous books in the computer field. Shane currently lives in Las Vegas, Nevada with his wife.

SQL SERVER 2000

SQL Server™ 2000 Administration

MARK A. **LINSENBARDT**
M. SHANE **STIGLER**

Osborne/**McGraw-Hill**

Berkeley New York St. Louis San Francisco
Auckland Bogotá Hamburg London Madrid
Mexico City Milan Montreal New Delhi Panama City
Paris São Paulo Singapore Sydney
Tokyo Toronto

Osborne/**McGraw-Hill**
2600 Tenth Street
Berkeley, California 94710
U.S.A.

For information on translations or book distributors outside the U.S.A., or to arrange bulk purchase discounts for sales promotions, premiums, or fund-raisers, please contact Osborne/**McGraw-Hill** at the above address.

SQL Server™ 2000 Administration

1234567890 CUS CUS 01987654321

Book p/n 0-07-212616-7 and CD p/n 0-07-212617-5
parts of
ISBN 0-07-212618-3

Publisher	**Copy Editor**
Brandon A. Nordin	Claire Splan
Vice President & Associate Publisher	**Proofreader**
Scott Rogers	Susie Elkind
Editorial Director	**Indexer**
Wendy Rinaldi	James Minkin
Associate Acquisitions Editor	**Computer Designers**
Ann Sellers	Jani Beckwith
Project Editor	Roberta Steele
Mark Karmendy	**Illustrator**
Acquisitions Coordinator	Michael Mueller
Tim Madrid	**Series Design**
Technical Editor	Peter F. Hancik
Jerry Raymond	

This book was composed with Corel VENTURA™ Publisher.
Microsoft is a registered trademark of Microsoft Corporation. SQL Server is a trademark of Microsoft Corporation.

This book is dedicated to the
memory of Robert Samuelson.

AT A GLANCE

CONTENTS

ACKNOWLEDGMENTS

I believe in my heart that the true reason that any author continues to write is just so we get to say thank you to so many different people. Here, in the few words that are invariably found at the beginning of a book, we get to draw attention to people who shine so brightly in our lives. Thank you to the members of the editorial and production staff at Osborne/McGraw-Hill, who worked so hard to get this book done. Thanks also to my good friends Hal Ross and David Ben-Shimon, who provided us with the powerful servers we needed for testing, some good advice, and a little criticism. Thanks Shane, for everything.

The writing of a book takes more than putting down the words. There are always those who take away some of the stress, make the world look a little brighter, and encourage us when we don't think we can finish another page. Thank you so much Craig, for doing all the little things that I was too lazy to finish. Thank you Mom for telling me to sleep, when to eat, and for everything else that gives me hope. Thank you Karl and Dana, for being patient. I know I don't tell either of you this enough, but I love you. Thank you Dad for being my image of strength.

Mark Linsenbardt

A technical writer really has only one chance to thank the people behind the scenes who make the writer's work possible—not just the people who work for the publisher, but also those individuals who have inspired or helped in any number of ways in the writer's success.

That being said, I would like to thank Wendy Rinaldi for making this book possible; Julian Mallin for providing healthy competition for me; and the following individuals for numerous reasons: Jerry Raymond, Wes Jones, Jamie Morrison, Connie Morrison, Robin and Terry Dunlap, Jim Parris, my Samuelson family, Don and Debbie Stigler, and Sharon and Christi Stigler.

I also want to thank my partner Mark Linsenbardt for all his tireless work on this project. I really could not have done it without you.

I would also like to add a special thanks to my father-in-law, Bob Samuelson. Bob passed away during the writing of this book, but his memory will live on for quite some time to come. He was one of the kindest people I ever met, and inspired me to want to be a better person. Bob, you will be missed.

Shane Stigler

CHAPTER 1

Installation

*Check Page 9

This book is written with the experienced network administrator in mind. In order to save time here, and because we are all quite capable of following the simple directions on the screen, this chapter deals only with the base requirements and the important choices that you will have to make during installation. For those who are new to SQL Server, have no fear. The CD that contains SQL Server automatically starts up when you put it in. If you have disabled the auto-start functionality of your CD-ROM drive, you can execute the SQL Server Installation Wizard by double-clicking your mouse on the AUTORUN.EXE file in the root directory of the CD. The wizard is intelligent software and will identify the operating system and software requirements on your system and tell you the order in which you should proceed. Like any other Microsoft product that you have installed, you will have to answer a variety of questions such as installation path, registration name, and server name. Other questions are asked and you can fill them in quite easily. In the text that follows, you will learn about the base requirements for Microsoft SQL Server and the important SQL Server-specific choices that you will have to make during the installation process.

PLATFORM CHOICE

Since Microsoft Windows NT (the operating system required for SQL Server) is capable of running on different platforms, you technically have the choice as to the type of processor on which you would like to run Microsoft SQL Server. Your choices are simple.
You can run SQL Server on the Intel x86-based processor or on Digital Equipment Corporation's Alpha processor.

As you probably know, Microsoft Windows NT 4.0 is capable of supporting up to four processors as it comes, and up to 32 processors in a single server with a customized hardware abstraction layer (HAL). Microsoft SQL Server is capable of leveraging that multiple-processor support and utilizing multiple processors to execute a single task. For example, a large query that would normally dominate a server's operating time can have its execution divided among the installed processors on that machine under SQL Server 7. Since the processors can work together to perform tasks, the addition of even a single processor can tremendously increase the efficiency of your server.

Since processor development moves very quickly, you should evaluate your choices at the time of purchase and take into account factors such as performance, cost, and the availability of compatible processors based on that architecture. Become aware of hardware ability and cost well before the time to purchase arrives. Combining multiple processors at lower levels can sometimes be just as or more effective than a faster processor, and may actually cost less.

Now that you know the type of processors that SQL Server can function on, you will probably want to become familiar with some of the other hardware requirements. Understanding the minimum levels of acceptable hardware are, after all, vital to creating a successful server. As always, research and planning are the keys to making certain that the server you purchased is right for your environment.

Hardware Requirements

As you are undoubtedly aware, software packages typically have a minimum hardware requirement, which must be met in order for the software to function. SQL Server is no different and has its own specifications, which vary depending on your choice of platform. The following table details the hardware requirements for Microsoft SQL Server.

Computer	Intel x86-based computer and compatible systems must be equal to a Pentium 166 or higher. DEC Alpha and compatible systems are also acceptable.
Hard Disk Space	A typical installation requires 170MB of free disk space. Compact installations require a minimum of 65MB. Installing the Management Tools Only option requires a minimum of 82MB.

Memory	The Standard version of SQL Server requires 32MB of memory. The Enterprise version requires 64MB. (Additional memory is recommended in both cases.)
File System	SQL Server can function on either FAT- or NTFS-formatted file systems. (NTFS is recommended.)
Operating System	SQL Server can function on Windows NT Server 4.0 or Windows 2000 in standard version, Windows NT Server Enterprise Edition 4.0 or Windows 2000 in the Enterprise version, and can function in the Desktop version on either of these operating systems as well as Windows NT Workstation 4.0 or Windows 9x.
Additional Requirements	SQL Server 2000 also requires Internet Explorer 5.0.

Remember that the table lists the minimum requirements for running a SQL Server and not the optimal configuration. In almost all cases, for example, more memory will result in a smoother-running server that is less problematic and functions with greater efficiency than one configured with base levels of memory. Additionally, you will always need to have much more available hard disk space than is actually being used for storing the SQL Server program files, because the user databases will consume space as you create or install them.

INSTALLATION—THE IMPORTANT CHOICES

The installation of SQL Server 2000 is a bit different from previous releases of SQL Server, and gives you some choices during the first part of the install that were previously unavailable, referenced differently, or that were performed using different techniques.

Initial Choices

To begin with, the primary installation screen gives you the choice of installing to a Local Computer, installing to a remote server, or installing a virtual server. The following steps will assume that you are installing your first SQL Server and so you should choose Local Computer at the Computer Name dialog box, as shown in Figure 1-1. Notice that when you choose the Local Computer option you are unable to type a server name, and that SQL Server Setup automatically selects the name of your server. You will learn how to install remote and virtual servers later in this chapter.

The next dialog box that you come to is named Installation Selection. This dialog box is where you will choose the type of SQL Server installation you are going to perform. Your choices are to create a new installation of SQL Server, to upgrade or remove components from an existing installation, to maintain a virtual server, or to record an unattended installation file for use with unattended installations later. Later in the chapter, you will learn how to use the features for unattended installations and how to manage a virtual server; for now

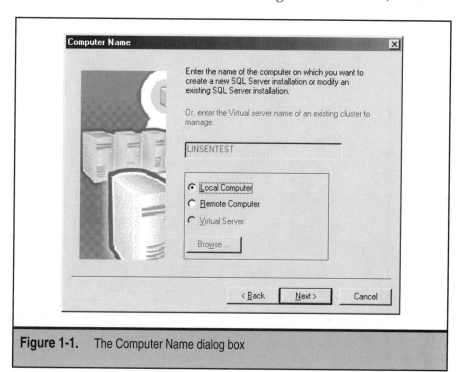

Figure 1-1.   The Computer Name dialog box

you should choose to create a new installation of SQL Server. You will then be prompted for your name and company info, followed by the Licensing screen. After affirming your license agreement, you are presented with the Installation Definition dialog box, which is shown in Figure 1-2. This dialog box gives you the following choices:

▼ **Client Tools Only**   Installs the network libraries, data access components, and management tools for SQL Server. Choose Client Tools Only if you intend to use this computer to manage an existing SQL Server remotely.

■ **Server And Client Tools**   Performs a complete installation of SQL Server. This is the default option.

▲ **Connectivity Only**   Installs the network libraries and Microsoft data access components, but no management tools. Use this selection if the computer you are installing on must participate in SQL Server communication, but will not house a server or be used for management purposes.

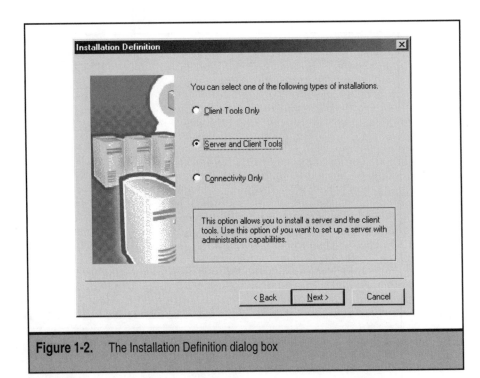

Figure 1-2.   The Installation Definition dialog box

You should choose Server and Client Tools to create a complete SQL Server installation. The next screen displayed is the Instance Name dialog box. This dialog box is present due to a new feature in SQL Server 2000, which lets you install multiple instances of SQL Server on the same computer. When you do this, each installation of SQL Server is called a *named instance*. Later in this chapter, we will discuss the advantages to installing multiple instances of SQL Server; for now, simply leave the default checkbox selected and move on.

Having selected a default instance, Setup will display the Setup Type dialog box, which lets you choose from Typical, Minimum, or Custom installation. This is a common dialog box for Microsoft Products and does not require an explanation, though you should note that Minimum and Typical installations do not let you make advanced choices such as character set and sort order. For your first installation, you should choose a Custom installation so that you can see the choices displayed. Note that if you choose not to change anything during the custom install, you will have the same results as a Typical installation. The Setup Type dialog box also lets you choose the path for installation files, as you can see in Figure 1-3.

Having chosen to do a Custom install, you will next be prompted to select components for your install. We recommend that you make no changes here, since the selections already made are the most common components, leaving out only those components required for advanced design and development, which is outside the scope of this book.

Service Account Selection

One of the more important choices you can make during installation is how to install the SQL Server Services. These choices are made in the Services Accounts dialog box shown in Figure 1-4.

You use this dialog box to designate the Windows NT account that SQL Server services will logon with. This choice is very important because not all accounts are created equal. In order to achieve the greatest flexibility with your server, you must choose a global domain user account as the account type because both system

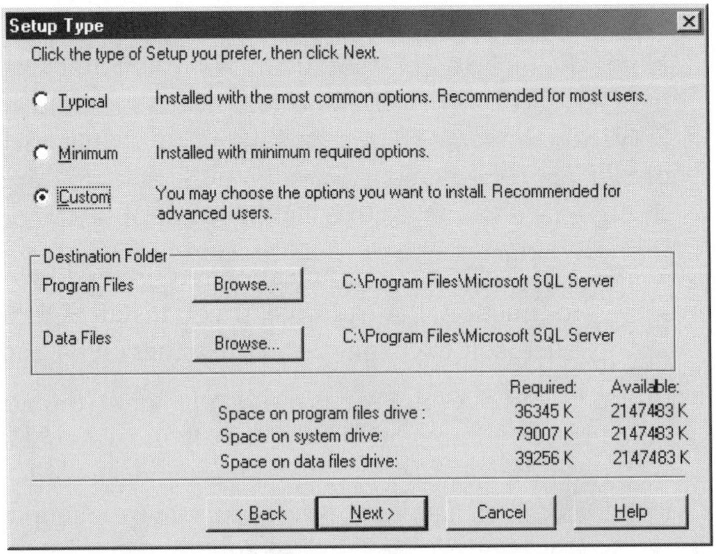

Figure 1-3.   The Setup Type dialog box

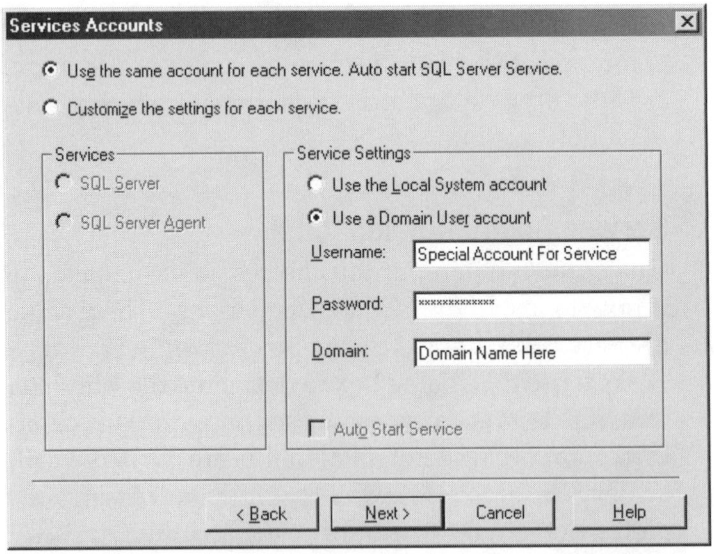

Figure 1-4.   The Services Accounts dialog box

and local user accounts are unable to cross domains. You should create a new account and use that account for all SQL Server services. You should never use the Administrator account as a service account because the normal changing of the Administrator password will affect your installation, and at a minimum, increase your management workload when changing passwords. Consider the following when choosing a services account.

▼ Inter-service communication requires a domain user account to function. For example, if you install SQL Server and Microsoft Exchange Server together on the same machine and want the services to communicate with each other, you must use a domain user account. The same functionality is produced in Windows 2000, though the storage of users and their rights is handled differently.

■ Using SQL Server to send notifications through e-mail requires a domain user account. Notifications and other types of mail usage is best enabled using Microsoft Exchange Server, which is most functional when using a domain user account.

■ Multiserver jobs require a domain user account.

■ A domain user account must either be a member of the local Administrators group on the machine or be a member of the SYSADMIN role in SQL Server.

▲ If you want communication and functionality to span multiple domains, you must use a global domain user account.

The experienced administrator will create the account before starting the installation process so that the account is waiting for him or her when the time comes. If, however, you did not remember to create an account, do not panic. You can always start User Manager for Domains over the top of the SQL Server Setup Wizard, create the account, and then close User Manager and proceed with installation.

In the worlds of both Windows NT and Windows 2000, it is very common for certain kinds of software to install themselves as services. Because this method of application design is so common, there are certain properties that are associated with user accounts that require special attention when a service uses the account to logon. The following list contains some general rules that all service-related accounts should follow.

▼ The account should always be set so that the password does not expire.

■ The account should not be set up using an account template.

■ The account should not have any denied logon hours.

■ Administrators should implement a plan for changing the password of system accounts to prevent security breaches.

■ Administrators who have enabled auditing should watch the service accounts as well as user accounts for unauthorized attempts to access restricted areas.

▲ Service accounts should have nondescript names in environments where security is a concern because intruders will look for service accounts due to their high levels of access.

Paying attention to the service account details will bypass many potential problems for you and free up your time for other duties. During installation, you specify the services account from the Services Logon Account dialog.

TIP: You can specify a separate account for each service as an added security measure in high-security environments.

During installation, you can also choose to auto-start or not auto-start services at the time of system boot. This choice depends on your own environment. SQL Server uses a maximum of four possible services at any time but can run on as little as one. Also, you can make choices for only the SQL Server and SQL Server Agent services, but we will discuss the functionality of all four here. The four services and their responsibilities are listed in the following table.

MSSQLServer	This service is the heart of SQL Server and is required in order for SQL Server to run.

SQLSERVERAgent	This service controls administrative features such as scheduling, jobs, and operators. SQL Server can run without this service running but has diminished capabilities.
Microsoft Distributed Transaction Coordinator	This optional service is only required if you are implementing distributed transactions. It is not required in a common installation of SQL Server.
Microsoft Search	This optional service produces full text catalogs and indexes for greater user flexibility. It is not required in a common installation of SQL Server.

You can control the auto-start setting for each of these services based on your own environment. By default, the Setup Utility auto-starts MSSQLServer, but does not do so for the SQL Server Agent service.

The Services Accounts dialog box will let you use the same account for each of the SQL Server services, which is fine for most installations, or you can choose to use a unique account for each service. If you choose to use a unique account for each service, the dialog box will let you choose each service in turn, and specify information for it.

NOTE: You cannot choose to auto-start the SQL Server Agent account from Setup.

Collation Settings

One of the major changes in SQL Server 2000 installation is the elimination of the need to select a character set during installation. Previous versions of SQL Server required you to separately specify a character set or code page (character set and code page are synonymous terms), and in SQL Server 7.0, you were additionally required to specify a Unicode collation.

In SQL Server 2000, you are no longer required to choose a code page. Instead, SQL Server operates using a collation that matches the operating system that you are installing SQL Server on. This new selection is called a *Windows collation* and it includes the character set, sort order, and Unicode collation all in a single designator.

When you choose a Windows collation, you will choose based on the common language of the region that you are installing for. Microsoft operating systems install based on the same criteria and refer to this setting as a *locale*. You will additionally choose a sort order type by selecting all the applicable options from the given list, which includes Binary, Case Sensitive, and Accent Sensitive. For example, if you want to install SQL Server for the U.S. English locale, you would clear the SQL Collation checkbox on the Collation Settings screen and choose the Latin1_General collation designator. For standard installations, you would also select the Accent Sensitive option, but would not select either the Binary or Case Sensitive settings. This would specify that you wanted to store data using the U.S. English locale, in a case-insensitive manner, allowing accent specifications to be included in the storage of data. By excluding the Binary option, you are specifying that SQL Server will store the data using standard dictionary order.

If your server will operate independently, or will replicate with only other SQL Server 2000 servers, these settings will be ideal. However, if you wish to coexist, or replicate with earlier versions of SQL Server, you will have to use SQL Collation settings in order to provide the backwards-compatibility required to achieve error-free communication. Understanding that many organizations will be upgrading to 2000 on a step-by-step basis, Microsoft includes SQL Collation as a support feature enabling you to replicate with older versions. By default, the standard SQL Server 2000 Setup program will select the U.S. English SQL Collation (SQL_Latin1_General_CP1_CI_AS), which is compatible with the default install for earlier versions of SQL Server. We recommend that you leave the default selection as you are learning, and make more advanced choices as your knowledge of SQL Server 2000 increases. In SQL Server 2000, these choices are all made from the same dialog box called Collation Settings, as shown in Figure 1-5.

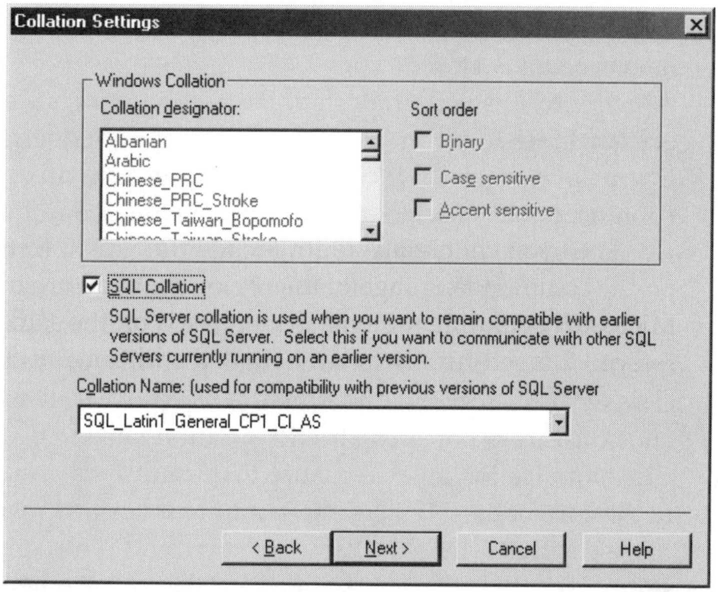

Figure 1-5.   The Collation Settings dialog box

The sort order options are very important and, though you do not specify these options when using a SQL collation, the choices you make when using a Windows collation can impact the performance of your server a great deal. In the following text, we will explore some of the issues surrounding sort order and what things you should take into consideration when making selections.

Sort Order

As you know, part of choosing a Windows collation is specifying the Sort Order options. If you have ever had to alphabetize a list of names, you have the concept of a sort order down pat. *Sort order*, then, is simply the way that the data you are storing gets organized. Another accurate description is that sort order determines the way data is compared, what data is considered equal during comparison, and in what sequence (order) data is returned as a standard query result (a query that does not specify its own sort order). Be careful not to confuse server sort order with the sort order specified in a query. At query level, you are merely determining the way the data is displayed, whereas in server sort order, you are affecting the way data is actually stored.

Sort order is very important because a poor choice here could cause queries to return incorrect data sets from queries. For example, if you have chosen to include case sensitivity as an option, and are running a query to find a list of people named Smith, your result set would include only data that matched the case specified in the query. If you specified "Smith," the result set would return all those entries that matched Smith, but would ignore any entries that had been made as "smith" or "SMITH" or any other variation of case. In order for the case-sensitive sort order to function correctly, well-established rules and software-enforced restrictions would need to be in place at the client application level to ensure that users always entered the data in the correct case. If the same example is applied to a server without case-sensitivity, then the same query would return all examples of smith regardless of the case in which they were entered.

You should not assume, however, that case-sensitive sort orders are a poor choice. Sort orders are chosen for performance more so than ease of design. For example, binary sort order is the fastest and simplest sort order available but lacks conventionality and may return result sets in a manner that is confusing to users. Additionally, many companies that produce and sell applications that use SQL Server as a base choose a specific sort order for internal reasons. The impact of this choice on the administrator is that frequently you will have to ensure that all databases that have been developed in-house are built to use a specific sort order merely to assure compatibility with another database. Most of the time, the database designer dictates the sort order. If you are designing a database and want to know more about sort order choice, please refer to one of the other books in this series that are devoted to database design.

CAUTION: Remember always that any change to the Collation Settings after install requires the rebuilding of all databases on that server.

TIP: You can use the system stored procedure SP_HELPSORT to check or verify the current sort order on any given SQL Server.

Network Libraries

The next dialog box displayed during installation is called Network Libraries, shown in Figure 1-6. SQL Server communicates with client computers using network libraries carried over standard transport protocols such as TCP/IP or NWLINK-IPX/SPX. As you are probably aware, network communication is established by packaging data into specially formatted packets that are sent across the network from one machine to another in a common format that each computer can understand. Inside this packet, there is information that specifies things like destination and sending computer as well as the data itself. One way to look at SQL Server network libraries would be as

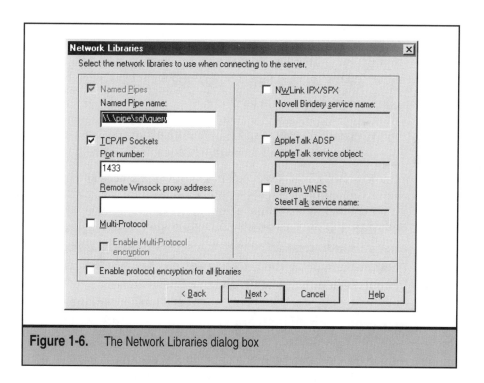

Figure 1-6. The Network Libraries dialog box

pools of code that tell SQL Server how to format its data so that another SQL Server can understand it. The networking components of Windows NT then add additional formatting to the data so that it may actually be sent across the network. In order for the client to communicate with the server, the client's network library must match one of the network libraries installed on the server. SQL Server supports the following network libraries:

▼ Named Pipes

■ TCP/IP Sockets

■ Multiprotocol

■ NWLink IPX/SPX

■ AppleTalk ADSP

▲ Banyan VINES

The Setup utility selects Named Pipes and TCP/IP as the default network libraries for the server, and additionally selects Named Pipes as the network library for client management tools. When choosing a network library, you should especially take into consideration these facts:

▼ Using Windows NT Authentication requires one of the default server network libraries.

▲ Using Windows NT Encryption requires setting the Multiprotocol Encryption option.

SQL Server 7.0 includes two tools for changing the default network libraries. To change the server network library, use the Server Network Utility; to change the client default network library, use the Client Network Utility.

In SQL Server 2000, you can also choose to include protocol encryption for all network libraries. This setting will provide additional security for your implementation of SQL Server, but will slow the performance of the protocols and may impact your server. As a result, we recommend that you do not enable protocol encryption unless you know the impact to your environment. For more information on protocol encryption, see Books Online.

UNATTENDED INSTALLATION

Network administrators have enjoyed the value of automated or unattended installation for some time now. Microsoft products in particular have a long history of including designs for automated install. Microsoft SQL Server 7.0 is no different and is shipped including the ability to be installed automatically.

Most administrators never need the unattended install feature of SQL Server because they only install a few servers and prefer to manage those installs personally. There is, however, a surprising amount of environments in which SQL Server must be installed repeatedly and frequently or on a large scale. In these instances, it can be quite valuable to use the tools that Microsoft provides to create an automated install.

Creating an unattended installation can be as easy as typing a command line, or as difficult as having to customize an installation file for each of your locations prior to running the installation. In order to provide the greatest amount of flexibility, Microsoft included a number of pre-configured Command and Initialization files that control the installation and additionally provide you with the ability to easily customize the files to suit your specific needs. Additionally, SQL Server 2000 includes the ability to record an automated script from Setup. You will remember from earlier in this chapter that one of the choices available during Setup is to record an unattended install file. This option lets you install SQL Server normally, but will record your selections as you install. You use this feature on a test server, making the selections that you will use on the remaining installs, and when finished, you copy the resulting SETUP.ISS file to another location for future use. In the following section, you will learn how to use an ISS file to create an automated install.

The Files

Unattended installation is accomplished through the use of two files, a command file and an initialization file. The command file simply runs a complex command line that reads the processor architecture as a variable and then executes the Setup Utility for the correct processor. The Setup Utility is told by the command line to obtain its variable settings from an Initialization file and then runs in a hands-free mode until completion. The files are divided into sets for simplicity and are included with the SQL Server CD. There are a total of six command files and five initialization files, which are described in the following table:

SQL70INS.BAT with SQL70INS.ISS	Performs a Typical installation of SQL Server.
SQL70CST.BAT with SQL70CST.ISS	Performs a Custom installation of SQL Server (defaults to Typical components).
SQL70CLI.BAT with SLQ70CLI.ISS	Installs the Server Management Tools only.
DESKEINS.BAT with DESKEINS.ISS	Performs a Desktop version Typical installation of SQL Server. This is the file set required to automatically install SQL Server on a Windows 9.*x* operating system.
DESKECST.BAT with DESKECST.ISS	Performs a Desktop version Custom (defaults to Typical components) installation of SQL Server. This is the file set required to automatically install SQL Server on a Windows 9.*x* operating system.
SQL70REM.BAT	Performs an unattended uninstall of SQL Server. You must include the installation path in the command line in order to use this command file.

How to Do an Unattended Installation

To perform an unattended installation of SQL Server you must, of course, first choose the type of installation that you require for your environment. Having done so, you can perform the installation in a few ways:

▼ You can simply choose the appropriate command file for your selection and execute it.

■ You can customize one of the files to better suit your specific needs and then execute the matching command file.

▲ You can create a completely new initialization file and then execute the command manually from the console or command prompt.

Many organizations can use the files that are provided by Microsoft without customization at all. These organizations can do so because the installation type that they require is of a standard nature and requires no customization. For those organizations that do require specific customization, you can create a new initialization file using the Setup Utility as described earlier. Now, the normal way to use this file would be to execute the complex command line that begins the Setup Utility with the ISS file. If, however, you simply change the name of the SETUP.ISS file to SLQ70CST.ISS, you can use the SQL70CST.BAT command file to execute the installation. (This method prevents you from having to memorize the correct syntax for the SQL Server Setup Utility.) You can also manually call to the initialization file by specifying the F1 switch when you execute the Setup Utility, for example:

```
setupsql -f1 c:\ sample.iss -s
```

(The –S parameter sets the installation to silent mode.) As always, you should experiment and practice this technique in a safe environment prior to using it in a production environment.

Systems Management Server—Power Tip
Microsoft Systems Management Server (SMS) can also use the initialization files that you create or copy from the SQL Server CD. Please refer to SMS documentation for more complete directions.

SQL Server Instances

SQL Server 2000 includes the ability to install multiple instances of SQL Server on the same computer. This is a new concept, and at this point is used primarily for testing applications and learning SQL Server. There are basically two types of instances: the default instance, which is the first installation of SQL Server that you have installed, and named instances, which are additional installations on the same machine. The basic advantage of a named instance is that it gets its own unique set of Databases and Users that are kept separate from the default and other named instances. Additionally, you can use the feature to create the same named instance on multiple computers, which can then be combined in a virtual server configuration, as seen in the following section. Other components are either unique or shared by all instances on a server. For more information on using instances, refer to Books Online.

Virtual Servers

As you know, Windows NT and Windows 2000 support the clustering of servers. This technique lets you install several servers and have them work on tasks together as if they were one. Additionally, clustered servers allow you to create a high-response, fail-over scheme that lets one server take the place of another in the case of failure.

SQL Server 2000 supports this feature directly, so you can take advantage of clustering by installing SQL Server as a virtual server. You install a virtual server from SQL Server Setup by simply indicating your choice in the initial setup screen, and then by typing in the identity of the server cluster. Combining servers that are installed as the same named instance on multiple computers will let SQL Server act as a single server spread across multiple physical machines. SQL Server will then be available as a clustered install, and will take advantage of all features of the clustered environment. For more information on server clustering, see any text on Microsoft Cluster Server.

TESTING YOUR INSTALLATION

Now that you have installed SQL Server, you will probably want to take a few minutes and test your installation to ensure that everything is exactly as you want. In the following text, you will be guided through many of the items you should be looking for when testing your installation of SQL Server. You will start by taking a very basic look at the files that were copied, then check out the status of the SQL Server services, and end by testing some of the SQL Server features to ensure that everything works.

The Files

The basis for any software installation and its ability to function is always, of course, reduced to a series of files that are installed on the system. In the case of SQL Server 7, it is not necessary that you check each and every file to ensure that it was copied correctly because the Setup Utility would have almost assuredly produced an error during the copy process if one had in fact taken place. You should, however, take the time to ensure that the correct directory structure is in place and that you did not make a mistake when you chose the installation path. By default, the relational database engine and all of the management install tools are in the C:\PROGRAM FILES\ MICROSOFT SQL SERVER directory. You have the option of changing the drive specification or directory name during installation and should check the installation against your own notes if you did so. In addition to the files that are copied to the SQL Server root working directory, a number of system files are copied to the system root directory in order to provide some of the functionality that the operating system will require in order to run SQL Server.

Take the testing stage very seriously and you will find that many of the problems that take administrators by surprise are avoided. There are many possible problems that can be avoided if care is taken to inspect the installation prior to implementing business databases. Over the next few pages, you will learn what potential problem areas to look for and how to actually look. The wise administrator will take what is learned here and expand upon it, looking with an increasingly meticulous eye at his or her installations.

The Services

As you now know, SQL Server is primarily run through the use of Windows NT services. Upon the completion of install, you will want to manually check that the services you chose to install are in fact installed, running, and configured to either auto-start or not auto-start, depending on your environment's needs. If you want your SQL Sever to automatically start when the system starts or re-starts, you must at a minimum ensure that the MSSQLServer service and the SQLSERVERAgent service are configured to auto-start. Take the time here to actually stop and start the services. Sometimes a problem can be identified while the service is actually starting or stopping, and you will be much better off if you know about a problem before the server is introduced into a production environment.

Just after install is also an excellent time to practice starting and stopping your SQL Server in various modes. For example, at some point you will probably have to start a SQL Server in minimal configuration mode in order to solve a configuration problem such as the over-allocation of memory. Starting the server in this mode can only be done from the command prompt using the –f option. Learning to start and stop SQL Server services from the command prompt before you are in a situation that requires it is generally a good idea for administrators and consultants alike.

Testing in the Real World

Testing an installation of Microsoft SQL Server is perhaps the most overlooked step in successful administration. This is partly due to the fact that Microsoft has created a very thorough Setup Utility, and partly due to the human tendency to assume that we did it correctly. In the real world, some of the most common problems within SQL Server are caused by incorrect settings at the time of install. You should therefore always take the time to test any installation of SQL Server, and additionally perform some of the test procedures that we cover here.

Now that you have ensured that the SQL Server files have been installed where you want them to be and that the SQL Server services are installed using the proper type of account, you will want to connect to the SQL Server. For a Typical installation, you will want to connect to SQL Server in a couple of ways. This will test management tools as well as the SQL Server itself. First connect using SQL Enterprise Manager and register your server name. For the purpose of this discussion, assume you are using Windows NT Authentication. If you were using Standard authentication you would see a dialog box that would let you choose to automatically log on, or be prompted for logon credentials each time you connected. Authentication types and other security issues are discussed in more detail in Chapter 3.

Once the server has been registered, you can subsequently connect to the server by simply clicking on the plus sign found to the left of the server name. When connected, you will see a red mark next to the server name. While connected in Enterprise Manager, take the time to expand and view the databases that are installed. By default, the SQL Server Setup Utility installs six databases:

▼ MASTER

■ MODEL

■ MSDB

■ TEMPDB

■ NORTHWIND

▲ PUBS

During installation, you can choose not to install the PUBS or NORTHWIND databases because they are test user databases that are not required for SQL Server to function. The remaining databases, however (called the *system databases*), must be present in order for SQL Server to provide the functionality that it is capable of. Frequently, administrators will skip this part because they know that SQL Server will not function correctly without these databases, but you should use this time to obtain information from and document the starting condition of the system databases for later use.

In addition to checking the system databases, while you are connected in Enterprise Manager take the time to check the system logins that were created during installation. To view SQL Server logins, click on the LOGINS folder. There should be three logins already present on the server, as seen in the following list:

▼ BUILTIN\Administrators

■ DOMAINNAME\Sqlserverserviceaccountname

▲ SA

These logins were created during the installation process and represent the three most important logins that will ever be created.

The BUILTIN\Administrators group is only present if you installed SQL Server on a Windows NT Server or Windows NT Server Enterprise Edition and also chose to use Windows NT Authentication. It represents any member of the Windows NT local Administrators group and has administrative access on the server.

The DOMAINNAME\Sqlserverserviceaccountname is the login account that the SQL Server service account uses to logon to the server with. You do not use this login for any purpose other than to check its ability to connect, but should be aware of it due to the inherent security risk involved with this account. This login also has administrative access on the server.

The SA login is a default login, which is created for server management. SA is always created during installation and is always created without a password. You should give the SA login a password as soon as you can, and make plans to change the password on a regular basis as a general security step. The SA login is the complete manager of the entire server and has an alias of DBO in all databases by default. This means that the SA login has complete power everywhere in the server.

The three default logins are not created in Desktop installations on Windows 9.*x* and are by no means the last logins you will have to manage in other installation types. Chapter 3 will discuss logins in detail and provide some sound advice on managing them.

Troubleshooting Installation

Every administrator at some point has a problem during installation that must be solved. The primary difference between a good administrator and a poor one is how fast he or she can determine the amount of time that troubleshooting will require. Sometimes it will be faster to find the problem and fix it, and other times it will be much faster to simply re-install the software.

Over the next few pages, you will learn the most common problems that arise from installing SQL Server and how to address them. Also included are some Transact-SQL statements that will help you determine the condition of your SQL Server.

Standard Troubleshooting

The most common problems that occur during the installation of SQL Server tend to fall within the three basic categories of user error, hardware deficiency, and compatibility. While each of these categories contain problems that could be avoided by planning and testing, as an administrator you may have to review problems caused by another person's installation, or you might simply have made a mistake and not realized it. The next few paragraphs will cover each of these areas and what to look for.

User error, of course, refers to the person who installed the server to begin with. Problems associated with user error can sometimes be found and solved quickly, but in many cases are better solved by re-installing the software. To locate and solve a user-error problem within SQL Server, first review the System and Application logs in the Windows NT Event Viewer. Many times problems stemming from user error will result in logged events that will help you identify the cause. The next step is to review all of the possible choices that the user had during installation and ensure that those settings are correct for your network.

Hardware deficiency is very easy to determine and is one of the first things to check if a SQL Server installation fails or produces unexpected results. Manually check all of the hardware in the system using operating system tools, other hardware management software, or physical checks. Compare the hardware against the list of minimum requirements to ensure that the computer meets those requirements. If your sever meets the minimal hardware requirements but seems to have trouble running the server, check to see that all the hardware components were listed on the Windows NT Hardware Compatibility List (HCL). It is possible for a computer running Windows NT that has been functioning normally with hardware not on the list to develop problems with SQL Server because of the increased load.

Compatibility issues most typically result from incorrectly loaded service packs and other software. Compatibility issues are solved by examining the required software and re-installing suspect software. Many times a compatibility issue can only be solved by re-installing the Windows NT or 2000 Server itself, all service packs, and any additional software that is required, and then re-installing SQL Server.

Real World Tips

Now that you have learned what to look for when troubleshooting a SQL Server, let's take a look at the act of troubleshooting itself. There are some characteristics that all good troubleshooters have in common. The first of these is that they do not assume anything is correct. Just because you performed the installation five minutes ago, does not mean that you did everything right. Even if you remember doing it right, check it anyway. Top troubleshooters follow a logical path that begins with the simplest possible problem and progresses in stages to the most difficult. If you begin troubleshooting an installation by looking at the structure of databases when the actual problem is insufficient memory, you will likely spend a lot of wasted time. Master troubleshooters document each and every test, check, or observation as they go. Creating a record of what you did will not only help you keep track of your progress and prevent you from duplicating effort, but will additionally provide you with a valuable document that keeps common problems fresh in your mind and that others can learn from.

When an installation of SQL Server does not produce the expected results, the first thing to do is stop and actually look at the problem. Many new administrators begin looking for causes to problems before they truly understand what is happening, or even follow a troubleshooting list without thinking about the problem itself at all. Once you understand that there is a problem, stop and actually look at the symptom you noticed. Frequently, you will find that just by looking at the symptom, you will discover the problem with little or no further steps required.

CHAPTER 2

System Architecture
of SQL Server

Throughout this book, we will look at specific features of the Microsoft SQL Server engine. In this chapter, we will examine what makes up that engine and how it works. If you are interested only in the functional operations of SQL Server and want to consider everything as a black box operation, you can safely skip this chapter. Here we will focus on what happens inside the engine. We will also point out system behavior that might affect application development and suggest ways to deal with it.

Additionally, the understanding of SQL Server database structure that you will gain herein will help you develop and implement your databases effectively, should you participate in the development process. In addition to architecture explanations, this chapter discusses the types of databases found in SQL Server and also describes two types of structural elements: database objects and system tables.

THE SQL SERVER ENGINE

Figure 2-1 shows the general architecture of SQL Server. For simplicity, we have made some minor omissions and simplifications and ignored certain "helper" modules.

Now let's look in detail at the major modules.

The Net-Library

The Net-Library (often called Net-Lib; in this book we will use the two terms interchangeably) abstraction layer enables SQL Server to read from and write to many different network protocols, and each such protocol (such as TCP/IP sockets) can have a specific driver. The Net-Library layer makes it relatively easy to support many different network protocols without having to change the core server code.

A Net-Library is basically a driver that is specific to a particular network inter-process communication (IPC) mechanism. (Be careful not to confuse *driver* with *device driver*.) All code in SQL Server, including Net-Library code, makes calls only to the Microsoft Win32 subsystem. SQL Server uses a common internal interface between

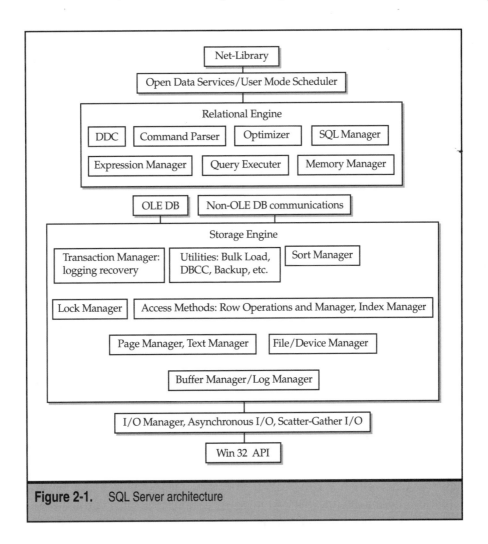

Figure 2-1. SQL Server architecture

Microsoft Open Data Services (ODS), which manages its use of the network, and each Net-Library. If your development project needs to support a new and different network protocol, all network-specific issues can be handled by simply writing a new Net-Library. In addition, you can load multiple Net-Libraries simultaneously, one for each network IPC mechanism in use.

SQL Server uses the Net-Library abstraction layer on both the server and client machines, making it possible to support several clients simultaneously on different networks. Microsoft Windows

NT/2000, Windows 95, and Windows 98 each allow multiple protocol stacks to be used simultaneously on one system. Net-Libraries are paired. For example, if a client application is using a Named Pipes Net-Library, SQL Server must also be listening on a Named Pipes Net-Library. (You can easily configure multiple Net-Libraries using the SQL Server Network Utility, which is available under the Programs\Microsoft SQL Server 2000.0 folder from your Start button.)

It is important to distinguish between the IPC mechanisms and the underlying network protocols. IPC mechanisms used by SQL Server include Named Pipes, RPC, SPX, and Windows Sockets. Network protocols used include TCP/IP, NetBEUI, NWLink (IPX/SPX), Banyan VINES SPP, and Appletalk ADSP. Two Net-Libraries, Multiprotocol and Named Pipes, can be used simultaneously over multiple network protocols (NetBEUI, NWLink IPX/SPX, and TCP/IP). You can have multiple network protocols in your environment and still use only one Net-Library.

On machines running Windows 95 or Windows 98, you can also use shared memory as an IPC mechanism. This is considered both the IPC and the network protocol and is available only for local connections in which the client is running on the same machine as SQL Server. In addition, SQL Server running on Windows 95 or Windows 98 machines does not support Named Pipes as an IPC.

The Multiprotocol Net-Library uses the RPC services of Windows 2000, Windows NT/2000, Windows 95, or Windows 98. It could just as well have been called the "RPC Net-Library," but "Multiprotocol" better conveys its key benefit. Because the Multiprotocol Net-Library uses the RPC services of the operating system, it can encrypt all traffic (including requests, data, and passwords) between the client application and the SQL Server engine.

Both Named Pipes and RPC services in Windows 2000 support impersonation of security contexts to provide an integrated logon capability (also known as Windows NT/2000 Authentication). That is, instead of requiring a separate user ID/password logon each time a connection to SQL Server is requested, SQL Server can impersonate the security context of the user running the application that requests the connection. If that user has sufficient privileges (or is part of a Windows NT/2000 domain group that does), the connection is established. Note that Windows NT/2000 Authentication is *not* available when SQL Server is running on Windows 95 or Windows 98. When you connect to SQL Server running on Windows 95 or Windows 98, you must specify a SQL Server logon ID and password.

Understanding Net-Library's Existence

If RPCs had been available years ago, Net-Library might never have been invented. When SQL Server ran only on OS/2, it supported only Named Pipes. The developers wanted to broaden this support to SPX and TCP/IP and potentially other protocols, so they developed Net-Library as an abstraction layer. Now RPC services are available with so many network protocols that RPC alone might have met the need.

Determining Which Net-Library Is Fastest

Strictly speaking, the TCP/IP Sockets Net-Library is the fastest Net-Library. In a pure network test that does nothing except throw packets back and forth between Net-Library pairs, it is perhaps 30 percent faster than the slowest Net-Library. But for local area network (LAN) environments and applications, the speed of the Net-Library probably makes little difference, because the network interface is generally not a limiting factor in a well-designed application.

On a LAN, however, turning on encryption with the Multiprotocol Net-Library will cause a performance hit—it is the slowest Net-Library option when encryption is turned on. But again, most applications probably would not notice the difference. Your best bet is to choose the Net-Library that matches your network protocols and provides the services you need in terms of unified logon, encryption, and dynamic name resolution.

Open Data Services

Open Data Services (ODS) functions as the client manager for SQL Server; it is basically an interface between server Net-Libraries and server-based applications, including SQL Server. ODS manages the network: it listens for new connections; cleans up failed connections; acknowledges "attentions" (cancellations of commands); coordinates threading services to SQL Server; and returns result sets, messages, and status back to the client.

SQL Server clients and the server speak a private protocol known as *tabular data stream* (*TDS*). TDS is a self-describing data stream. In other words, it contains tokens that describe column names, datatypes, events (such as cancellations), and status values in the "conversation" between client and server. The server notifies the client that it is sending a result set, indicates the number of columns and datatypes of the result set, and so on—all encoded in TDS. Neither clients nor servers write directly to TDS. Instead, the open interfaces of DB-Library and ODBC at the client emit TDS. Both use a client implementation of the Net-Library.

ODS accepts new connections, and if a client unexpectedly disconnects (for example, if a user reboots the client computer instead of cleanly terminating the application), resources such as locks held by that client are automatically freed.

You can use the ODS open interface to help you write a server application, such as a gateway. Such applications are called *ODS server applications*. SQL Server is an ODS server application, and it uses the same DLL (OPENDS70.DLL) as all other ODS applications.

NOTE: Depending on your system and what software is installed, you may find other versions of the OPENDS library file present on the system.

ODS Read and Write Buffers

After SQL Server puts result sets into a network output buffer that is equal in size to the configured packet size, the Net-Library dispatches the buffer to the client. The first packet is sent as soon as the network output buffer (the write buffer) is full or, if an entire result set fits in one packet, when the batch is completed. In some exceptional operations—such as one that provides progress information for database dumping or provides database consistency checker (DBCC) messages—the output buffer is flushed and sent even before it is full or before the batch completes.

SQL Server has two input buffers (read buffers) and one output buffer per client. Double-buffering is needed for the reads because while SQL Server reads a stream of data from the client connection, it must also look for a possible attention. (This allows that "Query That Wouldn't Die" to be canceled directly from the issuer. Although the ability to cancel a request is extremely important, it is relatively unusual among client/server products.) Attentions can be thought of as "out-of-band" data, though they can be sent with network protocols that do not explicitly have an out-of-band channel. The SQL Server development team at Microsoft experimented with double-buffering and asynchronous techniques for the write buffers, but these did not improve performance substantially. The single network output buffer works very nicely. Even though the writes are not posted asynchronously, SQL Server does not need to write through the operating system caching for these as it does for writes to disk.

Because the operating system provides caching of network writes, write operations appear to complete immediately with no significant latency—that is, no significant time expires between the request for a write and the occurrence of the write itself. But if several writes are issued to the same client and the client is not currently reading data from the network, the network cache eventually becomes full and the write is blocked. The previous sentence is incomplete. This is essentially a throttle. As long as the client application is processing results, SQL Server has a few buffers queued up and ready for the client connection to process. But if the client's queue is already stacked up with results and is not processing them, SQL Server stalls sending them, and the network write operation to that connection has to wait. Since the server has only one output buffer per client, data cannot be sent to that client connection until it reads information off the network to free up room for the write to complete. (Writes to other client connections are not held up, however; only those for the laggard client are affected.)

SQL Server adds rows to the output buffer as it retrieves them. Often, SQL Server can still be gathering additional rows that meet the query's criteria while rows already retrieved are being sent to the client.

Stalled network writes can also affect locks. For example, if READ COMMITTED isolation is in effect (the default), a share lock can normally be released after SQL Server has completed its scan of that page of data. (Exclusive locks used for changing data must always be held until the end of the transaction, to ensure that the changes can be rolled back.) However, if the scan finds more qualifying data and the output buffer is not free, the scan stalls. When the previous network write completes, the output buffer becomes available and the scan resumes. But, as stated above, that write will not complete until the client connection "drains" (reads) some data to free up some room in the pipe (the virtual circuit between the SQL Server and client connection).

If a client connection delays processing results that are sent to it, concurrency issues can result because locks are held longer than they otherwise would be. A sort of chain reaction occurs: If the client connection has not read several outstanding network packets, further writing of the output buffer at the SQL Server side must wait, because the pipe is full. Since the output buffer is not available, the scan for data might also be suspended, because no space is available to add qualifying rows. Since the scan is held up, any lock on the data cannot be released. In short, if a client application does not process results in a timely manner, database concurrency can suffer.

The size of the network buffer can also affect the speed at which the client receives the first result set. As mentioned earlier, the output buffer is sent when the batch, not simply the command, is done, even if the buffer is not full. (A *batch* is one or more commands sent to SQL Server to be parsed and executed together. For example, if you are using OSQL.EXE or the Query Analyzer, a batch is the collection of all the commands that appear before a specific GO command.) If two queries exist in the same batch and the first query has only a small amount of data, its results are not sent back to the client until the second query is done or has supplied enough data to fill the output buffer. If both queries are fast, this is not a problem. But suppose the first query is fast and the second is slow. And suppose the first query returns 1,000 bytes of data. If the network packet size is 4,096 bytes, the first result set must wait in the output buffer for the second query to fill it. The obvious solution here is either to make the first command its own batch or to make the network packet size smaller. The first solution is probably the best one in this case, since it is typically difficult to fine-tune your application to determine the best buffer size for each command. But this does not mean that each command should be its own batch. Quite the contrary. In fact, under normal circumstances, grouping multiple commands into a single batch is most efficient and recommended because it reduces the amount of hand-shaking that must occur between client and server.

ODS Default Net-Libraries

By default, SQL Server on Windows NT/2000 always listens on Named Pipes as well as on TCP/IP and Multiprotocol. SQL Server running on either Windows 95 or Windows 98 listens on the shared memory library instead of on Named Pipes, but it also has TCP/IP and Multiprotocol available. You can add other Net-Library interfaces. On Windows NT/2000, you can also remove any of the Net-Libraries, but it is best not to remove Named Pipes. All the other Net-Libraries on Windows NT/2000 require an actual network. Because Named Pipe services exist in Windows NT/2000 even when no network is present, using Named Pipes leaves you a back door into SQL Server even if your network becomes totally nonfunctional. Similarly, SQL Server on either Windows 95 or Windows 98 always listens over the shared memory IPC by default, so you should avoid removing this option. Even with no network (which is a more likely scenario in Windows 95 and Windows 98 than in Windows NT/2000), shared memory is still available for inter-process communication.

Figure 2-2 shows the path from the SQL Server client application to the SQL Server engine and indicates where the Net-Library interface fits in. On the server side, ODS provides functionality that mirrors that of ODBC, OLE DB, or DB-Library at the client. Calls exist for an ODS server application to describe and send result sets, to convert values between datatypes, to assume the security context associated with the specific connection being managed, and to raise errors and messages to the client application.

ODS uses an event-driven programming model. Requests from servers and clients trigger events to which your server application

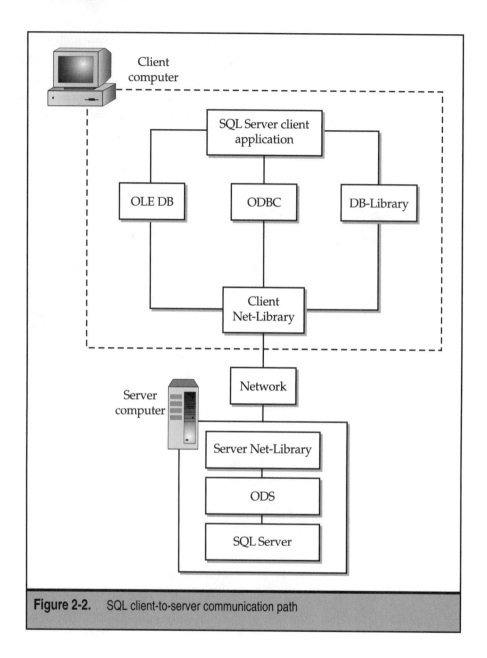

Figure 2-2.   SQL client-to-server communication path

must respond. Using the ODS application programming interface (API), you create a custom routine, called an *event handler,* for each possible type of event. Essentially, the ODS library drives a server application by calling its custom event handlers in response to incoming requests.

ODS server applications respond to the following events:

▼ **Connect Events**   When a connect event occurs, SQL Server initiates a security check to determine whether a connection is allowed. Other ODS applications, such as a gateway to DB/2, have their own logon handlers that determine whether connections are allowed. Events also exist that close a connection, allowing the proper connection cleanup to occur.

■ **Language Events**   When a client sends a command string, such as a SQL statement, SQL Server passes this command along to the command parser. A different ODS application, such as a gateway, would install its own handler that accepts and is responsible for execution of the command.

▲ **Remote Stored Procedure Events**   These events occur each time a client or SQL Server directs a remote stored procedure request to ODS for processing.

ODS also generates events based on certain client activities and application activities. These events allow an ODS server application to respond to changes to the status of the client connection or of the ODS server application.

In addition to handling connections, ODS manages threads (and fibers) for SQL Server. It takes care of thread creation and termination and makes the threads available to the User Mode Scheduler (UMS). Since ODS is an open interface with a full programming API and toolkit, other independent service vendors (ISVs) writing server applications with ODS get the same benefits that SQL Server derives from this component, including symmetric multiprocessing (SMP)-capable thread management and pooling as well as network handling for multiple simultaneous networks. This multithreaded operation enables ODS server applications to maintain a high level of performance and availability and to transparently use multiple processors under Windows NT/2000, because the operating system can schedule any thread on any available processor.

THE RELATIONAL ENGINE AND THE STORAGE ENGINE

The SQL Server database engine is made up of two main components: the relational engine and the storage engine. Unlike versions of SQL Server prior to 7, these two pieces are clearly separated, and their primary method of communication with each other is through OLE DB. The relational engine comprises all the components necessary to parse and optimize any query. It requests data from the storage engine in terms of OLE DB rowsets and then processes the rowsets returned. The storage engine comprises the components needed to actually access and modify data on disk.

The Command Parser

The command parser handles language events raised by ODS. It checks for proper syntax and translates Transact-SQL commands into an internal format that can be operated on. This internal format is known as a *query tree*. If the parser does not recognize the syntax, a syntax error is immediately raised. Starting with SQL Server 6, syntax error messages identify where the error occurred. However, nonsyntax error messages cannot be explicit about the exact source line that was the cause of the error. Because only the parser can access the source of the statement, the statement is no longer available in source format when the command is actually executed. Exceptions to the calling sequence for the command parser are EXECUTE(*"string"*) and cursor operations. Both of these operations can recursively call the parser.

The Optimization Component

The optimizer takes the query tree from the command parser and prepares it for execution. This module compiles an entire command batch, optimizes queries, and checks security. The query optimization and compilation result in an execution plan.

The first step in producing such a plan is to *normalize* the query, which potentially breaks down a single query into multiple, fine-grained queries. After the optimizer normalizes the query, it *optimizes* it, which means that the optimizer determines a plan for executing that query. Query optimization is cost-based; the optimizer chooses the plan that it determines would cost the least, based on internal metrics that include estimated memory requirements, estimated CPU utilization, and the estimated number of required I/Os. It considers the type of statement requested, checks the amount of data in the various tables affected, looks at the indexes available for each table, and then looks at a sampling of the data values kept for each index or column referenced in the query. The sampling of the data values is called *statistics*. Based on the available information, the optimizer considers the various access methods and join strategies it could use to resolve a query and chooses the most cost-effective plan. The optimizer also decides which indexes, if any, should be used for each table in the query, and, in the case of a multitable query, the order in which the tables should be accessed and the join strategy to be used.

The optimizer also uses pruning heuristics to ensure that more time is not spent optimizing a query than it would take to simply choose a plan and execute it. The optimizer does not necessarily do exhaustive optimization. Some products consider every possible plan and then choose the most cost-effective one. The advantage of this exhaustive optimization is that the syntax chosen for a query would theoretically never cause a performance difference, no matter what syntax the user employed. But if you deal with an involved query, it could take much longer to estimate the cost of every conceivable plan than it would to accept a good plan, even if not the best one, and execute it. For example, in one product review, SQL Server (and some other products) consistently executed one complex eight-table join faster than a product whose optimizer produced the same "ideal" execution plan each time, even though SQL Server's execution plan varied somewhat. This was a case in which a pruning technique produced faster results than pure exhaustive optimization. In general, though, you will typically get the same execution plan no matter what equivalent syntax you use to specify the query. Some products have no cost-based optimizer and rely purely on rules to determine the query execution plan. In such cases, the syntax of the query is vitally important. (For example, the execution would start with the first table in the FROM clause.) Such products sometimes claim to have a "rule-based optimizer." This might simply be a euphemism for "no optimizer"—that is, any optimization that took place was done by the person who wrote the query.

The SQL Server optimizer is cost-based, and with every release it has become "smarter" to handle more special cases and to add more query processing and access method choices. However, by definition, the optimizer relies on probability in choosing its query plan, so sometimes it will be wrong. (Even a 90 percent chance of choosing correctly means that something will be wrong one in ten times.) Recognizing that the optimizer will never be perfect, you can use SQL Server's *query hints* to direct the optimizer to use a certain index—for example, to force the optimizer to follow a specific sequence while working with the tables involved, or to use a particular join strategy.

After normalization and optimization are completed, the normalized tree produced by those processes is compiled into the execution plan, which is actually a data structure. Each command included in it specifies exactly which table will be affected, which indexes will be used (if any), which security checks must be made, and which criteria (such as equality to a specified value) must evaluate to TRUE for selection. This execution plan might be considerably more complex than is immediately apparent. In addition to the actual commands, the execution plan includes all the steps necessary to ensure that constraints are checked. (Steps for calling a trigger are a bit different than those for verifying constraints. If a trigger is included for the action being taken, a call to the procedure that comprises the trigger is appended. A trigger has its own plan that is branched to just before committing the changes. The specific steps for the trigger are not compiled into the execution plan, like those for constraint verification.)

A simple request to insert one row into a table with multiple constraints can result in an execution plan that requires many other tables to also be accessed or expressions to be evaluated. The existence of a trigger can also cause many additional steps to be executed. The step that carries out the actual INSERT statement might be just a small part of the total execution plan necessary to ensure that all actions and constraints associated with adding a row are carried out.

The Manager Service

The SQL manager is responsible for everything having to do with managing stored procedures and their plans. It determines when a stored procedure needs recompilation based on changes in the underlying objects' schemas, and it manages the caching of procedure plans so that they can be reused by other processes.

The SQL manager also handles auto-parameterization of queries. In Microsoft SQL Server 2000, certain kinds of ad hoc queries are treated as if they were parameterized stored procedures, and query plans are generated and saved for them. This can happen if a query uses a simple equality comparison against a constant, as in the following statement:

```
SELECT * FROM pubs.dbo.titles
WHERE type = 'business'
```

This query can be parameterized as if it were a stored procedure with a parameter for the value of `type`:

```
SELECT * FROM pubs.dbo.titles
WHERE type = @param
```

A subsequent query, differing only in the actual value used for the value of `type`, can use the same query plan that was generated for the original query.

The Expression Manager Component

The expression manager handles computation, comparison, and data movement. Suppose your query contains an expression like this one:

```
SELECT @myqty = qty * 10 FROM mytable V
```

The expression service copies the value of `qty` from the rowset returned by the storage engine, multiplies it by ten, and stores the result in `@myqty`.

The Query Execution Component

The query executor runs the execution plan that was produced by the optimizer, acting as a dispatcher for all the commands in the execution plan. This module loops through each command step of the execution plan until the batch is complete. Most of the commands require interaction with the storage engine to modify or retrieve data and to manage transactions and locking.

Communication Between the Relational Engine and the Storage Engine

The relational engine uses OLE DB for most of its communication with the storage engine. The following description of that communication is adapted from the section titled "Database Server" in Books Online. It describes how a SELECT statement that processes data from local tables only is processed:

1. The relational engine compiles the SELECT statement into an optimized execution plan. The execution plan defines a series of operations against simple rowsets from the individual tables or indexes referenced in the SELECT statement. (*Rowset* is the OLE DB term for a result set.) The rowsets requested by the relational engine return the amount of data needed from a table or index to perform one of the operations used to build the SELECT result set. For example, this SELECT statement requires a table scan if it references a table with no indexes:

   ```
   SELECT * FROM ScanTableV
   ```

2. The relational engine implements the table scan by requesting one rowset containing all the rows from ScanTable. This next SELECT statement needs only information available in an index:

   ```
   SELECT DISTINCT LastName
   FROM Northwind.dbo.Employees
   ```

3. The relational engine implements the index scan by requesting one rowset containing the leaf rows from the index that was built on the `LastName` column. The following `SELECT` statement needs information from two indexes:

```
SELECT CompanyName, OrderID, ShippedDate
FROM Northwind.dbo.Customers AS Cst
JOIN Northwind.dbo.Orders AS Ord
ON (Cst.CustomerID = Ord.CustomerID)
```

4. The relational engine requests two rowsets: one for the clustered index on `Customers` and the other for one of the nonclustered indexes on `Orders`. The relational engine then uses the OLE DB API to request that the storage engine open the rowsets. As the relational engine works through the steps of the execution plan and needs data, it uses OLE DB to fetch the individual rows from the rowsets it requested the storage engine to open. The storage engine transfers the data from the data buffers to the relational engine. The relational engine then combines the data from the storage engine rowsets into the final result set transmitted back to the user.

Not all communication between the relational engine and the storage engine uses OLE DB. In fact, some commands cannot be expressed in terms of OLE DB rowsets. The most obvious and common example of non-rowset-expressible return values is when the relational engine processes data definition language (DDL) requests to create a table or other SQL Server object.

The Access Methods Manager

When SQL Server needs to locate data, it calls the access methods manager. The access methods manager sets up and requests scans of data pages and index pages and then prepares the OLE DB rowsets to return to the relational engine. It contains services to open a table, retrieve qualified data, and update data. The access methods manager does not actually retrieve the pages; it makes the request of the buffer manager, which ultimately serves up the page already in its cache or reads it to cache from disk. When the scan is started, a look-ahead mechanism qualifies the rows or index entries on a page. Retrieving rows that meet specified criteria is known as a *qualified retrieval*. The access methods manager is employed not only for queries (selects) but also for qualified updates and deletes (for example, UPDATE with a WHERE clause).

A session opens a table, requests and evaluates a range of rows against the conditions in the WHERE clause, and then closes the table. A session descriptor data structure (SDES) keeps track of the current row and the search conditions for the object being operated on (which is identified by the object descriptor data structure, or DES).

Additional Components of the Access Methods Manager

The row operations manager and the index manager can be considered components of the access methods manager, because they carry out the actual method of access. Each is responsible for manipulating and maintaining its respective on-disk data structures, namely rows of data or B-tree indexes. They understand and manipulate information on data and index pages.

The Row Operations Manager

This component retrieves, modifies, and performs operations on individual rows. It performs an operation within a row, such as "retrieve column 2" or "write this value to column 3." As a result of the work performed by the access methods manager, lock manager, and transaction manager, the row will have been found and will be appropriately locked and part of a transaction. After formatting or modifying a row in memory, the row operations manager inserts or deletes a row.

The row operations manager also handles updates. SQL Server 2000 offers three methods for handling updates. All three are direct, which means that there is no need for two passes through the transaction log, as was the case with deferred updates in earlier versions of SQL Server. SQL Server 2000 has no concept of a deferred data modification operation.

The three update modes in SQL Server 2000 are as follows:

▼ **In-Place Mode**   This mode is used to update a heap or clustered index when none of the clustering keys change. The update can be done in place, and the new data is written to the same slot on the data page.

■ **Split Mode**   This mode is used to update nonunique indexes when the index keys change. The update is split into two operations—a delete followed by an insert—and these operations are performed independently of each other.

▲ **Split with Collapse Mode**   This mode is used to update a unique index when the index keys change. After the update is rewritten into `delete` and `insert` operations, if the same index key is both deleted and then reinserted with a new value, it is "collapsed" into a single update operation.

If you want to reorganize a table—for example, to reestablish a FILLFACTOR value or to make data more contiguous after a lot of data modification has occurred—you can use a clustered index, which makes the reorganization easy. You simply rebuild the clustered index, which rebuilds the entire table. In the case of a `delete`, if the row deleted is the last row on a data page, that page is deallocated. (The only exception occurs if that page is the only one remaining in the table. A table always contains at least one page, even if it is empty.)

The Index Manager

While the row operations manager works with individual rows, the index manager maintains and supports searches on B-trees, which are used for SQL Server indexes. An index is structured as a tree, with both a root page and intermediate- and lower-level pages (or branches). A B-tree groups records that have similar index keys, thereby allowing fast access to data by searching on a key value. The B-tree's core feature is its ability to balance the index tree. ("B" stands for *balanced*.) Branches of the index tree are spliced together or split apart as necessary so that the search for any given record always traverses the same number of levels and thus requires the same number of page accesses.

The traverse begins at the root page, progresses to intermediate index levels, and finally moves to bottom-level pages, called *leaf pages*. The index is used to find the correct leaf page. On a qualified retrieval or delete, the correct leaf page is the lowest page of the tree at which one or more rows with the specified key or keys reside. SQL Server supports both clustered and nonclustered indexes. In a nonclustered index, shown in Figure 2-3, the leaf level of the tree (the leaf page of the index) contains every key value in the index along with a row locator for each key value. The row locator is also called a *bookmark* and indicates where to find the referenced data. A row locator can have one of two forms. If the base table has no clustered index, the table is referred to as a *heap*. The row locators in nonclustered index leaf pages for a heap are pointers to the actual rows in which the data can be found, and these pointers consist of a Row ID (RID), which is a file number, a page number, and a row number on the page. If the base table has a clustered index, the row locators in any nonclustered index leaf pages contain the clustered index key value for the row.

After reaching the leaf level in a nonclustered index, you can find the exact location of the data, though the page on which that data resides must still be separately retrieved. Because you can access the data directly, you do not need to scan all the data pages for a qualifying row. Better yet, in a clustered index, shown in Figure 2-4, the leaf level actually contains the data row, not simply the index key. A clustered index keeps the data in a table physically ordered around the key of the clustered index, while the leaf page of a clustered index is in fact the data page itself.

Because data can be physically ordered in only one way, only one clustered index can exist per table. This makes the selection of the appropriate key value on which to cluster data an important performance consideration.

You can also use indexes to ensure the uniqueness of a particular key value. In fact, the PRIMARY KEY and UNIQUE constraints on a column work by creating a unique index on the column's values. The optimizer can use the knowledge that an index is unique in formulating an effective query plan.

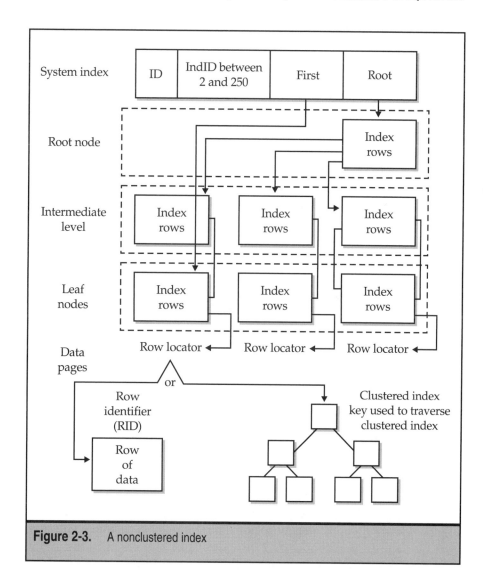

Figure 2-3.   A nonclustered index

Internally, SQL Server always ensures that clustered indexes are unique by adding a 4-byte, universally unique identifier (UUID) to clustered index key values that occur more than once. This UUID becomes part of the key and is used in all levels of the clustered index and in references to the clustered index key through all nonclustered indexes.

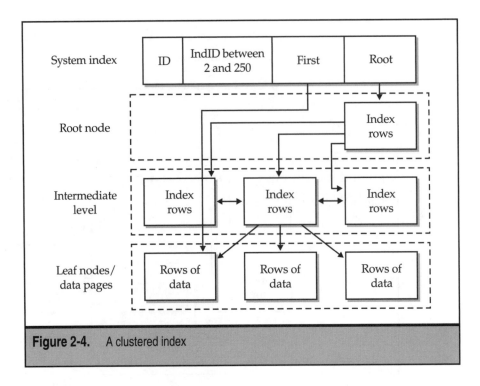

Figure 2-4.   A clustered index

Since SQL Server maintains ordering in index leaf levels, you do not need to unload and reload data to maintain clustering properties as data is added and moved. SQL Server will always insert rows into the correct page in clustered sequence. For a clustered index, the correct leaf page is the data page in which a row will be inserted. For a nonclustered index, the correct leaf page is the one into which SQL Server inserts a row containing the key value (and data row locator) for the newly inserted row. If data is updated and the key values of an index change, or if the row is moved to a different page, SQL Server's transaction control ensures that all affected indexes are modified to reflect these changes. Under transaction control, index operations are performed as atomic operations. The operations are logged and fully recovered in the event of a system failure.

Locking and Index Pages

As we will see in the section on the lock manager, pages of an index use a slightly different locking mechanism than regular data pages.

A lightweight lock called a *latch* is used to lock upper levels of indexes. Latches are not involved in deadlock detection because SQL Server 2000 uses "deadlock-proof" algorithms for index maintenance.

You can customize the locking strategy for indexes on a table basis or index basis. The system stored procedure `sp_indexoption` lets you enable or disable page or row locks with any particular index or, by specifying a table name, for every index on that table. The settable options are `AllowPageLocks` and `AllowRowLocks`. If both of these options are set to FALSE for a particular index, only table-level locks are applied.

The Page Manager and the Text Manager

The page manager and the text manager cooperate to manage a collection of pages as named databases. Each database is a collection of 8K disk pages, which are spread across one or more physical files. (In the next chapter, you will find more details about the physical organization of databases.)

SQL Server uses six types of disk pages: data pages, text/image pages, index pages, Page Free Space (PFS) pages, Global Allocation Map (GAM and SGAM) pages, and Index Allocation Map (IAM) pages. All user data, except for the *text* and *image* datatypes, are stored on data pages. The *text* and *image* datatypes, which are used for storing large objects (up to 2GB each of text or binary data), use a separate collection of pages, so the data is not stored on regular data pages with the rest of the rows. A pointer on the regular data page identifies the starting page and offset of the text/image data. Index pages store the B-trees that allow fast access to data. PFS pages keep track of which pages in a database are available to hold new data. Allocation pages (GAMs, SGAMs, and IAMs) keep track of the other pages; they contain no database rows and are used only internally.

The page manager allocates and deallocates all types of disk pages, organizing extents of eight pages each. An *extent* can be either a uniform extent, for which all eight pages are allocated to the same object (table or index), or a mixed extent, which can contain pages from multiple objects. If an object uses fewer than eight pages, the page manager allocates new pages for that object from mixed extents.

When the size of the object exceeds eight pages, the page manager allocates new space for that object in units of entire uniform extents. This optimization prevents the overhead of allocation from being incurred every time a new page is required for a large table; it is incurred only every eighth time. Perhaps most important, this optimization forces data of the same table to be contiguous (for the most part). At the same time, the ability to use mixed extents keeps SQL Server from wasting too much space if a database contains many small tables.

To determine how contiguous a table's data is, you use the DBCC SHOWCONTIG command. A table with a lot of allocation and deallocation can get fairly fragmented, so rebuilding the clustered index (which also rebuilds the table) can improve performance, especially when a table is accessed frequently using table scans.

The Transaction Manager

A core feature of SQL Server is its ability to ensure that transactions follow the ACID properties. (ACID stands for *atomicity, consistency, integrity,* and *durability.*) Transactions must be *atomic*—that is, all or nothing. If a transaction has been committed, it must be recoverable by SQL Server no matter what—even if a total system failure occurs one millisecond after the commit was acknowledged. In SQL Server, if work was in progress and a system failure occurred before the transaction was committed, all the work is rolled back to the state that existed before the transaction began. Write-ahead logging makes it possible always to roll back work in progress or roll forward committed work that has not yet been applied to the data pages. Write-ahead logging ensures that a transaction's changes—the "before and after" images of data—are captured on disk in the transaction log before a transaction is acknowledged as committed. Writes to the transaction log are always synchronous—that is, SQL Server must wait for them to complete. Writes to the data pages can be asynchronous, because all the effects can be reconstructed from the log if necessary. The transaction manager coordinates logging, recovery, and buffer management. These topics are discussed later in this chapter; at this point, we will just look at transactions themselves.

The transaction manager delineates the boundaries of statements that must be grouped together to form an operation. It handles transactions that cross databases within the same SQL Server, and it allows nested transaction sequences. (However, nested transactions simply execute in the context of the first-level transaction; no special action occurs when they are committed. And a rollback specified in a lower level of a nested transaction undoes the entire transaction.) For a distributed transaction to another SQL Server (or to any other resource manager), the transaction manager coordinates with the Microsoft Distributed Transaction Coordinator (MS DTC) service using operating system remote procedure calls. The transaction manager marks *savepoints,* which let you designate points within a transaction at which work can be partially rolled back or undone.

The transaction manager also coordinates with the lock manager regarding when locks can be released, based on the isolation level in effect. The isolation level in which your transaction runs determines how sensitive your application is to changes made by others and consequently how long your transaction must hold locks to protect against such changes. Four isolation-level semantics are available in SQL Server 2000: Uncommitted Read (also called "dirty read"), Committed Read, Repeatable Read, and Serializable.

Your transactions' behavior depends on the isolation level. We will look at these levels now, but a complete understanding of isolation levels also requires an understanding of locking, because the topics are so closely related. The next section gives an overview of locking.

Understanding the Nature of Uncommitted Reads

Uncommitted Read, or dirty read, lets your transaction read any data that is currently on a data page, whether or not that data has been committed. For example, another user might have a transaction in progress that has updated data, and even though it is holding exclusive locks on the data, your transaction can read it anyway. The other user might then decide to roll back his or her transaction, so logically those changes were never made. If the system is a single-user system and everyone is queued up to access it, the changes would never have been visible to other users. In a multiuser system, however, you read the changes and possibly take action on them. Although this scenario is not desirable, with Uncommitted Read you will not get stuck waiting for a lock, nor will *your* reads issue share locks (described below) that might affect others.

When using Uncommitted Read, you give up assurances of having strongly consistent data so that you can have the benefit of high concurrency in the system without users locking each other out. So when should you choose Uncommitted Read? Clearly, you do not want to choose it for financial transactions in which every number must balance. But it might be fine for certain decision-support analyses—for example, when you look at sales trends—for which complete precision is not necessary and the tradeoff in higher concurrency makes it worthwhile.

Contrasting Committed with Uncommitted Reads

Committed Read is SQL Server's default isolation level. It ensures that an operation will never read data that another application has changed but not yet committed. (That is, it will never read data that logically never existed.) With Committed Read, if a transaction is updating data and consequently has exclusive locks on data rows, your transaction must wait for those locks to be released before you can use that data (whether you are reading or modifying). Also, your transaction must put share locks (at a minimum) on the data that will be visited, which means that data is potentially unavailable to others to use. A share lock does not prevent others from reading the data, but it makes them wait to update the data. Share locks can be released after the data has been sent to the calling client—they do not have to be held for the duration of the transaction.

TIP: Although you can never read uncommitted data, if a transaction running with Committed Read isolation subsequently revisits the same data, that data might have changed or new rows might suddenly appear that meet the criteria of the original query. Rows that appear in this way are called *phantoms*.

Repeatable Read

The Repeatable Read isolation level adds to the properties of
Committed Read by ensuring that if a transaction revisits data or
if a query is reissued, the data will not have changed. In other words,
issuing the same query twice within a transaction will not pick up
any changes to data values made by another user's transaction.

Preventing nonrepeatable reads from appearing is a desirable
safeguard. But there is no free lunch. The cost of this extra safeguard
is that all the shared locks in a transaction must be held until the
completion (COMMIT or ROLLBACK) of the transaction. (Exclusive
locks must always be held until the end of a transaction, no matter
what the isolation level, so that a transaction can be rolled back if
necessary. If the locks were released sooner, it might be impossible to
undo the work.) No other user can modify the data visited by your
transaction as long as your transaction is outstanding. Obviously,
this can seriously reduce concurrency and degrade performance. If
transactions are not kept short or if applications are not written to be
aware of such potential lock contention issues, SQL Server can appear
to "hang" when it is simply waiting for locks to be released.

TIP: You can control how long SQL Server waits for a lock to be released
by using the session option LOCK_TIMEOUT.

Serializable

The Serializable isolation level adds to the properties of Repeatable
Read by ensuring that if a query is reissued, rows will not have been
added in the interim. In other words, phantoms will not appear if
the same query is issued twice within a transaction. More precisely,
Repeatable Read and Serializable both affect sensitivity to another
connection's changes, whether or not the user ID of the other
connection is the same. Every connection within SQL Server has its
own transaction and lock space. We use the term "user" loosely so as
to not obscure the central concept.

Preventing phantoms from appearing is another desirable
safeguard. But once again, there is no free lunch. The cost of this
extra safeguard is similar to that of Repeatable Read—that is, all the

shared locks in a transaction must be held until completion of the transaction. In addition, enforcing the Serializable isolation level requires that you not only lock data that has been read, but also lock data *that does not exist!* For example, suppose that within a transaction we issue a SELECT statement to read all the customers whose ZIP code is between 98000 and 98100, and on first execution no rows satisfy that condition. To enforce the Serializable isolation level, we must lock that "range" of potential rows with ZIP codes between 98000 and 98100 so that if the same query is reissued, there will still be no rows that satisfy the condition. SQL Server handles this by using a special kind of lock called a *range lock*. The Serializable level gets its name from the fact that running multiple serializable transactions at the same time is the equivalent of running them one at a time—that is, serially—without regard to sequence. For example, transactions A, B, and C are serializable only if the result obtained by running all three simultaneously is the same as if they were run one at a time, in any order. Serializable does not imply a known order in which the transactions are to be run. The order is considered a chance event. Even on a single-user system, the order of transactions hitting the queue would be essentially random. If the batch order is important to your application, you should implement it as a pure batch system.

The tough part of transaction management, of course, is dealing with rollback/rollforward and recovery operations. We will return to the topic of transaction management and recovery a bit later. But first we will further discuss locking and logging.

The Lock Manager

Locking is a crucial function of a multiuser database system such as SQL Server. Recall that SQL Server lets you manage multiple users simultaneously and ensures that the transactions observe the properties of the chosen isolation level. At the highest level, Serializable, SQL Server must make the multiuser system perform like a single-user system—as though every user is queued up to use the system alone with no other user activity. Locking guards data and the internal resources that make this possible, and it allows many users to simultaneously access the database and not be severely affected by others' use.

The lock manager acquires and releases various types of locks, such as shared read locks, exclusive locks for writing, intent locks to signal a potential "plan" to perform some operation, extent locks for space allocation, and so on. It manages compatibility between the lock types, resolves deadlocks, and escalates locks if needed. The lock manager controls table, page, and row locks as well as system data locks. (System data, such as page headers and indexes, is private to the database system.)

The lock manager provides two separate locking systems. The first enables row locks, page locks, and table locks for all fully shared data tables, data pages and rows, text pages, and leaf-level index pages and index rows. The second locking system is used internally only for restricted system data; it protects root and intermediate index pages while indexes are being traversed. This internal mechanism uses *latches,* a lightweight, short-term variation of a lock for protecting data that does not need to be locked for the duration of a transaction. Full-blown locks would slow the system down. In addition to protecting upper levels of indexes, latches protect rows while they are being transferred from the storage engine to the relational engine. If you examine locks by using the `sp_lock` stored procedure or a similar mechanism that gets its information from the syslockinfo table, you will not see or be aware of latches; you will see only the locks for fully shared data. However, some counters are available in Performance Monitor to monitor latch requests, acquisitions, and releases. Locking is an important aspect of SQL Server, primarily for the many developers who are keenly interested in locking because of its potential effect on application performance.

NOTE: Counters and other performance monitoring and management issues are discussed in Chapter 8.

Other Managers in SQL Server

Also included in the storage engine are managers for controlling utilities such as bulk load, DBCC commands, backup and restore operations, and the Virtual Device Interface (VDI). VDI allows ISVs to write their own backup and restore utilities and to access the SQL

Server data structures directly, without going through the relational engine. There is a manager to control sorting operations and one to physically manage the files and backup devices on disk.

MANAGING MEMORY

One of the major goals of Microsoft SQL Server 2000 was to scale easily from a laptop installation on Windows 95 or Windows 98 to an SMP server running on Windows NT/2000 Enterprise Edition. This requires an extremely robust policy for managing memory. By default, SQL Server 2000 adjusts its uses of system memory to balance the needs of other applications running on the machine as well as the needs of its own internal components. SQL Server can also be configured to use a fixed amount of memory. Whether memory allocation is fixed or dynamically adjusted, the total memory space is considered one unified cache and is managed as a collection of various pools with their own policies and purposes. Memory can be requested by and granted to any of several internal components.

The Buffer Manager and Memory Pools

The buffer pool is a memory pool that's the main memory component in the server; all memory not used by another memory component remains in the buffer pool. The buffer manager manages disk I/O functions for bringing data and index pages into memory so that data can be shared among users. When other components require memory, they can request a buffer from the buffer pool.

Another memory pool is the operating system itself. Occasionally, SQL Server must request contiguous memory in larger blocks than the 8K pages that the buffer pool can provide. Typically, use of large memory blocks is kept to a minimum, so direct calls to the operating system account for a very small fraction of SQL Server's memory usage.

The procedure cache can be considered another memory pool, in which can be stored query trees and plans from stored procedures, triggers, or ad hoc queries. Other pools are used by memory-intensive queries that use sorting or hashing, as well as by special memory objects that need less than one 8K page.

Access to In-Memory Pages

Access to pages in the buffer pool must be fast. Even with real memory, it would be ridiculously inefficient to have to scan the whole cache for a page when you are talking about hundreds of megabytes, or even gigabytes, of data. To avoid this inefficiency, pages in the buffer pool are hashed for fast access. *Hashing* is a technique that uniformly maps a key (in this case, a dbid-fileno-pageno identifier) via a hash function across a set of hash buckets. A *hash bucket* is a page in memory that contains an array of pointers (implemented as a linked list) to the buffer pages. If all the pointers to buffer pages do not fit on a single hash page, a linked list chains to additional hash pages.

Given a dbid-fileno-pageno value, the hash function converts that key to the hash bucket that should be checked; in essence, the hash bucket serves as an index to the specific page needed. By using hashing, even when large amounts of memory are presently in use, you can find a specific data page in cache with only a few memory reads (typically one or two).

TIP: Finding a data page might require that multiple hash buckets be accessed via the chain (linked list). The hash function attempts to uniformly distribute the dbid-fileno-pageno values throughout the available hash buckets. The number of hash buckets is set internally by SQL Server and depends on the total size of the buffer pool.

Access to Free Pages (Lazywriter)

A data page or an index page can be used only if it exists in memory. Therefore, a buffer in the buffer pool must be available into which the page can be read. Keeping a supply of buffers available for immediate use is an important performance optimization. If a buffer is not readily available, many memory pages might have to be searched simply to locate a buffer to use as a workspace.

The buffer pool is managed by a process called the lazywriter, which uses a clock algorithm to sweep through the buffer pool. Basically, the lazywriter thread maintains a pointer into the buffer pool that "sweeps" sequentially through it (like the hand on a clock). As it visits each buffer, it determines whether that buffer has been referenced since the last sweep, by examining a reference count value in the buffer header. If the reference count is not 0, the buffer stays in the pool and its reference count is adjusted in preparation for the next sweep; otherwise, the buffer is made available for reuse: It is written to disk if "dirty," removed from the hash lists, and put on a special list of buffers called the free list.

NOTE: The set of buffers through which the lazywriter sweeps is sometimes called the LRU (for least recently used list). It does not, however, function as a traditional LRU because the buffers do not move within the list according to their use or lack of use; the lazywriter "clock hand" does all the moving. Also note that the set of buffers that the lazywriter inspects actually includes more than pages in the buffer pool. It also includes pages from compiled plans for procedures, triggers, or ad hoc queries.

The reference count of a buffer is incremented each time the buffer's contents are accessed by any process. For data or index pages, this is a simple increment by 1. But objects that are expensive to create, such as stored procedure plans, get a higher reference count that reflects their "replacement cost." When the lazywriter clock hand sweeps through and checks which pages have been referenced, it does not use a simple decrement. It divides the reference count by 4. This means that frequently referenced pages (those with a high reference count) and those with a high replacement cost are "favored" and their count will not reach 0 anytime soon, keeping them in the pool for further use.

The lazywriter hand sweeps through the buffer pool when the number of pages on the free list falls below its minimum size. The minimum size is computed as a percentage of the overall buffer pool size but is always between 128K and 4MB. Currently, the percentage is set at 3 percent, but that could change in future releases of SQL Server 2000.

User threads also perform the same function of searching for pages for the free list. This happens when a user process needs to read a page from disk into a buffer. Once the read has been initiated, the user thread checks to see if the free list is too small. (Note that this process consumes one page of the list for its own read.) If so, the user thread performs the same function as the lazywriter: It advances the clock hand and searches for buffers to free. Currently, it advances the clock hand through 16 buffers, regardless of how many it actually finds to free in that group of 16. The reason for having user threads share in the work of the lazywriter is that the cost can be distributed across all the CPUs in an SMP environment.

Keeping Pages in the Cache Permanently

Tables can be specially marked so that their pages are never put on the free list and are therefore kept in memory indefinitely. This process is called *pinning* a table. Any page (whether data, index, or text) belonging to a pinned table is never marked as free and reused unless it is unpinned. Pinning and unpinning is accomplished using the *pintable* option of the `sp_tableoption` stored procedure. Setting this option to TRUE for a table does not cause the table to be brought into cache, nor does it mark pages of the table as "favored" in any way; instead, it avoids the unnecessary overhead and simply does not allow any pages belonging to a pinned table to be put on the free list for possible replacement.

Because mechanisms such as write-ahead logging and checkpointing are completely unaffected, such an operation in no way impairs recovery. Still, pinning too many tables can result in few or even no pages being available when a new buffer is needed. In general, you should pin tables only if you have carefully tuned your system, plenty of memory is available, and you have a good feel for which tables constitute hot spots.

Pages that are "very hot" (accessed repeatedly) are never placed on the free list. A page in the buffer pool that has a nonzero use count, such as one that is newly read or newly created, is not added to the free list until its use count falls to 0. Prior to that point, the page is clearly hot and is not a good candidate for reuse. Very hot pages might never get on the free list, even without their objects' being pinned—which is as it should be.

Protection against media failure is achieved using whatever level of RAID (redundant array of independent disks) technology you choose. Write-ahead logging in conjunction with RAID protection ensures that you never lose a transaction. (However, a good backup strategy is still essential in case of certain situations, such as when an administrator accidentally clobbers a table.) SQL Server always opens its files by instructing the operating system to write through any other caching that the operating system might be doing. Hence, SQL Server ensures that transactions are atomic—even a sudden interruption of power results in no partial transactions existing in the database, and all completed transactions are guaranteed to be reflected. (It is crucial, however, that a hardware disk-caching controller not "lie" and claim that a write has been completed unless it really has been or will be.)

Checkpoints

Checkpoint operations minimize the amount of work that SQL Server must do when databases are recovered during system startup. Checkpoints are run on a database-by-database basis. They flush dirty pages from the current database out to disk so that those changes will not have to be redone during database recovery. (A *dirty page* is one that has been modified since it was brought from disk into the buffer pool.) When a checkpoint occurs, SQL Server writes a checkpoint record to the transaction log, which lists all the active transactions. This allows the recovery process to build a table containing a list of all the potentially dirty pages.

Checkpoints are triggered when:

▼ A database owner explicitly issues a `checkpoint` command to perform a checkpoint in that database.

■ The log is getting full (more than 70 percent of capacity) and the database option `trunc. log on chkpt.` is set. A checkpoint is triggered to truncate the transaction log and free up space.

▲ A long recovery time is estimated. When recovery time is predicted to be longer than the *recovery interval* configuration option, a checkpoint is triggered. SQL Server 2000 uses a simple metric to predict recovery time, because it can recover, or redo, in less time than it took the original operations to run. Thus, if checkpoints are taken at least as often as the recovery interval frequency, recovery will complete within the interval. A recovery interval setting of 1 means checkpoints occur every minute. A minimum amount of work must be done for the automatic checkpoint to fire; this is currently 10MB of log per minute. In this way, SQL Server does not waste time taking checkpoints on idle databases. A default recovery interval of 0 means that SQL Server will choose an appropriate value automatically; for the current version, this is one minute.

Checkpoints and Performance Issues

A checkpoint is issued as part of an orderly shutdown, so a typical recovery on restart takes only seconds. (An orderly shutdown occurs when you explicitly shut down SQL Server, unless you do so via the `shutdown with nowait` command. An orderly shutdown also occurs when the SQL Server service is stopped through the Windows NT/2000 Service Control Manager or the `net stop` command from an operating system prompt.) Although a checkpoint speeds up recovery, it does slightly degrade run-time performance.

Unless your system is being pushed with high transactional activity, the run-time impact of a checkpoint probably will not be noticeable. It is minimized via the *fuzzy checkpoint* technique, which reflects the changes to the data pages incrementally. You can also use the recovery interval option of `sp_configure` to influence checkpointing frequency, balancing the time to recover versus any impact on run-time performance. If you are interested in tracing how often checkpoints actually occur, you can start your SQL Server with trace flag 3502, which writes information to SQL Server's error log every time a checkpoint occurs.

Accessing Pages via the Buffer Manager

The buffer manager handles the in-memory version of each physical disk page and provides all other modules access to it (with appropriate safety measures). The memory image in the buffer pool, if one exists, takes precedence over the disk image. That is, the copy of the data page in memory might include updates that have not yet been written to disk. (It might be dirty.) When a page is needed for a process, it must exist in memory (in the buffer pool). If the page is not there, a physical I/O is performed to get it. Obviously, because physical I/Os are expensive, the fewer the better. The more memory there is (the bigger the buffer pool), the more pages can reside there and the more likely a page can be found there.

A database appears as a simple sequence of numbered pages. The database ID (dbid), file number (fileno), and page number (pageno) uniquely specify a page for the entire SQL Server environment. When another module (such as the access methods manager, row manager, index manager, or text manager) needs to access a page, it requests access from the buffer manager by specifying the dbid, fileno, and pageno.

The buffer manager responds to the calling module with a pointer to the memory buffer holding that page. The response might be immediate if the page is already in the cache, or it might take an instant for a disk I/O to complete and bring the page into memory. Typically, the calling module also requests that the lock manager perform the appropriate level of locking on the page. The calling module notifies the buffer manager if and when it is finished dirtying, or making updates to, the page. The buffer manager is responsible for writing these updates to disk in a way that coordinates with logging and transaction management.

Large Memory Issues

Systems with hundreds of megabytes of RAM are not uncommon. In fact, for benchmark activities, Microsoft runs programs under development with a memory configuration of as much as 2GB of physical RAM. Using SQL Server on a DEC Alpha processor, or using the Enterprise Edition of SQL Server, allows even more memory to be used. In the future, Windows NT/2000 will support a 64-bit address space, and memory prices probably will continue to decline, so huge data caches of many gigabytes will not be so unusual. The reason to run with more memory is, of course, to reduce the need for physical I/O by increasing your cache-hit ratio.

Read Ahead

SQL Server supports a mechanism called read ahead, whereby the need for data and index pages can be anticipated and pages can be brought into the buffer pool before they are actually read. This performance optimization allows large amounts of data to be processed effectively. Unlike in previous versions of SQL Server, read ahead is managed completely internally, and no configuration adjustments are necessary. In addition, read ahead does not use separate Windows NT/2000 threads. This ensures that read ahead stays far enough—but not too far—ahead of the scan of the actual data.

There are two kinds of read ahead: one for table scans and one for index ranges. For table scans, the table's allocation structures are consulted to read the table in disk order. There are up to 32 extents (32×8 pages/extent $\times$ 8,192 bytes/page = 2MB) of read ahead outstanding at a time. The extents are read with a single 64K scatter read. (Scatter-gather I/O was introduced in Windows NT/2000 4, Service Pack 2, with the Win32 functions `ReadFileScatter` and `WriteFileScatter`. These functions allow SQL Server to issue a single read or write to transfer up to eight pages of data directly to or from SQL Server's buffer pool.) If the table is spread across multiple files in a filegroup, SQL Server attempts to keep at least eight of the files busy with read ahead instead of sequentially processing the files.

For index ranges, the scan uses level 1 of the index structure, which is the level immediately above the leaf, to determine which pages to read ahead. It tries to stay a certain number of pages ahead of the scan; that number is currently about 40 plus the configuration value for `max async I/O`. When the index scan starts, read ahead is invoked on the initial descent of the index to minimize the number of reads performed. For instance, for a scan of `WHERE state = 'NV'`, read ahead searches the index for `key = 'NV'`, and it can tell from the level 1 nodes how many pages have to be examined to satisfy the scan. If the anticipated number of pages is small, all the pages are requested by the initial read ahead; if the pages are contiguous, they are fetched in scatter reads. If the range contains a large number of pages, the initial read ahead is performed, and thereafter, every time another 16 pages are consumed by the scan, the index is consulted to read in another 16 pages. This has several interesting effects:

▼ Small ranges can be processed in a single read at the data page level whenever the index is contiguous.

■ The scan range (for example, state = 'NV') can be used to prevent reading ahead of pages that will not be used, since this information is available in the index.

▲ Read ahead is not slowed by having to follow page linkages at the data page level. (Read ahead can be done on both clustered indexes and nonclustered ones.)

NOTE: Scatter-gather I/O and asynchronous I/O are available only to SQL Server running on Windows NT/2000. This includes the desktop edition of SQL Server if it has been installed on Windows NT/2000 Workstation.

The Log Manager

All changes are "written ahead" by the buffer manager to the transaction log. Write-ahead logging ensures that all databases can be recovered to a consistent state even in the event of a complete server failure, as long as the physical medium (hard disk) survives. A process is never given acknowledgment that a transaction has been committed unless it is on disk in the transaction log. For this reason, all writes to the transaction log are synchronous—SQL Server must wait for acknowledgment of completion. Writes to data pages can be made asynchronously, without waiting for acknowledgment, because if a failure occurs the transactions can be undone or redone from the information in the transaction log.

The log manager formats transaction log records in memory before writing them to disk. To format these log records, the log manager maintains regions of contiguous memory called *log caches*. Unlike in previous versions, in SQL Server 2000 log records do not share the buffer pool with data and index pages. Log records are maintained only in the log caches.

To achieve maximum throughput, the log manager maintains two or more log caches. One is the current log cache, in which new log records are added. The log manager also has two queues of log caches: a flushQueue, which contains log caches waiting to be flushed, and a freeQueue, which contains log caches that have no data and can be reused.

When a user process requires that a particular log cache be flushed (for example, when a transaction commits), the log cache is placed into the flushQueue (if it is not already there). Then the thread (or fiber) is put into the list of connections waiting for the log cache to be flushed. The connection does no further work until its log records have been flushed.

The *log writer* is a dedicated thread that goes through the flushQueue in order and flushes the log caches out to disk. The log caches are written one at a time. The log writer first checks to see if the log cache is the current log cache. If it is, the log writer pads the log cache to sector alignment and updates some header information. It then issues an I/O event for that log cache. When the flush for a particular log cache is completed, any processes waiting on that log cache are awakened and can resume work.

THE SQL SERVER KERNEL AND INTERACTION WITH THE OPERATING SYSTEM

The SQL Server kernel is responsible for interacting with the operating system. It is a bit of a simplification to suggest that SQL Server has one module for all operating system calls, but for ease of understanding, you can think of it in this way. All requests to operating system services are made via the Win32 API and C run-time libraries. When SQL Server runs under Windows NT/2000, it runs entirely in the Win32 protected subsystem. Absolutely no calls are made in Windows NT/2000 Privileged Mode; they are made in User Mode. This means that SQL Server cannot crash the entire system, it cannot crash another process running in User Mode, and other such processes cannot crash SQL Server. SQL Server has no device `driver_level` calls, nor does it use any undocumented calls to Windows NT/2000. If the entire system crashes (giving you the so-called "Blue Screen of Death") and SQL Server happens to have been running there, one thing is certain: SQL Server did *not* crash the system. Such a crash must be the result of faulty or incompatible hardware, a buggy device driver operating in Privileged Mode, or a critical bug in the Windows NT/2000 operating system code (which is doubtful).

TIP: The Blue Screen of Death—a blue "bug check" screen with some diagnostic information—appears if a crash of Windows NT/2000 occurs. It looks similar to the screen that appears when Windows NT/2000 initially boots up.

A key design goal of both SQL Server and Windows NT/2000 is scalability. The same binary executable files that run on notebook computers run equally well on symmetric multiprocessor superservers with loads of processors. SQL Server includes versions for Intel and RISC hardware architectures on the same CD-ROM. Windows NT/2000 is an ideal platform for a database server because it provides a fully protected, secure, 32-bit environment. The foundations of a great database server platform are preemptive scheduling, virtual paged memory management, symmetric multiprocessing, and asynchronous I/O. Windows NT/2000 provides these, and SQL Server uses them fully. The SQL Server engine runs as a single process on Windows NT/2000. Within that process are multiple threads of execution. Windows NT/2000 schedules each thread to the next processor available to run one.

Threading and Symmetric Multiprocessing

SQL Server approaches multiprocessor scalability differently from most other symmetric multiprocessing (SMP) database systems. Two characteristics separate this approach from other implementations:

▼ **Single-Process Architecture**   SQL Server maintains a single-process, multithreaded architecture that reduces system overhead and memory use. This is called the Symmetric Server Architecture.

▲ **Native Thread-Level Multiprocessing**   SQL Server supports multiprocessing at the thread level rather than at the process level, which allows for preemptive operation and dynamic load balancing across multiple CPUs. Using multiple threads is significantly more efficient than using multiple processes.

To understand how SQL Server works, it is useful to compare its strategies to those generally used by other products. On a non-threaded operating system such as some UNIX variants, a typical SMP database server has multiple DBMS processes, each bound to a specific CPU. Some implementations even have one process per user, which results in a high memory cost. These processes communicate using shared memory, which maintains the cache, locks, task queues, and user context information. The DBMS must include complex logic that takes on the role of an operating system: It schedules user tasks, simulates threads, coordinates multiple processes, and so on. Because processes are bound to specific CPUs, dynamic load balancing can be difficult or impossible. For the sake of portability, products often take this approach even when they run on an operating system that offers native threading services, such as Windows NT/2000. SQL Server, on the other hand, uses a clean design of a single process and multiple operating system threads. The threads are scheduled onto a CPU by a User Mode Scheduler.

SQL Server always uses multiple threads, even on a single-processor system. Threads are created and destroyed depending on system activity, so thread count is not constant. Typically, the number of active threads in SQL Server ranges from 16 to 100, depending on system activity and configuration. A pool of threads handles each of the networks that SQL Server simultaneously supports, another thread handles database checkpoints, another handles the lazywriter process, while another handles the log writer. A separate thread is also available for general database cleanup tasks, such as periodically shrinking a database that is in auto-shrink mode. Finally, a pool of threads handles all user commands.

The Worker Thread Pool

Although SQL Server might seem to offer each user a separate operating system thread, the system is actually a bit more sophisticated than that. Because it is inefficient to use hundreds of separate operating system threads to support hundreds of users, SQL Server establishes a pool of worker threads.

When a client issues a command, the SQL Server network handler places the command in a "queue," and the next available thread from the worker thread pool takes the request. Technically, this queue is a Windows NT/2000 facility called an IOCompletion port. The SQL Server worker thread waits in the completion queue for incoming network requests to be posted to the IOCompletion port. If no idle worker thread is available to wait for the next incoming request, SQL Server dynamically creates a new thread until the maximum configured worker thread limit has been reached. The client's command must wait for a worker thread to be freed.

Even in a system with thousands of connected users, most are typically idle at any given time. As the workload decreases, SQL Server gradually eliminates idle threads to improve resource and memory use.

The worker thread pool design is efficient for handling thousands of active connections without the need for a transaction monitor. Most competing products, including those on the largest mainframe systems, need to use a transaction monitor to achieve the level of active users that SQL Server can handle without such an extra component. If you support a large number of connections, this is an important capability.

TIP: In many cases, you should allow users to stay connected—even if they will be idle for periods of, say, an hour—rather than have them continually connect and disconnect. Repeatedly incurring the overhead of the logon process is more expensive (in terms of overhead) than simply allowing the connection to remain live but idle.

Active Versus Idle

In the previous context, a user is considered idle from the database perspective. The human end user might be quite active, filling in the data entry screen, getting information from customers, and so forth. But those activities do not require any server interaction until a command is actually sent. So from the SQL Server engine perspective, the connection is idle.

When you think of an active user versus an idle user, be sure to consider the user in the context of the back-end database server. In practically all types of applications that have many end users, at any given time the number of users who have an active request with the database is relatively small. A system with 1,000 active connections might reasonably be configured with 150 or so worker threads. But this does not mean that all 150 worker threads are created at the start—they are created only as needed, and 150 is only a high-water mark. In fact, fewer than 100 worker threads might be active at a time, even if end users all think they are actively using the system all the time.

A thread from the worker thread pool services each command to allow multiple processors to be fully utilized as long as multiple user commands are outstanding. In addition, with SQL Server 2000, a single user command with no other activity on the system can benefit from multiple processors if the query is complex. SQL Server can break complex queries into component parts that can be executed in parallel on multiple CPUs. Note that this intraquery parallelism occurs only if there are processors to spare—that is, if the number of processors is greater than the number of connections. In addition, intraquery parallelism is not considered if the query is not resource-expensive to run, and the threshold for what constitutes "expensive" can be controlled with a configuration option called *cost threshold for parallelism*.

Under the normal pooling scheme, a worker thread runs each user request to completion. Because each thread has its own stack, stack switching is unnecessary. If a given thread performs an operation that causes a page fault, only that thread, and hence only that one client, is blocked. (A page fault occurs if the thread makes a request for memory, and the virtual memory manager of the operating system must swap that page in from disk since it had been paged out. Such a request for memory must wait a long time relative to the normal memory access time, because a physical I/O is thousands of times more resource-expensive than reading real memory.)

Now consider something more serious than a page fault. Suppose that while a user request is being carried out, a bug is exposed in SQL Server that results in an illegal operation's causing an access violation (for example, the thread tries to read some memory outside the SQL Server address space). Windows NT/2000 immediately terminates the offending thread—an important feature of a truly protected operating system. Because SQL Server makes use of structured exception handling in Windows NT/2000, only the specific SQL Server user who made the request is affected. All other users of SQL Server or other applications on the system are unaffected and the system at large will not crash. Of course, such a bug should never occur and in reality is indeed rare. But this is software, and software is never perfect. Having this important reliability feature is like wearing a seat belt—you hope you never need it, but you are glad it's there in case a crash occurs.

NOTE: Since Windows 95 and Windows 98 do not support SMP systems or thread pooling, the previous discussion is relevant only to SQL Server running on Windows NT/2000. The following discussion of disk I/O is also only relevant to SQL Server on Windows NT/2000.

Disk I/O on Windows NT/2000

SQL Server 2000 uses two Windows NT/2000 features to improve its disk I/O performance: scatter-gather I/O and asynchronous I/O. The following descriptions were adapted from Books Online:

▼ **Scatter-Gather I/O**   As just mentioned, scatter-gather I/O was introduced in Windows NT4, Service Pack 2. Previously, all the data for a disk read or write on Windows NT had to be in a contiguous area of memory. If a read transferred in 64K of data, the read request had to specify the address of a contiguous area of 64K of memory. Scatter-gather I/O allows a read or write to transfer data into or out of noncontiguous areas of memory.

If SQL Server 2000 reads in a 64K extent, it does not have to allocate a single 64K area and then copy the individual pages to buffer cache pages. It can locate eight buffer pages and then do a single scatter-gather I/O that specifies the address of the eight buffer pages. Windows NT/2000 places the eight pages directly into the buffer pages, eliminating the need for SQL Server to do a separate memory copy.

▼ **Asynchronous I/O**   In an asynchronous I/O, after an application requests a read or write operation, Windows NT/2000 immediately returns control to the application. The application can then perform additional work, and it can later test to see if the read or write has completed. By contrast, in a synchronous I/O, the operating system does not return control to the application until the read or write completes. SQL Server supports multiple concurrent asynchronous I/O operations against each file in a database. The maximum number of I/O operations for any file is controlled by the max async io configuration option. If max async io is left at its default of 32, a maximum of 32 asynchronous I/O operations can be outstanding for each file at any time.

Types of Databases

Each SQL Server has two types of databases: system databases and user databases. Structurally, there is no difference between system and user databases, as both types of databases store data. However, SQL Server recognizes and requires system databases for its own use. System databases store information about SQL Server as a whole. SQL Server uses these databases to operate and manage the system. User databases are databases that users create. One copy of SQL Server can manage one or more user databases. When SQL Server is installed, SQL Server Setup creates four system databases and two sample user databases.

System Databases

The following table describes the system databases:

Database	Description
Master	Controls the user databases and operation of SQL Server as a whole by keeping track of information such as login accounts, configurable environment variables, database locations, and system error messages
Model	Provides a template, or prototype, for new user databases
Tempdb	Provides a storage area for temporary tables and other temporary working storage needs
MSDB	Supports SQL Server Agent and provides a storage area for scheduling information and job history
Distribution	Stores history and transaction data used in replication

TIP: The Distribution database is installed only when you configure SQL Server for replication activities.

While it is possible to modify and delete data in the system databases, this is not recommended. You should create all user objects in user databases and use system stored procedures only to read and modify data in the system databases.

There is one case in which you can modify a system database directly. If you want certain objects that you create (such as stored procedures, datatypes, defaults, and rules) to be added to every new user database, you can add these objects to the Model database. The contents of the Model database are copied into every new database.

User Databases

The Pubs and Northwind sample databases are installed when you install SQL Server. These provide useful examples for you to use when learning how to work with SQL Server. They are not required for SQL Server to operate correctly.

Database Objects

A database is a collection of data stored in tables, along with objects that support the storage, retrieval, security, and integrity of this data. The following table summarizes the SQL Server database objects.

Database Object	Description
Table	Stores data as a collection of rows and columns
Datatype	Defines the type of data values allowed for a column or variable; SQL Server provides system-supplied datatypes; users can create user-defined datatypes
Constraint	Used to define integrity rules for a column or set of columns in a table; the standard mechanism for enforcing data integrity
Default	Defines a value that is stored in a column if no other value is supplied
Rule	Defines an expression that is used to check the validity of values that are stored in a column or datatype

Database Object	Description
Index	A storage structure that provides ordering and fast access for data retrieval and that can enforce data uniqueness
View	Provides a way to look at data from one or more tables or other views in a database
Stored procedure	A named collection of Transact-SQL statements or batches that execute together
Trigger	A special form of a stored procedure that is executed automatically when a user modifies data in a table

TIP: In Enterprise Manager, system databases and system objects are hidden by default. You can change the default by editing the server registration information and checking the Show System Databases and System Objects option.

Referring to SQL Server Objects

You can refer to SQL Server objects in several ways. You can specify the full name of the object (its fully qualified name), or you can specify only part of the object's name and have SQL Server determine the rest of the name from the context in which you are working.

Fully Qualified Names

The complete name of a SQL Server object includes four identifiers: the server name, the database name, the owner name, and the object name, in the following format:

```
server.database.owner.object
```

Any name that specifies all four parts is known as a fully qualified name. Each object created in SQL Server must have a unique, fully qualified name. For example, there can be two tables named Orders in the same database only if they belong to different owners. In addition, column names must be unique within a table or view.

Partially Specified Names

When referencing an object, you do not always have to specify the server, database, and owner. Leading identifiers can be omitted. Intermediate identifiers can also be omitted as long as their position is indicated by periods. The valid formats of object names are as follows:

```
server.database.owner.object
server.database..object
server..owner.object
server...object
database.owner.object
database..object
owner.object
object
```

When you create an object, SQL Server uses the following defaults if different parts of the name are not specified:

▼ The server defaults to the local server.

■ The database defaults to the current database.

▲ The owner defaults to the username in the specified database associated with the login ID of the current connection. (Usernames are mapped to login IDs when they are created.)

A user who is a member of a role can explicitly specify the role as the object owner. A user who is a member of the db_owner or db_ddladmin role in the Northwind database can specify the DBO user account as the owner of an object. This practice is recommended.

The following example creates an order_history table in the Northwind database:

```
CREATE TABLE northwind.dbo.order_history
  (
    OrderID INT,
    ProductID int,
    UnitPrice money,
    Quantity int,
    Discount decimal
  )
```

Most object references use three-part names and default to the local server. Four-part names are generally used for distributed queries or remote stored procedure calls.

Understanding the Importance of System Tables

System tables store information, called metadata, about the system and objects in databases. *Metadata* is information about data.

The Database Catalog

Each database (including the `Master` database) contains a collection of system tables that store metadata about that specific database. This collection of system tables is called the database catalog.

The System Catalog

The SQL Server system catalog, found only in the `Master` database, is a collection of system tables that stores metadata about the entire system and all other databases. System tables all begin with the `sys` prefix. The following table identifies some frequently used system tables:

System Table	Database	Function
sysxlogins	Master	Contains one row for each login account that can connect to SQL Server; if you need to access information in sysxlogins, you should do so through the syslogins view
sysmessages	Master	Contains one row for each system error or warning that SQL Server can return

System Table	Database	Function
sysdatabases	Master	Contains one row for each database on a SQL Server
sysusers	All	Contains one row for each Windows NT/2000 user, Windows NT/2000 group, SQL Server user, or SQL Server role in a database
sysobjects	All	Contains one row for each object in a database

Metadata Retrieval

You can query a system table as you would any other table to retrieve information about the system. However, you should not write scripts that directly query the system tables, because if the system tables are changed in future product versions, your scripts might fail or might not provide accurate information.

CAUTION: Writing scripts that directly modify the system tables is strongly discouraged. Changing a system table might make it impossible for SQL Server to operate normally.

When you write applications that retrieve metadata from system tables, you should use system stored procedures, system functions, or system-supplied information schema views. Each of these is described in the sections that follow.

System Stored Procedures

To make it easier for you to gather information about the state of the server and database objects, SQL Server provides a collection of prewritten queries called *system stored procedures*. The names of most system stored procedures begin with the `sp_` prefix. The following table describes three commonly used system stored procedures:

System Stored Procedure	Description
`sp_help` `[object_name]`	Provides information on the specified database object
`sp_helpdb` `[database_name]`	Provides information on the specified database
`sp_helpindex` `[table_name]`	Provides information on the index for the specified table

Many other stored procedures are used to create or modify system information or database objects by modifying the system tables. For example, the system stored procedure `sp_addlogin` creates a new login account in the `master..sysxlogins` system table. As you have seen, there are system stored procedures that modify and query the system tables for you so that you do not have to do so directly.

Views That Provide Information About the Database's Design

Information schema views provide an internal, system table-independent view of the SQL Server metadata. These views conform to the ANSI SQL standard definition for information schema. Information schema views allow applications to work properly even if future product versions change the system tables significantly.

In SQL Server, all information schema views are owned by a predefined `information_schema` user. Each information schema view contains metadata for the data objects stored in a particular database. You can obtain a complete list of the views by searching for Information_schema views in Books Online.

SUMMARY

In this chapter, we have looked at the general workings of the SQL Server engine, including the key modules and functional areas that make up the engine. We have also covered issues dealing with integration with Windows NT/2000. By necessity, we have made some simplifications throughout the chapter, though the information provided should provide some insight into the roles and responsibilities of the major subsystems in SQL Server, the general flow of the system, and the interrelationships among subsystems.

The retrieval of metadata—information about objects and their configuration—has been made much easier in Microsoft SQL Server 2000. Information schema views, new to this version, provide a means to retrieve valuable information from system tables without writing a query against these tables yourself. SQL Server continues to support the use of system stored procedures, which can be recognized by their sp_ prefix, to gather valuable information for database objects. In Chapter 3, we will move on to a consideration of how user databases are created under SQL Server 2000.0, and examine many of the issues that are likely to confront you as an administrator in managing those user databases.

CHAPTER 3

Implementing Security

Security is probably the oldest problem faced by network administrators through the years. Security issues in Microsoft SQL Server are still very much present and are in fact much more common in recent years than ever before. Security has always been an issue because the data of any organization must be protected to a greater or lesser extent. Protecting data is actually a multitude of tasks that range from simple backups, which are performed to ensure that the data is protected from both physical damage as well as corruption, to advanced methods of protecting against intruders, which protects the data from unauthorized access or willful damage. In this chapter, you will focus on and learn about the security aspects of SQL Server that protect data from unauthorized access. You will learn about protecting data through backups in Chapter 6.

The very first thing to understand is, of course, why we want to prevent unauthorized users from accessing data on our SQL Servers. Data, as you know, comes in a very wide variety, each of which has different properties that may require protection. The first reason to protect data, and the one that applies equally to all kinds of data, is protection from willful damage such as that caused by a disgruntled employee or that rare hacker who acquires access to a network solely for destructive purposes. Imagine for a second that your network has been penetrated and there is an unauthorized user who has obtained access to your SQL Server. The intruder intends to do damage to whatever he or she can and is executing destructive code right now. What data are you most afraid will be lost? What data can you afford to lose? Is your job at risk? Is your organization at risk? The threat of a network penetration is very real, and while not all penetrations are done by hackers with damage in mind, much of the data we store in SQL Servers has the potential to do some damage if it falls into the hands of our competition. Suppose, for example, that a recently fired employee decides to use his or her access to the SQL Server in order to obtain and sell the organization's customer list. That list could potentially cost the organization business merely because the competition now knows who the clients are, how to contact them, and who to contact.

No matter if your goal is to prevent a hacker from doing damage to your network and data, or to prevent competition from obtaining confidential information, the answer is always the same. You must take steps to ensure that your network and SQL Server have the appropriate security measures in place to prevent unauthorized access.

SOME NEW ANSWERS TO AN OLD PROBLEM

Microsoft SQL Server implements security at two levels. The first level of security is server access and deals with the authentication of users. SQL Server 7 can perform user authentication by checking a login and password against information stored inside the SQL Server (SQL Server Authentication), or by accepting a login that has had its password verified previously by Windows NT or Windows 2000 (Windows NT Authentication). You should note here that although Windows NT and Windows 2000 can handle security authentication differently, SQL Server treats all Windows-based methods of authentication the same. As a result, the term "Windows NT Authentication" is used in Enterprise Manager, and will be used throughout this book to indicate a Windows-based authentication method.

Many administrators feel that SQL Server Authentication presents the best solution because an additional level of security is present. Put another way, the security is increased when using SQL Server Authentication because the user must know the Windows NT User Account Name, the password for the account name, the SQL Server login Name, and the password for the SQL Server login Name in order to gain access to the SQL Server. When using Windows NT Authentication, a user only need know the Windows NT User Account Name and its associated password in order to gain access to the SQL Server with the access level that has been granted to that user account or any group that the user account is a member of. SQL Server can also combine the two types of authentication in order to support users who are authenticated within the Windows NT Domain, as well as users who are connecting from outside the domain.

UNDERSTANDING SQL SERVER LOGINS

To better understand the authentication types, you should take a look at the way that SQL Server actually stores login information. To begin with, you should know that logins are stored as entries inside of SQL Server; a user may then login with one of those entries to obtain access to the server. In order to be the most technically accurate, you should know that the login name is actually stored inside the Master Database. Login names are specific to the server and not to databases, which means that while having an authenticated login will grant access to the server, it does not expressly grant access to any databases. SQL Server must have a login created in order to provide access to the server no matter what type of authentication you use. If you are using SQL Server Authentication, the SQL Server will validate the attempted entry by matching the entered login Name and password with entries found in the Master Database. If you are using Windows NT Authentication, SQL Server will validate the attempted entry by matching the Windows NT username with the login Name stored in the Master Database and will trust that Windows NT validated the password. When using Windows NT Authentication, SQL Server obtains the username over the network automatically. If the username matches an existing login, SQL Server will grant access to the user based on the matching login. If the username obtained over the network does not match an existing SQL Server login, SQL Server will check to see if the username is a member of any Windows NT groups that have a valid login. If the username is a member of any group with a valid login, SQL Server will grant access to the user based on the login for the group that has the highest level of access.

When SQL Server is installed, there is a special login created called *SA*. SA stands for System Administrator and is a special login because it has complete control over the entire server by default. You must be sure to take special care when dealing with the SA login because it cannot be dropped (removed) from the server and represents the single greatest threat to security in any SQL Server installation. The SA login is created at the time of installation and is created without a password. The very first thing an administrator should do after validating the SQL Server install is assign a password to the SA login. You can assign the SA login a password either by accessing the properties of the login in SQL Enterprise Manager or by executing the SP_PASSWORD system stored procedure. For example, if you want to assign a password using Enterprise Manager, perform the following steps:

1. Expand the Logins folder in Enterprise Manager.
2. Double-click your mouse on the SA login.
3. Type a password into the Password field.
4. Click the OK button.

If you want to assign a password to the SA login account using a system stored procedure, connect to SQL Server using Query Analyzer and execute the following Transact-SQL statement:

```
exec sp_password NULL, password, 'SA'
```

In the example above, you are specifying that the SP_PASSWORD stored procedure is to be run using the following variables. The NULL reference is used in place of an old password. If there had been an existing password present and you were using the stored procedure to change it, you would specify the password here. The password reference is merely a placeholder that tells you to insert your chosen password here. The final reference SA is the specification that tells the stored procedure what login to operate on. For a complete listing of the syntax, please review the details in Books Online.

You can specify the type of authentication that SQL Server uses by accessing the properties page for the server inside Enterprise Manager. On the Security Tab, you can choose the authentication type and have a choice between SQL Server and Windows NT, or Windows NT Only, as seen in Figure 3-1.

While technically you can set the authentication mode using Transact-SQL, the specifications modify a variety of SQL-DMO objects, and is a process that really requires SQL programming experience. Since this book is written specifically for the administrator, the authors advise you to manage the authentication mode using SQL Enterprise Manager.

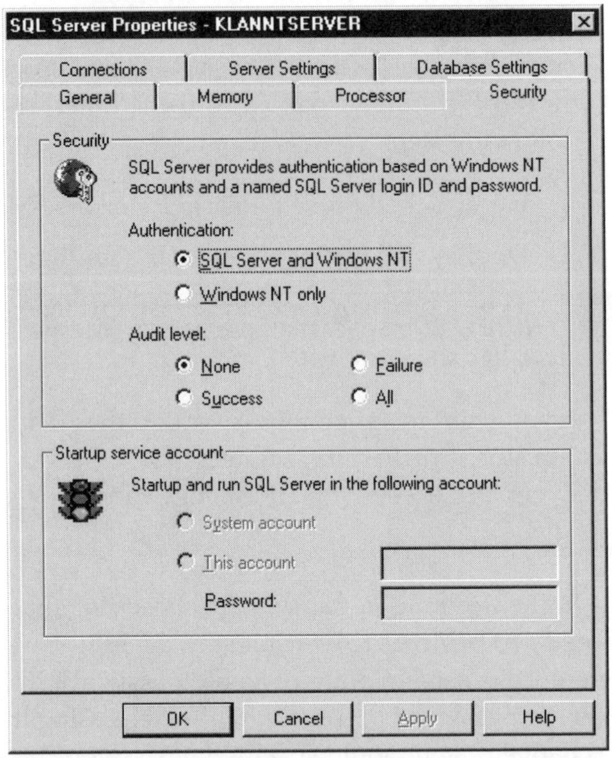

Figure 3-1. Changing the authentication mode from Enterprise Manager

Sometimes as an administrator, you will have to grant database access to a large group of Windows NT users at the same time. As you have learned, a SQL Server login is required in order for a user to access a SQL Server. When using Windows NT Authentication, you can create SQL Server logins that are matched to specific Windows NT groups. This means that you can have a single SQL Server login, which applies to many Windows NT users at the same time. For example, if you have created a customer management database on your SQL Server and you want to grant access to every sales person in the organization, you can simply create a Windows NT group called Sales that contains all of the Windows NT user accounts that represent salespeople. Then you can create a single SQL

Server login that matches the name of the Windows NT group, create a user inside the Customer Management database that is matched to the login, and grant that user permissions to the database objects that the sales force requires. Having performed these steps, any Windows NT user account who is made a member of the Sales Group will inherit the right to logon to the SQL Server and access the Customer Management Database.

NOTE: SQL Server treats groups from Windows NT and Windows 2000 the same.

UNDERSTANDING DATABASE USERS

Once you have created the SQL Server logins, you will want to grant permissions to users and groups of users so that they may perform tasks inside databases. By default, there are no users inside any database except a special user called DBO, which stands for database owner. The DBO is the owner of the database itself and has total control of the database and its objects. It is the DBO who should create all objects inside the database in order to prevent problems, which may be caused by multiple owners. Once the database is complete, you will want to create users who can access the database and obtain information, but who cannot control the structure of the database itself. You would not, for example, want to grant all users the right to delete tables because the potential for loss of data would then be increased by a wide margin.

In order for a user to have access to a database, the administrator must expressly grant database permission to that login. Administrators grant permissions in databases by creating objects called users in the database itself. Do not confuse this kind of user with the Windows NT or 2000 user account, which is maintained by the operating system. Keeping the SQL Server login and the database user permission separate is what lets you as an administrator grant a user access to one database on a server, while keeping the same user out of other databases stored on the same server. For example, a user who has a SQL Server login named Bob requires access to the Customer database in order to do his job, but does not require access to the Financial database. As the administrator, you would create a user inside the Customer database using Bob's SQL Server login and grant that database user whatever permissions were necessary to perform his or her duties. Because Bob does not have his SQL Server login mapped to a user in the Financial database, Bob will have access to the SQL Server, Bob will have access to the Customer database, but Bob will not have access to the Financial database.

In the example above, user Bob was restricted from accessing the Financial database because no user existed in the database that mapped to Bob's SQL Server login. If you were asked the question of how to grant Bob access to the Financial database, the obvious answer would be to create a user inside the Financial database that mapped to Bob's SQL Server login. There is, however, another way to accomplish the same goal. SQL Server 7 lets you apply permissions to multiple users simultaneously through the use of special database objects called *roles*. You can think of roles as if they were groups because they are conceptually containers into which you will place logins and users so that the permissions that you applied to the role are carried over and are applied to the login or user. SQL Server uses two basic types of roles to assign permissions. In the following text, you will learn about each type of role, what roles are predefined in each type, and what permissions are assigned to the predefined roles.

UNDERSTANDING SERVER ROLES

The first type of role that you will use to assist in the assignment of permissions is a server role. Server roles are special containers that have the right to perform certain server operations. When you add a SQL Server login to a server role, you are effectively granting the same server rights to that login. Server roles contain SQL Server logins because the rights that they convey are server-wide in nature and do not apply specifically to a database.

As an administrator in a medium to large organization, you will use server roles to help you delegate the miscellaneous duties of SQL Server administration. For example, if your organization has multiple implementations of SQL Server installed in different departments, and you no longer have enough time in the day to manage all the various tasks on all of the servers that your job requires, you may want to have a trusted employee in each department assist in some general SQL Server management tasks, such as creating databases or managing disk space on his or her departmental server. Because the employee in each case is not really a trained SQL Server administrator, and because that person has the potential to unintentionally create problems, you do not want to grant that user complete control over the system. Instead, you will want to grant that user a specific set of rights that pertain specifically to the tasks that you want him or her to perform. SQL Server provides you with seven predefined server roles to make this task easier. In the following sections, you will learn about each server role and when to use it.

Database Creators

One of the more useful server roles is the Database Creators role. This role grants to its members the right to create, rename, and modify databases. As a network administrator, you will undoubtedly find that many times your severs are somewhat volatile in that the actual user databases on the system are changed frequently as new databases are installed and old databases removed. We have found this to be true in a surprisingly large number of environments ranging from universities and computer training institutions to corporate environments. These deployments frequently move data around in the enterprise by creating new databases on a regular basis, performing a wide variety of changes to data, then saving the data to an environment other than SQL Server and deleting the databases. Universities and computer training institutions have unique needs and are often starting over with fresh installations of SQL Server on a weekly basis.

In the corporate environment, it can be especially valuable to have other people who are able to create new databases. The larger the organization, the larger this need becomes. You can easily grant a SQL Server login the right to create databases by adding that login to the Database Creators role.

Disk Administrators

The Disk Administrators role is somewhat self-explanatory in that members of this role inherit the ability to manage SQL Server disk files from within SQL Enterprise Manager or through a variety of stored procedures DISK INIT or DISK REINIT.

The Disk Administrators role has a lower level of functionality than it did in older versions of SQL Server because of the way SQL Server 7 stores databases. Many of the stored procedures that this role has permission to run are supported in SQL Server 7 only to provide backward compatibility. For example, the SP_DISKDEFAULT stored procedure set the status of a device to determine if it could store databases by default. In SQL Server 6.5, this procedure would determine the correct device for database storage in the event a user did not specify a device when creating or altering a database. Since SQL Server 7 stores databases directly to file, there is no longer a need for specifying a default device.

Process Administrators

The Process Administrators role is a unique role in that it really has only one purpose. Members of this role inherit the ability to kill processes. Administrators must sometimes kill a process in order to free resources that are locked and restore database functionality. If in your environment you have a network user who has sufficient knowledge to identify a lock that is impacting database performance, you can add the login for this user to the Process Administrators role, thereby granting that user the ability to kill those processes and free up the database. This can be particularly helpful in larger deployments where multiple SQL Servers are installed and the administrator cannot constantly monitor or manage them all.

Security Administrators

Because of its name, the Security Administrators role is perhaps the most confused server role supported by SQL Server. Members of this role inherit the ability to create server logins, modify the condition of statement permissions such as CREATE TABLE to a state of grant, deny, or revoke for all users. What this means to you as an administrator is that the members of this group can create new logins for database users, specify the default database for logins, and grant a low level of statement permissions to logins.

Administrators are often confused by the name of the Security Administrators role and believe that members of this role can perform all of the necessary functions required to manage a SQL Server security model. Though the security model for each deployment of SQL Server is different, most installations that the authors have seen involve complex permission management that is beyond the scope of this role alone.

Server Administrators

The Server Administrators role grants to its members the right to manage some of the different variables that control how SQL Server functions. Members of this role should have a high level of SQL Server knowledge and be trusted to make important decisions such as altering the default locking level of the server or shutting the server down. You will only add users to this role when they are members of your support staff or are employees trusted with maintaining the functionality of the server.

Setup Administrators

This role is particularly useful in large deployments where replication is being used. Members of this role inherit the ability to set up replication and manage extended stored procedures. You will add users to this role so that they can manage the replication environment on remote install sites. For example, if you are the administrator of a large SQL Server installation involving servers that are spread over a large geographical area, you may want to assign a trusted user from each site into this role so that there is an employee at the location of each server. If there is a user who has the ability to assist you in setting up replication from that location, you will not be required to travel to each install site in order to create or manage replication. You will learn more about setting up and managing replication in later chapters.

System Administrators

The System Administrators role is perhaps the most important server role that you will ever manage. Members of this role inherit all rights on the server, making them equal to the SA in default permissions. Typically, you will only add users to this role if they are senior members of the support staff who have an exceptionally high level of SQL Server knowledge and experience. Adding users to this role is basically making those users equal to the SA account and is a step that must be taken with extreme caution.

One of the most common abuses of this role is to assign members to the role due to their rank in the organization. You may find in some organizations that users who are ranked at the management or executive level frequently desire a level of access that is unnecessary for them to complete their duties and is granted only as a matter of principle. System administrators themselves are often the culprits in this type of permission abuse.

Many times the system administrator has day-to-day duties, which have nothing to do with the management of the SQL Server but involve using the database as a normal network user. In instances like this, we have found that many administrators perform their day to day duties logged on as the SA or have assigned their standard user account to the System Administrators role. This practice, however, is not in keeping with a good security model and increases the potential for unintentional damage to the database or SQL Server itself. As a general rule of thumb, you should only log on to the SQL Server as SA or as a System Administrator in order to perform administrative duties. All other duties that can be performed as a login with lesser privileges should, in fact, be performed with a normal login instead of SA or as a member of the System Administrators role.

TIP: You can photocopy Table 3-1 and keep it handy when planning or managing a SQL Server security model.

Depending on your environment, you may use one or all of the fixed server roles that are available in SQL Server. As you can see from the following table, the rights that are granted through the use

Role Name	Purpose	Executable Commands

Database Creators	Create and alter databases	Add member to `dbcreator`
		`ALTER DATABASE`
		`CREATE DATABASE`
		`Extend Database`
		`SP_RENAMEDB`

Disk Administrators	Manage files	Add member to `diskadmin`
		`DISK INIT`
		`DISK MIRROR`
		`DISK REINIT`
		`DISK REMIRROR`
		`SP_ADDUMPDEVICE`
		`SP_DISKDEFAULT`
		`SP_DROPDEVICE`

Process Administrators	Manage processes	Add member to `processadmin` `KILL`

Security Administrators	Manage security	Add member to `securityadmin`
		Grant/Deny/Revoke `CREATE DATABASE`
		Read the error log
		`SP_ADDLINKEDSRVLOGIN`
		`SP_ADDLOGIN`
		`SP_DEFAULTDB`
		`SP_DEFAULTLANGUAGE`
		`SP_DENYLOGIN`
		`SP_DROPLINKEDSRVLOGIN`
		`SP_DROPLOGIN`
		`SP_GRANTLOGIN`
		`SP_HELPLOGINS`
		`SP_REMOTEOPTION UPDATE PART`
		`SP_REVOKELOGIN`

Server Administrators	Manage server configurations	Add member to `serveradmin`
		`DBCC PINTABLE`
		`RECONFIGURE`
		`SHUTDOWN`
		`SP_CONFIGURE`
		`SP_TABLEOPTION`

Setup Administrators	Manage extended stored procedures	Add member to `setupadmin` Add/Drop/Configure Linked Servers Mark a stored procedure as startup
System Administrators	Any function	Can perform any task or function

Table 3-1.   Predefined Server Roles in the SQL Server 2000 Environment

of server roles do not affect the permissions of specific databases and provide you with no means of easily assigning database permissions to groups of users. To assign database permissions using roles, you will use database roles, which are discussed in the following section.

UNDERSTANDING DATABASE ROLES

Now that you understand the function of server roles, understanding database roles will be no trouble at all. As you know, server roles contain logins and apply server rights to those logins by passing their own rights onto the logins that they contain. In the same way, database roles pass their database permissions onto the users contained within them. Database roles can contain users just like databases contain users and are applied permissions to objects within the database to enable users to perform various database functions such as selecting data, updating data, or deleting data. There are actually two kinds of database roles. SQL Server automatically installs a set of predefined database roles with certain permissions already assigned to them. These database roles are general in nature and provide you with a means to assign general permissions to standard database objects. Additionally, you can create custom database roles and assign appropriate permissions, which gives you the ability to create very specific permission sets. You can use these two kinds of database roles to establish and maintain database security at an extremely precise level so that while database users have access and permissions to the objects that they need, they do not have permissions to objects that they do not need. SQL Server 7 provides you with ten database roles that have the appropriate permission level to perform specific tasks. In the text that follows, you will learn more about each of the database roles and how to use them to your advantage.

Understanding the Public Role

The first database role you will want to understand is the Public role. The Public role is very important because all SQL Server logins are members of this group by default. Additionally, the Public role exists in all databases by default and cannot be dropped (removed). As an administrator, you must be very careful about permissions that you assign to the Public role because a mistake could let any user into areas of the database you would under normal circumstances take steps to protect. Knowing the importance and special membership properties of the Public role is vital to effectively managing a SQL Server. There are actually many reasons to use the Public role. For example, if you have a database that contains standard employee information like name, desk phone number, building, department, and so on, you may want to grant all employees permission to view this information. You could add users for every login on the server and then grant each user permission to view the data, but a much more simple solution would be to simply grant the permission to the Public role. By granting the SELECT permission to the Public role, you have effectively granted the same permission to every valid login on the SQL Server because all valid logins belong to the Public role automatically. By default, the Public role is granted SELECT permissions on the system tables and views in all databases, but the permissions are controllable and you can change them if necessary.

Examining Predefined Database Roles

Now that you understand the Public role, you will want to take a look at the rest of the predefined database roles and what their purpose is. Remember as you review the following text, that only the Public role automatically contains all logins and users. Each of the database roles in the table must have users added to it in order to apply its inherent permissions. Remember also that in addition to using the predefined database roles, you will want to create new database roles and customize them to your specific needs. You will learn more about creating custom database roles later in this chapter.

The DB_OWNER (DBO) Database Role

If the most important database role to understand is Public, then certainly the DB_OWNER role is the second most important. In some ways, DB_OWNER is more important than the Public role because of the permissions that are automatically assigned to this role. Users who have been assigned to the DB_OWNER role have the same permissions as the database owner. This means that any database user that you add to the DB_OWNER role has all permissions in the database and can perform any task. From an administrative perspective, database users who can perform any action are extremely dangerous because the potential for unintentional damage is very high. If, for example, a database user who was recently added to the DB_OWNER role attempted to delete a table as a demonstration to another user because up until last week that user was unable to delete a table, the results could be disastrous. Imagine the impact that the loss of a single important table could have on your server. You will only assign a database user to the DB_OWNER role if that user is an assistant administrator and must have all permissions in a database.

The DB_ACCESSADMIN Role

DB_ACCESSADMIN is a role that grants its members the right to add new users to the database. You should understand that this is actually a very important database role because while it grants its members the ability to add new users, the users are created with the default database permissions. Members of the DB_ACCESSADMIIN are unable to change the permissions for that user or any other user. This means that you can add a login to this group and the result is that that user will only be able to add new users to the database when necessary. Adding additional permissions or modifying database membership is beyond the scope of this group and would only be possible if the login was added to more than one role

The DB_SECURITYADMIN Role

This role is a powerful tool for you because it grants its members the right to manage all permissions and ownerships in the database. This means that you can add an employee who will act as a single database administrator to this role for the specific database, and that user will be able to add, remove, and modify the ownership of all database objects and alter permissions such as the SELECT permission or the UPDATE permission on those objects to database users. Additionally, the members of this role can modify role membership in the database so that they are able to assign or remove permissions to multiple database users at the same time.

The DDLADMIN Role

The DDLADMIN role is the primary role into which you will place users who are active in the capacity of assistant system administrator. This role grants to its users the right to issue Data Definition Language (DDL) statements such as `create table` or `create index`. Developers and database users alike will use the SQL Data Definition Language to create database objects. You will assign users to this role when their job requires the ability to create such objects.

The DB_BACKUPOPERATOR Role

The DB_BACKUPOPERATOR role is perhaps the most commonly used role in any SQL Server deployment because no matter what the size of the SQL Server installation, the need to perform backups is always present and frequently is performed by an individual other than the primary system administrator. You will assign a user to this role so that the user is able to perform backups on a specific database and in place of the system administrator. Members of this role can issue Database Consistency Checker (DBCC) commands such as `dbcc checkdb` because DBCC commands are useful in determining the status of the database and managing transaction logs. Role members can additionally issue manual checkpoint commands in order to clear a database transaction log, and backup statements in order to actually perform backups.

The DB_DATAREADER Role

As you have learned, many of the predefined database roles are designed to provide the administrator with assistant users who can perform certain managerial actions on a database. The DB_DATAREADER role is no different and is designed to grant its members the right to grant other database users the SELECT permission on database objects. This is a useful role because most management-level employees can safely determine if a network user should be able to view data or not. Since the SELECT permission only grants the ability to view data, it is generally considered to be a permission with a low potential for damage. You should not, however, add all users to this role because then all users would potentially have access to all data including data that is considered confidential in nature and should be protected from standard users on a need-to-know basis.

The DB_DATAWRITER Role

The DB_DATAWRITER role grants its members the right to assign the INSERT, UPDATE, and DELETE permission to any object in the database. As an administrator, you must be careful with this role because unlike the DB_DATAREADER role, the DB_DATAWRITER role represents a greater potential threat to database damage and data loss than many other database roles. Database users who are members of this role need to understand that the granting of permissions that allow for the deletion of data is a task that must be taken very seriously because of the potential threat that it represents.

The DB_DENYDATAREADER Role

This role is the sister role to the DB_DATAREADER role and grants to its members the right to revoke the SELECT permission from any user for any object in the database. It is easy to see why many administrators assign the same database users to this role and to the DB_DATAREADER role—because they deal with the same permission and should therefore be managed by the same person. One interesting use of this role, however, is its use in ultra-secure environments where the databases contain highly confidential information that is highly sought after and therefore subject to intentional unauthorized access such as military or government classified data. In scenarios like this, the DB_DENYDATAREADER role, in conjunction with other roles, is assigned to users whose primary duties are simply to monitor user activity and find holes in the security structure or disable unauthorized access when such attempts are discovered.

The DB_DENYDATAWRITER Role

This role is the sister role to the DB_DATAWRITER role and grants to its members the right to revoke the SELECT permission from any user to any object in the database. This role is also typically assigned to an assistant permissions administrator who also is a member of the DB_DATAWRITER role in the same way that the DB_DENYDATAREADER role can be used creatively in high security environments.

Table 3-2 details all of SQL Server's built-in database roles.

When you are planning your security model, you should photocopy this table and keep it handy so that you can accurately plan for the use of predefined database roles or custom database roles. Good planning is always at the root of a sound security model and the ability to grant permissions on a group level will let you better control the database objects and users.

Understanding Custom Database Roles

Now that you understand the function of the predefined database roles, you will want to take a closer look at custom database roles and how they can help you control your database users. To begin with, you should understand that a custom database role is still just a database role and, as such, will contain database users and have permissions applied to it. The difference is only that you will create the custom database role and you will assign the role its permissions. Creating a custom database role is actually very simple. You can perform this operation either from SQL Enterprise Manager or using a system stored procedure. The first and perhaps most commonly used method of creating a custom database role is performed using SQL Enterprise Manager. If you use the tools in Enterprise Manager to create a new database role, you will be presented with the option of creating a standard role or an application role. Since you are

Built-in Database Role	Description
DB_OWNER	Has all permissions in database.
DB_ACCESSADMIN	Can add or remove user IDs.
DB_SECURITYADMIN	Can manage all permissions, object ownerships, roles, and role memberships.
DB_DDLADMIN	Can issue all DDL, but cannot issue GRANT, REVOKE, or DENY statements.
DB_BACKUPOPERATO	Can issue DBCC, CHECKPOINT, and BACKUP statements.
DB_DATAREADER	Can grant SELECT permissions on any object.
DB_DATAWRITER	Can grant INSERT, UPDATE, and DELETE permissions on any object.
DB_DENYDATAREADER	Can deny or revoke SELECT permissions on any object.
DB_DENYDATAWRITER	Can deny or revoke INSERT, UPDATE, and DELETE permissions on any object.

Table 3-2.   SQL Server's Built-in Database Roles

currently learning about custom database roles, you will want to focus on creating a standard role. You will learn more about application roles and how to manage them later in this chapter. To create a new role, perform the following steps:

1. Expand the database in Enterprise Manager and right-click your mouse on the Roles folder.

2. Choose the New Database Role option from the pop-up menu.

3. Type a name for the role in the Name field.

4. Click the Add button.

5. Add at least one database user from the list presented and click the OK button.

6. Click OK again.

Now that you have created a database role, you will probably want to apply permissions to the role. Before you start applying permissions, you should become familiar with the different types of SQL Server permissions, where to apply them, and how they impact the database.

EXPLORING DATABASE PERMISSIONS

As a SQL Server administrator, you undoubtedly want to ensure that your network users have access to the SQL Server and databases that they need, with the permissions that are appropriate to perform their duties. You may also want to ensure that while network users have every permission that they absolutely require to do their job, that they do not have permissions that exceed the required levels of access. This concept has been at the heart of database administration for many years. Network users who have too much access are likely to explore in areas that they should not, and possess a higher potential to cause database damage. Because the network users should be restricted from accessing all areas of the database, database management systems like SQL Server implement a mechanism to secure certain areas of the data while allowing access to others. SQL

Server 7 accomplishes this through the use of permissions. The two basic types of database permissions are statement permissions and object permissions, which are detailed in the following sections.

Understanding Statement Permissions

Statement permissions are those permissions that grant a user the ability to execute certain Transact-SQL statements. Statement permissions pertain to the creation and management of database objects such as tables, views, or stored procedures. The following is a list of the available statement permissions:

BACKUP DATABASE	CREATE STORED PROCEDURE (SP)
BACKUP LOG	CREATE TABLE
CREATE DEFAULT	CREATE VIEW
CREATE RULE	

Within the Enterprise Manager, statement permissions are managed from the properties page of a specific database. To manage statement permissions, perform the following steps:

1. Expand the list of databases in SQL Enterprise Manager.

2. Right-click on the database you want to manage permissions for.

3. Choose the Properties option from the pop-up list that appears.

4. Click on the Permissions tab in the upper-right side of the dialog box.

Looking at the Statement Permissions window, you will notice that the database users and roles are listed on the far-left side, with the statement permissions themselves listed in order to the right of each user or role, as seen in Figure 3-2.

Once you have accessed the Statement Permissions window for a particular database, you will want to assign statement permissions to database users and roles as applicable. Before you start clicking, you

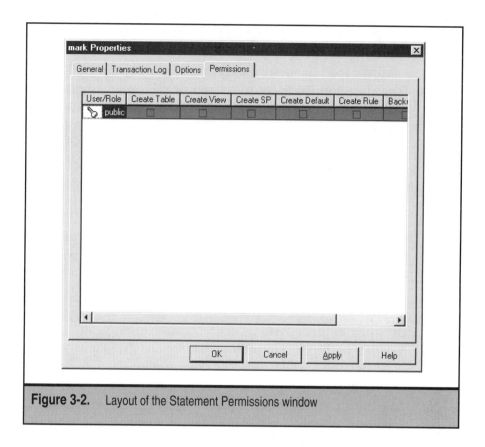

Figure 3-2. Layout of the Statement Permissions window

should understand that permissions can be in one of three states at any one time. A permission, whether it is a statement permission or an object permission, can be set to one of the conditions described in the following table:

Granted	SELECT ✓	In this condition, the database user or role is able to perform the action that the permission specifies.
Denied	SELECT ☒	In this condition, the database user or role is unable to perform the action that the permission specifies even if the permission is granted elsewhere.
Revoked	SELECT ☐	In this condition, the database user or role is unable to perform the action that the permission specifies. The user or role can, however, inherit the permission from another role and then be able to perform the action.

As you may have guessed, you can also manage the state of permissions using Transact-SQL. To control these permissions, you will use statements such as GRANT, REVOKE, and DENY followed by specifications that determine user or role and the permission being controlled. For example, if you want to grant the CREATE TABLE permission to a database user named Howard using Transact-SQL, connect to the server using Query Analyzer and execute the following statement:

```
USE CUSTOMERS
GRANT CREATE TABLE TO HOWARD
```

Using the same principle, if you wanted to later revoke that permission, you would simply connect in the same way and execute the following statement:

```
USE CUSTOMERS
REVOKE CREATE TABLE FROM HOWARD
```

One of the most important distinctions to make when dealing with permissions is understanding the difference between the REVOKED and DENIED permission. When a permission is in a REVOKED state, the database user is not expressly granted the permission and cannot perform the action that that permission specifies. The database user can, however, inherit permission from a role and be granted the ability to perform the action that way. When a specific permission is in a DENIED state, the database user has been expressly denied the ability to perform the action that is specified by that particular permission. The DENIED condition overrides all inherited permissions and the database user is unable to perform the specified action until the permission is no longer in a state of denial. For example, if you want to deny a user access to a specific database resource, but that user is a member of a database role that has been granted access to the resource, you can apply the DENIED permission state to the user specifically. By applying the DENIED permission state, that user is no longer able to access the database even though he or she belongs to a role that has been granted access permissions. The concept of denying permissions at the user level can be done on an as-needed basis or on a mass scale. For example, you can expressly deny all users all permissions as a matter of policy and thus ensure that only those users who actually require access are granted permission. This model works well for high-security environments, but tends to create too much work in organizations that are less concerned with security. The other way to use the deny-at-user method of security management is to grant permissions for any group of users who will typically need permission and only deny users who should *not* have the permission. This method results in less work for the administrator on a day-to-day basis, but allows for a greater quantity of mistakes and a lower level of base security.

As you have learned, statement permissions are those permissions that enable a database user or role to execute certain Transact-SQL statements. The state of permissions also applies to object permissions, as you will learn next.

EXPLORING OBJECT PERMISSIONS

As you now know, there are two basic types of database permissions supported under SQL Server 7. Since you have just learned about statement permissions, you will probably want to take a look at object permissions and how they can impact the database.

Object permissions deal with the ability of a database user or role to perform certain tasks on database objects. Object permissions are the same as statement permissions in that they can exist in a condition of GRANTED, DENIED, or REVOKED. You apply object permissions directly to the database user or role by accessing the Properties page. For example, if you wanted to grant a database user the SELECT permission for objects within the Northwind database, you would perform the following steps:

1. Expand the desired database in SQL Enterprise Manager.
2. Click on the Users folder.
3. Double-click on the user you want to grant permissions for.
4. Click on the Permissions button at the top of the dialog box.

Looking at the Permissions window, you will notice that the database objects are listed on the left side of the display and are in alphabetical order. All you have to do in order to set a specific permission is find the database object that you want to apply the permissions for in the left field, then scroll right until you find the permission that you want to apply and click in the checkbox. The Object Permissions windows is illustrated in Figure 3-3.

You can, of course, also control the state of permissions at the object level using Transact-SQL. Remember from the earlier section on statement permissions that there are three conditions that a permission can be in: GRANTED, DENIED, and REVOKED. You can control the state of permissions within the database by issuing the Transact-SQL statement that matches the name of your desired condition. For example, if you want to grant the SELECT permission

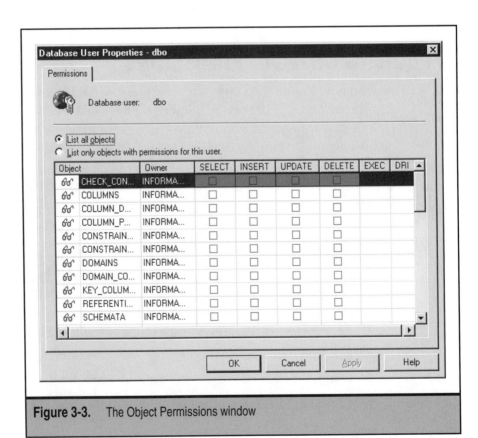

Figure 3-3. The Object Permissions window

for the Products table in the Northwind database to a user named Howard, connect to SQL Server using Query Analyzer and execute the following statement:

```
USE NORTHWIND
GRANT SELECT ON PRODUCTS TO HOWARD
```

In the same way, if you later want to revoke this permission from Howard, connect to the SQL Server in the same way and execute this statement:

```
USE NORTHWIND
REVOKE SELECT ON PRODUCTS FROM HOWARD
```

There are more types of object permissions than there are statement permissions and you will have to spend a little more time navigating the Permissions window. In the table below, you will find a complete list of available object permissions.

Permission	Description
SELECT	Lets a user view the contents of an object such as a table or view.
INSERT	Lets a user add new data to the contents of an object such as a table or view.
UPDATE	Lets a user change existing data in the contents of an object, such as a table, or to a table through a view.
DELETE	Lets a user remove data from the contents of an object, such as a table, or from a table through a view.
EXECUTE	Lets a user run an executable object such as a stored procedure.
DRI (Derived Relational Integrity, also known as the REFERENCES permission)	Lets a user invoke relational integrity for an object referenced by a table that the user does not have the SELECT permission for.

Most of the available object permissions are very easy to understand and can be easily applied by any administrator, with the exception of the DRI permission. The DRI permission stands for Derived Relational Integrity and is a permission that lets a user reference the data in a foreign constraint even if the user does not have the SELECT permission on the referenced data source. For example, if a database user named Howard has the INSERT permission for the Customers table, Howard is typically able to add rows to the table without incident. If, however, the Customers table contains a foreign key constraint that references the StateABB table, then SQL Server must validate any new data added to the referenced field. This would be a common scenario in which an unchanging table named State had a list of acceptable abbreviations for states and was called upon by other tables to verify the validity of abbreviations for state. If Howard does not have the SELECT permission for the StateABB table, SQL Server would technically be unable to validate the data being entered into the Customers table because Howard does not have the permission required to look at the reference table (StateABB). The DRI permission solves this problem because it lets you assign a user the right to reference a foreign data source without having to assign that user select rights to that source. In this example, granting the DRI permission for the State field in the Customer database to Howard will enable SQL Server to reference the StateABB table when Howard attempts to insert a new row into the Customer table. This way you are providing Howard with the ability to do his job, while still preventing him from being able to change data stored in the StateABB table.

During the planning stages of your security model, part of what you will do is determine what permissions are required by the various users in order to perform their jobs. Once you understand what users require, you will then divide the users into logical groups so that users who require similar permissions can be organized into roles.

You will normally apply object permissions to database roles, because doing so creates a means of assigning permissions to a group of users at the same time. When you need to restrict a database user from accessing a specific resource, you will apply the DENIED permission directly to the user account. If you assign database permissions this way, you will create an environment wherein no user can unintentionally obtain permissions to a database object simply because that user belongs to a database role that has those permissions.

UNDERSTANDING THE APPLICATION ROLE

As you have now learned, the two general kinds of roles are server roles and database roles. Within the database role category, there is a special kind of role called an application role. Application roles are special because they contain no database users. Instead, an *application role* applies its inherent permissions to any login who has the correct password to activate the role.

The advantage of application roles is that you, as the administrator, can apply permissions directly to an application that is performing specific tasks on your SQL Server. No matter what login was used to obtain access to the server, once the application role is activated, that login has the permissions that were applied to that role until the connection is terminated or the user changes databases.

You can use application roles to solve interesting problems found in the corporate structure. We have found in some organizations, for example, that an executive-level employee with little or no SQL Server knowledge or experience desires access to the SQL Server with high levels of permission so that he or she can run detailed reports from the server. As an administrator, this scenario can quickly become a nightmare because the executive represents a serious potential threat to the data. The potential threat is present because of the separation found in many large organizations between the executive echelon and those in charge of data security. Many executives or middle managers are considered exempt from normal security standards because they are implicitly trusted. This presents a breach of security because while the executives themselves may be worthy of such trust, their network access accounts and SQL Server logins are not. Because the executive strata of many companies enjoy high levels of access and are not required to conform to security standards, hackers and other unauthorized intruders will frequently target those accounts as methods of entry.

To solve this problem, you can first create a custom database front-end application that is only capable of generating the desired reports. Once the application has been developed and tested, you can create an application role on the SQL Server and grant the role the required permissions to generate the reports. During the development process you will want to modify the front-end application so that it sends a Transact-SQL statement to the SQL Server, which activates the application role.

The end result of this creation is that you can reduce the permissions for the executive to a very low level, which in turn reduces the potential threat to security. The executive can still obtain the required reports because the front-end application, operating through the application role, has the required permissions and is able to access the data it needs to generate reports.

Creating an application role is no more difficult than creating a custom database role and can actually be performed from the same dialog box in SQL Enterprise Manager or by using a stored procedure. To create an application role using Enterprise Manager, perform the following steps:

1. Expand the database you want to create an application role for in Enterprise Manager.

2. Right-click on the Database Roles folder.

3. Choose the New Database Role option from the pop-up list that appears.

4. Type a name for the role in the Name field.

5. Click in the Application Role checkbox.

6. Type a password into the Password field.

7. Click the OK button.

To create an application role using Transact-SQL, execute the SP_ADDAPPROLE system stored procedure. For example, if you wanted to create an application role named EXECREPORTS with a password of PASSWORD, you would connect to the SQL Server using Query Analyzer and type in the following SQL statement:

```
EXEC SP_ADDAPPROLE EXECREPORTS, PASSWORD
```

Once you have created the application role, you will want to activate it. From within Query Analyzer or another program into which you can directly type TRANSACT-SQL statements, you simply execute another stored procedure. If you want to have a custom application perform the step for you, it becomes a little more difficult. While the scope of actually performing Transact-SQL statements from within a specific programming language is beyond the scope of this book, you should be aware that most application types capable of connecting to a SQL Server typically are easily configured to send such statements. To activate an application role from Query Analyzer, you will execute the SP_SETAPPROLE system stored procedure. For example, if you want to activate the EXECREPORTS application role that was created in the previous example, you would connect to the SQL Server using Query Analyzer and type in the following statement:

```
EXEC SP_SETAPPROLE EXECREPORTS .
```

When you activate the role, SQL Server will prompt you to enter the password and provide you with a dialog box in which to do so.

TIP: If, as an administrator, you are in a position to dictate how your application developers connect to the server from a custom front end, you should specify that the developers use SQL-DMO (Data Manipulation Objects) to take advantage of application role support.

As a SQL Server administrator, you will use application roles to enhance your security model and control database access. Some of the other features that can enhance the security are stored procedures and views. In the text that follows, you will learn how to use stored procedures and views to control database access and improve security.

MANAGING SECURITY CREATIVELY

So far in this chapter, you have learned about the intuitive tools that aid you in the creation and management of a SQL Security model. You have learned about the different types of SQL Server logins and how they are implemented on a server. You have learned how to map logins into database users, which are the objects that are actually assigned permissions. You have learned about server, database, and custom roles and how you add logins and users to roles in order to manage permissions effectively. In most of the standard deployments of SQL Server, these tools are sufficient to manage the security and ensure that the data is secure while still providing the users with a high level of functionality.

Sometimes managing security can be difficult. In some environments, the data is considered to be so confidential that users who access the data from a single table should not be able to access all of the fields. Other times, the administrator is faced with a problem that is produced due to internal politics or organizational structure and finds that the standard methods of managing security are not enough. In the next section, you will learn some creative ways to manage security that can be applied to large SQL Server deployments as well as small ones.

Managing Security Using System Stored Procedures

As a SQL Server administrator, there may be instances when you will need to grant a user the ability to perform a task or series of tasks in a database, but for security reasons you may be unable or unwilling to grant that user permissions to the data sources. For example, assume you have created a database solution that includes an archive table to store deleted records in once they have been removed from the customer table. The process is fairly simple in that a record should be first copied to the archive table, then and only then removed from the primary table. The problem that you encounter is that typically, as an administrator, you will not want to trust that the average network user will always copy a record to the archive table prior to deleting it from the primary table. You can solve this problem by performing the following steps:

1. Create a stored procedure that copies a specified record or set of records from the primary table to the archive table and then remove those records from the primary table.

2. Assign the required permissions including the DELETE permission to the stored procedure.

3. Assign normal permissions to the database users but do not assign the DELETE permissions to the database user.

4. Assign the database users the EXECUTE permission for the stored procedure.

The end result of this scenario is that the users are able to remove the old records by executing the stored procedure. Since the stored procedure always copies records into the archive table before removing them from the primary table, there is no chance that the database users will forget to archive prior to deleting old records. Remember that the database users do not have the DELETE permission and are unable to remove records directly. Database users must execute the stored procedure in order to remove archives and remove old records. This method of managing permissions creatively is a very effective means of protecting your data. As you will learn in the next section, you can also use views to creatively grant database users the ability to perform certain tasks while still maintaining a high level of security.

Managing Security Using Views

You have probably noticed that even people with the best of intentions sometimes make mistakes that have dire consequences. It is this very concept, along with the knowledge that there are some people in the world who will attempt to access your servers with harmful thoughts in mind, that drives the administrator to design security measures on any system. As you learned in the previous sections, there are a variety of creative ways to implement security measures and still provide your network and database users with a high level of functionality. One such technique is to require database users to access the data stored in tables through views.

The idea behind this concept is simple. If you have a table that contains certain fields that you do not want all users to access, you can create a view that can access only the fields that you specify. With the appropriate permissions applied to the view instead of the table, database users are unable to access the table directly and so cannot access restricted fields. For example, database user Gladys requires access to all fields in the Customer data table that contain contact information such as name, address, and phone number. Gladys should not, however, be permitted to access the customer financial data in the same table (assume the table contains all these fields), because this type of confidential information is not needed by Gladys in order to complete her job. The problem is that if you were to grant the SELECT permission for Gladys to the Customer Data table, she would be able to access the financial data by default. You can solve this problem by performing the following steps:

1. Create a view that contains only the contact fields.
2. Apply all required permissions to the view.
3. Do not apply any permissions to the Customer Data table.
4. Instruct Gladys to use the view in order to perform her job.

In the example above, you are creating a scenario where permissions must pass through one object into another. More specifically, you are trusting that the permissions you apply to the view will then apply to the table so as to provide Gladys with the required access. This scenario will work well, so long as the table and view both have the same owner. If the database user who owns the table is different than the database user who owns the view, when you apply permissions to the view, they will not carry through to the table and the example will not work.

This problem is called a *broken ownership chain*, and can happen easily if the database is designed poorly or if many users have been granted the permission to create objects. It is because of broken ownership chains that experienced database designers are frequently of the opinion that database structure is best managed by always having one database owner create all objects.

Frequently, self-taught administrators make the mistake of thinking that adding a user to the DB_OWNER database role is the same as actually having the same user create all objects, which is not true. Members of the DB_OWNER role are still separate users and take ownership of objects when they create them. If members of this role create various objects and then other members create subobjects, you will still suffer from the problem of a broken ownership chain.

Fortunately, there is a way to have multiple users act as a single user within a database for the creation of objects. This method of creation is typically only used during the development of a major database, and you should avoid performing this action on a live database unless you have no other choice. To map multiple logins to a single database user, you will apply what is called an *alias* to the multiple logins. The database must already have the user stored within it, and you will simply apply an alias to one or more additional logins. This action is performed using a system stored procedure called SP_ADDALIAS and is done from Query Analyzer or a similar program capable of connecting to a SQL Server and issuing Transact-SQL statements manually. For example, if you wanted to alias the SQL Server login Cathy to the database user DBO inside the Customers database, connect to SQL Server using Query Analyzer and execute the following statement:

```
USE CUSTOMERS
EXEC SP_ADDALIAS CATHY, DBO
```

The concept of having logins assigned to a database as an alias brings up an interesting and hard-to-track problem that represents a potential hole in the SQL Server security model. The problem is that when a login obtains access to a database through the use of an alias, SQL Enterprise Manager does not display the presence of the login when you look at the user list for a database. This means that you can look at a database, check to see that the users are all as they should be, and move on without ever knowing that another user has access through an alias.

The solution to this problem is solved with a stored procedure called SP_HELPUSER. As an administrator, you will use the SP_HELPUSER stored procedure to determine not only what users are defined within a database, but additionally what logins are mapped to an existing user through an alias. For example, if you wanted to determine the users and mapped logins in the Customers database, you would connect to SQL Server using Query Analyzer and execute the following statement:

```
USE CUSTOMER
EXEC SP_HELPUSER
```

The query will run the stored procedure and return a list of users. At the bottom of the user list, you will see a list of logins that have been mapped to an existing user and which user they are mapped to. This problem and solution are an excellent example of why SQL administrators are well served by learning Transact-SQL and familiarizing themselves with the system stored procedures.

There is an additional method of ensuring that objects are created the right way, but this method assumes that the users who are creating objects will follow the proper procedure when they do so. Basically, an object in SQL Server is referenced properly by its fully qualified object name, which is described elsewhere in this book. A fully qualified name follows the structure SERVERNAME.DATABASENAME.OWNER.OBJECT. This means that if you are referencing the Customers table in the Northwind database, on a server named SQLTEST, the fully qualified name would be SQLTEST.NORTHWIND.DBO.CUSTOMERS. If you feel that you can trust all users who have the right to create objects, simply tell them to create the objects using the owner name of DBO when creating objects. We do not recommend this method, as it requires trusting your users, but it can be used in certain situations where political restrictions prevent you from aliasing users. You will learn more about object names later in this book.

SUMMARY

In this chapter, you learned how to create and manage a SQL Server security model. You began the chapter by learning about the SQL Server and Windows NT Authentication modes, how each can be used effectively to enhance the security of your deployment, and about the strengths and weaknesses of each. As you moved through the chapter, you learned about SQL Server logins and that a login is required no matter what type of authentication mode you choose in order to access a SQL Server. Learning about SQL Server logins led you to examine how they map into database users and what the job of a user is inside a database. You examined server, database, and custom roles and read examples of how you can group logins and users inside these roles so that you can assign permissions to multiple employees or network users at the same time. With the thought of assigning permissions in mind, you have closely looked at both statement and object permissions and what permissions are assigned to roles by default. Having learned that permissions must exist in order for database users to perform tasks within the database, you have learned how to assign permissions to logins, users, roles, stored procedures, and database objects in both SQL Enterprise Manager and by using Transact-SQL or stored procedures. In the hope that you will take the base SQL Server security knowledge and use it creatively to manage difficult deployments, you have learned some interesting ways to manage security and hopefully have examined some of the more common problems that can exist in an organization, but that are rarely talked about in courses or other books.

Now that you have a grasp on the security concepts that you will apply to SQL Server and its objects, you will undoubtedly want to learn more about the structure of databases, the new way that SQL Server stores the data, and some details about the general management concepts and techniques that you are likely to encounter as the administrator of a SQL Server. In the next chapter, you will deal with these topics and more, building on the knowledge you already have so that you will know your server and databases at a very personal level and will be able to solve almost any problem.

CHAPTER 4

The Structure of Data in SQL Server

S QL Server is, as you know, a *relational database management system* and, as such, deals specifically with storing high volumes of data in an efficient manner. To better understand the way that SQL Server handles your data, it is important that you understand the various levels at which SQL Server will place data. In this chapter, you will learn about the structure of databases. We will begin by examining the smallest unit of storage recognized by SQL Server and work our way through until we have discussed the files themselves and how we can improve file performance using both advanced hardware configurations and special configurations within SQL Server.

UNDERSTANDING PAGES

The smallest unit of storage recognized by SQL Server is called a *page*. A single page is 8K in size and is the unit on which SQL Server actually stores data. Books Online defines a page as "a fixed-length block of contiguous virtual addresses copied as a unit from memory to disk and back during paging operations." This means that the computer operating SQL Server actually has to read from disk the entire page to access any of the data stored in that page. Additionally, SQL Server does not allocate the entirety of a page before moving on to use space in another. This means that, at any time, there is a portion of page space that is unused but that nonetheless takes up space as allocated by SQL Server. This percentage is configurable and is known as the *fill factor*. You will learn more about the fill factor later in this chapter, and it is enough for now to know what a page is.

UNDERSTANDING EXTENTS

SQL Server groups pages for the purpose of allocating space inside the database for storage. SQL allocates eight pages at a time in a unit of storage called an *extent*. The way that data is actually allocated is determined by the extent. As users fill the database with information, this data is stored in pages until the extent is filled to a specified percentage. SQL Server maintains two types of extent, commonly referred to as uniform extents and mixed extents.

Uniform extents are extents that comprise continuous data from a single object. As you have learned, SQL Server databases are composed of objects that in turn hold data, configuration information, and other types of general data necessary to SQL Server. A uniform extent contains data from only one object and is therefore owned by that object.

Mixed extents are composed of data that spans multiple objects. This simply means that different SQL Server objects, such as a database table, index, or even multiple tables, own the data contained within the extent.

When tables and indexes are created within SQL Server, the objects are allocated into mixed extents. When the object reaches a point that it can fill an extent completely, SQL Server then changes the extent into a uniform extent. Uniform extents are desired because SQL Server can more easily manage them than it can mixed extents—for the simple reason that the pages within the extent all maintain information about a common object, and therefore are simpler to maintain than mixed extents.

Additionally, mixed extents create a higher potential within the database for a condition called *lock escalation* to occur. To better understand why you do not want your database to suffer from lock escalation, you will have to explore the concept of a lock.

UNDERSTANDING THE IMPACT OF LOCKS ON DATABASES

Within a database, no single user or process can access the same data, at the same time, for the purpose of updating. Put another way, you cannot have two or more users trying to change the data in a single row at the same time. Because of the way that SQL Server stores and manages data, sometimes data from more than one row is stored within the database in such a way that a user attempting to access one row is prevented from doing so because another user is already accessing data in another row that is stored in the same area. Figure 4-1 shows how rows within a given page might cause an access conflict.

When SQL Server prevents a user from accessing data that another user is accessing, the condition that occurs is known as a *lock*. Locking is a normal part of database operation and is a feature that helps to validate your data by ensuring that a user attempting to change data is first made aware of the data's current state within the server. When a user is prevented from reaching data because another user is accessing different data, the database becomes less efficient. In some cases, a lock that begins at the row level can escalate to a point where it is locking an entire page, an extent, or even an entire table. Database administrators frequently call this scenario lock escalation.

Solving the problem of lock escalation is typically a developmental task and is performed by the database developer, because it usually involves altering the structure of the database. As an administrator, you play an important part, because you are the individual who identifies the problem and provides much of the research required to identify the cause accurately.

NOTE: You will learn more about researching and monitoring SQL Server in Chapter 8.

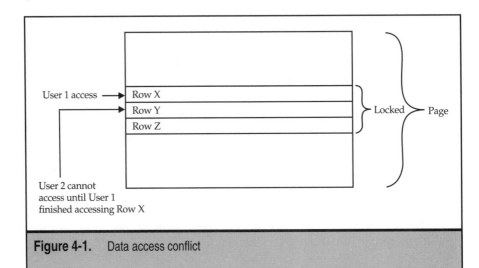

Figure 4-1.   Data access conflict

To help prevent lock escalation, SQL Server converts all mixed extents into uniform extents as soon as there is enough data from a single object to dominate the extent and be assigned ownership. Additionally, SQL Server leaves room in each page composing the extent; that room in turn gives the table or index the ability to grow without losing efficiency. In the next section, you will learn more about this free space and why SQL Server maintains it.

TIP: When SQL Server converts a mixed extent to a uniform extent, it performs a two-step process on the excess data in the extent. If existing uniform extents have space available, objects of that type(s) are moved into those extents. For any objects for which a uniform extent with available space does not exist, SQL Server creates a new mixed extent and places all the remaining objects into the new, mixed extent.

UNDERSTANDING THE DEFAULT FILL FACTOR SPECIFICATION

As you know, SQL Server stores data in pages. What you should also know is that the data is organized according to the server sort order that you specified during installation. When a table or index is created, SQL Server organizes the data into the proper order. Later, as you add new data, the data you are adding might need to be placed into a page that is already full in order to maintain the sort. When this happens, SQL Server creates a new page and moves half the rows from the current page into the new page, which makes room for the new data. This division is known as a *page split*.

Sometimes, new data can cause SQL Server to page split many times as it reorganizes the table or index. Reorganizing a database can sometimes be processor- and memory-intensive, resulting in higher server load and, naturally, reduced productivity. Depending on the number of new pages created, as well as other issues in the database, SQL Server might create some pages in mixed extents, moving them into uniform extents as more pages in the index are created, or might create pages in existing uniform extents with page space available, or some combination of both. Needless to say, all that additional processing takes time.

To help solve this problem, SQL Server can leave a predefined amount of empty space in each page so that when new data needs to be added, there is available room for storage, resulting in fewer page splits. In SQL Server 2000, the setting that defines the amount of free space is called the *default fill factor*. Default fill factor has always been a configurable option in SQL Server; you can override this setting and take manual control of this factor. Specifying it determines the efficiency of the database because doing so determines free space within an index at the time of creation and is a vital part of how SQL Server manages data. For example, if your database is a read-only database that provides information to the network users but is never updated, then there is no need for the pages to have any free space at all, and the default fill factor might be set so that little or no space is reserved.

When the index for the database table is created, a default fill factor of zero percent means that no free space exists in the pages, with the exception of a small amount left free in the upper area of the index tree. This setting is actually very close to a default fill factor setting of 100, except that in this case SQL Server will create clustered and nonclustered indexes with all pages 100 percent full and with no room left in the index tree.

TIP: While it is presumed that you know the difference between a clustered and a nonclustered index, it is valuable to reconsider their construction briefly. Clustered indexes have one row in `sysindexes` with `INDID = 1`. The pages in the data chain and the rows in them are ordered on the value of the clustered index key. All inserts are made at the point at which the key value in the inserted row fits in the ordering sequence. Nonclustered indexes, on the other hand, have the same B-tree structure as clustered indexes, with two significant differences: The data rows are not sorted and stored in order based on their nonclustered keys, and the leaf layer of a nonclustered index does not consist of the data pages. Instead, the leaf nodes contain index rows. Each index row contains the nonclustered key value and one or more row locators that point to the data row (or rows if the index is not unique) having the key value.

Put another way, if you specify a setting of zero percent, SQL Server will leave a small amount of room in the pages that were created first, but other than that will fill all pages to capacity. The space left free provides SQL Server with a means for easily adding new data about database objects, such as adding a column to a table or a new filter to a long-standing query. If you specify a setting of 100 percent, SQL Server will fill all pages to capacity, not even leaving space for the modification of database objects. This setting, in particular, would be more appropriate for a well-tested and proven database, one specifically designed for read-only operations.

If your database has the potential to be frequently updated, however, you will need a default fill factor setting of somewhere between 20 and 80 percent. You will determine the amount of free space within the index by specifying a percentage. For example, if you want your indexes to be created with 50 percent of the allocated storage space free for input, specify a default fill factor setting of 50 percent. This way, when the index is created, a percentage of free space is left in the extent so that if changes are made to the data or new records are added, there will be room to insert the data at the correct point in the index without having to re-create the index again. In the event that you do not leave sufficient space, SQL Server will again have to create new pages and extents to support the index, resulting in the performance decreases discussed previously.

TIP: Determining how much of a default fill factor to set is complex and difficult. The number of indexes, both clustered and nonclustered, the number of new records inserted in each indexed table, and a whole series of additional considerations will all come into play when you make your decisions about fill factors. While our extensive experience with a wide variety of databases lets us make some general comments about fill factors, the determination will be unique and specific to each database you create.

It is important that you understand that SQL Server does not maintain the pages or extents at any specific level of free space. The default fill factor setting is only applied at the time the index is created and is a default setting that you can override when creating any index using the CREATE INDEX Transact-SQL statement. For example, the Transact-SQL statement to create a new index called CUSTBYNAME on the CustomerName column of the Customers table is as follows:

```
create index CUSTBYNAME on Customer (CustomerName)
```

Note the use of the column name CustomerName, which is enclosed within parentheses. You had to specify here that the name of the column on which you wanted to index within the table is CustomerName.

Now assume your server has a default fill factor setting of 25 percent and you want to create a new clustered index named CUSTBYNAME for the Customers table with a default fill factor of 50 percent. To create a new index using Transact-SQL, connect to SQL Server using Query Analyzer or a similar program capable of executing Transact-SQL statements manually and directly to a SQL Server, and then execute the following statement:

```
CREATE CLUSTERED INDEX CUSTBYNAME
ON Customers (CustomerName)
WITH FILLFACTOR=50
```

The re-creation of indexes because of page splitting can be a time-consuming and highly processor-intensive operation. For the administrator, this can substantially affect the performance of your SQL Server. Because incorrect default fill factor settings could cause the database to be inefficient, you must be extremely careful about your fill factor choices if you decide to manage fill factor settings manually. Microsoft recommends that you let your SQL Server manage the default fill factors for you, and we agree. Remember that you can always take manual control during the creation of a new table or index.

TIP: As a rule, you should adjust fill factor settings only for each table or index. You should definitely avoid adjusting the default fill factor setting in all but the most exceptional design situations.

If you choose to take manual control of the default fill factor, you can modify its settings using a slider in Enterprise Manager by following the steps below:

1. Within Enterprise Manager, right-click on the SQL Server.

2. Click the Database settings tab.

3. Using your mouse, drag the slider in the Default Fill Factor area to the left or right until the percentage matches what you want.

4. Click OK.

As with most administrative actions that you can perform in Enterprise Manager, you can also change the default fill factor setting for a SQL Server using Transact-SQL. Default fill factor is a server configuration and, as such, is modified using the SP_CONFIGURE stored procedure. For example, to modify the default fill factor on your server to a setting of 50 percent, connect to SQL Server using Query Analyzer and execute the following statement:

```
sp_configure 'fill factor', 50
go
reconfigure
go
```

TIP: Taking control of the default fill factor setting in SQL Enterprise Manager is a system-wide setting and sets the default for all databases.

Now that you understand the basic structure and allocation units that SQL Server uses to store data, you will want to take a close look at the files that ultimately store the database. The following section takes a probing look at the structure of database files and explains how SQL Server 2000 uses them.

EXPLORING DATABASE FILES

As you might already know, SQL Server 2000 stores databases directly to files. This is a relatively new method of storage for

Microsoft SQL Server, because versions prior to 7.0 had to register specific files and preallocate space into a unit of storage called a *device*. The device concept has always been described as an important one because it let you preallocate an area of disk space that a database could then use. This ensured that the database would not suffer from disk fragmentation as it grew. Another praised aspect of the device structure is that a device can be created on a nonpartitioned area of a physical disk. This ability added to the security features of SQL Server, because only SQL Server could access any database objects or data that they contain. While SQL Server 7.0 and 2000 still technically support the use of devices, they now use them primarily to identify the location of permanent backup storage files. SQL Server no longer requires files to be recognized as devices and can access the disk files directly.

NOTE: Everyone's opinion about the elimination of disk devices varies; however, Microsoft's original logic behind the usage of devices was to protect against fragmentation of the data storage. In the field, however, most companies were deploying SQL Servers on stand-alone computers anyway, so disk fragmentation was not the issue administrators thought it would be. In general, eliminating devices makes managing SQL Servers substantially simpler, but does lead to certain laziness issues, as discussed elsewhere in this chapter. On the whole, we believe serious administrators would agree that eliminating devices is a boon for management, but can force some adjustments in the thought process.

To provide a level of backward compatibility with older versions of SQL Server, Microsoft has included limited support for devices. Device support is one instance where the issues are equally important to developer and administrator alike. The importance of devices to the developer derives mostly from the scripted installation files that execute Transact-SQL statements as part of an install for many database applications; developers providing product support for SQL Server must be cautious when creating or modifying such scripts. For the administrator, the task of supporting devices expands to include support of older databases that were developed within the organization, and also ensures that new databases will not cause problems when implemented on an existing SQL Server deployment.

One of the more interesting aspects of SQL Server's support for devices lies in the Transact-SQL statements DISK INIT and DISK REINIT. These two statements were among the primary tools that a SQL Server 6.5 administrator would use.

The DISK INIT statement is included in the Transact-SQL library for SQL Server. In previous versions of SQL Server, you would use this statement to create a device on which you would place a new database. In SQL Server 7 or 2000, you can use this statement to create a device to support older database designs, but should be aware of how the statement truly works so that you avoid potential problems. To help you understand some issues not immediately apparent, we will use this reference from Books Online as an example of the DISK INIT statement:

```
DISK INIT name = 'testdb_data',
                Physname = 'c:\testdb_data.dat',
                Vdevno = 9,
                Size = 10240
DISK INIT name = 'testdb_log',
                Physname = 'c:\testdb_log.dat',
                Vdevno = 8,
                Size = 10240
CREATE DATABASE testdb
                ON testdb_data = 10
                LOG ON testdb_log = 10
```

In SQL Server 6.5, the first DISK INIT statement would create a device named testdb_data. The testdb_data device would be stored as a physical file named TESTDB_DATA.DAT on the C: drive and would have a size of 10,240 2K pages, or roughly 20MB. The reference Vdevno stands for Virtual Device Number and is an internal tracking number for SQL Server. If you were to execute the first part of the statement alone, it would look like this:

```
DISK INIT name = 'testdb_data',
                Physname = 'c:\testdb_data.dat',
                Vdevno = 9,
                Size = 10240
```

In newer versions of SQL Server, however, executing this statement alone has a different effect, in that no physical disk space is reserved by the operating system. Running this statement will create a reference inside the MASTER Database that identifies the device, though the file would not be created. In SQL Server 6.5, the same statement would both make an entry in the MASTER Database and also create the disk file, effectively reserving that space for future use. In SQL Server 7 or 2000, however, the disk files are not created until the CREATE DATABASE statement is executed, as you will see in the text that follows.

The second part of the statement is equally important because while SQL Server 6.5 was capable of storing both a database and its associated Transaction Log in a single physical disk file, SQL Server 2000 is not. To create a database in SQL Server 2000, you must specify a separate physical file for both the database and the log. In the example, the second part of the statement creates a device on which the log will reside. If you were to execute this portion of the statement alone, it would look like this:

```
DISK INIT name = 'testdb_log',
               Physname = 'c:\testdb_log.dat',
               Vdevno = 8,
               Size = 10240
```

In SQL Server 6.5, if you ran this part of the statement by itself, it would create a single device named testdb_log, which is stored on the C: drive in a file named TESTDB_LOG.DAT and which would have a size of about 20MB. In the new SQL Server, however, it will only create the device inside SQL Server and store the information in the MASTER Database. You could later use the CREATE DATABASE statement to create the physical disk.

The last portion of the example statement is the CREATE DATABASE reference. This part of the example is what actually creates a database in SQL Server, creates physical disk files on the computer, and creates a Transaction Log for the database to use along with its associated disk files. When run alone, the CREATE DATABASE statement would look like this:

```
CREATE DATABASE testdb
            ON testdb_data = 10
            LOG ON testdb_log = 10
```

In this example, the CREATE DATABASE statement includes parameters that will work only if the devices were previously created. For example, if you ran this statement alone, without having first run the DISK Init statements that created testdb_data and testdb_log, the CREATE DATABASE statement would fail.

You should understand that this does not mean that the CREATE DATABASE statement must always be preceded by a DISK Init statement, as it was in SQL Server 6.5—but rather that the statements are supported within SQL Server 7 and 2000, using the syntax exemplified here.

To better understand the way that SQL Server creates and manages databases, it is important for you to comprehend the database file structure. In the following sections, you will learn about database files. These are the actual disk files in which SQL Server stores databases. In SQL Server, database files come in three basic forms: *Transaction Log files*, *database files*, and *extended database files*. SQL Server uses each of the file types in a different way to accomplish data storage. To differentiate between file types, each type is assigned a different file extension so that you, the operating system, and SQL Server can tell the difference between them. The three file extensions used are .MDF for a primary database file, .NDF for a secondary or extended database file, and .LDF for a Transaction Log file.

NOTE: one easy way to remember these files is just to remember the words Main, Next, and Log. Take the first initial and add DF to the end, and you have a valid name, as well as an understanding of what the file is for.

Over the next few sections, you will learn about each of these files and how SQL Server uses them to both protect and store data. At the same time, you will gain valuable insight into the workings of SQL Server and the methodology of transaction-based storage. Now that we have used the phrase *transaction-based storage*, it is probably wise to begin with a discussion of the Transaction Log and how it works in SQL Server.

Understanding the Transaction Log

Because data, or rather the transactions that create data, is basically stored first in the Transaction Log, it is the first file that you should understand. To truly understand the Transaction Log, you will first need to learn a few things about the structure of SQL Server and the lengths that it goes to in order to ensure that the data is secure and that all executed transactions are run either completely or not at all.

When a user sends a Transact-SQL statement to SQL Server, the information is first delivered to the buffer cache. This is simply physical computer memory that SQL Server has allocated for its use. Naturally, as Transact-SQL statements enter the server, it is to this memory location that they are first delivered. Once in the buffer cache, SQL statements basically stand in line and wait for an opportunity to begin executing. If the buffer cache is filled to capacity, the transaction being sent has to wait at the client side until delivery can be made. This is in practice a very rare problem, and one that is typically only found on installations with an extreme case of insufficient memory. In most deployments, the transaction enters into the buffer cache without incident and simply waits for its turn to execute.

When a statement begins to execute, the execution is recorded in the Transaction Log. Statements are stored in a SQL Server-specific format that is similar to a machine language. Conceptually speaking, each executable line of Transact-SQL code is recorded line by line as it executes on the server. At regular intervals, SQL Server will initiate a process called a *checkpoint*, which basically moves information from the Transaction Log into the database. You will learn more about the checkpoint process later in this chapter. As you will see later, in general, a checkpoint occurs after each transaction completes.

When a new transaction begins to execute, SQL Server additionally places a marker inside the Transaction Log, at the beginning of a new transaction, specifying that the transaction has begun to execute. This marker is called a BEGIN TRANSACTION (or BEGIN TRAN) statement. When the transaction has completed, SQL Server places another marker at the end of the statement that specifies that the transaction is complete, called a COMMIT TRANSACTION (COMMIT TRAN) statement.

By using this method, the SQL Server ensures that all transactions are recorded as they execute. Because there are both BEGIN TRAN and COMMIT TRAN markers, if something were to happen to the SQL Server while a transaction was in progress, the Transaction Log would thus have recorded the beginning of a transaction but not its completion.

Each time SQL Server starts, the server initiates a process known as *automatic recovery*. The automatic recovery process scans the Transaction Log and moves completed transactions into the database. In addition, transactions that lack an end marker are removed from the Transaction Log as if they never existed.

Most database administrators, developers, and reference texts use some common terms to describe the automatic recovery process. We have tried to use different and friendlier terms here, but you should *still* learn the correct terminology so that you can recognize it in online help and reference texts when needed. For example, the typical description of the automatic recovery goes like this:

At SQL Server start, the automatic recovery process is initiated. During the recovery process, SQL Server scans the Transaction Log and rolls committed transactions forward *(stores them in the database)*, and rolls uncommitted transactions backward *(deletes them from the database)*.

The following sections detail the types of transactions supported in SQL Server and how you can use them best.

Understanding Transaction Types

Because understanding the automatic recovery process is vital to your success as a SQL Server administrator, and because it is actually transactions themselves that make the process possible, we will spend a little time here to ensure that you completely understand the transaction process and know how SQL Server 2000 implements transactions.

Transactions are commands issued in a language that is understood by SQL Server. These commands contain data and instructions on how to process data. As you know, SQL Server processes transactions in such a way that a transaction must complete totally, or not at all. You should be aware that there are times when SQL Server cannot accomplish this because of the way the data is changed. Said another way, certain operations inside SQL Server are called *nonlogged operations*. These operations make no record in the Transaction Log and therefore represent a potential for data loss. In addition to nonlogged operations, SQL Server supports two basic types of transaction: implicit and explicit transactions.

Implicit transactions are those that SQL Server completes without additional direction from the SQL code itself. In other words, the actual statement does not instruct SQL Server to begin a transaction or to end the transaction. Implicit transactions are short transactions that typically take up no more than a single line. For example, the following line of Transact-SQL can be safely executed as an implicit transaction:

```
BACKUP DATABASE testdb to disk = 'c:\mssql\backup\testdb.bak'
```

In the example above, the statement begins and ends an entire transaction in a single line of code. When executed, this statement will immediately begin to back up the database named TESTDB. SQL Server will enter this line into the Transaction Log and automatically consider it a complete transaction. When the transaction is complete, SQL Server will make an entry in the Transaction Log, indicating that it is a committed transaction. When the next checkpoint is issued, SQL Server will roll this transaction forward because it is committed. If, however, the SQL Server crashes during the execution, then the transaction is not recorded as complete, and will be rolled back during the automatic recovery process.

The statement in the example is considered an implicit transaction because it relies on SQL Server to determine whether the statement is committed or not. If this had been a part of a larger transaction, and you wanted to manually determine whether the transaction was committed, you would use an explicit transaction.

Explicit transactions are ones that are completely controlled by the operator. Said another way, an explicit transaction is one over which you take complete control, telling SQL Server where the transaction begins and when it commits. To use the example shown previously (something of a stretch, granted, but useful for our purposes), you might want to create an explicit transaction that backs up all the databases on a server, or fails and rolls back—meaning that none of the backups are considered to have been completed.

More commonly, explicit transactions will be used to enforce some type of data integrity issue. To that end, typically, with explicit transactions you will use statements that help maintain complex data integrity.

Effectively Handling Locking Conflicts

When one user has a page locked and another user tries to view data on that page, no conflict occurs. On the other hand, when yet another user attempts to edit data on that same page, he or she experiences an error.

You will not always want SQL Server's own error handling to take over when a locking conflict occurs. For example, rather than having SQL Server display its generic error message indicating that a record is locked, you might want to display your own message and attempt to lock the record a couple of additional times. To do something like this, it is necessary that you and your developers learn to interpret each locking error so that you and your network applications can decide how to respond.

Locking conflicts occur in the following situations:

▼ A user tries to edit or update a record that is already locked.

▲ A record has changed or been deleted since the user first started to edit it.

Understanding Database Files

As you have learned, after being recorded in the Transaction Log, Transact-SQL statements are then run against the SQL Server, which in some cases produces data that must be stored. Occasionally the Transact-SQL statements make configuration changes on the server or merely read data and return results to the client. Since this section is devoted to the topic of database files, we will restrict ourselves at this point to talking about those statements that create data.

Once the SQL Server has created the data for storage, the data is placed into a database file. The two basic types of database files are called *primary database files* and *secondary* or *extended database files*. In this section, you will learn about primary database files and what their role is in SQL Server storage. You will learn about extended database files in the next section.

The file extension for a primary database file is .MDF. Each and every database on your server has a primary database file, which it uses to store data. As you know, the data is actually stored in tables, sorted using indexes, and additionally managed by other database objects. It is within the database file that SQL Server stores all the database objects, and therefore you can safely say that the database file is the root unit of storage.

SQL Server 2000 supports the creation, access, and deletion of disk files directly from within the SQL Server interface. This means that you no longer have to create devices or remove devices and then use another program to delete the disk file. In some ways, SQL Server's ability to delete the disk file is an advantage. For example, not having to remember to manually delete the disk file means that you will not use up valuable disk space with deleted databases, and also that your job as an administrator is less difficult.

In other ways, SQL Server's ability to delete disk files is a disadvantage. If you—or another network user with high levels of permission—inadvertently (or intentionally) deletes an entire database, for example, you will thereafter be unable to reattach the database from the file because the file is gone. This means that you will have to rely on your backup to restore that particular database to the server. You will learn more about backups, restores, and the backup process in Chapters 6 and 7.

Primary database files also are the initial unit that SQL Server uses to create file groups. File groups also use extended database files, which you will learn more about in the text that follows; for now, simply understand that they exist.

When you first create a database, the name of the primary database file is automatically generated, using the name of the database. For example, if you created a database named TESTDB and did not specify any name at the time of creation, SQL Server would name the primary database file TESTDB.MDF. At the same time, SQL Server would also create the Transaction Log, which you learned about in the previous section, and name it TESTDB.LDF. When the file is created, extended information that is not readily apparent to you is also included in the file. Part of this extended information specifies what file group this file is a part of. In the case of a primary database file, the file itself is always part of the primary file group. You can prove this to yourself simply by connecting to the SQL Server using Query Analyzer and executing the following statement:

```
sp_helpdb Testdb
```

The code example above will execute the SP_HELPDB stored procedure on the TESTDB database. The information returned includes a reference to the file group where you can plainly see that the primary database file (TESTDB.MDF) is a member of the primary file group. You can also obtain file group information by examining the properties of a database in Enterprise Manager, by following these steps:

1. Within Enterprise Manager, expand the Databases folder.
2. Right-click on the database you wish to examine.
3. Choose Properties from the pop-up list.

In the Database Files area on the right side, you will see a listing that clearly identifies the file grouping for a specific file. You will use this same dialog box to create databases from scratch if you are doing so from within Enterprise Manager. Creating databases, as well as managing many of the other settings for a database, is covered in a later section of this chapter.

Understanding Extended Database Files

In the previous section, you learned about the primary database file and about the existence of file groups. In this section, you will learn about extended database files and how SQL Server uses them to manage growing databases, enhance database performance, and assist you in performing logical backups of a database.

As you now know, a database always has a primary database file. This is not true of the extended database file, which is not always present in a database structure. You can use extended database files to increase the size of a database that has run out of disk space, to enhance the performance of a database that is suffering from hardware constraints, or to enhance the performance of a database that is too large to function efficiently.

You can create extended database files when you initially create the database, or at any time after that as an add-on to a preexisting database. For example, if you have a database that is running out of disk space, you can solve the problem by simply adding an additional disk to the server and then creating an extended database file on the new disk. As the database reaches the end of space on the original disk, it will automatically begin to store data on the new file (on the new disk) and continue to run without incident.

Additionally, you can use an extended database file to solve problems that arise from insufficient hardware. For example, one of the most common problems that can occur in a database arises when users are executing read operations against the database at the same time as other users are trying to execute write operations against it. The problem is that there is only one set of heads in the physical disk drive that are capable of *either* reading *or* writing data at one time. Because of this, one of the processes is forced to wait as the other process continues to execute. This problem is commonly referred to as *disk contention*.

You can solve the problem of disk contention by adding a new disk to the server and separating the database objects so that tables containing data that will be mostly write operations and indexes that will be used primarily for reading are on different physical disks. This way, users who are reading data and others who are writing it are accessing different disk drives and thus different heads to execute their respective tasks. Since there is double the amount of hardware functionality in the server, there is roughly double the amount of gained productivity in the database environment.

The example above will not always apply to your particular environment, of course, and you will have to carefully examine the database to determine if this solution will work for you. Additionally, you should have database development experience and knowledge before attempting to divide a database into different files, because the division must make sense in terms of performance; it can also affect the functionality of database management tasks, such as backups.

File groups can give you a tremendous administrative advantage because they let you specify a file group at the time of backup, when the backup will archive all files that are part of that group. For example, if you divided the objects of a database up so that the administrative tables were in one file group and the financial tables were in another, you would be able to specify the administrative file group during the backup procedure, and SQL Server would automatically back up all files that are members of that group—but not back up members of the financial file group.

Like extended database files themselves, you can create secondary file groups (a generalized term that refers to any file group *other* than the primary file group, which in turn implies that you must have a primary file group before you can have a secondary file group, just as you must have a database file before you can create an extended database file). You create the secondary file groups either at the time of database creation or at any point thereafter when you add an extended database file. Because SQL Server can create and manage databases using Enterprise Manager or Transact-SQL, you must be able to specify a secondary file group in either location. For example, if you wanted to add an extended database file to the CUSTOMERS database using Enterprise Manager, you would connect to the SQL Server and perform the following steps:

1. Within Enterprise Manager, expand the Databases folder.

2. Right-click on the database for which you wish to add an extended file.

3. Choose Properties from the pop-up list.

4. In the Database Files area of the window, click in the name field, just below the existing filename.

5. Type a name for the new database file.

If you wanted to add a new extended database file to an existing database, the process is a little different. For example, if you want to add an extended database file to the CUSTOMERS database using Transact-SQL, you would simply connect to the SQL Server using Query Analyzer and execute the following statement:

```
ALTER DATABASE Customers
ADD FILE (name = 'customer1_dat',
        filename = 'c:\MSSQL\data\customer1_dat.ldf',
        size = 1mb)
```

As you can see from the statement above, adding an extended database file is a relatively simple process, no matter your choice of tools. The statement adds a new file to the CUSTOMERS database with a name of CUSTOMER1_DAT and an initial size of 1MB. All other file variables are assumed to be defaults. You will learn more about each of the variables for database files later in this chapter. When you add an extended file, you might or might not decide to create a new file group, just as you might or might not create multiple file groups when you initially create a database. You will learn about the creation of a database in the following section.

TIP: As noted earlier, file groups are purely an administrative issue. The addition of file groups to your database is a step that will be unique in every situation. Do not, however, think you need to create file groups simply because you can. As a rule, they should be created only to respond to a specific administrative purpose.

CREATING A DATABASE

Luckily, the process of creating a database in SQL Server 2000 is easier than it has been in any previous version. The reason for this is mostly the new file storage techniques, which in turn have altered the syntax of the CREATE DATABASE statement in Transact-SQL.

SQL Server 2000 provides you with two powerful tools with which to create databases—right out of the box. The first and user-friendliest of the two is the SQL Enterprise Manager. You can create a database in Enterprise Manager with precious few steps, since many of the settings for a database can be set to default by simply omitting any specification. For example, you can create a new database in Enterprise Manager by following the steps in the example below. You should understand that performing this example depends on your server's having been installed with all the defaults selected.

Assume for the purpose of this example that the database you want to create should be named TEST.

1. Connect to SQL Server with Enterprise Manager and right-click on the Databases folder.

2. Choose the New Database option from the pop-up menu.

3. Type **TEST** into the Name field in the New Database dialog box.

4. Click OK.

As you learned in Chapter 2, SQL Server will create a database using the defaults that are identified by copying the settings in the MODEL Database. You will recall from Chapter 2 that an administrator will only make changes to the MODEL Database if he or she wants nearly all new databases to have the same settings, database users, database roles, and the like.

If you have made changes to the MODEL Database and want to create a database that does not comply with the settings that you have set in the model, you can always specify different settings at the time of creation. You can make such specifications either from Enterprise Manager or by using Transact-SQL. A fitting example of creating a database with very specific settings different from those defined in the MODEL Database would be as follows.

Assume for the purpose of this example that you want to create a database called TEST, that you want to span two different database files, and that you also want to create a secondary file group called Secondary. To try this example at your own computer, perform the following steps:

1. Connect to SQL Server using Query Analyzer and log in.

2. In the TSQL window, type in and execute the following statement:

```
use master
CREATE DATABASE TEST ON Primary
    (name = 'test',
    filename = 'c:\data\test.mdf')
go
ALTER DATABASE TEST
    ADD FILEGROUP Secondary
go
ALTER DATABASE TEST
    ADD FILE (name = 'test2', filename = 'c:\MSSQL\data\test2.ndf')
    TO FILEGROUP Secondary
```

The statement in the example will specify all the following: the creation of a new database named TEST, which has two file groups named Primary and Secondary; that a single database file exists in each file group (TEST.MDF and TEST2.LDF); the name of the Transaction Log; and the physical locations of these files. The statement will assume that all other possible specifications such as SIZE, MAXSIZE, and FILEGROWTH should be copied from the specifications in the MODEL Database. You could also specify each of these settings manually by adding them to the statement.

You should note that, because of the logical manner in which SQL Server processes transactions, we had to first create the database, then add a new file group, and finally add the additional file to the database and its file group. You will need to become familiar with the syntax for such statements before you can create them on your own. For a complete reference to the syntax, refer to the Books Online program or *SQL Server 7: The Complete Reference* by Gayle Coffman (Osborne/McGraw-Hill, 1998). You will find this work to be correct syntactically even for the 2000 edition of SQL Server.

Remember as you proceed that not all the possible variables for the CREATE DATABASE or ALTER DATABASE statements were used in the example. In the following text, you will explore each of the possible database specifications and their purpose. This section ends with a table that captures all the specifications in an easy-to-reference format. Like other tables you have found in this book, you are advised to photocopy the table and keep it close at hand until such time as you are completely confident with all specifications.

INTRODUCING DATABASE SPECIFICATIONS

In this section, you will learn about each of the possible database specifications and their purpose. While memorizing these specifications is not necessary, especially when using Enterprise Manager, you would be well served to learn them just in case a situation arises in which you are required to create a database using Transact-SQL and must remember the specifications to do so. From a management perspective, those in your organization, from executives to your own support staff, will be impressed by your ability to execute complex SQL statements, which in turn increases both job security and income potential.

Database Name

The database name is the most important of the possible specifications, because it is the only one that must be included in a CREATE DATABASE statement. This specifies the logical name of the database as SQL Server recognizes it. For example, if you wanted to create a database named NEWDATA, you would at an absolute minimum have to specify the name NEWDATA as part of the CREATE DATABASE statement for the database to be created. The following is an example of the CREATE DATABASE statement using only the Database Name parameter:

```
CREATE DATABASE Testdb
```

This example will create a database named TESTDB. The database will use all the default specifications, which SQL Server copies from the MODEL database, and will place the physical disk files in the default data storage folder. In an unmodified installation, the default folder will be C:\mmsql7\data\.

Using the NAME Parameter with CREATE DATABASE

NAME is the first of the optional parameters that you will learn about for use with the CREATE DATABASE statement. This parameter identifies the logical name of a database file. If you want to create a new database that places its primary database file on a different physical disk than the one containing the default directory, you must specify a new NAME and FILENAME in the CREATE DATABASE statement. SQL Server uses the NAME option for internal recognition of the database file. This is important because SQL Server must have a logical name that it can then map to a physical filename in order to access and properly manage the database file.

Variable parameters such as NAME and FILENAME must always be enclosed in parentheses when executed in Transact-SQL. Additionally, you must always enclose the actual value in single quotations. For example, to create a new database on the D: drive in a folder named Data, but using all other default variables, you would connect to the SQL Server using Query Analyzer and execute the following statement:

```
CREATE DATABASE TEST ON
    (NAME = 'TEST_DATA',
    FILENAME = 'D:\DATA\TEST_DATA.MDF')
LOG ON
    (NAME = 'TEST_LOG',
    FILENAME = 'D:\DATA\TEST_LOG.LDF')
```

Notice that in the example the variable strings containing NAME and FILENAME are enclosed in parentheses. Notice also that the actual value for each is enclosed in single quotations. If you wanted to create your own database using the same specifications, you would simply alter the NAME, FILENAME, and folders to match your needs.

If you are using Enterprise Manager to create the database, the NAME parameter appears to you as the Name field in the upper portion of the Database Properties dialog box. Specifying the logical name of the database here is intuitive and an easy action to perform.

Managing Filenames with the FILENAME Parameter

Since you just learned about the NAME parameter, the next thing you will want to take a look at is the FILENAME specification. FILENAME is the counterpart to NAME in that it is the physical filename that is recognized by the operating system. SQL Server maps the logical name that was specified in the NAME parameter to the FILENAME parameter in the MASTER Database so that it can access and manage the database file properly. As you just learned, SQL Server must have both parameters or the CREATE DATABASE statement will fail.

This parameter can be handled differently when using Enterprise Manager to create the database. Enterprise Manager will automatically create the FILENAME parameter by taking the data you entered into the Name field and adding it to the default data storage path. If your SQL Server is installed using all defaults, that path is C:\MSSQL\DATA\.

You can also specify a different path or name for the database files in the Database Properties dialog box simply by clicking your mouse in the Filename field and manually typing in the desired information. Look back at the example given for the NAME parameter to see an example of the FILENAME parameter in use.

File Group Specification During the Creation Process

This parameter is possibly the most easily confused specification in the CREATE DATABASE statement because it is not easily recognized as an optional parameter. If, for instance, you look at an example of syntax in either Books Online or another reference, you will see the CREATE DATABASE statement listing the file group parameter like this:

```
CREATE DATABASE [DATABASE NAME] ON PRIMARY
```

In the example above, the section that reads ON Primary is the reference to the file group specification. You will recall from earlier sections that there is always a primary file group in any database. It is for this reason that the syntax in Books Online always lists primary in its examples. In simple statements that do not specify file group parameters, you can choose to leave off the designation `Primary`. Because of the way that SQL Server manages databases, when you are creating a database that will span multiple file groups using Transact-SQL, you must first create a database and then alter it. To clarify this point, let's review the example from the earlier "Creating a Database" section:

```
USE MASTER
CREATE DATABASE TEST ON PRIMARY
    (NAME = 'TEST',
    FILENAME = 'C:\DATA\TEST.MDF')
GO
ALTER DATABASE TEST
    ADD FILEGROUP SECONDARY
GO
ALTER DATABASE TEST
    ADD FILE(NAME = 'TEST2', FILENAME =
    'C:\MSSQL\DATA\TEST2.NDF')
    TO FILEGROUP SECONDARY
```

In the example, you can plainly see that there are two file group parameters specified (`On Primary` and `To Filegroup Secondary`). Once seen as a working example, the syntax becomes clear and easy to follow. Since there must always be a primary file group in any database, you can specify the primary file group first, but are not required to do so. Additional file groups can be added in any order you choose. The order in which you create the additional file groups has no impact on the way SQL Server processes them, but you must create the file group before you can add a database file to it.

As with many of the other parameters discussed here, Enterprise Manager provides an easy way to create file groups, either at the time of database creation or when you add new database files later. Within the Database Properties dialog box is a field that identifies the file group name. By default, this field always says Primary, because the primary file group is always present. Although you cannot change the name of the primary file group, each time you add a new database file to the structure of the database you have the opportunity to create a new file group. To create a file group using Enterprise Manager, simply click your mouse in the file group field and type in a new name. As you add more and more database files, you will note that file groups that you have created are available for you to use; they take the form of a drop-down list.

Specifying the Database's Initial *SIZE*

The SIZE parameter is very straightforward and easy to understand. This parameter specifies the initial size of the database at the time it is created. If you leave off this parameter, the database defaults to being created at the same size as the MODEL Database. You will use this parameter when you want to create a new database that has an initial size that is different from that of the model. You should be aware that because of the syntactical restrictions in Transact-SQL, you must specify the NAME and FILENAME parameters if you intend to use the SIZE specification. For example, if you wanted to create a new database named TESTDB and wanted to specify that it had an initial size of 3MB, you would connect to SQL Server using Query Analyzer and execute the following statement:

```
CREATE DATABASE TESTDB
    (NAME = 'TESTDB',
    FILENAME = TESTDB.MDF',
    SIZE = 3MB)
    LOG ON
    (NAME = 'TESTDBLOG',
    FILENAME = 'TESDBLOG.LDF',
    SIZE = 1MB)
```

The statement listed in the above example will create a database named TESTDB that has a primary database file that is 3MB large and that has a Transaction Log file that is 1MB large. Note the use of the NAME and FILENAME parameters. If you had tried to execute the command without using NAME and FILENAME, the statement would return an error from the Transact-SQL engine and would not complete.

If you are creating the database using Enterprise Manager, the Size field is easy to spot, and you can specify the database initial size simply by typing in your desired size. You can also use this field to alter the size of a database at any time. You should be careful to ensure that you are on the Database tab and not the Log tab when specifying size, because the field appears on both tabs and applies to the respective file for that tab.

Limiting Database Growth with MAXSIZE

If you were to create a database using SQL Enterprise Manager, you would note that there is an area inside the Database Properties dialog box in which you specify the maximum size to which the database will grow. When using Transact-SQL to create a database, you will use the MAXSIZE parameter to specify the maximum growth potential of the database. This setting is particularly useful when you choose to auto-grow a database in increments. As with other optional parameters, you must specify the NAME and FILENAME specifications to use the MAXSIZE variable. For example, if you want to create the TESTDB database and specify that it has a maximum size of 100MB, you would connect to SQL Server using Query Analyzer and execute the following statement:

```
CREATE DATABASE TESTDB ON PRIMARY
    (NAME = 'TESTDB',
    FILENAME = 'C:\MSSQL\DATA\TESTDB.MDF',
    MAXSIZE = 100MB)
```

Using the example above, the TESTDB database will be created with an initial size of 1MB because that is the default size that SQL Server reads from the MODEL Database. All other unspecified parameters will also be read from the model. Because you specified the MAXSIZE parameter, the primary file will have a maximum possible size of 100MB.

When you designate a database as being able to auto-grow, if left unchecked, the database has the potential of eventually taking up all the available disk space. You will learn more about auto-growing a database in the next section.

Controlling the Nature of a Database's Expansion with FILEGROWTH

The FILEGROWTH parameter specifies that you want to auto-grow a database and to what amount of disk space or percentage of database size you want to auto-grow it. This specification can be an important decision for an administrator because, while it adds tremendous functionality to SQL Server, it also has the unfortunate potential to produce a certain level of complacency in an administrator. The auto-growth feature lets SQL Server automatically grow a file by a predetermined percentage or measurement of disk space in the event that the database approaches the level at which the defined size is insufficient. To the administrator, this means that it will forevermore be unlikely that he or she will have to get up at three o'clock in the morning to extend the size of a database that has grown too large for its space. The concept of not having to worry about any aspect of SQL Server administration is, however, typically a bad idea because the administrator can begin to overlook potential problems.

For example, assume that you have a database that is roughly 3GB and resides on a physical disk that has an initial capacity of 8GB. Because there is sufficient space available for use, many administrators will add non-SQL Server data files to the same disk. Now assume that there is only 500MB left on the disk that is available for allocation. The default specification for FILEGROWTH is 10 percent. This means that your 3GB database will grow by approximately 300MB when it tries to auto-grow. In this example, when the database auto-grows, there will be only 200MB available on the disk available for use. At this point, problems in the operating system might cause the administrator to take note of the problem and add space. If, however, the administrator fails to add space, the next time the database needs to auto-grow there will not be sufficient space in which to do so.

FILEGROWTH can also cause problems in smaller databases for an entirely different reason. For example, if you have a database that is only 1MB in size initially but auto-grows in 10-percent increments, it is likely that you will experience a much higher level of fragmentation. Between the times that the database auto-grows, additional files or programs might take up the physical disk space that is adjacent to the storage of the database, which will result in poor database performance because of fragmentation.

TIP: To make this crystal clear, the general guidelines you should use are: The larger the database size, the more appropriate percentage growth is, while the smaller the database size, the more appropriate incremental growth is.

When using Enterprise Manager, you can choose from within the Database Properties dialog box to turn the auto-grow specification on or off, the number of megabytes to grow at a time, or a percentage of current database space on which to base the growth.

If you are using Transact-SQL to create or alter a database, you must use the FILEGROWTH parameter. In the same way that many of the other optional parameters require other parameters to work, the FILEGROWTH specification requires that you have specified the NAME and FILENAME parameters, otherwise it will not function. For example, in the following code fragment, the statement creates the TESTDB database and specifies that the primary file will be set to grow in 5MB increments:

```
CREATE DATABASE TESTDB ON
    (NAME = 'TESTDB',
    FILENAME = 'C:\MSSQL\DATA\TESTDB.MDF',
    FILEGROWTH = 5MB)
```

Note that the example uses both the NAME and FILENAME parameters. If you had not specified these parameters and instead tried to execute the statement with just the FILEGROWTH parameter, the statement would not function and SQL Server would return an error. You should also at this point note that there is no specification for the Transaction Log. Leaving out this parameter is acceptable, and you only need to include the log parameter if you want the Transaction Log to have properties other than the defaults. The next section details the log parameter and its use.

TIP: As you become more familiar with the workings of a given database, you might want to exercise greater control over how the log is constructed, its size, and so on. In such cases, you can always use the Transact-SQL ALTER DATABASE statement to change the log's nature. On the whole, log sizes depend on the type of activities you are performing with a given database, and using the default at creation is generally an acceptable place to start.

Specifying Information About the Transaction Log with the LOG Parameter

As you know, SQL Server databases store data only after that data, or rather the transactions that produced that data, have been recorded into the Transaction Log. When you create a database, you must also create a Transaction Log for the database. When you are using Enterprise Manager to create the database, the Transaction Log settings are managed from the Log tab in the dialog box. When you are creating a database using Transact-SQL, however, you must specify in the CREATE DATABASE statement the properties of the Transaction Log. Additionally, if you use the LOG parameter in Transact-SQL, you must also specify the location of the database file or files and include at a minimum the NAME and FILENAME parameters for those files.

For example, if you wanted to create a database that had two database files and two Transaction Log files, you would connect to SQL Server using Query Analyzer and execute a statement similar to the following:

```
CREATE DATABASE TESTDB ON PRIMARY
    (NAME = 'TESTDB',
    FILENAME = 'C:\MSSQL\DATA\TESTDB.MDF')
    LOG ON (NAME = 'TESTBLOG',
    FILENAME = 'C:\MSSQL\DATA\TESTDBLOG.LDF')
GO
```

```
ALTER DATABASE TESTDB
ADD FILE
     (NAME = 'TESTDB1',
     FILENAME =  'C:\MSSQL\DATA\TESTDB1.NDF')
GO
ALTER DATABASE TESTDB
     ADD LOG FILE
     (NAME = 'TESTDB_LOG1',
     FILENAME =  'C:\MSSQL\DATA\TESTDB_LOG1.LDF')
```

As you can see in the example, the CREATE database statement is a complete specification that includes the NAME and FILENAME parameters for both the primary database file and the Transaction Log. Because of the step-by-step methodology that SQL Server uses, the statements must be broken into a CREATE Database statement, as well as two ALTER database statements that add the additional files for the database and Transaction Log. The complete statement will create the TESTDB database with two database files plus two Transaction Log files, all of which will be located in the C:\MSSQL\data\ folder.

If your intent was simply to place the Transaction Log on a different physical disk, and you wanted to do so using Transact-SQL, your statement would be similar to the following:

```
CREATE DATABASE TESTDB ON PRIMARY
     (NAME = 'TESTDB',
     FILENAME = 'C:\MSSQL\DATA\TESDB.MDF)
LOG ON
     (NAME = 'TESTDBLOG',
     FILENAME = 'D:\MSSQL\LOGS\TESTDBLOG.LDF')
```

In this example, the statement simply places the Transaction Log on the D: drive, into a folder that you created for just that purpose. You should note here that you must have previously created the directory structure on the D: drive for the statement to work. SQL Server will not create any folders outside the defaults on the installation drive.

As you can see, the Transact-SQL statement LOG is the way that you tell SQL Server where to create the Transaction Log, how many files it will span, and other associated properties. Once you have entered the LOG parameter, other parameters such as NAME, FILENAME, and FILEGROWTH apply to the Transaction Log file or files, just as they do to a database file that is used for permanent storage (see Table 4-1).

Specification	Description
Database Name	The logical name of the database as recognized in SQL Server
NAME	The logical name of the physical database file
FILENAME	The physical name of the database file as recognized by the operating system (specified as a complete path)
Primary, Secondary, etc.	The logical name of the file group as recognized by SQL Server
SIZE	The initial size of the database when it is created (specified in megabytes)
MAXSIZE	Determines the maximum physical size that the database file can grow; this specification is performed for each database file in the CREATE statement
FILEGROWTH	Specifies that the auto-grow feature should be set to on, and at what increment the file will grow when auto-expanded
Log on	Specifies that the statement will deal with the transaction log from this point forward; also, NAME, FILENAME, FILEGROWTH, and MAXSIZE can all be specified for the transaction log

Table 4-1. Transaction Log Specifications

Throughout this section, you have again and again seen references to Enterprise Manager as well as syntax for use with Transact-SQL. If you have looked at the Database Properties dialog box inside Enterprise Manager, you are probably curious about the third tab that is present, named Database Options. Database options are special settings for a database that let you control your database in a variety of ways. In the following section, you will learn about each of these options as well as methods for using them.

EXPLORING DATABASE OPTIONS

Managing databases on SQL Server can be a complex task. As an administrator, you might have to deal with situations that require very specific settings within the database. For example, if you are restoring a database from backup, you must ensure that no users attach to the database and attempt to change data until the restoration is complete. To accomplish this you will, among other things, set the database into *single-user mode*.

Single-user mode ensures that only one user can connect to the database at a time. The single-user mode property is considered a database option. Database options are typically set from within the Database Properties dialog box, on the Database Options tab. You can, however, also set database options by executing the SP_DBOPTION stored procedure. In the section that follows, we will discuss each of the database options, explain how to set them using Transact-SQL and Enterprise Manager, and provide you with some valuable tips on how to use them to your advantage.

Before we begin to examine each of the options, it is important that you fully understand how to use the SP_DBOPTION system-stored procedure. In each instance of use, this stored procedure uses an easy-to-follow set of variable parameters. To execute this procedure, we recommend that you always set your statement to use the MASTER Database first, to avoid potential problems that could occur as a result of being in the wrong database when executing the procedure. To set your current database using Transact-SQL, simply type in the following line, press ENTER, and press TAB. The initial line will look like this:

USE MASTER

Now that the current database has been set, you can enter the
stored procedure. Because it is not the only line of code in the
window, you must preface the name of the procedure with the word
exec. Exec stands for execute and will tell SQL Server that you want to
execute the procedure from within the MASTER Database and using
the listed parameters. For example, if you want to use Query
Analyzer to set database options, perform the following steps:

1. Connect to SQL Server using Query Analyzer.

2. Type **use master**.

3. Press ENTER.

4. Press TAB.

5. Type **exec SP_DBOPTION**.

When you follow these instructions, the Query Analyzer window
should look like the image found in Figure 4-2.

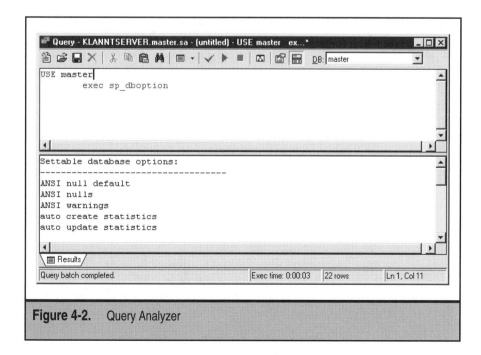

Figure 4-2.   Query Analyzer

If you always begin any instance of the SP_DBOPTION stored procedure by following the steps listed above, you will have a much lower potential for problems and are likely to succeed at the desired setting for your database.

TIP: Using the use [databasename] construct is a useful management technique, particularly when creating stored procedures, to ensure that the user always accesses the correct data source. However, with stored SQL files, you might want to omit the statement, particularly if you have a number of identical databases stored on the same server and want to be able to use the query on any of them.

Single-User Mode

The advantage in setting a database into single-user-only mode is obviously that only one user at a time can connect to the database. This prevents other users from access to a database that is perhaps unstable, has maintenance actions being performed on it, or is likely to be altered one or more times in a given time span by the administrator. Preventing users from accessing the database is a crucial aspect of database management that you will use repeatedly. The single-user-only mode is frequently set as an addition to the DBO Use Only option. This is because there might be more than one user whom the database recognizes as the DBO (database owner). Setting both the DBO Use Only and Single-User mode at the same time effectively ensures that no other users, regardless of database privileges, can access the database simultaneously.

Setting the single-user option on a database from within Enterprise Manager is a relatively simple process in which you simply access the Properties page for the database, change to the Options tab, and click on the Single User checkbox.

Setting the single-user option using Transact-SQL, however, is a touch more complicated, but is still a simple process if you understand the syntax of the SP_DBOPTION stored procedure. For example, if you wanted to set the TESTDB database into Single-User mode using Transact-SQL, you would simply connect to SQL Server using Query Analyzer and execute the following statement:

```
use master
    exec sp_dboption 'Testdb', 'SINGLE USER', TRUE
```

As a test, if you have created the TESTDB database, connect to SQL Server using Enterprise Manager and access the Properties page for the database. Note that the Single User option is not selected. Now connect to SQL Server using Query Analyzer and perform the steps listed in the procedure. Go back to Enterprise Manager and check the Options tab again. (You might have to close the window and reopen it to let SQL Server refresh the screen.) You should see that there is a checkmark in the Single User checkbox and that the option is now set.

Setting the DBO Use Only Flag

As you have learned, DBO stands for Database Owner, the database user who has unlimited rights and privileges in the database. Setting the database option DBO Use Only is a way of telling SQL Server that only this user can access the database at certain times. You would set this option for a variety of reasons. For example, if you were conducting active development of a database situated on a production server, you would want to prevent users from accessing the database until you were finished. As a developer, you would alias your development team to the DBO database user so that those individuals would have access to the database, while other users would not. As another example, if you were performing maintenance on the database or restoring the database from backup, you would want to prevent users from accessing the database until you had completed the maintenance or the restoration. You could set the DBO Use Only option to prevent standard network users from connecting to the database. Users who had an alias of DBO in the database would still have access, so that if they were part of the maintenance, their user accounts would still be able to access the database. If you wanted to prevent all users except you from accessing the database, you could set the DBO Use Only along with the Single-User mode options. This would effectively restrict all users except you from accessing the database until you either severed your connection or turned the options off.

In the same way that the Single User option is set within Enterprise Manager, you can simply access the Properties page of the database and make your selection on the Options tab.

To set the option with Transact-SQL, connect to SQL Server using Query Analyzer and execute the following statement:

```
USE MASTER
    EXEC SP_DBOPTION 'TESTDB', 'DBO USE ONLY', TRUE
```

Once the database option has been set to True, you can remove the setting using the exact same syntax, changing only the True to False as seen below:

```
USE MASTER
    EXEC SP_DBOPTION 'TESTDB', 'DBO USE ONLY', FALSE
```

This syntax will apply to all the options that are covered in the following sections. We will no longer include all the descriptions, but merely a syntactical example.

TIP: As you will learn in later chapters, creating a replication set on a large existing database can be problematic, at best. Placing the database into Single-User, DBO Use Only mode can help solve the problems created when building the replication's initial snapshot—a concept you will learn about in later chapters. We discuss this consideration further later in this chapter.

Auto-Shrink

One of the more common occurrences in database manipulation is the removal of existing records. Deleting outdated or unnecessary records is a task that must be done in almost all databases. When you remove a record in SQL Server, it leaves behind an empty space that might or might not be reallocated by a new record. Sometimes the process of validating or archiving data requires the removal of many records at the same time. When this occurs, a large amount of previously used disk space could be available for other uses, except for the fact that the database does not take up less space on disk merely because there is free space inside it.

To remedy this situation, SQL Server provides you with two mechanisms for shrinking the size of an existing database that no longer requires its current allocation of physical disk space. The first of these solutions is a Transact-SQL statement that manually performs the shrink process. This statement is classified as one of the Database Consistency Checker (DBCC) commands and is executed as follows:

```
DBCC SHRINKDATABASE
```

Executing this command will shrink the database as a background operation. This means that SQL Server will shrink the database when it has time, and will not interrupt more important transactions to do so.

Many administrators have databases that are extremely volatile and that might grow or contract in required size on a regular basis. As you know, SQL Server 2000 can automatically expand a database as needed to store data. By implementing the second solution, which is to set the database option Auto-Shrink, SQL Server also gains the ability to shrink that database as necessary to provide the maximum amount of hands-free functionality. An example of the Transact-SQL statement is listed below:

```
use master
    exec sp_dboption 'Testdb', 'AUTOSHRINK', TRUE
```

Truncate Log On Checkpoint

The Truncate Log On Checkpoint database option is probably the most dangerous of them all. This option is dangerous because when set, the database Transaction Log clears itself of all committed transactions each time a checkpoint is issued, or about once a minute by default. As you can imagine, this could have disastrous results if set on a database that relies on the Transaction Log for safety in the event of database damage.

The option is sometimes useful for certain types of databases that benefit from this action and are safe to auto-truncate. As an administrator, though, you must be very cautious about setting this option on databases and must take every possible step to ensure that SQL Server will benefit from the setting without putting the data at risk.

An example of the Transact-SQL setting is listed here:

```
use master
    exec sp_dboption 'Testdb', 'TRUNC LOG ON CHKPT', TRUE
```

Read Only Mode

The Read Only option is pretty much self-explanatory. This option sets the database so that while network users can still execute read operations such as a SELECT statement against the database, they cannot execute write operations such as an UPDATE statement.

As an administrator, you will use this setting from time to time on most production databases to prevent users from updating data while you perform managerial operations on the database. For example, we have found in several installations that support medium-sized databases of over 1GB that, to effectively set up transactional replication, you must first set the database to Read Only mode. In these instances, when we tried to set up replication without setting the database to Read Only mode, SQL Server would hang during the process of setting up the database for replication. Setting the database to Read Only mode solved the problem, which arose because SQL Server could not add the required triggers to the database tables while users were continually updating data in those tables.

As always, you can set the Read Only option from within Enterprise Manager by accessing the Properties page of the database. An example of the Transact-SQL statement is listed here:

```
use master
    exec sp_dboption 'Testdb', 'READ ONLY', TRUE
```

Auto-Create Statistics

From this section on, you will deal with options that are less well known and perhaps often overlooked because of administrator confusion about their proper use. The first of these parameters is the Auto-Create Statistics option. This option sets the database so that it can automatically generate unspecified statistical information needed for query optimization. For example, suppose that you executed a standard SELECT query against a large table. Information that the query might need to perform well might include both the primary and foreign keys in the table, as well as whatever rules of referential integrity were in place. The query could be set to gather this information from a previously created set of statistics, but such a set might have to be frequently updated in some instances. Setting the Auto-Create Statistics option enables the database to generate this information as needed. An example of the Transact-SQL statement is listed below:

```
use master
    exec sp_dboption 'Testdb', 'AUTO CREATE STATISTICS', TRUE
```

Auto-Update Statistics

This option is directly related to the Auto-Create Statistics option because it deals specifically with the same information. As you have learned, when a query executes, it needs certain information to run efficiently within the server. The statistics page that was previously built, or the Auto-Create Statistics option, automatically creates a set of statistical information that the query can use to process the data efficiently.

Auto-Update Statistics is used when you have previously created a statistics set that your queries will check for statistical data. Once created, the set might need to be updated from time to time as the structure of the table changes. As an administrator, you can manually change this information by re-creating the statistics page, or you can specify the Auto-Update Statistics option on the database itself.

As with many other options, you can specify the Auto-Update Statistics option on the database by accessing the Properties page for the database and placing a checkmark in the appropriate checkbox on the Options tab. Setting the option using Transact-SQL is exemplified below:

```
use master
    exec sp_dboption 'Testdb', 'AUTO UPDATE STATISTICS', TRUE
```

Effectively Using the Auto-Close Option

If you have ever tried to make structural changes to a database that has been recently accessed by a user, you can fully appreciate the Auto-Close option. This option enables a database to automatically close all connections cleanly when the last user exits the database. Setting this option immediately frees up all resources that SQL Server allocated to the database. Freeing the resources can be beneficial when dealing with an infrequently used database, but can actually cause a frequently used database to perform less efficiently because SQL Server will release the resources, then have to reallocate them when a user connects to the database. In an environment where there are multiple databases, the affected database could conceivably acquire a smaller amount of resources because other databases reserved them first.

Like other parameters, the Options tab of the Database Properties dialog box will let you easily set the option from within Enterprise Manager. An example of the Transact-SQL statement to set the option is listed below:

```
use master
    exec sp_dboption 'Testdb', 'AUTOCLOSE', TRUE
```

Using the Select Into/Bulk Copy Option

The Select Into/Bulk Copy option is a common option that some administrators who operate in more volatile environments might use on a regular basis. This option sets the database to a mode similar to Single User mode and DBO Use Only if they were set simultaneously. Use this option when you want to copy a large amount of information into the database in a single (nonlogged) operation and you do not want users to access the database while the operation is being carried out.

CAUTION: Remember, nonlogged operations are not recorded into the Transaction Log. As you will learn in Chapter 6, nonlogged operations that are not backed up immediately are one of the greatest risks to data security in any environment. Make sure to perform backups as soon as possible after performing any nonlogged operation, particularly a bulk copy.

Once set, the Select Into/Bulk Copy option will prevent any single-row operations from executing and will only allow Select Into or BCP (Bulk Copy Program) operations to be performed on the database.

Many times you will want this option to be set on a new database so that you might populate some tables before letting users connect to the database. You can set this option either from Enterprise Manager or by using Transact-SQL as shown below:

```
use master
     exec sp_dboption 'Testdb', 'SELECT INTO/BULK COPY', TRUE
```

Using the ANSI NULL Default Option

This option merely specifies the default status for column creation within the database. Once the option is set to True, columns will be created as NULL by default. If the option is set to False, the columns will be created as NOT NULL automatically. The Transact-SQL statement to turn this option on is shown here:

```
use master
     exec sp_dboption 'Testdb', 'ANSI NULL DEFAULT', TRUE
```

Determining When to Use the Recursive Triggers Option

This is an interesting option that is normally defined by the developer because it affects the way that a database will execute *triggers.* Triggers are special objects in databases that contain predefined sets of Transact-SQL. When a condition within the database changes, triggers can be set to perform other operations as a result. For example, if you wanted to ensure that all related data in all tables is deleted when a record from the primary table is deleted, you would construct a trigger that executes whenever a record is deleted. The trigger could be designed so that it deletes all information related to the deleted record from all tables in the database.

When the Recursive Triggers option is set to True, triggers are fired more than once as a result of a single action within the database. For example, suppose that you made a modification to the Customer table, which executed a trigger that updated data in the Products table. For the purpose of this example, let us assume that the Products table also has a trigger set, so that when data is modified within the table, information in the Customer table is altered. Using this example, it is conceivable that changing data in the Customer table would trigger changes in the Products table, which in turn would trigger changes in the Customer table again. If the Recursive Triggers option is set to True, the trigger in the Customer table might execute repeatedly as other triggers modify data. If the Recursive Triggers option is set to False, the Customer table trigger will execute only once, when you or another database user modifies data, and will not reexecute when another trigger modifies data. Depending on the desired result, the database developer should specify whether this option should be enabled or disabled for the database. As an administrator, you will rarely modify this option unless instructed by the developer.

The standard methods of setting this option both from within Enterprise Manager and when using Transact-SQL are performed in the same way as other database options.

Specifying the Use of Quoted Identifiers with Transact-SQL

The Quoted Identifiers option simply sets the database so that database users might use double quotation marks to specify variables. For example, throughout this chapter you have seen again and again how variable parameters are encased within single quotation marks. If you try to execute Transact-SQL statements using double quotation marks, an error code is returned. If you set the Quoted Identifiers option to True, you could then use double quotation marks in Transact-SQL statements within the database without returning an error. Setting this option is performed in the same way as other database options, and can be performed from either Enterprise Manager or using Transact-SQL by using the SP_DBOPTION stored procedure.

Detecting the Existence of Torn Pages

During the years when previous versions of SQL Server used an 8K page, one frequent problem was that pages could become "torn" (that is, corrupted) when the server suddenly became unavailable because of power failure or critical errors on the operating system. Even though SQL Server now uses a 2K page, data is still written to disk in 512-byte increments. This means that SQL Server uses four disk operations to write a single page. If the power were to fail between the time SQL Server wrote the first 512-byte increment and the remaining increments, a torn page is produced.

During the automatic recovery process, torn pages are typically detected and either fixed (because the transaction is rolled back) or not fixed, in which case SQL Server will mark the database as *suspect*. When a database is marked suspect, administrators usually perform a variety of system checks, including running statistical Transact-SQL statements against the database. In such cases, one of two results is possible: They are able to locate and correct the problem, or they are unable to do so and end up restoring the database from backup.

Setting the Torn Page Detection option enables the database to detect the presence of torn pages, with the end result being that the database will be marked suspect. As an administrator, you will set this option only in extreme cases where database integrity is at a level of importance far above the norm. For example, in databases that store cryptology keys or complex password arrangements, the loss of a single byte might have great impact on the database functionality. In cases such as this, you will set the Torn Page Detection option to True. In most other cases, this option is not necessary, and while the impact on performance is minimal, it can add up when used unnecessarily.

The option might be set using either Enterprise Manager or Transact-SQL in the form of the SP_DBOPTION stored procedure, using the same syntax previously covered in this chapter.

PERFORMANCE CONSIDERATIONS

Disk contention occurs when two read or write operations need to be carried out on the same physical disk at the same time. Disk contention can be solved in a variety of ways, among which is the use of file groups, as you learned earlier.

Depending on your hardware choices, your benefit to using file groups as a solution to disk contention might have varied results. For example, many implementations of hardware-controlled *redundant arrays of independent disks* (RAID) array storage systems far exceed the gain found using file groups. If this is the case, you might actually be diminishing the efficiency of your database by splitting the files into file groups.

Performance, then, is an exceedingly complex issue that will require you to know more than just the workings of SQL Server to properly identify the correct solution for your environment. While the necessary knowledge of hardware and other concepts is outside the scope of this book, some general tips might help you make a quick determination. The following is a list of rules that we use as guidelines when attempting to design a database solution:

▼ Use file groups when multiple disks are present but when no RAID system has been implemented.

■ If a RAID system is present, obtain read/write information from the manufacturer prior to making a decision.

■ Always monitor the read/write operations of the database before deciding on hardware.

■ Double the amount of memory required by the system.

▲ Double the processor speed required for the system each time the number of users is increased by half.

While this list is certain to assist you in making good choices, nothing can substitute for planning and research. The best implementations of SQL Server always have a history of good planning and sometimes unconventional solutions. We once witnessed a SQL Server solution in which the system administrator purchased a refrigerator, customized its interior, drilled holes in the sides for cabling, and then installed the server in the refrigerator. This solution seems extreme and perhaps even funny, but it solved a unique problem for a server that had to run in a desert climate, in a building with no air conditioning. The result was that a system that went through more than five physical drives in one year has not failed again, from that time to the time of this writing. As you are bound to find, sometimes the seemingly most unreasonable solution is the correct choice.

SUMMARY

In this chapter, you learned about databases. You learned how SQL Server creates and manages databases, about the files that comprise databases, and about various database options.

Specific to the task of administrator, you learned how to create and alter databases using both Enterprise Manager and Transact-SQL, about the structure of data, and about the Transaction Log, and you also obtained some tips on performance and optimization.

In the following chapter, you will learn more about moving and manipulating data in your environment, experiment with a number of the tools included with SQL Server, and discover some practical tips on controlling the flow of data.

CHAPTER 5

Transferring Data and Managing Distributed Data

As a system administrator, you must understand how to manage data and transfer it between applications and environments. Almost all environments require some degree of data transfer for one or more of the following reasons:

▼ To move data to another server or location

■ To make a copy of data

■ To archive data

▲ To migrate data

The process of copying data from one environment to another typically involves

▼ Identifying the data source

■ Specifying the data destination

▲ Manipulating or transforming the data between the source and destination (optional)

Simple importing and exporting of data is the most basic form of data transfer. Even this simple process can transform data if, for example, you specify a different datatype for a column or save a file in another product version or format.

A SQL Server administrator frequently needs to transfer data between heterogeneous environments. For example, you might transfer sales information from an Oracle database to a SQL Server database or transfer data from an online transaction processing system to a data warehouse.

UNDERSTANDING WHY YOU WILL TRANSFORM DATA IN MANY ENVIRONMENTS

Migrating and transferring data between different environments is a common occurrence that often involves the manipulation or transformation of data. Transforming data can be as simple as mapping transformation datatypes or as complex as programming data logic to handle data transformations.

During data transformation, missing values can be added and column values summarized, decoded, decomposed, converted, and translated to a common measure or format. The captured data typically is integrated, made consistent, validated, and restructured before it is stored at the destination.

TIP: The SQL Server Transfer Manager found in previous versions of SQL Server is no longer available. Data Transformation Services (DTS) provides all of the functionality formerly provided by the SQL Server Transfer Manager.

When you transform data, you may want to perform one of several tasks. The following sections describe these tasks.

Changing the Format of the Data

Transforming data frequently requires changing its format. Suppose, for example, that a value of 1 or 0 is stored in the `Active_Customer` column in your database, but the data that you want to transfer into your database represents the value as the text "TRUE" or "FALSE." You can convert the "TRUE" and "FALSE" values to 1 and 0 values when you transfer the data into your database. Numeric and date formats are frequently changed.

Restructuring and Mapping Data

Restructuring and mapping data frequently involves combining data from multiple data sources, tables, and columns into a single data set at the destination. For example, you can preprocess the data (this is known as *data aggregation* or *summarization*) and store the preprocessed data at your destination. For example, for a common report, you may have to run a query that extracts data from multiple tables. If you wanted to store the data for said report to perform other functions or manipulations later, you may choose to use DTS to pull the data from the two separate tables and store it in a single table for later use.

Making Data Consistent

When you import data from another source, you should make sure that the new data is consistent with the existing data. This is sometimes called *data scrubbing*. Data can be inconsistent in several ways:

▼ The data is consistent, but the representation is not consistent with how you want to store it at the destination. For example, suppose that a credit rating is represented by the values 1, 2, and 3. Making the data consistent may require translating these values to the character string values of "Good", "Average", and "Poor."

▲ The data representation is correct, but it is inconsistently represented. For example, a company name may be stored in several ways, such as ABC Corp., ABC, or ABC Corporation. In this instance, you can make the data consistent by requiring that the destination always store the company name as ABC Corporation.

TIP: You generally can make your data consistent by translating codes or values to readable strings or by converting mixed values to single values.

Validating Data

When you validate data, you verify the accuracy and correctness of the data that you import. For example, you can require that data meet a specific condition before it can be included with your destination data. Or you can verify that a customer ID already exists at the destination before you transfer additional information for the customer into the destination data.

If you discover any invalid data, try to determine where the fault originated and correct the processes that are contributing to the error. Save invalid data to a log for later examination to determine why it is incorrect.

Tools for Transferring Data in SQL Server

SQL Server provides several tools and Transact-SQL statements for transferring data. The data that you can transfer is typically in the form of tables or files. The method you choose for importing or exporting data depends on a variety of user requirements, including:

▼   The format of the source and destination data

■   The location of the source and destination data

■   Whether the import or export is a one-time occurrence or an ongoing task

■   Whether a command-prompt utility, Transact-SQL statement, or graphical interface is preferred (for ease of use)

▲   The type of import or export operation

Table 5-1 describes the tools that SQL Server provides for transferring data.

Tool	Description	Use
DTS Import Wizard and DTS Export Wizard	Allows users to interactively create DTS packages that can be used to import, export, and transform data.	Transferring data between heterogeneous data sources or transferring all of the objects in a SQL Server 2000 database to another SQL Server 2000 database.
DTS Designer	Allows experienced database administrators to import, export, and transform data and define complex data workflows.	Transferring homogeneous and heterogeneous data from multiple sources and for setting up complex workflows.
dtsrun utility	A command-prompt utility that allows you to execute existing DTS packages from a command prompt.	Executing a DTS package as part of a batch or scheduled job.

Table 5-1.   Tools for Transferring Data from Within SQL Server

Tool	Description	Use
Bulk copy program (bcp utility)	A command-prompt utility that imports and exports native SQL Server data files or ASCII text files.	Importing data into a SQL Server table from a file or exporting data from a SQL Server table to a file.
Transact-SQL statement	SELECT INTO and INSERT SELECT	Selecting data to add to a table from an existing SQL Server table—SELECT INTO creates a new table and INSERT SELECT requires an existing table.
	BULK INSERT	Copying a data file into a database table in a user-specified format. The fastest method of loading large amounts of data into a table.
	BACKUP and RESTORE	Copying a complete SQL Server database (all data and objects) to another SQL Server.
sp_attach_db	Attaches a database to a server.	Moving or copying a complete SQL Server database (all data and objects) to another SQL Server by copying the database files.
Replication	Maintains duplicate table schema, data, or stored procedure definitions from a source database to a destination database, usually on separate servers.	Maintaining copies of data intermittently on multiple databases (does not guarantee that the data will be consistent at the same point in time). An ongoing process.
Host Data Replicator	Provides replication to and from SQL Server and mainframe databases such as IBM DB2. Runs in conjunction with Microsoft SNA Server, a gateway and application integration platform that is part of BackOffice. Also supports data transformations such as conversion of date and timestamps. Data can replace existing tables or be merged on a row-by-row basis.	Transferring data between SQL Server and mainframe databases such as IBM DB2.

Table 5-1. Tools for Transferring Data from Within SQL Server *(continued)*

TIP: DTS is not intended to replace SQL Server replication. Replication is designed to provide exact copies of data to multiple destinations in an ongoing scenario that continues to update data at the remote source. Very little to no data changes or cleansing is performed in replication. Using DTS rather than replication requires executing a complete transformation for each destination. You will learn more about replication in later chapters.

CONSIDERING THE IMPLEMENTATION OF DTS

The method you choose for importing or exporting data depends on a variety of user requirements, including the format of the data, the location of the data, how often the transfer will be occurring, the type of import or export, and finally, ease of use.

Many organizations centralize data to improve corporate decision-making. However, this data often is stored in a large variety of formats on a number of different systems. By using DTS, you can import, export, and transform data among multiple homogeneous or heterogeneous sources and destinations using an OLE DB-based architecture. In the following sections, you will learn about DTS and how to create a DTS package.

 TIP: To migrate data from SQL Server 6.5 or 7.0 to SQL Server 2000, use the SQL Server Upgrade Wizard.

Overview of DTS

DTS is able to import, export, and transform data between SQL Server and any OLE DB, Open Database Connectivity (ODBC), or text file format. When you use DTS, you can

▼ Copy table schema and data between database management systems (DBMSs).

■ Create custom transformation objects that can be integrated into third-party products.

■ Build data warehouses and data marts in SQL Server by importing and transferring data from multiple heterogeneous sources interactively or automatically on a regularly scheduled basis.

▲ Access applications using third-party OLE DB providers. This allows applications for which an OLE DB provider exists to be used as sources and destinations of data.

DTS can be used with any OLE DB data source and destination; you are not required to use SQL Server 2000 for either source or destination. This makes DTS a general-purpose data transfer and transformation tool with a wide range of applications.

TIP: DTS moves table schema and data only between heterogeneous data sources. Triggers, stored procedures, rules, defaults, constraints, and user-defined datatypes can be transferred only if the source and destination are the same version of SQL Server.

The DTS Process

The process of transferring data is an integral part of all database management systems. DTS provides an extensible Component Object Model (COM)-based architecture that allows customers, independent software vendors (ISVs), and consultants to create new OLE DB data sources and destinations, tasks, and transformations.

With DTS, users create and execute a DTS package, which completely describes all of the work that is performed as part of the transfer and transformation process.

The DTS Package

A DTS package defines one or more data transformation steps. Steps are executed in a coordinated sequence, which you can control. Each step can perform a different type of operation. For example, step 1 might copy and transform data from an OLE DB source to an OLE DB destination by using the DTS Data Pump, step 2 might execute a script, and step 3 might load and execute an external program

(.EXE) or even a batch file (.CMD or .BAT). Figure 5-1 illustrates such a DTS package.

DTS packages are self-contained and can be executed from SQL Server Enterprise Manager or by using the `dtsrun` utility. DTS packages can be stored in the `msdb` database in SQL Server, linked to the Microsoft Repository, or saved as COM-structured storage files.

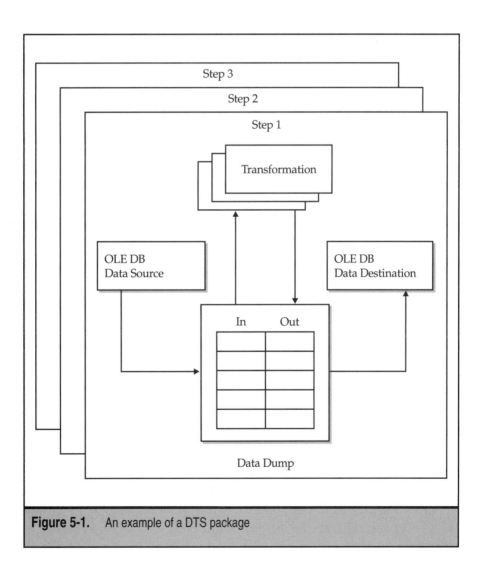

Figure 5-1. An example of a DTS package

The DTS Data Source and Destination

When you use DTS, the data source and destination can be heterogeneous. Using SQL Server as a data source or destination is not required. DTS may simply be the mechanism that transfers data between two data sources.

DTS uses OLE DB providers to import, export, and transform data. Using OLE DB allows access to a wide variety of data source and destination types. OLE DB is a COM interface-based data access mechanism. It can access any data storage format (databases, spreadsheets, text files, and so on) for which an OLE DB provider is available. An OLE DB provider is a software component that exposes an OLE DB interface. Each OLE DB provider is specific to a particular storage mechanism, such as SQL Server databases, Microsoft Access databases, or Microsoft Excel spreadsheets.

TIP: OLE DB is an evolutionary extension of ODBC. ODBC is limited to SQL-based relational databases; OLE DB provides access to any data format. OLE DB providers are conceptually the same as ODBC drivers. The OLE DB provider for ODBC makes it possible to use OLE DB applications, such as DTS, with any data source for which you have an ODBC driver.

Table 5-2 describes the OLE DB providers available with SQL Server. Other providers are available from third-party vendors.

Using DTS steps, it is also possible to create packages that do such things as performing high-speed non-logged inserts (using bcp or BULK INSERT), transforming and publishing data as HTML, or exporting data to pivot tables in Excel.

The DTS Data Pump

The DTS Data Pump is an OLE DB service provider that provides the infrastructure to import, export, and transform data between heterogeneous data stores. It is a high-speed, in-process COM server that moves and transforms OLE DB rowsets. The DTS Data Pump uses OLE DB because OLE DB provides access to the broadest possible range of relational and nonrelational data stores.

Data Source or Data Destination	Description
Native OLE DB	Accesses applications such as SQL Server, Excel, and Access, as well as workgroup and enterprise databases
ODBC	Accesses Oracle, Access, and DB2 by using the OLE DB provider for ODBC
ASCII text files	Accesses ASCII fixed-field-length text files and ASCII delimited text files by using the SQL Server DTS Flat File OLE DB provider
Customized	Supports third-party and ISV OLE DB providers

Table 5-2.   The OLE DB Providers Available with SQL Server

The DTS Data Pump provides the extensible COM-based architecture that allows complex data validations and transformations as the data moves from the source to the destination. The Data Pump exposes the source and destination OLE DB rowsets to scripting languages, such as VBScript, Microsoft JScript, and PerlScript, in a DTS package. This ability allows the expression of complex procedural logic as simple, reusable ActiveX scripts. Scripts can validate, convert, or transform column values as they move from the source through the Data Pump to the destination.

DTS Tools

DTS tools include the DTS Import Wizard, the DTS Export Wizard, DTS Designer, the `dtswiz` and `dtsrun` command-prompt utilities, and the Data Transformation Services node in the SQL Server Enterprise Manager console tree.

The DTS Import and DTS Export Wizards

The DTS Import and DTS Export Wizards offer many ways to customize or simplify the method in which data is copied from source to destination. With DTS wizards, you can

▼ Define DTS packages in an easy-to-use, interactive user interface. The result of using the wizard is a package that you can save and edit directly with DTS Designer if you want to.

■ Copy data between heterogeneous data sources.

■ Schedule DTS packages for later execution.

■ Copy an entire table or the results of a SQL query, such as a query that involves joins of multiple tables or even distributed queries. The Query Builder within the wizard allows users who are inexperienced with the SQL language to build queries interactively.

▲ Copy all of the objects from one SQL Server 2000 database to another.

TIP: When copying a table, the DTS wizards by default do not copy indexes, triggers, or constraints. If the table is to be created by the package, you can manually edit the Transact-SQL that is used to create the table and add the statements needed to create indexes, triggers, or constraints.

You can start the DTS Import Wizard and the DTS Export Wizard from SQL Server Enterprise Manager, from the Microsoft SQL Server 2000 program group on the Start menu, or by using the dtswiz command-prompt utility.

TIP: The DTS Import Wizard and the DTS Export Wizard are the same utility. You can move data into or out of SQL Server or any other OLE DB data source using either wizard. The text in the title bar of the utility changes depending on which wizard you select.

Importing and Exporting Data with the DTS Import and Export Wizards

Importing summary data into a new table using the DTS Import Wizard is a relatively straightforward process. In the following sections, we will consider some specific examples of how you can import and export data with the DTS. In the first example, we will consider the techniques you use to import data.

Importing Data from a SQL Query   To import data from a SQL query from within Enterprise Manager, perform the following steps (in the following steps, if an option is not specified, accept the default):

1. Right-click your server, point to All Tasks, and then click Import Data. This launches the Data Transformation Services Wizard. Click Next.

2. In Source, select Microsoft OLE DB Provider For SQL Server.

3. In Server, select (local).

4. Select Use Windows NT Authentication.

5. In Database, select Nwind (or any other database you want to use—though the printed example uses the Nwind database). Click Next.

6. In Destination, select Microsoft OLE DB Provider For SQL Server.

7. In Server, select (local).

8. Select Use Windows NT Authentication.

9. In Database, select Nwind. Click Next.

10. Select Use A Query To Specify The Data To Transfer. Click Next.

11. In Query Statement, type

```
SELECT ProductName, SUM(o.UnitPrice * Quantity) AS Total
FROM [Order Details]
```

```
INNER JOIN Products p ON o.ProductID = p.ProductID
GROUP BY ProductName
```

12. Click Parse. If you have typed the statement correctly, you will see the following confirmation message:

    ```
    The SQL statement is valid. Click OK to close the
    message.
    ```

    Click Next.

13. In the Table(s) list, click the value in the Destination Table column (the default value is Results). Since you are creating a new destination table, you cannot select its name from the drop-down list. Type in the name of the new table: **ProductTotals**.

14. Click the ellipsis button in the Transform column.

15. Check Drop And Recreate Destination Table. Uncheck Nullable for Total under Mappings. Click OK to close the Column Mappings and Transformations dialog box. Click Next.

16. Check only Run Immediately in the When section.

17. Check Save DTS Package and select SQL Server in the Save section. Click Next.

18. In Name, type **Nwind Product Totals**. In Description, type **Year to date product totals**.

19. For Server Name, select (local). Select Use Windows NT Authentication and then click Next.

20. Click Finish. The Transferring Data dialog box indicates the progress of the data transfer. An error will occur on the Drop Table ProductTotals step. This is expected, as the table does not already exist. It will not affect the data transfer.

21. A dialog box indicates when the transfer has completed successfully. Click OK to close the dialog box, and click Done to close the Transferring Data dialog box.

22. Expand your server, expand Data Transformation Services, and click the Local Packages icon. Note that your new DTS package is listed in the details pane.

23. Open SQL Server Query Analyzer.

24. To view the imported results in the `ProductTotals` table, execute the following Transact-SQL statement.

```
SELECT * FROM Nwind.ProductTotals
```

As you can see, although it consists of more than a few steps, building the DTS package and importing the data is actually a relatively simple process, easy to repeat once you understand the basic structure. Exporting data is similar—as you will see in the following section.

Exporting Data with the DTS Export Wizard   In this exercise, you will export data using the DTS Export Wizard and save the DTS package. The DTS package will copy a list of South American customers into a delimited text file. To export data, perform the following steps (as before, in the following steps, if an option is not specified, accept the default):

1. To begin exporting data by using the DTS Export Wizard, right-click your server, point to All Tasks, and then click Export Data. This launches the Data Transformation Services Wizard. Click Next.

2. In Source, select Microsoft OLE DB Provider For SQL Server.

3. In Server, select (local).

4. Select Use Windows NT Authentication.

5. In Database, select StudyNwind. Click Next.

6. In Destination, select Text File.

7. In File Name, type **c:\temp\Sacust.txt**. Click Next.

8. Select Use A Query To Specify The Data To Transfer. Click Next.

9. Click Query Builder. Click Customers and then click > to add all columns from the `Customers` table to the Selected Columns list.

10. In the Selected Columns list, click on Phone and click < to remove it from the list. Do the same for Fax. Click Next.

11. Move Country and CompanyName to the Sorting Order list. (Make sure that Country is above CompanyName.) Click Next.

12. Click Only Rows Meeting Criteria.

13. In the Column drop-down list, select [Customers].[Country]. In the Oper. drop-down list, select =. In Value/Column, type **'Argentina'** (include the single quotes). On the next line, select OR from the logical operator drop-down list. In the Column drop-down list, select [Customers].[Country]. In the Oper. drop-down list, select =. In Value/Column, type **'Brazil'** (include the single quotes). Click Next.

14. The query that will return only South American countries has been filled in for you in Query Statement. Click Parse. (If the statement is not valid, return to step 10.) Click Next.

15. For the file format, select Delimited.

16. Set the Column Delimiter to Tab. Click Next.

17. Check Run Immediately and Schedule DTS Package For Later Execution in the When section.

18. Click the ellipsis button next to Schedule DTS Package For Later Execution.

19. Click Weekly. Set the Weekly section to Every 1 Week(s) on Mon, Wed, and Fri.

20. In the Daily Frequency section, select Occurs Once At and set the time to 9:00 a.m. Click OK and then click Next.

21. In Name, type **South American Customers**. In Description, type **South American customer list**.

22. For Server Name, select (local). Select Use Windows NT Authentication. Click Next.

23. Click Finish. The Transferring Data dialog box indicates the progress of the data transfer.

24. A dialog box indicates when the transfer has completed successfully. Click OK to close the dialog box and click Done to close the Transferring Data dialog box.

25. Open Notepad to review the text file (C:\TEMP\
    SACUST.TXT). The file should contain all of the rows in
    which `Customer.Country` equals Argentina or Brazil.
    You should see all columns except Phone Or Fax.

Verifying that the Schedule Was Created   To view the schedule that was
created, in the Enterprise Manager console tree expand Management
and the SQL Server Agent icon and then click Jobs.

   In the details pane, right-click the job name, South American
Customers, and then click Properties. Review the properties of the
job that was created by the DTS Wizard. Note that the `job step`
command is not viewable because it is encrypted. Click OK to close
the job.

DTS Designer

DTS Designer is a graphical DTS package editor. The work surface
includes a toolbar and an extensible tool palette that you can use to
add package objects and specify workflow.

   When you create a new DTS package from the console tree, the
DTS Designer work surface opens in a new Microsoft Management
Console (MMC) window. Two tool palettes contain icons for
transformation tasks and data connections.

   Experienced users can use DTS Designer to integrate, consolidate,
and transform data from multiple heterogeneous sources, using
complex workflows to simplify the process of building a data
warehouse. The next lesson describes data transformations.

Transforming Data with DTS

Transforming data with DTS involves planning and designing
the transformation and creating and executing a DTS package. Data
transformation involves formatting and modifying data that is
extracted from the data source into merged or derived values that are
more useful at the destination. New values can easily be calculated
from one or more columns in the source rowset, and a single source
column can be decomposed into multiple destination columns.

Mapping Datatypes

DTS allows you to specify the attributes of the destination columns and to indicate how the source columns are mapped to the destination columns. Transformation flags specify whether data of one type in the source can be converted to another type in the destination. For example, you can allow datatype promotion, such as converting 16-bit integers to 32-bit integers, or datatype demotion, such as converting 32-bit integers to 16-bit integers (data may be lost in this case). You can also require an exact match between source and destination datatypes.

Each database defines its own datatypes as well as its column and object naming conventions. DTS attempts to define the best possible datatype matches between a source and destination. However, you can override DTS mappings and specify a different destination datatype, size, precision, and scale properties.

Merging and Separating Data

You can merge and separate data in two ways:

▼ **At the File Level**   You can combine information from multiple sources and place it into a single table, or you can take information from a single source and place it into multiple tables. Heterogeneous joins are an example of combining multiple sources into a single result set that is saved at the destination. Said another way, running a query that joins information from multiple tables and stores it in a single table is an example of a file-level data merge.

▲ **At the Column Level**   You can combine information from multiple columns and place it into a single column, or you can take information from a single column and place it into multiple columns. For example, you can summarize monthly sales totals for each product, or you can decompose a phone number that is stored in one column in order to store the area code in one column and the phone number in another.

Defining Transformation Steps

A DTS package is composed of one or more steps, which you can define. A step defines a unit of work that is performed as part of the transformation process. A step can

▼ Execute a SQL statement.

■ Move and transform homogeneous or heterogeneous data from an OLE DB source to an OLE DB destination, using the DTS Data Pump.

■ Execute a JScript, PerlScript, or VBScript script. These scripts can perform any operation that their scripting language supports, allowing the implementation of any complex procedural logic that is required. ActiveX scripts can also access and manipulate data by using ActiveX Data Objects (ADO) or any other COM Automation components.

■ Launch an external program.

▲ Retrieve and execute other DTS packages.

For example, you can create a DTS package that summarizes sales information for each product for a given month. The DTS package drops (if the table already exists) and creates the table on the destination, gets data from the source connection (OLE DB), processes the transformation (summarization), and finally sends the data to the destination connection (OLE DB).

Creating a DTS Package

When you use DTS to transfer and transform data, you create DTS packages that describe all of the work to be performed as part of the transformation process. You can create the DTS package interactively, using the DTS wizards or DTS Designer, or programmatically, using a language that supports OLE Automation, such as Microsoft Visual Basic.

Saving a DTS Package

Saving the DTS package allows you to modify it, reuse it, or schedule it for later execution. If you do not save the DTS package, it executes immediately. You must save the DTS package if you want to schedule it for later execution.

You can save a DTS package that you create in one of three ways:

▼ **To SQL Server**   Packages saved to SQL Server are referred to as Local packages and are stored in the msdb database. Local packages are the most efficient and are available to other SQL Servers. They are listed in the Local Packages node under Data Transformation Services in the console tree.

■ **To Microsoft Repository**   The Microsoft Repository is a database that stores descriptive information about software components and their relationships. It consists of a set of published COM interfaces and information models that define database schema and data transformations through shared metadata.

Saving a DTS package in the Microsoft Repository makes package metadata reusable and available to other applications. Using the Microsoft Repository also enables you to track data lineage at the package and row level of a table, which allows you to determine the source of each piece of data and the transformations that are applied to it.

When you save a package to the Microsoft Repository, the package is stored in the msdb database, but package metadata can be imported into the repository. Packages stored in this way are listed in the Repository Packages node under Data Transformation Services in the console tree. After you import the package metadata into the repository, you can view it using the Metadata Browser in the Metadata node under Data Transformation Services in the console tree.

▲ **To a File**   Saving a DTS package in a COM-structured storage file makes it easy to distribute the DTS package using e-mail or network file servers. DTS packages saved as files do not appear in the SQL Server Enterprise Manager console tree. To open a package file for editing, right-click Data Transformation Services in the console tree, point to All Tasks, and click Open Package.

Implementing Package Security

You can encrypt DTS packages that are saved to SQL Server or to COM-structured storage files in order to protect sensitive user names and password information. When a DTS package is encrypted, all of its collections and properties are encrypted, except for the package name, description, ID, version, and creation date.

DTS packages provide two levels of security: owner password and operator password, as considered in the following bulleted list:

▼ **Owner Password**   The owner password level of security provides complete access to all collections and properties. By default, DTS packages without owner passwords are not encrypted and can be read by any user with access to the package.

▲ **Operator Password**   The operator password level of security allows a user to execute but not edit or view the package definition. If an operator password is specified at the time of creation, an owner password must also be supplied.

Defining Workflows

With DTS, you can define a workflow that controls the execution sequence of each step. Control of flow logic and conditional processing is achieved using precedence constraints. DTS tasks can also be prioritized. The following sections discuss using DTS Designer to edit and customize packages.

Steps, Tasks, and Precedence Constraints

Workflows control the flow of execution for the package. A package is made up of data connections (sources and destinations) and tasks that are performed using those connections. The action of executing a task is controlled by a step. A step can be subject to one or more precedence constraints. A step with no precedence constraints executes immediately. If a step has precedence constraints, it cannot execute until all of its precedence constraints have been satisfied.

In DTS Designer, steps are represented by task icons and a solid data transformation arrow between two data connection icons. Precedence constraints are represented by dashed blue (Completion), green (Success), or red (Failure) arrows. An arrow points to the step that is subject to the precedence constraint; this is called the *destination step*. If the destination step is a data transformation, the arrow points to the source data connection of the step. An arrow points from the step that must be completed to satisfy the precedence constraint; this is called the *source step*. If the source step is a data transformation, the arrow points from the destination data connection of the step. To make your DTS Designer diagrams easier to read, you can add the same connection to the diagram more than once. When you do so, specify it as an existing connection. If a connection is involved in more than one transformation, it is recommended that you add the connection once for each transformation. If you do not, the diagram will have a single data connection icon with a large number of arrows (both data transformations and precedence constraints) pointing to and from it.

TIP: The terms *source* and *destination* are used to refer to both data connections and steps in DTS Designer. When working with a source or a destination, always make sure that you know whether it is a source or destination connection or a source or destination step.

In addition, arrows are used to represent both precedence constraints and data transformations in DTS Designer. When working with an arrow in a DTS diagram, make sure that you know whether it is a constraint or a data transformation arrow.

Steps are defined using the Workflow Properties dialog box. To open this dialog box, right-click on the destination step (either the task icon or the data transformation arrow if the step is a data transformation step). Then select Workflow Properties (you may need to point to Workflow to get to the Workflow Properties option) from the context menu. You can also open the Workflow Properties dialog box by right-clicking a precedence constraint arrow, but this is not recommended, as it is confusing and does not allow access to the General tab.

The Precedence tab of the Workflow Properties dialog box allows you to add precedence constraints to or remove them from the step. The order of precedence constraints in the list is not important. You can also add precedence constraints from the Workflow menu or from the toolbar in DTS Designer, but this is not recommended, as it is easy to confuse the destination and source steps using this method. The General tab of the Workflow Properties dialog box allows you to set workflow properties such as task priority and transaction management for the task of the destination step.

Precedence Constraint Types

The type of precedence constraint you select determines the requirement for executing a step:

▼ Success indicates that the source step must complete successfully before the destination step executes.

■ Failure indicates that the source step must complete with an indication of failure before the destination step executes.

▲ Completion indicates that the source step must simply complete (with failure or success) before the destination step executes.

Precedence constraints create a finish-start relationship between the step being executed (the source step) and the step that will be executed (the destination step). Given two steps, A and B, a precedence constraint says,

```
Step B cannot start until step A finishes
```

rather than saying,

```
If step A finishes, step B will start
```

which is important when multiple steps are involved, as a step may have many precedence constraints that all must be satisfied before it can execute.

Controlling Step Execution

Under the control of precedence constraints, steps execute in sequence, in parallel, or in a combination of these:

▼ Some steps must execute in a certain sequence. For example, data can be loaded into a table (step B) only after the table has been successfully created (step A).

■ Multiple steps can execute in parallel to improve performance. For example, a package can load data from Oracle and DB2 into separate tables simultaneously.

▲ Steps can use a combination of sequential and parallel execution. For example, a package can load data from several different heterogeneous files into a set of tables. The loading of data can be done in parallel, but only after the creation of the tables.

Figure 5-2 shows a package with six steps that demonstrate a combination of parallel and sequential execution. Steps A, B, and C have no precedence constraints and execute immediately. Step D waits for step A to complete successfully before executing. Step E waits for step D to complete with a failure before executing. Step F waits for step C to complete (with success or failure) before executing. Steps A, D, and E execute sequentially. Steps C and F

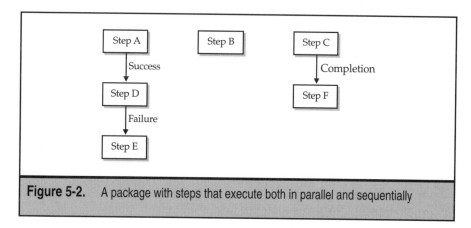

Figure 5-2.   A package with steps that execute both in parallel and sequentially

execute sequentially. Steps A (and its sequential steps), B, and C (and its sequential step) execute in parallel.

Figure 5-3 shows how one step can have multiple precedence constraints. In this case, step C can execute only when both step A and step B have successfully completed.

Conditional Processing

Conditional processing using basic IF-THEN-ELSE logic allows a DTS package to respond to run-time conditions that vary. To implement conditional processing, use a combination of steps with Success and Failure precedence constraints, as shown in Figure 5-4. In the figure, step B executes only if step A completes successfully. Step C will execute if step A fails. Step C would typically send a notification such as an e-mail message or would take corrective action that is in turn the condition for another precedence constraint that then allows the original step to be repeated.

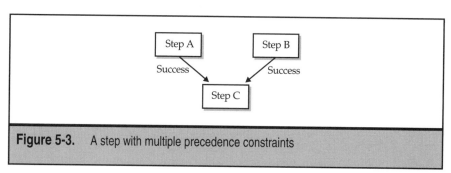

Figure 5-3.   A step with multiple precedence constraints

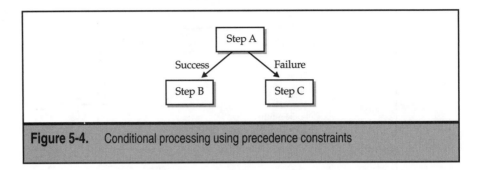

Figure 5-4. Conditional processing using precedence constraints

Specifying Task Priority

You can specify the priority of tasks. By default, each thread within the DTS package executes at the same priority as the DTS package. However, if some operations are more time-critical than others, you can assign an execution priority to each step. You can specify each step to execute at Idle, Normal, or High priority.

Creating a Package with DTS Designer

The best way to try this is to create a package using DTS Designer. In the following section, you will do just that; in the subsequent section, you will execute the package. The package will transfer some of the columns from the Products table in an Access database to a new table in a SQL Server database. The package will use a custom data transformation to look up and then convert data values from the Access table to new values in the SQL Server table. You will use an ActiveX script to convert the values.

TIP: The following package requires that you have Microsoft Access installed on the server. You can perform similar package design without Microsoft Access, obviously; this example just walks you through the methods you can use to share information amongst heterogeneous data sources.

Using DTS Designer to Create a Package   To create a package using the DTS Designer, perform the following steps:

1. Right-click Data Transformation Services in the console tree and then click New Package.

2. On the Data tool palette, click the Microsoft Access icon.

3. In New Connection, type **Access Connection**.

4. In File Name, type **C:\PROGRAM FILES\MICROSOFT OFFICE\SAMPLES\ NWIND.MDB**. Click OK to add the Microsoft Access data connection.

5. On the Data tool palette, click the Microsoft OLE DB Provider For SQL Server icon.

6. In New Connection, type **SQL Server Connection**.

7. In Database, select Nwind. Click OK to add the SQL Server data connection.

8. On the Task tool palette, click the Execute SQL Task icon.

9. In Description, type **Drop ProductsCopy**. In Existing Connection, select SQL Server Connection.

10. In SQL Statement, type the following T-SQL code:

```
DROP TABLE Nwind..ProductsCopy
```

11. Click Parse Query to confirm that you have typed the statement correctly. Click OK to close the dialog boxes and save the task.

12. On the Task tool palette, click the Execute SQL Task icon.

13. In Description, type **Create ProductsCopy**. In Existing Connection, select SQL Server Connection.

14. In SQL Statement, type the following T-SQL code:

```
CREATE TABLE StudyNwind..ProductsCopy (
    ProductID int NOT NULL ,
    ProductName nvarchar (40) NOT NULL ,
    QuantityPerUnit nvarchar (20) NULL ,
    UnitPrice money NULL ,
    IsAnimal char (3) NULL
    )
```

15. Click Parse Query to confirm that you have typed the statement correctly. Click OK to close the dialog boxes and save the task.

16. Click Package on the menu and click Save. In Package Name, type **Copy Access Products to SQL Server**.

17. The defaults in the Save DTS Package dialog box will save the package to SQL Server. Click OK to save the package.

18. On the taskbar, click Execute. This tests the package to see that the connections and tasks are working and also creates the table, which needs to be on the server when you add the data transformation. The first step will indicate that an error occurred; this is normal since the table cannot be dropped the first time the package is executed.

19. On the DTS Designer work surface, click Access Connection. Then hold down the CTRL key and click SQL Server Connection.

20. Click Workflow on the menu and click Add Transform. A data transformation arrow pointing from the Access connection to the SQL Server connection is added to the work surface.

21. Right-click the data transformation arrow and click Properties.

22. In Description, type **Copy data from Access to SQL Server**.

23. In Table Name, select `Products`. Click the Destination tab.

24. In Table Name, select `[Nwind].[dbo].[ProductsCopy]`.

25. Click the Advanced tab. Click the Lookups button.

26. Click Add. In the Name column, type **SQLLookup**. In the Connection column, select Access Connection, then click the ellipsis button in the Query column.

27. Type the following query in the code pane of the query builder:

```
SELECT CategoryName
FROM Categories
WHERE (CategoryID = ?)
```

28. Click OK to close the query builder, then click OK to close the Data Transformation Lookups dialog box and save the data lookup for your transformation.

29. Click the Transformations tab.

30. Click the line pointing from `SupplierID` to `QuantityPerUnit` and click Delete. Click the line pointing from `CategoryID` to `UnitPrice` and click Delete. Click the line pointing from `QuantityPerUnit` to `IsAnimal` and click Delete.

31. Click `QuantityPerUnit` in the Source Table and Destination Table columns and then click New. Click `UnitPrice` in the Source Table and Destination Table columns and then click New.

32. Click `CategoryID` in the Source Table column and `IsAnimal` in the Destination Table column. In New Transformation, select ActiveX Script and then click New.

33. Replace the default code in Script by typing the following VBScript:

```
Function Main()
  Select Case _
      DTSLookups("myLookup").Execute(DTSSource("CategoryID").Value)
    Case "Dairy Products", "Meat/Products", "Seafood"
      DTSDestination("IsAnimal") = "Yes"
    Case Else
      DTSDestination("IsAnimal") = "No"
  End Select
  Main = DTSTransformStat_OK
End Function
```

34. Click OK to save the transformation script.

TIP: To edit individual column transformations, you need to right-click on the lines pointing from the Source Table list to the Destination Table list.

35. Click OK to close the Data Transformation Properties dialog box and save your changes to the data transformation.

36. Right-click `Create ProductsCopy` on the work surface. Point to Workflow and click Workflow Properties.

37. In the Workflow Properties dialog box, click New to add a precedence constraint for the `Create ProductsCopy` step.

38. In the Source Step column, select `Drop ProductsCopy`. In the Precedence column, select Completion. Note that you cannot change the Destination Step because you are editing the precedence constraints for `Create ProductsCopy`, which is the destination step. Click OK to close the Workflow Properties dialog box and save the precedence constraints for `Create ProductsCopy`.

Next, you must add a precedence constraint for the data transformation step. Unlike the `Create ProductsCopy` step, which is represented by its icon, the data transformation step is represented by the arrow connecting the two data connections.

1. Right-click the data transformation arrow (the arrow from Access Connection to SQL Server Connection) on the work surface. Click Workflow Properties.

2. In the Workflow Properties dialog box, click New to add a precedence constraint for the data transformation step.

3. In the Source Step column, select `Drop ProductsCopy`. In the Precedence column, select Completion. Note that you cannot change the Destination Step because you are editing the precedence constraints for `Create ProductsCopy`, which is the destination step. Click OK to close the Workflow Properties dialog box and save the precedence constraints for `Create ProductsCopy`.

4. On the Package menu, click Save. Close the DTS Designer dialog box.

Executing the New Package   To ensure that you have created the package correctly, you should execute the package you have just created and then view the data in the new table. To execute the new package and verify its results, perform the following steps:

1. In the console tree, expand Data Transformation Services and click Local Packages.

2. Right-click Copy Access Products to SQL Server in the details pane and click Execute Package.

3. The Executing DTS Package dialog box appears and indicates the progress of each of the steps as the package executes.

4. Click OK and click Done to close the dialog boxes.

5. In the console tree, expand Databases, expand Nwind, and then click Tables.

6. In the details pane, right-click ProductsCopy (if you do not see this table, refresh your Enterprise Manager view), point to Open Table, and click Return All Rows. A grid displays the table that was created by the DTS package. Note the values in the IsAnimal column that were set by the ActiveX script and the lookup.

Executing and Scheduling a DTS Package

Each DTS package is self-contained after you create it. A package is a complete description of all the work to be performed as part of the transformation process. This section describes how to execute and schedule a DTS package that you have created.

Executing a DTS Package

After you save a DTS package, you can retrieve and execute it, using SQL Server Enterprise Manager or the dtsrun command-prompt utility.

The example given here shows the dtsrun command-prompt utility being used to execute a DTS package that creates and populates a summary table in the Nwind database on the SQL Server named SQLSERVER. The /U option specifies the sa login. If the specified login has a password, it must be specified with the /P option. Note that the name of the package is enclosed in double quotes; this is necessary if the name contains spaces. Remember that the DTS package is a complete description of all of the work to be performed as part of the transformation process.

```
dtsrun /SSQLSERVER /Usa /N"Nwind Product Totals"
```

Scheduling a DTS Package

You can schedule a saved DTS package for execution at a specific time, such as daily at midnight, or at recurring intervals, such as on the first or last day of the month or weekly on Sunday at 6 a.m.

You can schedule a DTS package for execution in the following ways:

▼ By using the DTS Import or DTS Export Wizards when you save the DTS package to the SQL Server msdb database.

▲ By using SQL Server Enterprise Manager to create a SQL Server job that executes the DTS package by running the dtsrun command-prompt utility. Do this manually for packages saved as files. For local packages and repository packages, right-click the package and select Schedule Package from the context menu.

INTRODUCTION TO LINKED SERVERS

SQL Server allows you to create links to OLE DB data sources called *linked servers*. This allows SQL Server clients to perform fully distributed queries and transactions. After linking to an OLE DB data source, you can

▼ Reference rowsets from the OLE DB data sources as tables in Transact-SQL statements sent to SQL Server. This means that client software does not need to use many different dialects of the SQL language and can access many different servers through a single connection to SQL Server.

▲ Reference multiple linked servers and perform either update or read operations against each individual linked server. A single distributed query can perform read operations against some linked servers and update operations against other linked servers. The types of queries executed against linked servers depend on the level of support for transactions present in the OLE DB providers.

Figure 5-5 illustrates how linked servers work.

Adding Linked Servers

A linked server definition specifies an OLE DB provider and an OLE DB data source.

An OLE DB provider is a dynamic-link library (DLL) that manages and interacts with a specific data source. An OLE DB data source is any data store accessible through OLE DB. Although

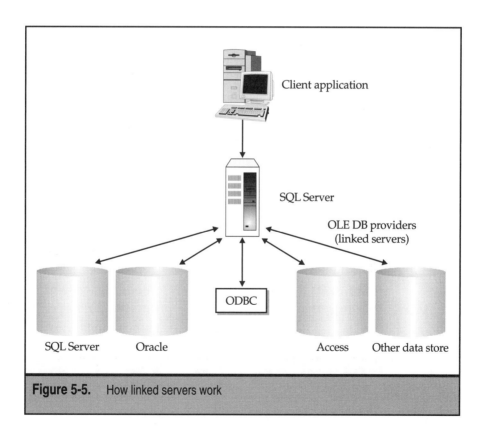

Client application

SQL Server

OLE DB providers
(linked servers)

ODBC

SQL Server   Oracle

Access   Other data store

Figure 5-5.   How linked servers work

data sources queried through linked server definitions are usually database servers (such as SQL Server or Oracle), OLE DB providers exist for a wide variety of files and file formats, including file-based databases (such as Microsoft Access and Microsoft Visual FoxPro), text files, spreadsheet data, and the results of full-text content searches. Table 5-3 shows examples of the most common OLE DB providers and data sources for SQL Server.

TIP: Microsoft has tested linked server support with the Microsoft OLE DB Provider for SQL Server, Microsoft OLE DB Provider for Jet, Microsoft OLE DB Provider for Oracle, Microsoft OLE DB Provider for Indexing Service, and Microsoft OLE DB Provider for ODBC. However, SQL Server distributed queries are designed to work with any OLE DB provider that implements the requisite OLE DB interfaces.

OLE DB Provider	OLE DB Data Source
Microsoft OLE DB Provider for SQL Server	SQL Server database, such as pubs or Northwind
Microsoft OLE DB Provider for Jet	Pathname of .MDB database file
Microsoft OLE DB Provider for ODBC	ODBC data source name (pointing to a particular database)
Microsoft OLE DB Provider for Oracle	SQL*Net alias that points to an Oracle database
Microsoft OLE DB Provider for Indexing Service	Content files on which property searches or full-text searches can be run

Table 5-3. Some of the Most Common OLE DB Providers and Data Sources for SQL Server

For a data source to return data through a linked server, the OLE DB provider (DLL) for that data source must be present on the same server as SQL Server.

When setting up a linked server, register the connection information and data source information with SQL Server. After registration is accomplished, the data source can always be referred to with a single logical name. You can create or delete a linked server definition with system stored procedures or through SQL Server Enterprise Manager.

For a table of the different parameter values that you need to specify when creating a linked server, see `sp_addlinkedserver` in Books Online.

Security Considerations for Linked Servers

When you execute a query against a linked server, SQL Server must provide a login name and password to the linked server on behalf of the user executing the query.

The login name and password provided to the linked server can be specified explicitly by adding a mapped login for the linked server. If many users need to use the linked server, it may not be practical to add mapped logins for each user. If a mapped login has not been created for a user who is trying to use a linked server, one of the following can occur:

▼ The user is denied access.

■ The user is mapped to a single login specified for all users that do not have a mapped login.

■ SQL Server provides no login or password. This works for data sources that do not enforce security.

▲ SQL Server provides the user's SQL Server login credentials. This requires that the user have the same login name and password on the linked server, and it is called *impersonation*.

When creating mapped logins for users, you can either specify a login name and password to be used on the linked server or specify that the user be impersonated on the linked server. Login mappings are stored on SQL Server, which passes the relevant login information to the linked server whenever necessary.

By specifying that users without login mappings must be denied access, you can control access to other data sources at the SQL Server level or provide access control to data sources that do not provide their own security. For example, you could place a Microsoft Access database file on a Windows NT drive and use NTFS permissions to disallow access to all users. Only users that have SQL Server logins would gain access to the Access database as a linked server.

System Stored Procedures for Working with Linked Servers

SQL Server provides system stored procedures for working with linked servers. For example, the sp_addlinkedserver system stored procedure is used to create a linked server definition, and the sp_linkedservers system stored procedure is used to view information about linked servers. Table 5-4 provides a list of system stored procedures that can be used for working with linked servers.

Executing a Distributed Query

When executing a distributed query against a linked server, include a fully qualified, four-part table name for each data source to be queried. This four-part name should be in the form

```
linked_server_name.catalog.schema.object_name
```

On SQL Server, catalog refers to the database name, and schema refers to the table owner. The following example shows a query that retrieves data from linked SQL Server and Oracle databases:

```
SELECT emp.EmloyeeID, ord.OrderID, ord.Discount
FROM SQLServer1.Northwind.dbo.Employees emp INNER JOIN
    OracleSvr.Catalog1.SchemaX.Orders ord
ON ord.EmployeeID = emp.EmployeeID
WHERE ord.Discount > 0
```

Configuring servers is a straightforward process. In the following section, we will discuss how to configure a Microsoft Access linked server from the Enterprise Manager.

System Stored Procedure	Purpose
sp_addlinkedserver	Create a linked server definition
sp_linkedservers	View information about linked servers
sp_dropserver	Delete a linked server definition
sp_addlinkedsrvlogin	Add a linked server login mapping
sp_droplinkedsrvlogin	Delete a linked server login mapping

Table 5-4.   Some of the System Stored Procedures at Your Disposal for Working with Linked Servers

Configuring a Microsoft Access Linked Server

Configuring an Access linked server can be done in ten steps. To configure the linking process, perform the following steps:

1. In the console tree, expand your server, expand Security, and then right-click Linked Servers. Click New Linked Server.

2. In Linked Server, enter the name **LINKEDJET** for the new linked server.

3. Under Server Type, click Other Data Source.

4. For Provider Name, select Microsoft Jet 4.0 OLE DB Provider from the list of providers.

5. In Data Source, enter the path to the linked server Microsoft Jet database **C:\PROGRAM FILES\MICROSOFT OFFICE\SAMPLES\NWIND.MDB**.

6. On the Security tab, click They Will Be Mapped To and type **Admin** in Remote User. This step maps all SQL Server logins to the login Admin, which is the default user name for Access databases that do not have security enabled.

7. Click OK to close the Linked Server Properties dialog box and add the new linked server.

8. In the console tree, expand LINKEDJET and then click Tables. In the details pane, you see a list of the tables from the Access NWIND.MDB file.

9. Switch to or open Query Analyzer. Select Northwind in the DB list box.

10. In the query pane, type and execute the following query:

```
SELECT ProductName, CategoryName,
DATALENGTH(ProductName)
FROM LINKEDJET...Products Prd JOIN Categories Cat
ON Prd.CategoryID = Cat.CategoryID
```

This query retrieves data from the Category table in the SQL Server Northwind database and joins it to data retrieved from the Products table in the Access NWIND.MDB database file.

The JOIN syntax of this query is valid in Transact-SQL but will not work in Microsoft Access (INNER JOIN would have to be specified). The query uses the Transact-SQL DATALENGTH function, which is not available in Microsoft Access. The DATALENGTH function returns the length of the data in the specified column. The value returned is twice the number of characters in the column because the data is stored using two-byte-per-character Unicode characters.

COPYING DATA WITH BULK COPY (BCP) AND THE DISTRIBUTED TRANSACTION COORDINATOR (DTC)

In the following sections, we will discuss how to use data from an external source to populate a SQL Server database. Older versions of SQL Server relied on the bulk copy program (bcp) for importing external data. Although bcp is still available, Microsoft recommends that you use Data Transformation Services (DTS) to move and transform data in SQL Server 2000. As you have already seen, DTS can move data out of or into any OLE DB or ODBC data source or destination.

Using the Bulk Copy Program

The *bulk copy program* (bcp) is a command-line utility that imports and exports native SQL Server data files or ASCII text files. Use bcp to import data into a SQL Server table from a file or to export data from a SQL Server table to a file. You can use the BULK INSERT Transact-SQL statement instead of the bcp program to copy data into a SQL Server table. BULK INSERT uses the same process as bcp but makes it possible to import data using Transact-SQL instead of the command-line utility. BULK INSERT cannot be used to copy data out of a SQL Server table.

Nonlogged Bulk Copies

Most of the time, all data modifications in a database are recorded in the transaction log. When you load a large amount of data with bcp, this logging slows performance and can cause the transaction log to become full. For this reason, bcp supports a non-logged mode of operation. *Non-logged bulk copies* only log the allocation of data pages; the insertion of new rows is not logged. For a non-logged bulk copy to be used, the following conditions must all be met:

▼   The Select Into/Bulkcopy Database option is set to TRUE.

■   The target table has no indexes, or if the table has indexes, it is empty when the bulk copy starts.

■   The target table is not being replicated.

▲   The TABLOCK hint is specified using the commandline -h argument.

TIP: In SQL Server 2000, bcp uses the ODBC bulk copy interface. In previous versions of SQL Server, bcp used the DB-Library bulk copy interface.

Configuring the Northwind Database for Bulk Copy   The easiest way to understand how bulk copy works is to try it. In this section, you will learn how to enable the Northwind database for bulk copying. You will then, in the next section, perform a non-logged bulk copy into the database. You will also create a new table called bcpProducts in the Northwind database. You will copy records into this table using the bulk copy program in the next section. To configure bulk copy, perform the following steps:

1.   Start SQL Server Enterprise Manager.

2.   Expand your server and then expand Databases.

3.   Right-click the Northwind database icon and then click Properties.

4.   Click the Options tab and verify that the Select Into/Bulk Copy option is checked. If it is not, check it and then click OK.

5.   In SQL Server Query Analyzer, enter the following SQL script to create the bcpProducts table in the Northwind database:

```
USE Northwind

if exists
    (select * from sysobjects where id =
    object_id(N'[dbo].[bcpProducts]') and
    OBJECTPROPERTY(id, N'IsUserTable') = 1)
  drop table [dbo].[bcpProducts]
GO

CREATE TABLE [dbo].[bcpProducts] (
    [ProductID] [int] IDENTITY (1, 1) NOT NULL ,
    [ProductName] [nvarchar] (40) NOT NULL ,
    [SupplierID] [int] NULL ,
    [CategoryID] [int] NULL ,
    [QuantityPerUnit] [nvarchar] (20) NULL ,
    [UnitPrice] [money] NULL ,
    [UnitsInStock] [smallint] NULL ,
    [UnitsOnOrder] [smallint] NULL ,
    [ReorderLevel] [smallint] NULL ,
```

```
        [Discontinued]  [bit]  NOT NULL
    )
GO
```

Importing Data with the bcp Utility   Now that you have created a new table, you can create a batch file that uses the bcp utility to import as many records as you place into a tab-delimited text file into the bcpProducts table in the Northwind database.

Open Notepad and type the following bcp command.

```
bcp Northwind..bcpProducts in
    "c:\newprods.txt -c -t",
    " -r\n -ec:\ newprods.err -b250 -m50 -SSQLSERVER -Usa -h"TABLOCK"
```

TIP: You must enter the whole command as a single line (do not insert any hard returns). The bcp arguments are case-sensitive so you must type the command exactly as it appears here. Replace the server name with your server name. For more information, search for "bcp utility" in Books Online.

An explanation of the arguments is given in the following table:

Argument	Value
Database and table	Northwind..bcpProducts
Data direction	In
Transfer file	C:\NEWPRODS.TXT (whatever you choose to name the file)
Data: character only	-c
Field terminator: comma	-t","
Row terminator: new line	-r\n
Error file	-e C:\NEWPRODS.ERR (whatever you choose to name the file)
Batch size	-b250
Maximum errors	-m50

Argument	Value
Server name (replace SQLSERVER with your server name if your server is not called SQLSERVER)	-SSQLSERVER
Username	-Usa
TABLOCK hint	-h"TABLOCK"

Save the file with the name RUNBCP.CMD in the C:\TEMP folder. From a command prompt, execute the C:\TEMP\ RUNBCP.CMD file. You are prompted for a password. Enter the password for the sa login and press ENTER, or just press ENTER if your sa password is blank.

The layout of the text file is pretty straightforward, as shown in the following line (other products would be entered into the file similarly, one product per line):

```
14,Sugar Free Chef Anton's Gumbo Mix,2,2,36 boxes,21.6000,5,0,0,1
```

DISTRIBUTING DATA WITH SQL SERVER

SQL Server provides many methods of distributing data. Two of the most commonly used tools are distributed transactions, which are controlled by the Microsoft Distributed Transaction Coordinator (MS DTC), and SQL Server replication. Figure 5-6 illustrates these two methods.

With both methods, it is possible to keep multiple copies of a table current and multiple databases closely synchronized. The extent to which your data must be current determines the model that you use.

Microsoft Distributed Transaction Coordinator

The Microsoft Distributed Transaction Coordinator (MS DTC), a feature of both SQL Server and Microsoft Transaction Server (MTS), ensures transaction integrity by managing updates across two or more servers.

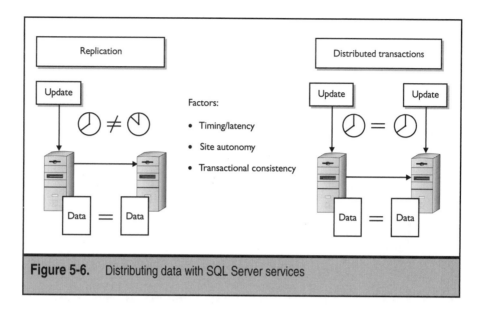

Figure 5-6.   Distributing data with SQL Server services

In a homogeneous environment that contains only SQL Servers, the MS DTC is invoked using the `BEGIN DISTRIBUTED TRANSACTION` statement or one of the SQL Server programming interfaces (OD BC or OLE DB). The MS DTC can also participate in heterogeneous environments by using MTS or other transaction monitors that are compatible with the UNIX XA standard for transaction processing.

The MS DTC provides *tight consistency* between data sites, ensuring that all updates to all copies of data are consistent at the same time. Creating tight consistency:

▼   Requires a high-speed network, because all updates must be committed in all databases in real time.

▲   Reduces database availability. If any of the distributed databases are unavailable, no updates can be made.

Because distributed applications can be vulnerable to hardware and network failures, use a tight consistency model only when data must be synchronized at all times and when you have a reliable high-speed network.

Replication

You can use *transactional replication* in place of the MS DTC for selected client functions, such as reporting and data warehousing. Replication provides data consistency but does not guarantee that all data will be consistent at the same time.

Replication allows you to:

▼ Update data intermittently on multiple databases.

▲ Resynchronize data following a system outage or failure.

TIP: Replication is covered in detail in Chapters 10 and 11 of this book.

INTRODUCTION TO DISTRIBUTED QUERIES

Distributed queries access data from multiple heterogeneous data sources stored on a local or remote computer. SQL Server supports distributed queries by using OLE DB, the Microsoft application programming interface for universal data access.

Distributed queries provide SQL Server users with access to:

▼ Distributed data stored in multiple computers that are running SQL Server

▲ Heterogeneous data stored in various relational and nonrelational data sources for which either an OLE DB provider or an ODBC driver exists

Accessing Remote Data

You can use two techniques for accessing an OLE DB data source from SQL Server: an *ad hoc query* or a *linked server query*. These two techniques are summarized in the following list:

▼ **Ad Hoc Query**   To access remote data when you do not expect to access a data source repeatedly over time, you can write an ad hoc query with the OPENROWSET function.

▲ **Linked Server Query**   To access remote data repeatedly, you can use a linked server and a four-part object name. A linked server is an OLE DB data source that is pre-registered on the local SQL Server so that when it is referenced, the local server knows where to look for the remote data and objects. Using linked servers is an efficient way to provide cross-SQL Server joins and other queries when you know in advance that certain data sources must be available.

Specifying Where to Process Distributed Queries

When you query an OLE DB data source, you can specify whether to process the query locally or on a remote server:

▼ **Local SQL Server**   For linked servers, SQL Server processes distributed queries on the local server by default.

▲ **Remote OLE DB Data Source**   You can use the OPENQUERY function with linked servers to specify that processing will occur on the remote server. When you use the OPENROWSET function to execute an ad hoc query on a remote data source, the query is processed remotely. This type of query is called a *pass-through query*.

Verifying Connection Settings

In any session issuing distributed queries, the ANSI_NULLS and ANSI_WARNINGS options must be set on. If you use OBDC or SQL Server Query Analyzer to issue distributed queries, these options are on by default. If you use the osql command-line utility, you must explicitly set these options on.

Executing an Ad Hoc Query on a Remote Data Source

You can access data ad hoc from remote sources by using an OLE DB provider. The OPENROWSET function allows you to connect to and access data from a remote source without setting up a linked server. You use the OPENROWSET function in the FROM clause of a query as if it were a table. Use the OPENROWSET function when you do not expect to access a particular data source repeatedly over time. You will implement the function as shown here:

```
OPENROWSET('provider_name',
    {'datasource'; 'user_id' ;
    'password' | 'provider_string'},
    {[catalog.][schema.]object | 'query'})
```

The arguments of the OPENROWSET function are straightforward. The provider_name argument is a unique, friendly name for the OLE DB provider corresponding to this data source. The datasource argument corresponds to the name of the data source as interpreted by the OLE DB provider. The user_id argument corresponds to the user name that will be passed to the specified OLE DB provider. The password argument contains the password to be passed to the OLE DB provider.

The provider_string argument corresponds to the OLE DB provider-specific connection string that identifies a unique data source. The catalog argument refers to the catalog or database in which the object resides. The schema argument contains the schema or owner for an object. The object parameter refers to a unique object name to act upon. The query parameter is a string containing a query to be sent to and executed by the provider. If a query is specified rather than a remote object name, the query is executed as a pass-through query.

Consider the following facts and guidelines when executing queries using the OPENROWSET function:

▼ You must provide catalog and schema names if the data source supports multiple catalogs and schemas (databases and object owners, in the case of SQL Server).

■ The user_id passed to the OLE DB provider determines the permissions associated with the connection.

▲ The OPENROWSET function can be used in place of a table name in the FROM clause of a SELECT statement.

How do you use the OPENROWSET function? Well, let's consider a simple example that joins the Orders table in the remote Microsoft

Access `Northwind` database with the `Customers` table in the Northwind database on the local SQL Server.

```
USE Northwind
SELECT cust.CompanyName,
    CONVERT(varchar(10), ord.OrderDate, 101) AS OrderDate
FROM Customers as cust
JOIN OPENROWSET('Microsoft.Jet.OLEDB.4.0',
    'C:\Program Files\Microsoft Office\Office\Samples\Northwind.mdb';
    'Admin'; '', Orders) AS ord
ON cust.CustomerID = ord.CustomerID
ORDER BY ord.OrderDate
```

SUMMARY

In this chapter, you learned about the data transfer process and the various tools you can use to transfer data in SQL 7.0. You can import and export data from SQL Server with several tools and Transact-SQL statements. Additionally, with the programming models and APIs that are available with SQL Server, such as the DTS object model, you can write your own programs to import and export data.

The method you choose for importing or exporting data depends on a variety of user requirements, including the format of the data, the location of the data, how often the transfer will be occurring, the type of import or export, and finally, ease of use.

DTS is a general-purpose data transfer and transformation tool with a wide range of applications. It provides the ability to copy table schema and data between DBMSs, create custom transformation objects, access applications using third-party OLE DB providers, and build data warehouses and data marts in SQL Server. DTS can be used with any OLE DB data source and destination; you are not required to use SQL Server 2000 for either source or destination.

DTS tools include the DTS Import Wizard, the DTS Export Wizard, DTS Designer, the `dtswiz` and `dtsrun` command-prompt utilities, and the Data Transformation Services node in the SQL Server Enterprise Manager console tree.

A linked server allows access to distributed, heterogeneous queries against OLE DB data sources. For example, information can be accessed from an Oracle or Access database by using a SQL Server connection. SQL Server provides system stored procedures to create and view information about linked servers. Once the linked server is created, a query can be run that uses both SQL Server tables and other OLE DB data sources.

The bulk copy program allows you to copy data into or out of SQL Server using ASCII text files that can be used with other databases. Although bcp is a fast way of transferring data and is the mechanism used by previous versions of SQL Server, Data Transformation Services is a more powerful and flexible way to transfer and transform data. SQL Server provides the Microsoft Distributed Transaction Coordinator and SQL Server replication for building true distributed applications.

CHAPTER 6

Implementing and Managing a Backup Solution

In the early days of computing, administrators were those lovely people who worked in the large rooms that made up the actual computer. These trusty people had the awesome responsibility of ensuring that data got processed and errors were kept to a minimum. Actually managing the day-to-day operations of a computer was the primary focus of the job, and administrators enjoyed a level of admiration for making everyone else's job easier.

THE ADMINISTRATOR DEFINED

With the innovation of the microcomputer and business applications, the administrator became widely unneeded and the position was all but eliminated in short order. Immediately following the dismissal of the administrator, the first technical problems came into being, and the position of administrator was restored.

This time the administrator position was more of a troubleshooting and preventative role including duties such as general repair and instruction. Somewhere in the middle of all this, the concept of data protection came into being.

Although protecting data includes many different tasks and concepts, at the root of any data protection scheme is the backup plan. Keeping a verified, valid copy of the data in a secure location has become one of, if not the most important task that falls within the scope of an administrator's duty.

As a SQL Server administrator, you must know how to design, plan, perform, schedule, and verify the backup plan in order to ensure that the data is secure. In this chapter, you will learn how to back up databases, how to plan a backup strategy, and how to control the backup utility and specify details using Transact-SQL. At the end of this chapter, you will be able to plan and implement a backup solution that is capable of protecting data in deployments ranging from a small database serving only a few users, to mass data warehouses serving thousands of users.

THE BACKUP PROCESS

Because planning and executing a backup strategy can be complex, we will begin by exploring how SQL Server actually performs a backup.

First off, you should understand that SQL Server backups are separate from normal system backups. The structure of a SQL Server backup is unique and must be performed by SQL Server or by a program that can control the behavior of SQL Server. If you plan to use a third-party backup utility, you should ensure that the product includes extensions, which let the product connect to and control SQL Server 2000.

The Transact-SQL engine within SQL Server actually supports the concept and functionality of backing up databases directly. The Transact-SQL statement that SQL Server uses to back up a database is BACKUP. In its simplest form, the BACKUP statement requires the database parameter and at least one backup device parameter. You can specify a disk file as a substitute for a backup device. For example, if you wanted to back up the TESTDB database to a physical disk file named TESTDBBACK on the C: drive using Transact-SQL, you would connect to SQL Server using Query Analyzer and execute the following statement:

```
use master
    backup database testdb to disk = 'c:\mssql7\backup\testdbback.bak'
```

In the example, you are telling SQL Server to back up the Testdb database by entering **backup database testdb**. You are then specifying the location to which SQL Server should send the backup by entering the disk and then the actual path to the file, which is encased in single quotation marks like this: 'C:\MSSQL7\BACKUP\ESDBBACK.BAK'.

As a result of this single-line statement, SQL Server will initiate a backup of the Testdb database and store the backup in the designated file. In the following sections, you will learn more about controlling the backup process using Transact-SQL and how to perform similar operations using the graphical tools in Enterprise Manager.

The SQL Server backup process is specifically designed to include aspects of the database that might otherwise be lost using a standard backup utility. Specifically, the backup process backs up the database schema, the file structure, the data, and portions of the Transaction Log that include all database activity that occurred during the backup. When combined, these features create a powerful tool that will help you protect and archive your data.

In order to execute the backup process on any database, you must be a member of the SYSADMIN server role, the DB_OWNER database role, or the DB_BACKUPOPERATOR database role. Though it is possible to manually assign the specific rights required to execute the statement, we recommend that you constrain yourself to using the predefined roles because it will be easier to manage rights.

SQL backup can store backups on any of three locations: *hard disk*, *tape*, and *named pipe*. The first of these locations simply stores the backup as a file on disk, the second stores the backup on a tape, and the third location allows for the installation of third-party mass storage devices on the network to which SQL Server can connect for the purpose of storing backups. For example, one of our larger clients implements a tape silo that houses and manages thousands of backup tapes. All of the SQL Servers in the network can connect to the silo using a named pipe and as a result, the administrative staff does not have to travel from server to server, changing tapes. Additionally, the silo is in a different building than the server, which accommodates one of the prime rules of backups, which is to always store the backup media at a location separate from the server's location.

The SQL Server backup process is designed so that network users can perform normal operations in the database while the backup is being performed. This feature is one of the aspects of the SQL Server backup utility that makes it more useful than standard backup tools. The following is a general example of how the backup process backs up data, while still letting users work in the database.

▼ The backup process causes a checkpoint to be issued in the Transaction Log and waits for all committed transactions to be rolled forward into the database.

■ The backup process records the log sequence number (LSN) at the point in the Transaction Log where the backup begins.

■ The backup process begins to back up the database. During this time, users can still work, and operations are recorded in the Transaction Log.

■ The backup process finishes backing up the database and begins to back up the Transaction Log. All transactions that were performed after the recorded LSN are backed up at this point.

▲ The backup process completes.

As you can see, the SQL Server backup process maintains functionality by letting users continue to access the database while the backup operation is performed. You should note that because the process uses the Transaction Log to accomplish this, only logged transactions can be carried out during the backup. You will learn more about SQL Server backup restrictions in the following section.

Restricted Activities

Part of the SQL Server backup process includes restrictions that prevent operations that could result in an ineffective backup. For example, if you were in the middle of backing up a large database, you would not want users to execute large non-logged operations in the database because these operations would not be included in the backup. Additionally, you would not want a network user to alter the structure of the database during a backup because part of the information stored in the backup is the database schema and file structure.

Because operations of this type have the potential to render a backup ineffective, SQL Server must incorporate certain restrictions to the backup process. The following activities are restricted during the backup process:

▼ You cannot create or modify a database while the backup process is operating.

■ You cannot create indexes while a database is being backed up.

■ You cannot perform non-logged operations during the backup process.

▲ The `auto-grow` function cannot initialize while the backup process is operating.

If you attempt to begin a backup while a restricted activity is occurring, the backup process will halt. If the backup process is already initialized and you attempt to start a restricted activity, SQL Server will not perform the activity and will return an error message.

WHEN TO BACK UP

If you were to ask any experienced administrator when you should perform backups, he or she would likely tell you "all the time" or "never stop." While these comments would be made in half-jest, they accurately convey the importance of the backup and actually help set the correct mindset for protecting data. Unfortunately, in the real world, constraints like user impact, cost, and database size prevent us from running complete backups every 15 minutes on all of our servers. Instead, we compromise and accept the limitations that are imposed upon us and plan our backup solution around these limitations. Understanding the data and data structure completely is vital to effectively planning a backup solution. With that thought in mind, the next few sections will provide you with some hints that may help you determine which databases to back up and when.

Backing Up System Databases

Since SQL Server derives so much functionality from the system databases, we will begin with some hints on when to back up system databases. Each database will be discussed separately so that you can easily reference each topic while planning your backup strategy.

The MASTER Database

You will remember from Chapter 2 that the MASTER Database stores information about each and every database, as well as data about logins, stored procedures, and other important information. Knowing that, you can safely assume that you must back up the MASTER Database each time any database is added, removed, or modified structurally, and must also back it up when logins change or when stored procedures are added. You can also safely assume that you do not have to back up the MASTER Database every time you back up user databases because the data in the MASTER Database will not change at a rate anywhere near that of a user database.

Knowing that the MASTER Database must be backed up whenever database structure changes are made can be tricky to remember. We have seen many installations wherein the backup strategy included every user database, but overlooked the MASTER entirely. The following is a list of events that should always remind you to back up the MASTER Database.

▼ When you execute the CREATE DATABASE, DROP DATABASE or ALTER DATABASE statements

■ When you execute the SP_ADDSERVER or SP_DROPSERVER stored procedure

■ When you execute the SP_ADDLINKEDSERVER stored procedure

■ When you modify the MODEL Database

■ When you modify the MSDB Database

■ After setting up replication

▲ At regular intervals, just in case

The MODEL Database

As you know, the MODEL Database is really just an empty shell that SQL Server uses as a template for the creation of new databases. Knowing that, you can safely assume that you only have to back up the MODEL Database when you make changes to it and once every now and again just to be safe. You should also remember to back up the MODEL Database following any changes made directly to it.

The MSDB Database

In Chapter 2, you learned that SQL Server uses the MSDB Database to store information for the SQL Server agent such as jobs, operators, and alerts. Since these tasks may change frequently in some deployments, and not so frequently in others, you will have to look carefully at the amount of changing data that is stored in the MSDB Database in order to best decide how often to back it up. As a general rule, if you are unsure how much of the data is changing, back up MSDB frequently. The amount of actual data being stored in the database is typically small in terms of data storage and should not impact the backup plan by much.

The TEMPDB Database

Since the TEMPDB Database holds only dynamic data, you do not have to back up this database.

The DISTRIBUTION Database

The DISTRIBUTION Database is probably the database that is most overlooked in backup plans. This is probably because replication is frequently set up after the backup solution is already in place. As you may know, the DISTRIBUTION Database contains different amounts of information depending on the type of replication that you have deployed. You will learn more about replication in Chapters 9 and 10.

Because the data in the DISTRIBUTION Database is very important, you must be sure to include the backup of this database in your regular backup plan, and we recommend that you treat the DISTRIBUTION Database in the same manner that you would treat any user database.

User Databases

If system databases are important because they contain data that SQL Server requires to function properly, user databases are important because they contain the data that you are running SQL Server for in the first place. No matter what kind of information you are storing in your SQL Server, if the data is volatile and changes frequently, you will need a backup solution that minimizes the damage that could result from corruption or complete data loss.

Because there are many different kinds of databases, and because the data sometimes changes frequently and other times not at all, the frequency of your backups will vary a great deal. You will need to understand the way your database functions in order to create the most efficient backup plan. For example, if your database stores information that is imported once a month from a vendor, and you use it for research purposes, it would be safe to say that you could back up this database only once every month. If, however, your database is one that users change every day, such as a retailer's inventory database, then you must plan your backups so that they happen frequently and regularly in order to provide the highest level of protection.

Unfortunately, knowing that infrequently changed databases can be backed up less frequently than those that are updated daily is not the end of the story. You must be very careful to back up any database that has its structure changed, such as when you add a new table or index, for example. Additionally, there are times when you will perform operations that are not recorded in the Transaction Log. You should back up the database as soon after performing a non-logged operation as is possible because SQL Server cannot provide the inherent database protection that is present following normal logged operations.

There are also some occasions when some unforeseen event causes you to perform an unusual operation on the database. Typically, if you have chosen or been forced to do something unusual on a database, you should first back up the database as a safety precaution. For example, if your database has run out of room on the physical disk, one common solution that provides temporary functionality is to truncate the Transaction Log. If you have truncated the transaction log, SQL Server no longer has the ability to auto-recover data if the server should fail. Knowing this, it is a good idea to back up the database at that time. This will give the network users database functionality, and buy you the time needed to implement a more permanent solution. The backup is vital to this scenario, because after truncating the log, if the server fails and no backup exists, the potential for data loss will be extremely high.

Although no amount of tips can replace a solid understanding of databases and a sound backup plan, we offer the following list of events that should always be followed by a backup, but remind you that there may be many occasions not covered by the list that nevertheless should be followed by a backup. In addition to your normal backup strategy, you should always back up databases at these times:

▼ When you create or alter a database

■ When you create indexes

■ After issuing non-logged operations such as SELECT INTO or UPDATETEXT

■ Prior to dismissing an employee who has high levels of database access, knowledge, or experience

- When there is an unusually high level of network errors
- After truncating the Transaction Log
- When an unusually high level of database errors are present
- ▲ When you get the feeling that you should

The last entry in the list may sound a bit funny at first. It is present because of many stories and experiences that we have encountered in various SQL Server deployments. You would be shocked at the number of times we have heard administrators say "Am I glad I did a backup." You would be equally surprised to hear the amount of times that an administrator has said "I knew I should have done a backup—I had a feeling." After hearing these words so many times, we now always advise new administrators to trust that feeling. At the end of the day, it's far better to have a backup that was not needed than to need a backup and not have one.

DESIGNING A BACKUP SOLUTION

Understanding the backup process and the restrictions that SQL Server applies during the process will help you understand when to perform backups, and what to do or not do during the process. What is lacking now is knowledge of the different types of backup, and how you can use them to design an effective backup solution.

Understanding Backup Types

Because the backup process can be a lengthy and processor/ memory-intensive operation in cases where the database is a large one, different types of backups are available so that you can design a backup plan that both protects the data, while also granting the highest level of functionality to the network users. Each type of backup has its unique strengths and weaknesses. In most scenarios, you will use a combination of different backup types because they are designed specifically to complement each other.

Full Backups

The foundation of any backup plan is the full backup. The full backup is a self-explanatory term that accurately describes the intent and function of this type of backup. Full backups include the entire database, portions of the Transaction Log, the database schema, and the file structure.

All backup strategies include the full backup at some point because the full backup provides a baseline that other backups work off of. Other types of backup such as a differential backup can only be performed if a full backup has been performed previously. If you tried to execute a differential backup prior to executing a full backup, SQL Server would halt the backup process and return an error to you.

Your backup solution should include a full backup at regular intervals because it will cut down on the amount of other backup types you must maintain, and will also reduce the amount of time and knowledge that you need to restore a database from backup. You will learn how to actually execute a full backup later in this chapter.

Differential Backups

The differential backup is the first of two types of backup concepts that help save time while backing up data and let you cut down on the impact that the backup process has on network users. Differential backups are backups that back up data that has changed since the last full backup.

In SQL Server, the differential backup backs up the data and parts of the data that have changed since the last full backup. Using the LSN that was recorded during the last full backup, the backup process is able to identify which portions of the database have changed and back up only those portions.

Because the differential backup requires that a full backup was performed previously, if you attempt to run the backup process with a specification of "Differential," and there is no recorded LSN from a full backup present, the backup process will fail and SQL Server will return an error.

TIP: Remember that you will need the full backup as well as the differential in order to restore the database. You should execute full backups at regular intervals and use the differential backup only as a time-saver.

Incremental Backups or Backing Up the Transaction Log

Almost any text that you read regarding the concept of data protection through backups will contain a section that explains incremental backups. Incremental backups back up all data that has changed since the last backup. The difference between a differential backup and an incremental backup is that the differential backup will back up all data that has changed since the last *full* backup, and the incremental backup will back up all changes since the last backup no matter if was full or differential.

The end result is that a differential backup will typically take up more time than an incremental backup will to execute. Conversely, restoring information from a plan that includes many incremental backups will require more time and may be more difficult to manage.

The SQL Server backup process does not include an option either in Enterprise Manager or using Transact-SQL for the incremental option. It would be safe to say that the process does not support incremental backups per se. The concept of the incremental backup is instead supported by backing up the Transaction Log. This means that you can create what amounts to an incremental backup simply by executing backups of the Transaction Log. By default, if you initialize the backup process, the Transaction Log is truncated. As you will learn later in this chapter, you must be very careful when using the backup process on a Transaction Log because in some cases, you will not want the log truncated.

Now that you understand the different types of backup, you will likely want to explore how SQL Server stores the backups themselves. In the following section, you will learn about permanent and temporary backup files, options for tape devices, and some special considerations for backing up to a named pipe.

Backup Locations

As you know, the SQL Server Backup Process is capable of backing up databases and Transaction Logs to three locations. The first of the locations we will discuss is the physical disk file. When you choose to back up a database to physical disk, you are trusting that the disk is secure and will not fail. Administrators usually perform backups of this type as a temporary solution, because they are about to do something unusual on the system. As a solution to data security, we do not recommend that your normal backup solution be performed only to disk. An exception may be a case wherein the database is first backed up to disk and then backed up to tape. No matter how you design your backup solution, you will be much safer if you always keep a recent backup on tape, which is stored in a different location than the server.

SQL Server actually supports backing up to disk two different ways. The first of these is to store the backup in a permanent disk file. A permanent disk file is a file that is registered within SQL Server as a device. While backup devices can actually be any of the possible locations, we will only discuss creating a disk device for now. You will create devices upon which to store data primarily to track the progress of backups and so that you can schedule the backup process to occur automatically. You will learn the details of task scheduling in Chapter 8.

Creating a Disk-Based Dump Device

Creating the permanent disk file is a relatively simple process and is one that you can do before you ever begin the backup process, or one that you can perform as you are executing a backup. To create a permanent backup file using SQL Enterprise Manager, simply follow the steps below:

1. Open the SQL Server Enterprise Manager.

2. Expand the Server Groups so that you can see the server or servers that are registered.

3. Click on the name of your server.

4. Select Tools | Backup Database.

At this point, the SQL Server Backup window will appear. The window should look like the image in Figure 6-1.

Now that you are in the correct window, you can easily create a new device by following these additional steps:

1. Click the Add button. SQL Server in turn will open the Choose Backup Destination dialog box.

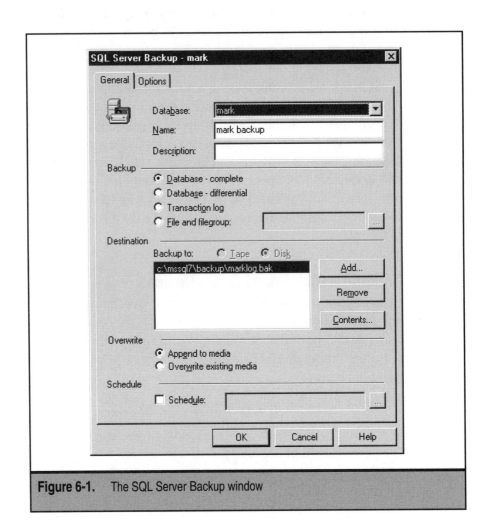

Figure 6-1. The SQL Server Backup window

2. Click once in the Backup Device checkbox.

3. From the drop-down list-box, choose the <New Device> option. SQL Server will open the Backup Device Properties dialog box.

4. Type a name for the device. (Notice that the path and filename is filled in automatically.)

5. Click OK. SQL Server will close the dialog box.

At this point a new device has been created. You can actually cancel out of the Backup Database dialog box and the device will still be present. Later, if you choose to create a backup and want to send the backup to the device, you will find it in the Backup Device drop-down list.

If you want to create the device using Transact-SQL, you must use the SP_ADDUMPDEVICE system stored procedure. This stored procedure is designed specifically to create backup devices in their various forms. There is a listing of the complete syntax in Books Online, but we will show you here how to use the statement one step at a time. In this section, you are only concerned with creating a disk-based device, so that is the syntax and example that we will use. To create a disk-based backup device using SP_ADDDUMPDEVICE, connect to SQL Server using Query Analyzer and execute the following statement:

```
use master
exec sp_addumpdevice 'disk', 'testdbback', 'c:\mssql7\backup\testdbback.bak'
```

The statement in the example will cause a device named TESTDBBACK to be created on the C: drive, in the default backup directory, with a physical name of TESTDBBACK.BAK. In the example, you can easily see the three most important parameters for this stored procedure. In the first parameter, you are specifying that this device will be disk-based and so use the 'DISK' specification. The second parameter is the logical name of the device. The name that SQL Server identifies the device by is another way of looking at this parameter. In the example, the logical name is TESTDBBACK. The final parameter you specify is the physical location, including path, where the device will be stored on the disk. In this case, the specification is C:\MSSQL7\BACKUP\TESTDBBACK.BAK. Because the device is now stored within SQL Server, you can reference it by logical name when you are performing a backup. In the next section, you will see how to use a device to actually perform a backup.

PERFORMING A FULL BACKUP

Now that you understand the importance of backups and the process by which they are accomplished within SQL Server, you will want to become familiar with how to perform backups. In this section, you will learn how to control the backup process using the graphical tools provided with Enterprise Manager and also using Transact-SQL.

The first thing any administrator learns when it comes to dealing with backups is how to execute a full backup of a database using Enterprise Manager and Transact-SQL. You will remember from the previous section that creating a dump device prior to executing a backup makes the process easier on you, and also lets you schedule backups to run automatically.

Once you have created the dump device, you can easily reference it by using the logical name in SQL Server. The logical name is valid in both Enterprise Manager and using Transact-SQL. For example, using the TESTDBBACK dump device that is created in the previous example, if you wanted to back up the TESTDB database using Enterprise Manager, you would simply follow these steps:

1. Open Enterprise Manager and expand the objects list to display your server.

2. Click on the name of your server once.

3. Select Tools | Backup Database.

4. Choose the database you want to back up from the Database drop-down list.

5. Type a name for the backup set in the Name field.

6. Optionally, type a description for the backup in the Description field.

7. Specify the type of backup that you want using the checkboxes in the Backup section (for a full backup choose Complete).

8. Click the Add button.

9. In the Choose Backup Destination dialog box, choose the Testdbback Backup Device.

10. Click OK.

At this point, the backup will begin and the process will continue until it completes or is interfered with. The backup utility interface is fairly intuitive and easy to follow, but many of you may find these steps lengthy compared to executing the BACKUP statement manually using Transact-SQL. To perform the exact same backup using Transact-SQL, connect to SQL Server using Query Analyzer and execute the following statement:

```
use master
    backup database testdb to testdbback
```

Again, the backup will begin and the process will continue until complete or interfered with by you manually, or by a critical error.

In the example, there are only two parameters needed for the statement to complete. You must, of course, list the name of the database that you want to back up, as seen in the reference TESTDB, and you must also indicate where to backup the database. Because you had already created the TESTDBBACK dump device, you could simply insert the logical name of the device and SQL Server will automatically figure out what the physical location is and send the backup to that location.

You may have noticed that while in Enterprise Manager, you could have chosen not to create or even use a device to store the backup. Instead, you could have specified a name in the File Name field and proceeded with the backup. Doing this would have created a backup to disk in much the same way that using a device would have. The difference between the two is that the device is considered to be a permanent file, recognized by SQL Server because it has a logical name registered within the MASTER Database. If you had chosen to specify a name in the File Name field, SQL Server would not store the name of the file as a device, you could not schedule the operation, and the file would be considered a temporary location.

Temporary backups are valid backups with many uses, including one-time backups such as a copy for another server, or testing backup procedures that you will later incorporate into the backup solution as permanent files. Creating a temporary backup is not much different than creating a permanent backup when using Enterprise Manager because only one change exists in the process. To create a temporary backup using Enterprise Manager, you will simply enter a file name and path into the File Name field on the Choose Backup Destination dialog box. When you complete the other steps as outlined in the previous section, the backup will complete, storing the database to a temporary file in the location that you specified.

Storing a temporary backup using Transact-SQL is also very similar, with the exception that you must now provide additional parameters to the statement. For example, if you want to store the TESTDB database to a temporary file named TEST.BAK in the default backup directory, connect to SQL Server using Query Analyzer and execute the following statement:

```
use master
    backup database testdb to disk = 'c:\mssql7\backups\test.bak'
```

In the example, we had to specify two additional parameters to make the statement work. In addition to the database name specification that must be present in all backup statements, we substituted the device reference with the specifications TO DISK, and the actual path and filename, which had to be encased in single quotes like this 'C:\MSSQL7\BACKUPS\TEST.BAK'. These changes make SQL Server understand that you wish the backup to be sent to a disk location as opposed to tape or named pipe, and that this will be a temporary backup sent to the location that you specified.

More than once in this chapter we have told you that backing up databases to disk provides a solid backup, but that storing your backups on disk alone is less secure than storing them to tape. While both disk-based backups and named pipe backups are both acceptable means of storing the backup structure, we feel that it is important to store your backups separately from the actual server, and have always found that this is easiest when the method of storage is a tape. With that thought in mind, you will probably want to know the steps required to send a backup to tape.

Creating a Full Backup to Tape

When using Enterprise Manager, the steps to create a full backup that is stored on tape are not much different than those to store the same backup on disk. All you have to do is choose a tape in the Choose Backup Destination dialog box, and the backup will be sent to tape. You have the option of creating a dump device that is tape-based, and can also create temporary backups using tape drives. Likewise, the difference in Transact-SQL is really not that much different, and all that is required is for you to change some of the parameters. For example, if you wanted to perform a full backup of the TEMPDB database and store it on a tape, you would connect to SQL Server using Query Analyzer and execute a statement similar to the following:

```
use master
    backup database testdb to tape = \\.\tape0
```

This statement sends the backup to the tape drive that is identified as number 0. The number 0 indicates that this is either the only tape drive installed on the system or that it is the first one. You should notice also that the location parameter is changed to TAPE rather than DISK. As an administrator, you will almost always type the backup parameter so that the DISK or TAPE reference is used. This is because the only reason to reference a named pipe is to support third-party applications. Unless you are a developer or are customizing third-party software, you are likely to never even use the option because most third-party software will already have installation routines that configure the backup process for you.

Now that you know how to create a full backup using Enterprise Manager and Transact-SQL, you are fully capable of planning an entire backup solution for smaller databases, and additionally can set the foundation for more complex solutions. The next step is to learn how to save resources and time so that the network users are impacted as little as possible. In the following sections, you will learn how to execute differential backups and how to back up the Transaction Log.

EXECUTING A DIFFERENTIAL BACKUP

As you know, the differential backup is designed to save time and resources by backing up only the data that has changed since the last full backup. In very large databases, performing a full backup can take tremendous amounts of time. SQL Server inherently supports differential backups as one method of solving that very problem. In this section, you will learn how to execute a differential backup using both Enterprise Manager and Transact-SQL.

To perform a differential backup using Enterprise Manager, remember that you must first have executed a full backup on the database. Once that has been accomplished, you can proceed with the creation of a differential backup by following the steps below:

1. Open Enterprise Manager.
2. Expand the object tree so that you can see the name of your server.
3. Click on the name of your server once.
4. Select Tools | Backup Database.
5. Choose the name of the database you want to back up in the Database field.
6. Type a name for the backup in the Name field.
7. Optionally, type a description for the backup in the Description field.
8. Click once in the Differential checkbox.
9. Click the Add button.
10. Choose a dump device or specify a location for a temporary backup in the Choose Backup Destination dialog box.

11. Click OK. SQL Server will close the Choose Backup Destination dialog box.

12. Click OK again.

Though the steps to perform the backup in Enterprise Manager are easy to follow, you may find as you did with the full backup that using the Transact-SQL statement is easier. For example, if you want to perform a differential backup of the TESTDB database using Transact-SQL, connect to SQL Server using Query Analyzer and execute the following statement:

```
use master
    backup database testdb to testdbbak with differential
```

In the example, you are sending the backup to a predefined dump device named TESTDBBACK. The parameters that you specify are simply the name of the database (TESTDB), the backup destination (TESTDBBACK), and the specification WITH DIFFERENTIAL, which tells SQL Server that this backup will be a differential backup. If you want the backup to be temporary, you would simply change the destination parameter and add the specification TO DISK. For example, if you want the same backup to be sent as a temporary backup to a file named TESTDIFF.BAK in the default backup folder, you would execute the statement like this:

```
use master
    backup database testdb to disk =
    'c:\mssql7\backups\testdiff.bak' with differential
```

As you can see, altering the result of a backup using Transact-SQL can be a simple process, so long as you understand which parameters to modify.

Let us pause at this point and examine what you now understand about planning a backup solution using just the full and differential backups. Taking the information one piece at a time, you will learn how to plan an effective backup solution.

To begin with, you now understand that all SQL Server backup solutions begin with the full backup. That means that the backup plan must include at least one full backup in order to function.

Additionally, you know that you should perform a full backup of the database on a regular basis so that the backup files require less management and in the event of database failure, the recovery process will be easy to understand and function efficiently. So in order to function, the backup solution must include one full backup of each database, and should include a plan to perform a full backup on each database on a regular basis.

In order to best determine when to perform the regularly scheduled full backups, you will have to monitor the time that it takes to perform the backup. Additionally, you should monitor the impact that the backup has on network users, and observe the impact that the backup has on the server resources. Once you understand the impact of the backup, you will be better able to decide how often it can be run while still providing a high level of database performance to users.

Once the databases have been backed up for the first time (full backup), you should perform a differential backup and observe how long it takes to complete. As with the full backup, you will want to monitor impact to users and the server while it is processing. You are doing this to see how much time and resources will be saved by running differential backups as opposed to full backups. In some cases, you may find that there is little gain and will decide to perform full backups only. As the database grows, the resources saved by running a differential backup will increase and your backup solution will change to reflect the inclusion of differential backups.

All of the backups that you perform have their frequency determined by the amount of data that you can afford to lose, versus the impact that the backup has to the organization and databases. For example, if you have a small database that is changed by only a few users on a daily basis, a full backup once or twice a day may be all that you perform. On the other hand, if you have a larger database with many users changing data, you may decide to perform a full backup once a day, and perform differential backups multiple times throughout the day.

Once the database grows to a certain point, or if your organization has a sufficient number of users, a point will be reached wherein the differential backup also has too great an impact on productivity if run throughout the day, and you will have to include additional backup plans in order to provide an effective solution. One of the primary means of extending the functionality of the backup plan is to perform Transaction Log backups. In the next section, you will learn how to perform a backup on a Transaction Log.

EXECUTING A TRANSACTION LOG BACKUP

Of all the types of backup that SQL Server supports, the one that has the lowest impact on the server and users is the Transaction Log backup. Transaction Log backups have little impact because they back up only the data that has changed since the last backup action (full backup or differential backup). In addition to this, Transaction Log backups back up only the actual Transact-SQL statements instead of the entire database schema and file structure as well as data. This means that you are actually backing up less data when backing up a Transaction Log than when backing up a database.

As an administrator, you will use Transaction Log backups as a means of supplying what amounts to incremental backups for the database. For example, if your organization has determined that it can tolerate no more than 15 minutes of lost data, and has a medium-sized to large database, you will design a backup solution that ensures that no more than 15 minutes goes by without a backup of some kind in place. While the following example should not be taken as a solution for all environments, in order to solve the problem in our scenario, the solution will be something similar to this:

▼ One full backup of the database every night

■ One differential backup every hour

▲ One Transaction Log backup ever 15 minutes

This solution provides protection by first producing a full backup at night. During the day, a differential backup is performed each hour, which provides a copy of all data that has changed since the previous night. You should remember that each and every differential backup will back up all the data that has changed since the last *full* backup. The final part of the solution is the Transaction Log backup, which happens every 15 minutes.

The end result of this backup solution is that no matter what time your database fails, you will lose no more than 15 minutes of data. In order to restore the database, you will need the full backup from the previous night, the most recent differential backup, and all Transaction Log backups that have taken place since the most recent backup. You will learn more about restoring databases later in this chapter.

As with other types of backup, you can perform a Transaction Log backup using either Enterprise Manager or Transact-SQL. Other third-party utilities may also be used but will not be discussed here because they are not included with SQL Server 7.0.

To perform a Transaction Log backup using Enterprise Manager, remember that you should have first performed a full backup. The full backup is not required as it is with the differential backup, but should still be performed to provide data security in the event of unexpected results. Once the full backup has been performed, you can execute the backup simply by performing the steps below:

1. Open Enterprise Manager.

2. Expand the object tree so that you can see the name of your server.

3. Click on the name of your server once.

4. Select Tools | Backup Database.

5. Choose the name of the database you want to back up in the Database field.

6. Type a name for the backup in the Name field.

7. Optionally, type a description for the backup in the Description field.

8. Click once in the Transaction Log checkbox.

9. Click the Add button.

10. Choose a dump device or specify a location for a temporary backup in the Choose Backup Destination dialog box.

11. Click OK. SQL Server will close the Choose Backup Destination dialog box.

12. Click OK again.

Once the final step is complete, SQL Server will begin to perform the backup. Because this is a Transaction Log backup, you can expect it to be complete much quicker than a regular or differential backup would be.

Like any other operation in SQL Server, you can execute this backup using Transact-SQL as well as Enterprise Manager. The syntax for this backup is slightly different and you should note the changes in the following example:

```
use master
    backup log testdb to testdblog
```

In the example, you will note that you have actually changed the BACKUP statement to include the specification LOG. The LOG specification tells SQL Server that a Transaction Log is being backed up. The remaining parameters are the same as a normal BACKUP statement including the database name and the backup destination. Just as with a normal BACKUP statement, you have the option of sending the backup to a device, or to a temporary location such as tape or a specified disk file.

Each time you perform a Transaction Log backup, the file should be considered untouchable until a full or differential backup is performed. This is because you will need all of the Transaction Log backups that have been performed since the last full or differential backup in order to restore the database. What this means to you as an administrator is that you must always back up Transaction Logs to different files or devices until such time as one of the other backup types are run. Once a full or differential backup has been performed, you can safely overwrite existing Transaction Log backups with new ones.

So now you know how to perform a full (normal), differential, and Transaction Log backup. You understand the place that each one plays in the backup solution, and you have obtained some general tips on how best to use each of the types.

BACKUP OPTIONS

In this section, we will explore some of the optional parameters that you may use with BACKUP statements or inside the Enterprise Manager.

The Options Tab

You may have noticed that there is an additional tab on the Backup Database dialog box that we have not at this point discussed. Up until now, you have learned just the bare minimum that is required for the backup process to function. Now that you have an understanding of how the process works, we will expand your knowledge so that you can exert a greater level of control over your backups.

Within Enterprise Manager, the Backup Database dialog box has a tab named Options. On this tab, which is shown in Figure 6-2, you can specify certain parameters that affect the way the backup will be performed. In the text that follows, each of the available options are described. At the end of the section, you will find another handy table that you can photocopy and keep with you for reference.

Verify Backup upon Completion

The Verify option tells SQL Server to check the media following the backup process. This verifies that the backup was stored safely and has no errors due to flaws in the backup media. Whenever possible, administrators are encouraged to use the Verify option because it makes the backup much more secure. Conversely, the Verify option impacts the length of time that it takes to perform the backup and has a higher impact on system resources. Only time and testing will tell you if using the Verify option is feasible in your deployment.

Eject Tape After Backup

Eject Tape is a simple option that tells SQL Server to eject the tape when the backup is complete. This option can help make the backup process easier in smaller deployments in particular by reminding people to change the tape. Sometimes, just seeing the tape sticking out of the server is enough to help someone remember to change it.

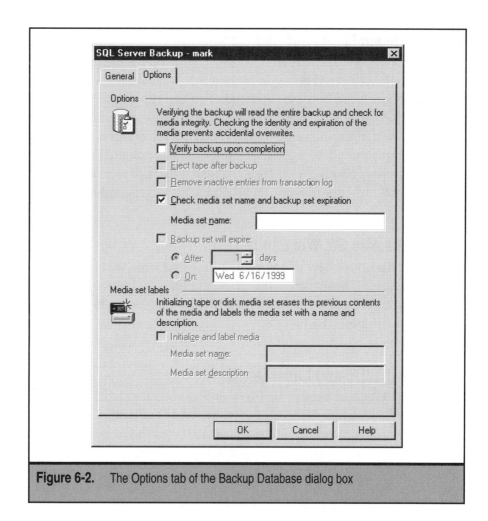

Figure 6-2.   The Options tab of the Backup Database dialog box

Remove Inactive Entries from Transaction Log

The backup process is designed so that at the end of the backup the database Transaction Log is truncated. This means that all committed transactions are removed from the Transaction Log. Truncating the Transaction Log is a process that should be performed in order to save space. However, there will be some cases wherein you want to perform a backup without truncating the log. This option grants you control over the process and lets you decide to truncate or not truncate the Transaction Log.

Check Media Set Name and Expiration

Check Media is a safety setting that protects the backup from being overwritten. When you place a mark in this checkbox, the Media Name field becomes enabled. You can type in the name of a particular tape here, and the Backup utility will check the media to see if it has the same name. If there is a conflict between names or the expiration date for the existing tape has not expired, the backup will be halted and the existing backup will be preserved. Typically, you will only use this option when backing up to tape.

Backup Set Will Expire

This option lets you specify a date and time that the backup will expire. The option is designed to help you identify backups that should not be overwritten, which in turn protects you from accidental backup loss.

Initialize and Label Media

This option really just turns on the ability to label the actual media. When checked, the Media Name and Description fields are enabled, into which you can then place labels for the backup media itself. Typically, you only use this option with backups to tape.

Append to Media/Overwrite Existing Media

While it is actually not on the Options tab, the Append to Media checkbox is technically a backup option. This option is a choice and you must select either it or Overwrite Existing Media. If you choose the Append to Media option, the backup process will perform the backup to the specified media, while leaving any existing backup sets in place. You will find the choice on the first tab.

When you choose the Overwrite Existing Media option, any existing backup sets stored on the media will be removed and replaced with the new backup set. Overwrite does, of course, replace the Append option.

Table 6-1 shows the various options that you can choose on the Options tab for the backup process. In the table, each option is listed with a brief description of its associated action.

Transact-SQL Backup Parameters

Like any other action that you can perform in Enterprise Manager, there are equivalent specifications for the BACKUP DATABASE and BACKUP LOG Transact-SQL statements that let you specify the variable options. In some cases, using Transact-SQL actually grants you a higher level of control than the Enterprise Manager utility. You will learn in the following sections how to execute backups using Transact-SQL with optional parameters that control the backup process.

BLOCKSIZE

This is a parameter that specifies the physical block size that will be used on the backup media while the backup is being stored. This specification is typically omitted and you will rarely use it. If your hardware or media choices recommend direct control of block size, you can obtain setting information from the technical manuals that came with the hardware or media. For disk-based storage, the backup process will automatically determine and apply the correct block size. When backing up to tape, BLOCKSIZE is only applied if you format the tape during the backup. Backups sent to a named pipe will default to a size of 65,536 unless you specify a different value.

For example, the following statement shows how you would use this option to specify a blocksize of 512 bytes:

```
use master
    backup database testdb to tape = \\.\tape0 with blocksize = 512
```

DESCRIPTION

A self-explanatory parameter, DESCRIPTION merely adds to the backup set a description of the backup in normal text. This information can be read from the backup set during a restore operation, as you will learn in the next chapter.

Option	Action
Verify Backup upon Completion	Performs a check of the media, ensuring that the backup was stored correctly.
Eject Tape After Backup	Automatically ejects the tape following the backup.
Remove Inactive Entries from Transaction Log	Specifies to clean up the transaction log following the backup by removing committed transactions.
Check Media Set Name and Expiration	Tells SQL Server to check the media name and expiration date prior to overwriting any data.
Media Set Name (under Check Media Set Name and Expiration option)	Lets you specify a name for the tape so that SQL Server can match the name against the media name already on the tape.
Backup Set Will Expire	Lets you specify how long SQL Server will protect this backup from being overwritten.
Initialize and Label Media	Tells SQL Server to label the tape when the backup begins.
Media Set Name	Lets you specify a name for the tape set. This option is used when the backup will span multiple tapes, and you want the media labeled with a set name.
Media Set Expiration	Lets you specify a description for the tape.

Table 6-1. Options for Backup Process

For example, the following statement shows how you would include a description that indicates this is a full backup:

```
use master
    backup database testdb to tape = \\.\tape0
    with description = 'full backup'
```

EXPIREDATE

This parameter specifies the date that this media will expire. This option is designed to protect against accidental overwriting of the media. The specification is only valid when applied to all backup sets on the media and, like the setting in Enterprise Manager, can only be applied to disk- and tape-based backups. Typically, you will only use this option when performing a backup to tape.

As an example, the following statement specifies an expiration date of the first of January in the year 2000:

```
use master
    backup database testdb to tape = \\.\tape0 with expiredate = '1/1/00'
```

RETAINDAYS

RETAINDAYS is an optional parameter designed to replace the EXPIREDATE option. This parameter specifies a number of days that must pass before the media can be overwritten with new backup sets.

An example of this parameter would be similar to the following statement where the backup media will be preserved for ten days:

```
use master
    backup database testdb to disk = 'c:\mssql7\backups\tesdb.bak'
    with retaindays = 10
```

FORMAT/NOFORMAT

These two options simply tell SQL Server to either format or not format a tape prior to performing a backup. If you specify the FORMAT option, the media header will be overwritten and all backup sets on the media will no longer be usable. Specifying NOFORMAT lets

SQL Server perform the backup without altering the media header, and leaves existing backup sets usable.

To specify that a tape should format, you would simply execute a statement similar to this:

```
use master
    backup database testdb to tape = \\.\tape0 with format
```

INIT/NOINIT

These two options are frequently confused with the FORMAT and NOFORMAT parameters because while their operation is different, the result is similar and easily confused. If you specify the INIT parameter, the media header will be overwritten and the backup set currently being processed will be placed at the beginning of the tape, effectively overwriting any existing backup. Existing backup sets on the media, however, will not be made unusable unless copied over. If you specify NOINIT, the backup set will be placed at the end of other existing backup sets and the header will be left intact. These options are the Transact-SQL equivalent to the Overwrite and Append options that are found in Enterprise Manager.

You would specify that the media should be initialized like this:

```
use master
    backup database testdb to tape = \\.\tape0 with init
```

MEDIADESCRIPTION

Another of the self-explanatory parameters available using Transact-SQL, the MEDIADESCRIPTION parameter specifies a simple text description for the backup media. It applies to the media itself and is not attached to a specific backup set. In the following example, you are describing the media as being a tape that should store only full backups:

```
use master
    backup database testdb to tape = \\.\tape0
    with mediadescription = 'full backups only'
```

MEDIANAME

A companion to the MEDIADESCRIPTION parameter, MEDIANAME specifies a simple text name for the backup media. This parameter also applies directly to the media and is not attached to any specific backup set. In this example, you are naming the media TESTDBBACKUPS:

```
use master
    backup database testdb to tape = \\.\tape0 with medianame = 'testdbbackups'
```

NAME

This parameter specifies a logical name for the backup set. Applying this parameter will let you easily distinguish between multiple backup sets that may be stored on the same media. Naming the backup set is a good idea and you should try to make the name functional so that you can easily identify what the backup set is. For example, in the following statement, you are naming the backup set FIRSTFULL so that you will know this backup set is the first full backup of the TESTDB database:

```
use master
    backup database testdb to tape = \\.\tape0 with name = 'firstfull'
```

NO_TRUNCATE

The NO-TRUNCATE option tells SQL Server not to clean up the Transaction Log after performing the backup. If specified, when the backup completes, the Transaction Log will be left intact. An example of a situation where you might want to use this parameter may be a case wherein you have lost or suffered a corruption of the main database files, but still have the Transaction Logs intact. As part of the recovery process, you want to back up the Transaction Log without purging it of committed transactions. To do this, you would simply place a clean tape in the drive and execute a statement like this:

```
use master
    backup log testdb to tape = \\.\tape0 with no_truncate
```

TRUNCATE_ONLY/NO_LOG

As a means to clear the Transaction Log quickly and without performing a real backup, the options TRUNCATE_ONLY and NO_LOG are available for use with the BACKUP LOG statement. These options perform basically the same operation, which is to clear the Transaction Log of committed transactions. You will use this option only in rare cases when you need to immediately make room on disk for a database to grow and can obtain sufficient space by reducing the size of the Transaction Log. Typically, this action is performed as a temporary solution that buys you enough time to install an additional disk. As an example, you could simply run the following statement to clear the Transaction Log of the TESTDB database:

```
use master
    backup log testdb to tape = \\.\tape0 with truncate_only
```

SKIP/NOSKIP

These two options enhance your control by telling the backup process to read or not to read the information contained in the tape headers. You should be careful when using this parameter because a setting of SKIP will let the backup process overwrite backup sets on media with an expiration date that has not expired. So if you wanted the backup process to skip reading the header information, you would connect to SQL Server using Query Analyzer and execute a statement similar to this:

```
use master
    backup database testdb to tape = \\.\tape0 with skip
```

UNLOAD/NOUNLOAD

These simple parameters tell the backup process whether or not to eject the tape after the backup has completed. If you want to eject the tape following a backup, the statement will look like this:

```
use master
    backup database testdb to tape = \\.\tape0 with unload
```

RESTART

An interesting parameter, the RESTART option tells SQL Server to begin the backup process where it left off when interrupted. The reason we have this parameter is for backup sets that span multiple tapes. When the SQL Server backup process runs out of room on a tape, it halts. You can continue the operation by inserting a new tape and running the original BACKUP statement with the RESTART parameter. As with many of the other options listed in this section, the statement is relatively unchanged and has only the added parameter RESTART added to the end. The following example shows how this parameter would be used:

```
use master
    backup database testdb to tape = \\.\tape0 with restart
```

STATS

STATS is a parameter that you will use mostly when you want to gather information about the backup process for the purpose of planning. This option causes SQL Server to display a message each time a percentile of the backup has completed. It lets you gauge the amount of time remaining for the backup to complete, but places additional strain on the server resources. For this reason, it is not commonly used. If you want to gauge the progress of your backup, you will have to use Transact-SQL because there is no option to do so within Enterprise Manager. The correct statement will look like this:

```
use master
    backup database testdb to tape = \\.\tape0 with stats
```

Like their counterparts in Enterprise Manager, each of the parameters listed above add to your control over the backup process. With these options, you can create a custom backup solution using only Transact-SQL.

Now that you have a firm grasp of SQL Server backup tools, you will want to take a look at some of the more advanced options provided by SQL Server that will help you customize your backup solution to suit any size deployment. In the following sections, we will delve into some less common backup techniques and methods.

ADVANCED BACKUP SOLUTIONS

The first thing to do is identify why you would ever need to get creative with the backup process. SQL Server is designed to store databases of various sizes, ranging from small databases that are less than 500MB to very large databases that may be many gigabytes or even terabytes in size. If you combine what you know about the SQL Server backup process with the average time frames that a normal server backup takes, and then add into the equation databases that are very large, you can easily see how the backup solution for an extremely large database will have to be innovative and well planned in order to provide a sound solution.

SQL Server 7 provides you with some unique features that will help you optimize your backup plan. The first trick that you will want to understand is the use of file groups. You will remember from earlier chapters that SQL Server 7 supports the division of a single database into multiple files. These files can then be broken into file groups, for the purpose of reference. Additionally, the use of file groups provides you with some flexibility in terms of the backup plan.

You can actually specify individual files or file groups in the backup statement. This means that you can actually back up only one file at a time or one file group at a time. The aspect about this process that most people may miss is that when you back up a file, the portions of the Transaction Log that have changed since the last backup are either flushed into the database or saved with the backup set. This means that you do not have to back up all of the files on the same day. For example, if you have a very large database that is divided into five different files, the basics of your backup solution could look something like this.

▼ Perform a full backup of all files.

■ Perform a full backup of one file on each day of the week at midnight.

▲ Perform a Transaction Log backup every two hours. (In an average organization, this means that you have four transaction log backups each day.)

If any one file is damaged, you will only need to restore that file and all Transaction Log backups that have been performed since the last time you performed any database file backup. It does not matter which file has failed; you will only need a maximum of five backups to effectively restore the server. You will learn more about restoring databases in the next chapter.

As with most things in the world of advanced computing, there is a catch. You must be very careful during the database design stage so that you group the database files in a way that lends itself to backups. Though this book is not meant for the developer specifically, you should know by now that it is possible to group tables and indexes of tables together, or you can separate them into different files. Sometimes, the developer will be tempted to divide the files in order to speed performance. While this is an excellent solution to access problems, it can actually add to backup problems because the backup process must back up tables and their indexes together. In simple terms, what this means to you as an administrator is that if your database is divided into different files, but the index for a table in one file is physically stored in another, then you will be forced to back up those two files together as a unit. This is one of many reasons why database developers and administrators should work together, so that a solid database design is created right from the beginning.

As you can see, backing up files or file groups can greatly reduce the amount of impact that the backup process has on the server and network users. Another feature of the backup process that can speed up your backups and reduce overhead is using multiple backup devices. You will remember from earlier in this chapter that you can add a device or specify a file in the Backup Database dialog box simply by clicking the Add button. Once you have added one location, you can add additional locations just by clicking the Add button again. If each of the locations that you specify are controlled by a different piece of hardware (such as two or more tape drives), the SQL Server backup process will automatically split the backup over multiple locations and divide the work between them. This means that by adding even a single tape drive to your server, you can reduce the amount of time that a backup takes by half. This process is commonly referred to as creating a *striped backup* and is one of the more common solutions to the problem of slow or high-impact backups.

> ### From the Field
>
> Actually performing the backups is a task that carries with it a great deal of responsibility. We have found that most organizations benefit from a log that details each backup, when it was performed, and by whom. The log should contain entries for the backups and two signature areas—one for the person who performs the backup and one for another person who verifies that the backup was completed. This type of log will prevent countless problems and circumvent numerous political issues as well.

SUMMARY

In this chapter, you have learned about backing up databases and how to use both Enterprise Manager and Transact-SQL to perform backups. You have even learned some tips for customizing a backup solution and how to create a backup plan. The next step is to learn how to use these backups if something goes wrong. In the following chapter, you will learn how to restore databases. You will learn some tricks that will help you control the restoration process, and even some tips on creating standby servers that are always ready to fill in should your main server require maintenance or unexpectedly fail.

CHAPTER 7

Restoring Databases

Now that you have learned how to plan and execute a complete backup plan for your SQL Server deployment, you will want to learn the details and procedures for restoring databases. Restoring from backup is a task that every administrator hopes that he or she will never have to perform, but must prepare for—just to be safe. Unfortunately, servers *do* fail, and many an administrator has experienced problems during the restore operation because he or she had not practiced restoring databases or did not fully understand the restore process. In this chapter, you will learn how to restore databases using both Enterprise Manager and Transact-SQL. You will learn methods for controlling the restoration and even acquire some tips for creating real-time standby servers.

UNDERSTANDING THE SQL SERVER RESTORE PROCESS

The very first thing you will want to understand is what happens during the restore process. The process and the SQL Server will automatically re-create both database files and their structure. Because the restore process works using actual Transact-SQL statements, all database objects are re-created and then filled with data. One major difference between the SQL Server 7 restore process and that of previous versions of SQL Server is that you do not have to delete (using the various drop-based stored procedures) damaged databases prior to restoring them. There are, however, some activities that you are still required to perform.

TIP: As mentioned in Chapter 6, changes to the schema must be backed up within the MASTER Database. If something happens that requires you to perform a restoration, make sure that you restore the MASTER Database first (to restore the server objects), and then perform the other database restorations as necessary.

Unlike the backup process, network users should not continue to use the database while it is being restored. You must therefore take precautions to ensure that users cannot connect to and use the database while you are performing the restoration. Unfortunately, SQL Server does not automatically restrict access to the database, and you will have to manually change database settings so that SQL Server will not allow access to the database during the restoration period. The database setting that you must change is the DBO Use Only option. You learned how to specify this setting in Chapter 4. Should you try to restore a database without first setting it so that it cannot be accessed, the restore operation will fail, a step that SQL Server takes to protect against inadvertent corruption of the data within the database.

Another task that you should perform prior to restoring a database is to back up the Transaction Log. This task is performed only if the database in question is still present on the server. For example, if you have a live database that has suffered damage by means of disk failure, and the Transaction Log is present on another disk, you should do the following: replace the damaged disk, back up the Transaction Log from the separate disk, restore the database to the new disk from backup, and finally restore the Transaction Log. This will ensure that the most recent transactions that had not yet been committed to the database will be restored as well. If you do not back up the Transaction Log, but then restore it as the final step in the restoration process, you might lose many changes to data that have taken place since the last time you backed up the Transaction Log. As a general rule, and as we have discussed previously, you will typically want to make sure that you have Transaction Log backups—whether differentials or incrementals—whenever you are backing up and restoring data.

It is important to understand that certain tasks must be accomplished prior to actually restoring the database. The most effective administrators have a series of steps in their strategically plotted and tested data recovery plan that include these tasks. You too should have a plan that details what steps to take whenever a problem with a database occurs. Because there are so many different reasons that databases could fail or be considered unusable in their current state, we cannot provide you with a plan that will work for all or even most scenarios. Your plans for data recovery are likely to be very specific and will take into consideration the different aspects of your organization and deployment. Two things that should always be in the plan, however, are the actions of setting the database that is to be restored into DBO Use Only mode, and backing up the Transaction Logs. Later in this chapter, you will learn how to control the restore process so that you can restore the Transaction Logs as the final step in a successful restoration.

RESTORING A DATABASE

You can restore a database in SQL Server using either Enterprise Manager or Transact-SQL. Enterprise Manager includes as part of its backup tools a set of dialog boxes devoted to restoring databases, and also some wizards that will guide you through the restoration. Because the wizards are well written and easy to understand, we will restrict ourselves to discussing the more complicated tools. Once you understand the Enterprise Manager interface and the parameters for control when using Transact-SQL, using the wizards will be child's play to you. The wizards are fairly complete, though they do lack some of the functionality that using Transact-SQL provides you—and in complex environments you will want to use Transact-SQL restorations (detailed later in this chapter) so that you can script complex restore processes.

RESTORING A DATABASE USING ENTERPRISE MANAGER

Because many administrators, both new and experienced, prefer graphical tools, you will first learn how to perform a restore operation using Enterprise Manager. To access the correct dialog boxes, simply follow these steps:

1. Start Enterprise Manager and expand the object list so that you can see your server name.

2. Click once on your server name.

3. Select Tools | Restore Database.

When you complete the steps, SQL Server will respond by displaying the Restore Database dialog box, as seen in Figure 7-1.

Restore Database is the primary dialog box that lets you control the restore process. You will begin all restore operations in this dialog box and will branch out from there to make specifications and reference files. For example, if you want to restore the TESTDB database, you will first open the Restore Database dialog box. The next step is to identify the location of the backup from which you want to restore. SQL Server was keeping track when you performed your backups, and if the database you want to restore is a current database on the server, you can simply choose the database from the Show Backups of Database field in the Parameters area of the dialog

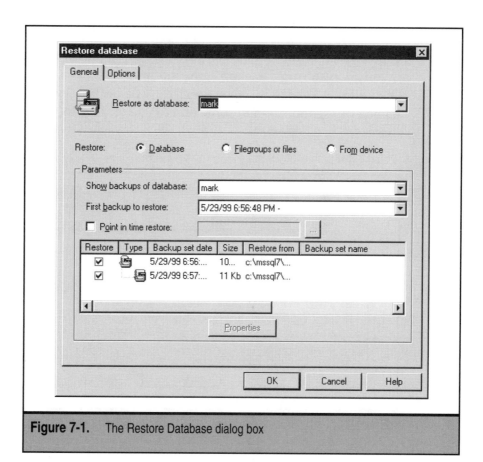

Figure 7-1.   The Restore Database dialog box

box. If you look closely at Figure 7-1 again, you will see the Parameters section of the dialog box, as shown in Figure 7-2.

When you choose a database in the Show Backups of Database field, the backups that have been performed will be displayed in a lower pane of the window. In this area, you can choose the backup from which you want to restore.

You will notice three radio buttons near the top of the dialog box that let you choose to restore a Database, Filegroups or Files, or From Device. These buttons grant you a high level of control over the restore process, letting you back up an existing database that was backed up to a different location or even on a different installation of SQL Server by choosing the From Device option. For example, if your server has failed completely because of disk failure and you are forced to reinstall SQL Server and then restore the databases, the new installation will have no record of backups and thus there will be no backup choices for the Database option. In this case, you will have to choose From Device and then specify a tape or file location. Similarly, if you are restoring a backup from another server, you will have to choose From Device and then specify a tape or file location (or a named pipe connection to some other mass storage location, as discussed in Chapter 6).

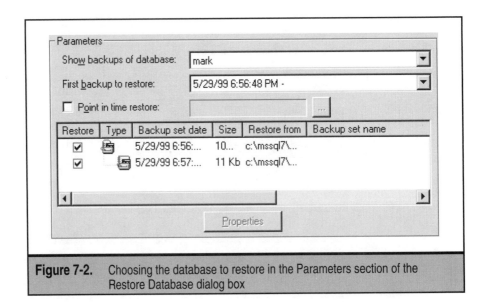

Figure 7-2.   Choosing the database to restore in the Parameters section of the Restore Database dialog box

In addition to the functionality provided by the From Device option, restorations using the Filegroups and Files option technically do not require you to have previously performed a filegroup or file backup. You can specify a file from a normal backup set to restore, which could be valuable in the case where you have separated files onto separate disks to enhance performance and are restoring the database to remedy a physical disk failure. While it is true that you would normally plan to back up files or filegroups to save resources during the backup process, knowing that you can back up single files from normal backups could be a powerful bit of knowledge that makes you shine.

Using the Database Radio Button

In the case of a normal backup, once you have chosen the appropriate backup you could just click the OK button and the restore process would begin. You do have some additional options, however, that you might want to take into consideration. For example, you might have more than one backup contained in the same media set and might want to specify which backup you want to restore first. Depending on your backup plan, specifying which backup to begin with might be either unnecessary or vital. As with all data recovery operations, you must be extremely cautious when restoring databases, because errors made at this time could affect the operation of the database later.

Another option that you have when using the Database radio button is to restore the database only to a specific point in time. Looking at your own server, you might notice that the Point in Time Restore checkbox is unavailable. If your Point in Time option is unavailable, it is because the backup set does not include a backup of the Transaction Log. SQL Server must have a backup of the Transaction Log to perform a Point in Time Restore operation. As you learned in the last chapter, your backup solution should always include backups of the Transaction Logs, because they add to the overall safety of the data and provide the administrator with more flexibility when dealing with restorations. The Point in Time Restore feature is a powerful tool that helps solve problems plaguing many other database management systems. For example, if your database is being restored because of a data corruption error, and you can identify the time when the database was corrupted, then you can use the Point in Time Restore feature to restore the database right up until the data was corrupted. Performing this type of a restoration can significantly reduce the amount of lost data and consumed time that might otherwise result from a data corruption.

To execute a Point in Time Restore, simply click in the Point in Time Restore checkbox. SQL Server will automatically display a Point in Time Restore dialog box in which you can specify the time and date that you want the restore process to stop. When the restore operation runs, it will restore all data up until the point that you specified and then halt. The database is left in a ready state, unless you specify one of the other states, as discussed later in this chapter.

Using the Filegroups or Files Radio Button

When you choose the Filegroups or Files radio button, the dialog box changes to reflect the different options that are now available to you. The first thing that you might notice is that the Point in Time Restore option is no longer available. This is because you cannot restore a database filegroup or specific file independently of the other files and still execute a point in time restoration. In place of the Point in Time Restore option, you will find a checkbox entitled Select a Subset of Backup Sets. When you place a checkmark in this box, SQL Server will automatically display a dialog box called Filter Backup Sets. You can use this dialog box to control which backup sets are displayed in the main Restore Database dialog box. By filtering the backup sets that are available for use, you can reduce the possibility of mistakes and ensure that the backups from which you are restoring are in fact the sets that you want

As seen in Figure 7-3, the Filter Backup Sets dialog box has three checkboxes that let you control which backup sets are displayed and thus available for use. The first checkbox enables control over the drive or tape device (when installed). This option lets you specify the drive or tape from which backups might be restored.

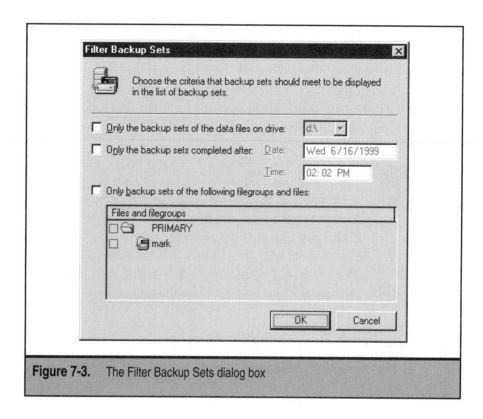

Figure 7-3. The Filter Backup Sets dialog box

The next option lets you take control over dates and times. Displaying only backup sets that were created after a specific point in time will also let you reduce mistakes and help you ensure that the backup sets you are using are in fact the ones that you want.

The third checkbox lets you specify only backup sets that contain data for certain files or filegroups. This option ensures that you do not use backup sets from other databases or even other filegroups when performing your restore.

When you combine the three options that are available in the Filter Backup Sets dialog box, you create a powerful set of restrictions that prevent you or other administrators from using the wrong backup sets during a restore. Because the display in a graphical utility like the restore tool can be easily misread or misinterpreted, the filter feature is a huge asset to you as an administrator, especially when your organization is large enough to support multiple administrators. If you want to make changes to the filter after the initial change, you can get back to the dialog box by clicking the Selection Criteria button on the Restore Database dialog box General tab. (Note that this button is only enabled when you use the Files or Filegroups option.)

TIP: One of the most common issues we encounter is the desire of administrators to manage filtering on remote machines—controlling the backups to which different individuals have access, and so on. Unfortunately, without additional scripting, you cannot control access in this manner from Enterprise Manager. In order to restore a database that does not exist, the user must have Create Database permissions. In order to restore a database that does exist, the user must have the permissions of Sysadmin or DBO.

Using the From Device Radio Button

The From Device radio button in the Restore Database dialog box lets you specify a tape or file location that might not be stored and maintained in SQL Server. This option is very helpful when you are moving a database to a different server or when you are restoring a database to a new installation of SQL Server.

When you choose this option, SQL Server automatically changes the main Restore Database dialog box to reflect the options that are now available for use. Because there is no information stored in SQL Server about the backup you are going to use, in addition to specifying the location of the backup, you must specify the type of backup that you are restoring from, or tell the restore utility to read the information directly from the backup media. To accomplish this, this dialog box has more checkboxes than do either the Database or Filegroups or Files radio buttons. You can see the Restore Database dialog box set to From Device in Figure 7-4.

As you can see, the dialog box basically has two sets of parameters. The first is the location of the backup set. To choose a backup set, you must click on the Select Devices button. When you do this, SQL Server will display the Choose Restore Devices dialog

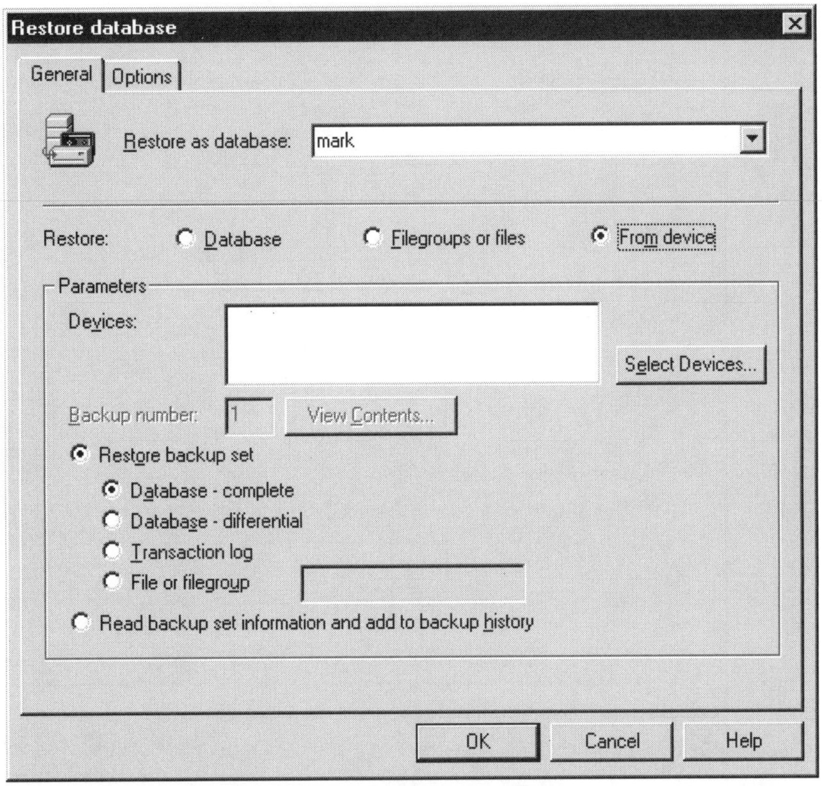

Figure 7-4. The Restore Database dialog box set to From Device

box. From here, you can specify a device or file location by clicking on the Add button, as seen in Figure 7-5.

Besides the Add button, you will notice that there are buttons that will let you Edit, Remove, or Remove All backup sets that might already be displayed in the window. Using these buttons, you can control which backup sets are displayed and are thus available for use in the restore operation. When you have finished choosing the backup locations, you can exit the dialog box by clicking the familiar OK button.

The next step is to designate what kind of backup is contained in the set specified. You have the option of having SQL Server read the

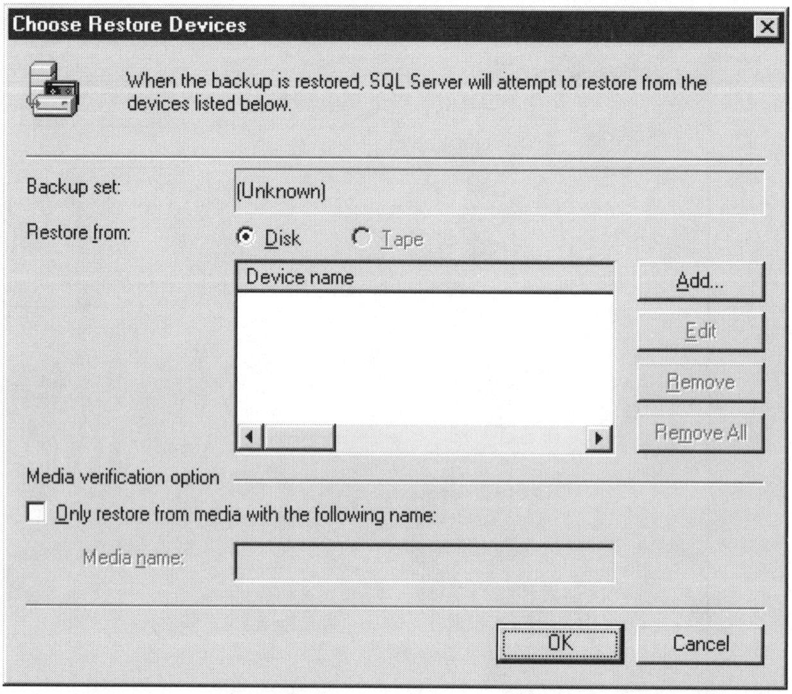

Figure 7-5. Specifying a device or file location from the Choose Restore Devices dialog box

information directly from the backup set by clicking in the Read Backup Set Information and Add to Backup History checkbox. When you choose this option, SQL Server will not actually restore any data, but will simply read the information stored with the backup and add it into the stored backup history that is maintained by SQL Server. You will then have to restart the restore process to actually restore data. This option is especially helpful when you are either reconstructing a failed SQL Server or building a new server that is a virtual copy of another.

If you want to restore data directly from the device, you must specify what kind of backup you are restoring from. The name and description will be good clues for you if you are unsure, providing that the backup was named and described effectively when it was created. You can choose from among a Complete or a Differential database backup, a Transaction Log backup, or a File or Filegroup backup. Once you have specified both a location for the backup set and the type of backup that is contained in the backup set, clicking OK will begin the restore process.

Understanding the Backup History

When performing either a Database or a File or Filegroup restoration, part of the restore information is obtained from the backup history maintained by SQL Server inside the MSDB Database. The backup history maintains a list of the backups that were performed, the date and time when they were created, what type of backup it was, and a few additional details. On some occasions, you might want to alter the location that SQL Server has stored for the backup. Technically, you could alter the backup history by editing data in the MSDB Database directly, but this is not a recommended practice.

TIP: Editing the MSDB Database directly is never a recommended practice, unless you are accomplishing certain specific tasks. For example, in one environment, we found a case where we could not delete or otherwise manage an alias. We edited the MSDB Database to free up the alias; however, we first had to enable the MSDB Database for editing before we could make the change—a process that was detailed in Chapter 2.

SQL Server permits editing the backup history by using the Restore tool. You can alter the path to the backup by following these steps:

1. Open the SQL Server Backup dialog box as usual and choose the database whose backup storage location you want to change.

2. Click the Properties button.

3. Click the Change button at the bottom of the dialog box.

4. Choose a disk or tape location, using the radio buttons that represent disk or tape.

5. Click the Edit button.

6. Choose a Filename or Device, using the representative radio buttons.

7. For a device, use the drop-down list box to select the correct device. For a filename, use the ellipsis button to select a new file.

Changing the storage location that SQL Server maintains is actually quite a rare scenario. We include the information here only in an attempt to be thorough. Typically, you will not need to change this location, but instead will use the From Device restore option when restoring databases of which SQL Server is unaware.

For SQL Server to maintain backup information, either the backup must have been performed on the server that you are using, or the information must have been read from the actual backup. This is true whether you are doing the restoration from Enterprise Manager or using Transact-SQL—a process that we will discuss in detail in the following sections.

RESTORING A DATABASE USING TRANSACT-SQL

As with any other managerial task in SQL Server, you can, if you choose, perform database restoration tasks using only Transact-SQL. The primary statement with which you restore databases is the RESTORE DATABASE statement. In the following sections, you will learn how to control the restore process using the RESTORE DATABASE statement with its optional parameters. You will begin with a simple restore and move on to more complex techniques. Each topic will include an example of Transact-SQL that you can run on your own server as part of the learning process.

Restoring a Database

The first step is to learn the absolute basics of the RESTORE DATABASE statement. For this statement to function, a few parameters must be included. First, you must include the database specification. When you attempt to restore a database or Transaction

Log, SQL Server must know what database you are attempting to restore. The database parameter is what tells SQL Server the database to which you are restoring data. The other option that is absolutely necessary is the location parameter. You must tell SQL Server specifically where to find the backup from which you want to restore. If you do not specify where the backup set is located, the RESTORE statement will fail, and SQL Server will return an error. As an example of a correct statement, assume that you want to restore the TESTDB database from a backup set stored on disk, in the default backup directory (C:\MSSQL7\BACKUP), which is named TESTDBBACK.BAK. To execute this operation, you would connect to SQL Server using Query Analyzer and execute the following statement:

```
use master
    restore database testdb
    from disk =   'c:\mssql7\backup\testdbback.bak'
```

Remember that the TESTDB database must have been backed up to this folder and the backup set must be named TESTDBBACK.BAK for this statement to work. Additionally, the backup must have been performed on this SQL Server, or the information about the backup must already have been added to the backup history. If SQL Server is unaware of this backup, the statement will not have enough information and will halt. Later in this chapter, you will see how to specify sufficient information to perform a restore without backup history information. Also, remember that if you were restoring the database from a backup device, the statement would be shorter because SQL Server would already know the physical location of the backup. For example, if you wanted to perform the same restoration, but the backup had been stored on a dump device named TESTDBBACK, the RESTORE statement would be this:

```
use master
    restore database testdb from testdbback
```

Notice that you do not need the disk parameter or the path to the file. Since SQL Server recorded where the device is stored, you no longer have to reference the exact backup type or path in the statement. In large environments where the administrative staff is of sufficient size, using dump devices can be helpful because the statements require less knowledge of the backups and of Transact-SQL itself.

Now that you understand the basics of the RESTORE statement, you can move into the realm of controlling the restore process using optional parameters. In the text that follows, you will learn to use each of the parameters in turn. Each description will include a statement that is based on restoring the TESTDB database. As you go through the parameters, remember that some of them are possible only when certain conditions are already true. When this is so, the description will include the specifics for when the parameter is valid. You must take care when reading the descriptions to be sure that you understand both the optional parameter and the conditions that must exist for it to be valid.

Using the DBO_ONLY Option with Restores

This parameter sets the database mode to DBO Use Only when the restore operation is complete. You will use this option when you want to perform other operations on the database before letting network users access it. The database will remain in DBO Use Only mode until you either change the setting in Enterprise Manager or set the condition to False using the SP_DBOPTION stored procedure. An example of the RESTORE statement using this option would be as follows:

```
use master
    restore database testdb
    from testdbback
    with dbo_only
```

While your own organizational needs will dictate how often you actually need to set a database into DBO Use Only mode, one common scenario occurs when you are restoring a database that has been set up for replication. When you restore the database, you might want to prevent users from accessing the database until after the replication has been set up again. This will prevent problems with the replication setup that might have been caused by users accessing the data.

Choosing Media Sets Using the With File Option

This option lets you take control of the backup media by choosing which backup set on the media will be used for the restoration. When you perform multiple backups to the same media, each backup is numbered as it is saved. When you restore a backup set and you want to use a set other than the most recent one, you must specify the number of the backup set. For example, if you want to restore the TESTDB database using the second backup set on the TESTDBBACK dump device, you will connect to SQL Server using Query Analyzer and execute the following statement:

```
use master
    restore database testdb from testdbback with File = 2
```

Take notice of the fact that in this case File comes after the word with. We point this out because the RESTORE statement actually supports the word File as two different options that correspond to the two locations where you can use File within the BACKUP statement, as you saw in Chapter 6. The first of these options lets you specify the number of the backup set used in the restoration, while the second lets you specify individual database files to restore. When the word File is preceded by the word with in the statement, you are using the parameter to specify a backup set. If, however, the word File came directly after the database name and was not preceded by the word with, then you would be specifying a database file to restore. Later in this chapter, you will learn more about restoring specific database files and filegroups.

Identifying Backup Sets with the MediaName Parameter

MediaName is a safety parameter that lets you specify a name for the entire backup set. As you have learned, the SQL Server backup process lets you name a backup set so that it can be identified later. The restore process includes a safety check that verifies the name specified during restore and then matches the one stored on the backup set. If you do not specify a name in the RESTORE statement, the safety check is not performed. Thus, you can think of the MediaName parameter as an additional safety check that helps you verify that you are restoring the correct backup set. An example of this parameter's use is as follows:

```
use master
    Restore database testdb
    from testdbback
    with medianame =   'backupsetname'
```

In the example, we use the word backupsetname as a placeholder for the actual name of the backup set. If you were trying to use this statement in a real restore operation, you would replace the word backupsetname with the actual name of the backup stored on the media. Remember that the backup set must also have been named when it was created, or the restore operation will halt.

Combining both the with File and MediaName parameters into a RESTORE statement creates a scenario which makes it very difficult to restore the wrong database. For example, if you restore the TESTDB database and specify backup set number 2, which has a MediaName of Secondary Backup, it is highly unlikely that another backup set anywhere in your collection of backups would match both parameters. The statement to accomplish this would look like this:

```
use master
    Restore database testdb from testdbback with file = 2,
    medianame = 'secondary backup'
```

Restoring to a Specified Location with the Move To Option

This option is particularly useful when you want to restore a database onto completely different physical drives from the ones on which it originally existed. It does not matter whether this is the same server where the database originated or whether the database is being restored to a completely different server, the Move To option lets you completely control the destination of the database files.

The syntax for this option is easy to understand, once put into the proper context. When moving database files to a different location, you must specify which database file you want to move, and where you want to move it. The syntax, therefore, is simply the logical name of the file preceded by the word move, and then the physical filename and path that specifies where you want the file to exist, preceded by the word to. As an example, assume that you want to move the database file TESTDB to the physical location D:\NEWFILES\TESTDB.MDF. To accomplish this during a restore, you will connect to SQL Server using Query Analyzer and execute the following statement:

```
use master
    restore database testdb from testdbback
    move 'testdb' to 'd:\newfiles\testdb.mdf'
    move 'testdb_log' to 'd:\newfiles\testdb_log.ldf'
```

You should note that the example uses two move operations. While there might be some occasions when you want to move a database file without moving the Transaction Log, such occasions are sure to be rare. The example moves both the main database file for the TESTDB database and its Transaction Log, because it is a fair assumption that if you want to move the database you will also want to move its Transaction Log. As an administrator, you must always be careful to take the Transaction Log into consideration before altering the structure of any database.

TIP: It is important to remember that a bad or unrecognized location for the log file and the database file will cause this statement to fail. This is because SQL Server parses the Transact-SQL statement before it begins to execute any part of the statement.

You must also be careful with your specified path variables when moving databases. Transact-SQL has no ability to recognize misspelled folder names or incorrect paths. If you specify an incorrect folder name or path, the statement will halt, returning an error. The error is nonspecific in nature, telling you only that SQL Server was unable to create the file.

Controlling How and When the Recovery Process Executes with the Recovery and Norecovery Options

Restoring databases becomes more difficult and complex when you have a complex backup strategy in place. When you are dealing with full backups alone, the process is fairly simple. However, if your backup strategy includes differential or Transaction Log backups as part of the plan, restoring the database becomes a bit tricky. This is because the restore process automatically initiates the automatic recovery process when it is complete. This means that when a database is restored, the Transaction Log is checkpointed and all noncommitted transactions are rolled back (removed). If a differential or Transaction Log backup was performed, you will need to execute multiple RESTORE statements to restore the database completely.

For example, if you had performed a full and then a differential backup on the database, whereupon the database failed, you would need to first restore the full backup, followed by the differential. Because the differential backup might contain completions for transactions that were incomplete at the time of the full backup, you do not want the recovery process to initiate until you have restored the differential backup. In the same way, if your backup solution included full backups combined with Transaction Log backups, during the restore process you would not want the recovery process to initiate until after the last Transaction Log backup had been restored.

Because a complex backup solution complicates the restore process, administrators must have the ability to control when the recovery process initiates. When using Transact-SQL, this control takes the form of the recovery and norecovery optional parameters. For example, if you want to restore the TESTDB database without initiating the recovery process, you will connect to SQL Server using Query Analyzer and execute the following statement:

```
use master
    restore database testdb from testdbback with norecovery
```

The exemplified statement leaves the TESTDB database in an unrecovered state. The database is inaccessible to users but can have additional backup sets restored to it. Simply said, if you want the database to recover following a restore, you specify the recovery option. If you do not want the database to recover after the restore, you specify the norecovery option. If you specify neither, SQL Server will use a default specification of recovery, and will automatically initiate the recovery process. This will be true in all cases, with the exception of the standby parameter, which also leaves the database in an unrecovered state. You will learn more about the standby parameter in the next section, and will additionally learn more about the standby process later in this chapter.

Creating a Hot-Standby Server with the Standby Option

This option actually takes us a little bit ahead of ourselves in this chapter, but needs to be included here so that you have thorough reference to the statement options. The standby option leaves the database in an unrecovered state, which is still accessible to network users on a read-only basis. Later in this chapter, you will learn how to create and maintain a hot-standby server—that is, a server that is always ready to take over if the main server fails. Hot-standby servers, as well as other unique server solutions, are good reasons for using the standby option. As an example of syntax, refer to the following statement:

```
use master
    restore database testdb from testdbback with standby
```

The Replace Option

As you know, SQL Server performs a safety check prior to executing a restore operation. This safety test is designed to protect existing databases from accidentally being destroyed during a restore. When the restore process is initiated, SQL Server verifies that the database name recorded in the backup set is the same as the name of the database on the server. If the names are different, the restore process halts and an error is returned. The safety check also verifies that the files contained in the backup set match the actual database files on the server. If the files are different, the restore process halts and an error is returned. (The restore process will not halt if the files are of a different size.)

On some occasions, you might want to override the safety check and restore a database over another database with a dissimilar name or over a database that has a different file structure from the one contained in the backup set. To accomplish this using Transact-SQL, you will add the `with replace` option to the end of the statement. For example, if you want to restore the TESTDB database and override the safety check when doing so, you will connect to SQL Server using Query Analyzer and execute the following statement:

```
use master
    restore database testdb from testdbback with replace
```

Continuing a Restore After a Server Failure with the Restart Option

The very fact that you are executing a RESTORE statement typically means that something went wrong. Unfortunately, the story sometimes does not end there, clean and neat. Since in the world of microcomputing the laws of a legendary gentleman named Murphy seem to hold sway, you can almost always assume that *if* something else can go wrong, it *will.* Because of this principle, the designers of the SQL Server restore process decided that you might actually experience a server stall, a locked restoration process, a full hard drive, or other similar problem while you are restoring a database. In cases where the database is particularly large, this can cause quite an impact on the time it takes to restore the database, to say nothing of the aggravation it causes. In cases like this, you have the option of starting a restore operation from the point where it left off when interrupted. When using Transact-SQL, the option that allows this is

restart. If, for example, you want to restore the TESTDB
database and want the restore process to begin where it left off,
you will connect to SQL Server using Query Analyzer and execute
this statement:

```
use master
    restore database testdb from testdbback with restart
```

Controlling the Tape Device

In the same way that you sometimes want to eject or not eject the
tape from the tape device during a backup operation, sometimes you
want to exercise the same control during a restore operation. To
accomplish this using Transact-SQL, the RESTORE statement
supports the unload and nounload parameters. The unload option
will rewind and eject the tape following the restore process, while
nounload will simply leave the tape in the condition that it was left
in following the restore process. Below you will find two examples,
one using unload and the second using nounload:

```
use master
    restore database testdb from testdbback with unload
use master
    restore database testdb from testdbback with nounload
```

Restoring Files and Filegroups

As you learned earlier in this chapter, the RESTORE statement
actually supports the word file as two completely different
parameters. In the first case, the word file is preceded by the word
with and specifies the number of the backup set on the backup
media that you want to use (see the with file option discussed
previously). The second parameter that can use the word file is
used when you want to specify a particular database file to restore. In
this case, the word file is not preceded by the word with, but is
instead part of the database specification. For example, if you want to

restore the database file TESTDB1 to disk and it must be specified because the backup set contains multiple files, you will connect to SQL Server using Query Analyzer and execute a statement like this:

```
use master
    restore database testdb
    file = 'testdb1'
    from testdbback
```

The logical filename TESTDB1 is referenced as a variable for the file parameter. SQL Server will use information stored in the backup history to determine where the file should be stored physically. Using this statement, only the TESTDB1 file will be restored, even if the backup set held files named TESTDB1, TESTDB2, TESTDB3, and TESTDBLOG.

Sometimes you might want to use a similar specification to restore an entire filegroup. You will remember from Chapter 6 that you can back up entire filegroups as a unit. When filegroups have been specified, you can choose to restore all the files in one filegroup, while leaving the others unrestored. Such a process is often beneficial in situations where one part of a database has been corrupted but others have not. It is also to be expected that you can restore from filegroups that you backed up to previously—otherwise, what is the point of using them in the first place? To restore a filegroup using Transact-SQL, connect to SQL Server as usual using Query Analyzer and execute a statement similar to the following:

```
use master
    restore database testdb
    filegroup = 'filegroupname'
    from testdbback
```

The example uses the word filegroupname as a placeholder to indicate the actual name of a filegroup. If you are using this statement to restore a real filegroup, you will substitute the name of the filegroup for the word filegroupname.

As you know, backing up individual files or filegroups has a restriction wherein you must back up database files and indexes together as one unit. Likewise, when you are restoring database files and filegroups, database files and indexes must be restored together as a unit, even if they are stored in different filegroups. For example, if you created the TESTDB database with two filegroups called Primary and Secondary, and you placed an index for the Customer table in the Secondary filegroup while the Customer table itself was stored in the Primary filegroup, you would have to back up and restore the Primary and Secondary filegroups together. This restriction is important to note and is a question you should ask of the developer whenever you take on administrative responsibility for a new database.

Restoring a Transaction Log

The log parameter is an item that is very easy to understand, but one that all new administrators seem to miss at the beginning. This might be because the log parameter actually changes the structure of the RESTORE statement instead of being an add-on parameter like so many others. To understand the way this parameter works, you simply need to know that when you are restoring a Transaction Log, you must use the word log instead of the word database. For example, if you wanted to restore the Transaction Log for the TESTDB database, you would connect to SQL Server as usual and execute this statement:

```
use master
    restore log testdb from testdbback
```

As you can see, the only change in the statement is the word log. If you had used the word database instead, the statement would restore the TESTDB database. Because you specified the word log, the statement will restore the Transaction Log only.

TIP: As noted earlier, unless you specify otherwise, the database will be left in a transaction-ready state because the recovery process will execute after the restoration completes.

Restoring to a Specific Point in Time

In the same way that you can restore to a specific point in time using Enterprise Manager, you can perform a Point in Time restoration using Transact-SQL. Using the stopat parameter lets you specify a date and time for the restoration to complete. No transactions that occur after this point will be restored.

You can use the `stopat` option only when restoring a Transaction Log; it is not valid for database restorations. While it is true that you can restore a database, and then its Transaction Log, you should note that it is the Transaction Log that makes the Point in Time restoration possible. As an example, assume that you want to restore the TESTDB Transaction Log, and want the restoration to stop at 12:00 A.M. on the first of January in the year 2000. To accomplish this, you will connect to SQL Server using Query Analyzer and execute the following statement:

```
use master
    Restore log testdb from testdbback
    With stopat = 'jan 01, 2000 12:00 am'
```

Now, suppose that you are restoring the entire database *and* the Transaction Log. In this case, you must first restore the database, and then the Transaction Log, so that you can include the `stopat` variable. The example for this new scenario would look like this:

```
use master
    restore database testdb from testdbback
    with norecovery
    restore log testdb from testdbback
    with recovery, stopat = 'jan 01, 2000 12:00 am'
```

Gathering Statistics

As you have learned, sometimes you will want to gather statistical information that helps you gauge the impact that a backup or restore process has on your server and users. When using Transact-SQL, you can specify that SQL Server should notify you every time a percentage of the process completes. For the RESTORE statement, this parameter is called `stats`. An example of the `stats` parameter is found below:

```
use master
    restore database testdb from testdbback with stats
```

If you want SQL Server to notify you as each percentage completes, you must remember to include the `stats` parameter before you begin the process. Interrupting a restore operation is not recommended, so if you forget this parameter we suggest that you let the operation complete and make a note to use it the next time you perform a restoration.

TIP: As a rule, we do not use the `stats` parameter. If you need to monitor the performance of a restoration activity, we recommend that you instead use the Performance Monitor. SQL Server monitoring and optimization is detailed in Chapter 9.

THE STANDBY SERVER

In a world where things frequently go wrong, where users are never happy, and where there is never enough time to complete the tasks you have, SQL Server has a possible solution for many of your problems. The solution is a concept called a *standby server*. The idea behind standby servers is actually not a new one, since administrators and other functionaries have been creating copies of important data for many years. The standby server is perhaps the ultimate backup. It is a complete mirror of a SQL Server maintained on another server machine that can either work on the network as a read-only server, or stand in readiness not connected to the network, just in case the main server fails. In either case, the server can solve many problems that you might face as an administrator.

Setting up a standby server is really not that difficult. For most administrators, the biggest problem will be obtaining another server to run the standby on. If you can obtain an additional server that can be dedicated for use as a standby server, you will begin your setup by simply installing SQL Server as usual.

Depending on what you want to do with your standby, you might name the server identically to the main production server or give it another name entirely. If, for example, you are using the server as a hot-standby server that is not accessed by network users, but merely sits waiting in case it is needed, then you will name the server so that it matches the production server exactly. If, however, you are using the server as a read-only server to cut down on the overhead of the main production server by handling data retrieval, then it must be on the same network and cannot be given the same name as the production server.

In either case, the creation of the standby server is performed the same way. You will begin by performing a full backup of the database or databases that you want to store on the standby server.

Once the full backup has been created, you will restore the database to the standby server using the `with standby` option. As you have learned, this option will restore the database in such a way that users can connect to the database for read-only operations, but cannot write, and will also leave the database in an unrecovered state so that additional backup sets can be restored to it.

As work progresses, throughout the day you will perform Transaction Log backups on the production server and restore them to the standby server. Each time you restore a Transaction Log, you will again use the `with standby` option.

TIP: A standby server is only as up to date as your backup and restore processes. If you do both backups and restores every hour, then the standby server will never be more than an hour out of date. However, for some enterprises, mission-critical data must be backed up more frequently—and using the technique detailed in this section can cause significant impacts to performance in such an environment. In such cases, other solutions, like clustered servers, are more appropriate.

If the production server crashes, or needs to be taken offline for any reason, you can bring the standby server into a state of complete readiness by completing a final restoration wherein you do *not* use the `with standby` option. For example, assume that you have created a standby server for the database TESTDB. You have the server online and it is sharing the network load for read-only operations. Now, assume that the production server has just crashed.

To bring the standby server online as the production server, you would complete the following steps:

1. Restore the most recent available backup to the standby server (do not use the `with standby` option).

2. Rename the standby server to the name of the production server.

3. Restart the standby server.

When the original production server is repaired, you can choose to repeat the steps on the original production server, or you can leave the standby server in place as the production server and make the original production server the new standby server. This choice will depend on the equality of computer hardware that is available in both machines, and perhaps some other organizationally specific considerations.

No matter how you decide to proceed with the servers, you should always start the standby server over again from scratch. Begin with a new full backup of the database, which you then restore to the standby server using the `with standby` option.

SUMMARY

In this chapter, you have learned to restore databases to SQL Server. You learned how to control the restore process using Enterprise Manager and Transact-SQL. You learned the syntax for the `RESTORE DATABASE` statement and how to create a standby server. In the next chapter, you will focus on monitoring your server. You will learn how to identify problems and forecast future needs. Because knowing how your server is performing will affect plans that are in place as well as those planned for the future, you will be able to include monitoring and statistical information in your overall plan and create a secure, dependable SQL Server deployment with growth potential.

CHAPTER 8

Monitoring and Optimization

Now that we have considered and discussed many of the issues that you will encounter in the design and subsequent maintenance of the data on your server, let us move on to concerning ourselves—at least for this chapter—with maintenance and performance of the server itself. Needless to say, while SQL Server will almost always execute quickly and efficiently out of the box—with few users, small tables, and so on—as your installation gets more substantial, you are likely to encounter performance issues regarding speed, size, and resources. Managing these issues and ensuring that performance is at the level your enterprise requires are two of the most important ongoing tasks you will face as a DBA.

While the most important optimization of your SQL Server will occur at the development level—through addressing a series of design issues that we will discuss briefly toward the end of the chapter—many of those issues are outside your direct control. In most environments, you have little ability to manage the way your developers design applications. You will, however, have extensive control over the running of the SQL Server itself. In this chapter, we look at the various ways that you will monitor the performance of your SQL Server, and also the various steps you will likely go through to optimize it so that it performs at the best possible levels. We will begin with a discussion of configuration issues, and then move on to an in-depth discussion of reasons to monitor SQL Server and common locations where performance is degraded.

CONFIGURATION ISSUES

Configuring the SQL Server correctly will provide you with performance benefits—though the benefits might not necessarily be terribly substantial. In a typical environment, you might see only a 5 percent performance increase from a reasonable configuration. By contrast, a misconfigured server might not only suffer from degraded performance, but at times might not work correctly at all. Effective and proper configuration is a key issue for proper server design.

Windows 2000 Configuration Settings

As mentioned previously, and as you might imagine from your own experience, a badly configured SQL Server can destroy the performance of your data storage as well as any applications running on the server. For example, a system with an incorrectly configured memory setting can break an application—because memory is not available to support it. SQL Server dynamically adjusts the most important configuration settings on your behalf.

In fact, unless you have a particularly compelling reason to do otherwise, you should generally accept these default configurations. In certain cases, adjusting the settings manually, rather than letting the SQL Server dynamically adjust them, might lead to minor performance improvements. However, your optimization time is generally better spent on application and database design, replication management, indexing, query tuning, and other such activities. Determining what configuration settings you might want to change requires a high familiarity with your environment; however, we will consider the most important settings in the following sections.

Task Management

As any good book on Windows 2000 Server management will tell you, the operating system processes threads of execution based on *priority settings* for the threads. Each thread has a base priority that is determined by the priority level of the process in which the thread is running. However, Windows 2000 will also dynamically adjust the priority level of each thread based on other considerations, such as whether the thread is responsible for input/output processing. One of the most common priority adjustments that Windows 2000 will automatically make on your behalf is to adjust the thread priority of the current foreground application to a higher level than the thread priority of background services.

While this setting is often appropriate, it is not appropriate in situations—such as the one you are likely to have on your SQL Server installation—where a server service is the primary application running on the server machine. In such cases, you will want to eliminate the favoring of foreground applications over background services. The SQL Server installation program will automatically make this adjustment on your behalf; however, you will often want to check this setting from time to time to ensure that no one in your organization has intentionally or inadvertently changed it, to the detriment of your SQL Server's performance.

To check or change the value of this configuration setting, right-click the My Computer icon on your Desktop. From the quick menu select Properties. In the System Properties dialog box on the Advanced tab, click Performance Options. Windows 2000 will display a Performance Options dialog box. Click the radio button Background Services.

Location of the System's Paging File

Whenever possible, you should place the Windows 2000 paging file on a different drive from those that contain the SQL Server files—both system files and data files. This particular choice is critical to performance if your system will be paging heavily—that is, if it does not have much physical memory. On the other hand, adding more memory to the system is often a better choice—and, if you find that your server is paging heavily, almost a mandatory one.

Additionally, you can change the SQL Server memory configuration settings to greatly reduce the amount of paging your system is doing. You can never eliminate paging on a Windows 2000 Server completely because the system will use available physical memory for paging disk I/O requests.

TIP: While the amount of memory to deploy with your SQL Server will be a direct function of the amount of traffic received by the server, we would not recommend deploying a server for any real-world implementation without at least 512MB of RAM. In the majority of the installations we have been working with, we have deployed at least 1GB of on-board RAM.

File System Selection

Whether you choose to use FAT or NTFS as your underlying file system will typically not have substantial impact on the performance of your SQL Server installation—at least not as it relates to speed.

However, the additional robustness and security features of NTFS will generally make it the optimal choice for your SQL Server installation. While most people do not necessarily consider the underlying stability of the files that make up a program as part of its optimization and performance, you can quickly change your tune if someone inadvertently deletes files on the server, making it not run correctly. NTFS security measures can help to protect against such risks.

Nonessential Services

One of the biggest issues we find in SQL Server performance is the existence and execution of nonessential services on the SQL machine. Such services will add overhead to the system and use resources that Windows 2000 could otherwise devote to the SQL Server itself. As a good starting point, do not use the SQL Server as a domain controller for your network. Moreover, do not use it as a group file or print server, Web server, or any other service that requires substantial network traffic and user communications.

In addition to such major server products (other good examples include Microsoft Message Queue (MSMQ) server and Microsoft Transaction Server (MTS) as well as any of the other Web-based Microsoft server products), you should also consider disabling the Alerter, Computer Browser, Messenger, and Task Scheduler services that Windows 2000 enables by default but that SQL Server does not require to execute properly.

Network Protocols

Finally, as far as Windows 2000 configuration settings are concerned, you should check and monitor the number of protocols that Windows 2000 supports for the server in question. You should run only the network protocols that you actually *need* for connectivity. Running multiple protocols will add additional overhead to the server and slow down the processing of the SQL Server. In most networks, TCP/IP and NetBEUI are the only required protocols; however, some mixed networks might also require that you install such additional protocols as NWLink and AppleTalk.

SQL Server Configuration Settings

As you might expect, changing configuration settings on the SQL Server itself can have an even more substantial impact on the performance of the server. Once again, SQL Server handles most of the default configuration for you and maintains the configuration throughout much of its lifetime. SQL Server has only 11 configuration options that are not considered "advanced," and none of these configuration options has any direct impact on performance. However, to view the advanced options—which will have direct impact on performance—you need to change the value of the Show Advanced Options setting, which you can do from Transact-SQL using the following code:

```
EXEC sp_configure 'show advanced options', 1
GO
RECONFIGURE
GO
```

You should change configuration options on the SQL Server only when you have a clear reason to do so. Moreover, you should closely monitor the effects of each change to determine whether the change improved or degraded performance. Always make and monitor changes one at a time.

The following sections consider the different configuration options that you can control from the SQL Server Properties dialog box, which you can display by right-clicking on the SQL Server in Enterprise Manager and choosing Properties from the pop-up menu. The sections are in the order, from left to right and front to back, of the option tabs on the dialog box.

The server-wide options that we discuss in the following sections are all set using the SP_CONFIGURE stored procedure. Many of them can also be set from within the SQL Enterprise Manager, but there is no single dialog box within the Enterprise Manager from which all configuration settings can be changed, or, for that matter, even viewed. However, most of the options that can be changed from within the SQL Server Enterprise Manager are controlled from one of the Properties tabs in the Properties dialog box, as mentioned previously.

TIP: If you use the `SP_CONFIGURE` stored procedure to change server settings, no changes will take effect until the `RECONFIGURE` command (or `RECONFIGURE WITH OVERRIDE`, in some cases) is issued on the server. Some changes will take effect immediately on reconfiguration, but the others will not take effect until the server is restarted. If an option's `run_value` and `config_value` as displayed by `SP_CONFIGURE` are different, then the server must be restarted for the `config_value` to take effect.

Obviously, we will not look at every configuration option in the following sections—other parts of this book have evaluated many of those options. Instead, we will focus on what the impact of setting many of the options will be on server performance. Furthermore, in general, we will spend most of this space discussing settings you *should not* change, and why doing otherwise can have a substantial negative impact on performance. Some of these options, for example, are resource settings that relate to performance only in that they consume memory. However, if you configure the options too high, they can rob the system of necessary memory for effective performance and substantially degrade the results you get from your server. Keep in mind that SQL Server automatically sets almost all the options discussed in the following sections, and your applications will, as a rule, work quite well without your ever looking at the settings, let alone modifying them.

Memory Options for the SQL Server

In previous versions of SQL Server, you had to manually configure memory usage. However, like so many other improvements, this is no longer the case in SQL Server 2000. In previous chapters, you have looked at the different ways in which SQL Server allocates memory, and when data is read from or written to the disk. But we did not discuss how much memory SQL Server actually uses for these various purposes or how to monitor the amount of the system's memory resources used by SQL Server.

Min Server Memory and Max Server Memory

By default, the SQL Server will automatically adjust the total amount of memory resources that it will use. However, you can use the Min Server Memory and Max Server Memory configuration options to take manual control of memory allocations. The default setting for Min Server Memory is 0MB, and the default setting for Max Server Memory is 2147483647 (bytes). If you use the SP_CONFIGURE stored procedure to change both of these options to the same value, you basically take control and tell the SQL Server to use a fixed memory size. Performing such a step will mimic the memory configuration behavior found in earlier versions of SQL Server. You can also use the SQL Server Enterprise Manager to set a minimum and maximum value for memory, using the Memory tab of the SQL Server Properties dialog box.

From within the Properties dialog box, you can set the minimum and maximum memory values using the slider bars displayed under the Memory tab. Note that the maximum amount of memory available for use is slightly less than the amount of physical memory available in the machine. The absolute maximum value (which corresponds to the default maximum value) is actually the largest value that can be stored in the Integer field of the Sysconfigures table. It is not related to the actual resources of your system. You can select a separate option button to indicate that you want to use a fixed size. Setting the minimum and maximum sliders to the same value has the identical effect.

Set Working Set Size

The Memory tab also includes a checkbox labeled Reserve Physical Memory for SQL Server. Selecting this checkbox is the equivalent to setting the configuration option Set Working Set Size to a value of 1, which reserves physical memory space for your SQL Server that is equal to the server's memory setting. Do this only if you do not want the SQL Server to dynamically adjust its memory usage. Setting the Set Working Set Size option means that the operating system does not swap out SQL Server pages even if they can be used more readily by another process when SQL Server is idle. If the Windows 2000

Virtual Memory Manager must page, it must then do so from other processes. This setting defaults to 0, which allows the Windows 2000 virtual memory manager to determine the working set size of the SQL Server.

As we have discussed previously, you should typically let the SQL Server take full control over the memory values, but if your server might be inactive for long periods of time, you can manually set Min Server Memory so that, when someone does finally submit a query, memory will already be available and allocated, ensuring that the query executes quickly. If you have other critical applications on the same server (as emphasized previously, not a recommended action), and these applications might have inactive periods, you can manually set Max Server Memory so that SQL Server will not use too much system memory and so that, when the other application becomes active again, memory will be available for it to use.

When SQL Server uses memory dynamically, the lazywriter queries the system periodically to determine the amount of free physical memory available. (We explained the lazywriter in detail in Chapter 2.) The lazywriter expands or shrinks the buffer cache to keep the operating system's free physical memory at 5MB (plus or minus 200K) to prevent paging. If less than 5MB is free, the lazywriter will release memory to the operating system that usually goes onto the free list. If more than 5MB of physical memory is free, the lazywriter will recommit memory to the buffer cache. The lazywriter recommits memory to the buffer cache only when it repopulates the free list; in other words, a server at rest does not grow its buffer cache.

SQL Server also releases memory to the operating system if it detects that too much paging is taking place. You can tell when SQL Server increases or decreases its total memory use by using the SQL Server Profiler to monitor the Server Memory Change event (in the Miscellaneous category). An event is generated whenever SQL Server's memory allocation increases or decreases by 1MB or 5 percent of the Max Server Memory, whichever is greater. You can look at the value of the data element named Event Sub Class to see whether the change was an increase or a decrease. An Event Sub Class value of 1 means a memory increase; a value of 2 means a memory decrease. We will discuss SQL Server Profiler in more detail later in this chapter.

Extended Memory Size

A third memory option, called the Extended Memory Size option, is intended for the SQL Server Enterprise Edition running under Windows 2000, which supports a full 64-bit address space. The extended memory size option refers to the Enterprise Memory Architecture (EMA), which allows memory beyond the 3GB range (or the 2GB range on Alpha processors) to be treated as a second-level cache. However, with certain hardware, you can use this feature with Windows NT 4 as well.

NOTE: In the original "beta" versions of Windows 2000, ALPHA processors were supported. However, prior to its actual release, Microsoft pulled ALPHA support.

User Connections

SQL Server 2000 dynamically adjusts the number of simultaneous connections to the server if the User Connections configuration setting is left at its default of 0. Even if you set this value to a different number, SQL Server does not actually allocate the full amount of memory needed for each user connection until a user actually connects. When SQL Server starts up, it allocates an array of pointers with as many entries as the configured value for user connections. Each entry uses less than 1,000 bytes of memory. When a user connects to SQL Server, that user is allocated 24K for three memory objects, each of which consists of a single (8K) page. These memory objects keep track of things such as the Process Status Structure (PSS) for each connection and the context area needed by the User Mode Scheduler (UMS) to keep track of the user's context as it moves the wait mode to a CPU and back again.

Needless to say, you should always let the SQL Server dynamically adjust the value of the User Connections option. If you configure the value too low, future connections will be denied access to SQL

Server. Even if you are trying to limit actual simultaneous users, this can backfire, because connections are not the same as users. One user can open multiple connections through the same application. If you are using a query tool such as the SQL Server Query Analyzer, a single user can easily have five, ten, or more connections opened at the same time. Each time the user starts a new query window with the New Query button, the client program and SQL Server will agree to open an entirely new connection for the query. Obviously, because of such performance, setting some fixed value for the number of allowable connections to the server is typically not the best idea.

Configuring Lock Settings

The Locks configuration option sets the number of available locks (of all types) for the server. The default is 0, which means that SQL Server will adjust this value dynamically. In such a case, the SQL Server will begin by allocating 2 percent of the memory allotted SQL Server to an initial pool of lock structures. When the pool of locks is exhausted, SQL Server allocates additional locks.

The dynamic lock pool does not allocate more than 40 percent of the memory available to SQL Server for itself. If too much memory is being used for locks, SQL Server will escalate row locks into table locks wherever possible to reduce the total number of locks in place. You should, therefore, leave this value at its default. If you manually supply a value for the maximum number of locks, once that number is reached, any query that executes and that requires additional locks will receive an error message, whereupon the batch will terminate.

Setting Scheduling Options

SQL Server 2000 has an algorithm for scheduling user processes that uses special UMS threads. These threads are created by using one or more Windows 2000 threads as SQL Server's own scheduler. Whether it is running in thread mode or fiber mode, SQL Server uses only one UMS thread per processor. Each SQL Server process is associated with exactly one UMS thread, and the process will remain with that thread for its lifetime. Windows 2000, in turn, will schedule each of the UMS threads on any of the available processors in the machine. Each UMS thread determines which of the SQL Server processes associated with that UMS thread should run at any given time.

The UMS, then, manages assignment of user connections to UMS threads to keep the number of users per CPU as balanced as possible. Four configuration options affect the behavior of the scheduler: Lightweight Pooling, Affinity Mask, Priority Boost, and Max Worker Threads. The following sections will examine each of these options.

Lightweight Pooling

By default, SQL Server operates in thread mode, which means that the UMS schedules Windows 2000 threads. However, SQL Server also lets user connections run in *fiber mode*, which you might use in your environment because fibers are less expensive to manage than threads. The Lightweight Pooling option has a value of 0 or 1; 1 means that SQL Server should run in fiber mode. Using fibers can yield a minor performance advantage, perhaps as much as a 5 percent increase in throughput when all the available CPUs on the server are operating at 100 percent. However, the tradeoff is that certain operations, such as running queries on linked servers or executing extended stored procedures, must run in thread mode. The cost of switching from fiber to thread mode for those connections can be noticeable, and in some cases can offset any benefit of operating in fiber mode.

If you are running in an environment with multiple CPUs, all of which are operating at 100 percent capacity, and if Performance Monitor shows a lot of context switching, setting Lightweight Pooling to 1 might have some performance benefit. With a system using more than four processors, the performance improvements should be even greater.

Affinity Mask

You can use the Affinity Mask setting to bind all the threads (or fibers) handled by one UMS thread to a certain processor. You should avoid doing this because this setting prevents Windows 2000 from using whatever processor is currently most available; instead, each UMS must then schedule its threads on the same processor.

You can also use this setting to limit the number of processors that SQL Server can use. Previous versions of SQL Server had a configuration option called SMP Concurrency that specified a maximum number of processors that SQL Server would use. That option is no longer available, but if you want to test the benefit of limiting the number of processors SQL Server uses, you can use an Affinity Mask to disable the use of some of the processors. For example, on an eight-processor system, setting the Affinity Mask to 63 decimal or 00111111 binary means that SQL Server can use only processors 0 through 5. Two processors are reserved for other, non-SQL Server activity.

The Affinity Mask option was added in SQL Server version 6.5 at the request of some major customers who ran SMP hardware with more than four processors. These sites were accustomed to similar options on UNIX or mainframe systems. Most sites do not need this option. To learn more about this setting, see the SQL Server documentation contained in Books Online.

Priority Boost

If the Priority Boost setting is enabled, SQL Server runs at a higher Windows 2000 scheduling priority. The default is 0, which means that SQL Server runs at normal priority whether you are running it on a single-processor machine or on an SMP machine. Enabling the Priority Boost option will allow the SQL Server process to run at high priority. There are probably few sites or applications for which setting this option will make much difference, so we recommend leaving it alone. But if your machine is totally dedicated to running SQL Server, you might want to enable this option (set it to 1) to see for yourself. It can potentially offer a performance advantage on a heavily loaded, dedicated system. Contrary to what you might have heard, changing this setting does not make SQL Server run at the highest Windows 2000 priority (which is real-time priority).

Max Worker Threads

SQL Server uses the Windows 2000 thread services by keeping a pool of worker threads (or fibers) that take requests off the queue. It attempts to evenly divide the worker threads among the UMS schedulers so that the number of threads available to each UMS is the setting of Max Worker Threads divided by the number of CPUs. With 100 or fewer users, there are usually as many worker threads as active users (not just connected users who are idle). With more users, it often makes sense to have fewer worker threads than active users. Although some user requests have to wait for a worker thread to become available, total throughput increases because less context switching occurs.

The Max Worker Threads setting is somewhat auto-configured. The default is 255; however, that does not mean that 255 worker threads are in the pool. It means that if a connection is waiting to be serviced and no thread is available, a new thread is created if the thread total is currently below 255. If this setting is configured to 255 but the highest number of simultaneously executing commands is, say, 125, the actual number of worker threads will not exceed 125. It might be less than that because SQL Server destroys and trims away worker threads that are no longer being used. You should probably leave this setting alone if your system is handling 100 or fewer simultaneous connections. In that case, the worker thread pool will not be greater than 100.

Even systems that handle 4,000 or more connected users run fine with the default setting of 255. When thousands of users are simultaneously connected, the actual worker thread pool is usually well below 255 since, from the back-end database's perspective, most connections are idle—even though the user might be doing plenty of work on the front end.

Disk I/O Options

No options are available for controlling SQL Server's disk read behavior. All the tuning options to control read ahead behavior that was included in previous versions of SQL Server are now handled completely internally. Two options are available to control disk write behavior. One controls the number of simultaneous write requests that can be issued, and the other controls the frequency with which the checkpoint process writes to disk.

max async IO

The Max Async IO option controls how many outstanding I/O operations SQL Server can have at a time. This number is specific to the speed of the I/O system of the hardware. The default setting of 32 is reasonable for most systems, but it is too low for systems with good I/O subsystems and high OLTP transaction rates. As usual, you should not change the default capriciously, but this setting probably warrants changing for such systems.

This setting governs the checkpoint, lazywriter, and recovery processes, since only during these operations do multiple outstanding I/O operations come into play. During the checkpoint process, large numbers of pages might need to be flushed. Recall that asynchronous I/O is never used for writing to the log, because write-ahead logging demands synchronous I/O to ensure recoverability. If you have a fast RAID (redundant array of independent disks) system and your checkpoint process flushes many pages (that is, if you have a high OLTP-type application), you can change this value and then measure the difference by monitoring the throughput of your application or benchmark test. (The SQL Server Benchmark Kit is a good proxy test for this setting, since this setting is more a function of what your hardware can handle rather than specific to your application. You can download the kit from Microsoft's Web site.) You can gauge your system's effectiveness with asynchronous I/O during the checkpoint process by watching the `Checkpoint Writes/sec` counter of the `SQLServer: Buffer Manager` object.

On systems with a fast I/O subsystem—multiple disks in a fast RAID environment—a setting of 32 might be too low to fully drive the hardware's capability, but you should change the setting only if you will empirically measure the result. If you set it too high, you might flood the system and hurt throughput. The large numbers of outstanding write operations issued by a checkpoint might result in other read activity being starved. Correctly setting this value results in throttling the checkpoint process, so you should see a less than 10 percent reduction in throughput even on a heavily loaded OLTP system while the checkpoint process is active. The white paper on Microsoft's Web site entitled "Microsoft SQL Server 2000 Performance Tuning Guide" includes the following advice:

> "A general rule of thumb for setting Max Async I/O for SQL Server running on larger disk subsystems is to multiply the number of physical drives available to do simultaneous I/O by 2 or 3. Then watch Performance Monitor for signs of disk activity or queuing issues. The negative impact of setting this configuration option too high is that it might cause Checkpoint to monopolize disk subsystem bandwidth that is required by other SQL Server I/O operations, such as reads."

Recovery Interval

The Recovery Interval option can be automatically configured. SQL Server setup sets it to 0, which means auto-configuration. In the current version, this means a recovery time of less than one minute, but that might change in later releases or service packs. This option lets the DBA control the checkpoint frequency by specifying the maximum number of minutes that recovery should take.

In earlier versions of SQL Server, the recovery interval was set in terms of minutes. In those versions, the default value was 5. In practice, this meant a checkpoint every 30,000 log records, which was almost always much less than every five minutes because the implementation was not scaled for today's faster systems. In SQL Server 7, recovery is more likely to match the Recovery Interval option, assuming that the system was busy before it came down. For databases with more than 20MB of log records, the Recovery Interval directly corresponds to the checkpoint frequency. Thus, a Recovery Interval of 5 means that checkpoints occur only every five minutes and all "dirty" pages are written to disk.

Query Processing Options

SQL Server 2000 introduces several options for controlling the resources available for processing queries. As with all the other tuning options, your best bet is to leave these options at their default values unless thorough testing indicates that a change might help.

Min Memory per Query

When a query requires additional memory resources, the number of pages it gets is determined partly by the Min Memory Per Query option. This minimum memory value for the sort is specified in kilobytes. Most people think this option is relevant only for sort operations that specifically request sorting through the use of an ORDER BY clause, but it also applies to the internal memory needed by merge join operations and by hash merge and hash grouping operations. In SQL Server 2000, sort and hash operations receive memory in a much more dynamic fashion than in previous versions, so you rarely need to adjust this value.

In fact, on larger machines, your sort and hash queries typically get much more than the Min Memory Per Query setting so that you will not restrict yourself unnecessarily. If you need to do a lot of hashing or sorting, however, and you have few users or a lot of available memory, you might improve performance by adjusting this value. On smaller machines, setting this value too high can cause virtual memory to page, which hurts server performance.

Query Wait

The Query Wait option controls how long a query that needs additional memory waits, if that memory is not available. A setting of –1 means that the query waits 25 times the estimated execution time of the query. A value of 0 or more specifies the number of seconds that a query waits. If the wait time is exceeded, SQL Server generates error 8645:

```
Server: Msg 8645, Level 17, State 1, Line 1
A time out occurred while waiting for memory resources to
execute the query. Re-run the query.
```

Even though memory is allocated dynamically, SQL Server can still run out of memory if the memory resources on the machine are exhausted. If your queries time out with error 8645, you can try increasing the paging file size on the server or even adding more physical memory to the server. You can also try tuning the query by creating more useful indexes so that hash or merge operations are not needed.

Index Create Memory

The Min Memory Per Query option applies only to sorting and hashing used during query execution; it does not apply to the sorting that takes place during index creation. Another option, Index Create Memory, lets you allocate a specific amount of memory for index creation. Its value is also specified in kilobytes.

Query Governor Cost Limit

You can use the Query Governor Cost Limit option to set a maximum length of time that a query will run. SQL Server will not execute queries that the optimizer estimates will take longer than this. The option is specified in seconds, but it might not map exactly to seconds on your machine. You should think of the value as an abstract cost of the query rather than an actual number of seconds. The cost figure was correlated to seconds on one test machine in the SQL Server development group, and no information is available on the exact specs of that machine.

You can come up with your own correlation using SQL Server Profiler. If you capture the Misc: Execution Plan events, the data element called Binary Data reflects the optimizer's estimated cost for each SQL statement. This value is compared to the Query Governor Cost Limit value. If you then also capture the Duration data for each SQL statement, you can compare the estimated cost with the actual duration. For example, if on the average, queries that show a cost (in the SQL Server Profiler trace) of 8 seconds actually take instead 10 seconds to run, you should specify a Query Governor Cost Limit of about 80 percent of what you will really allow. If you want to block all queries that are estimated to take longer than 1 minute to run, you should set the option to 48 (80 percent of 60 seconds). We will look at SQL Server Profiler in more detail later in this chapter.

Max Degree of Parallelism and Cost Threshold for Parallelism

Version 7.5 of Microsoft SQL Server lets you run certain kinds of complex queries simultaneously on two or more processors. The queries must lend themselves to being executed in sections. Here's an example:

```
SELECT avg(charge_amt), category
FROM charge
GROUP BY category
```

If the `charge` table has 100,000 rows and there are 10 different values for `category`, SQL Server can split the rows into groups and have only a subset of the groups processed on each processor. For example, with a 4-CPU machine, categories 1 through 3 can be averaged on the first processor, categories 4 through 6 on the second processor, categories 7 and 8 on the third, and categories 9 and 10 on the fourth. Each processor can come up with averages for only its groups, and the separate averages are brought together for the final result.

During query optimization, SQL Server looks for queries that might benefit from parallel execution. It inserts exchange operators into the query execution plan to prepare the query for parallel execution. An exchange operator is an operator in a query execution plan that provides process management, data redistribution, and flow control. The two main types of exchange operators that you will observe if parallel plans are generated are the *distribute* operator, which separates the processing into multiple streams, and the *gather* operator, which retrieves the separate results and combines them into a single result. Occasionally, you will also see a *redistribute* operator if the original streams need to be moved onto different processors at some point during the processing. Once exchange operators are inserted, the result is a parallel query execution plan.

A parallel query execution plan can use more than one thread; a serial execution plan, which is used by a nonparallel query, uses only a single thread. The actual number of threads used by a parallel query is determined at query plan execution initialization and is called the *degree of parallelism*. Even though a parallel plan might be developed, at execution time SQL Server might decide not to use it.

Data modification statements are always carried out on a single processor, but the search portion of the UPDATE, DELETE, and INSERT statements (in which SQL Server determines which rows to modify) might still be performed in parallel. In addition, even if the query is a SELECT query, parts of it might run single-threaded within a parallel plan.

SQL Server automatically determines the best degree of parallelism for each instance of a parallel query execution by considering the following:

▼ *Is SQL Server running on a computer with more than one processor?* (Only computers with more than one processor can take advantage of parallel queries.)

■ *How many concurrent users are active on the server?* SQL Server monitors its CPU use and adjusts the degree of parallelism at query startup time. It chooses lower degrees of parallelism if the CPUs are already busy. Parallel queries are valuable only if few users are on the system. Once a parallel query starts running, it consumes most of the CPU resources until it has completed.

■ *Is sufficient memory available for parallel query execution?* Each query requires a certain amount of memory to execute. Executing a parallel query requires more memory than a nonparallel query. The amount of memory required for executing a parallel query is equivalent to the amount of memory required for serial query execution multiplied by the degree of parallelism. If the memory requirement of the parallel plan cannot be satisfied, SQL Server automatically executes the serial plan for the corresponding query.

■ *What type of query is being executed?* Queries that consume a lot of CPU cycles are the best candidates for a parallel query (for example, joins of large tables, substantial aggregations, and sorting of large result sets). With simple queries, which are often found in transaction processing applications, the additional coordination required to execute a query in parallel outweighs the potential performance boost.

▲ *Are a sufficient number of rows processed in the given stream?*
If the query optimizer determines that the number of rows in a stream is too low, it does not introduce exchange operators to distribute the stream.

Once a query starts executing on multiple threads for parallel execution, the query uses the same number of threads until completion. SQL Server re-examines the optimal number of thread decisions each time a parallel query execution plan is retrieved from the cache. One execution of a query can result in the use of a single thread, and another execution of the same query (at a different time) can result in using two or more threads.

Two configuration options are available for controlling parallel queries. The Max Degree of Parallelism option indicates the maximum number of processors that are used to run queries in parallel. The default value of 0 means that SQL Server should use the number of available CPUs. A value of 1 means that SQL Server should suppress parallelism completely. Any other value restricts the degree of parallelism below the number of CPUs. If your computer has only one processor, the Max Degree of Parallelism value is ignored.

The second configuration option for controlling parallelism is Cost Threshold for Parallelism. You can specify that SQL Server should not even consider a parallel plan for a query with an estimated cost lower than this threshold. The unit of costing is the same one used by the Query Governor Cost Limit option. The default of five seconds is fine for most systems.

Be careful when you use either of these configuration options—they have server-wide impact. You can also use trace flag 8687 to turn off parallelism for individual connections. SQL Server Profiler lets you trace the degree of parallelism for each query captured. If you choose to monitor events in the SQL Operators category (DELETE, INSERT, SELECT, or UPDATE), the Event Sub Class data is a number indicating the degree of parallelism for that query. The values in the following table are possible for the Event Sub Class value for the SQL Operators events:

Value	Meaning
0	No parallelism was considered; for example, the computer executing the query contains only one processor or the estimated cost of the query execution is lower than the Cost Threshold for Parallelism value.
1	Parallel execution was considered, but the query was executed using a serial plan, because a parallel execution plan would have required an unavailable amount of resources.
>1	A portion of the query has been executed using a parallel execution plan with the degree of parallelism indicated by the value. Higher values mean greater parallelism.

Database Options

Several database options can affect performance. The Read Only and Single User options affect performance because they eliminate locking in some cases. If your database is used only for decision support (for example, a data mart), it might make sense to set your database to Read Only, as follows:

```
EXEC sp_dboption 'dbname', 'read only', TRUE
```

In this way, no locking is performed in the database, which has the end result of greatly reducing overhead. This option prevents changes from being made to the database. You can easily toggle it off to perform tasks such as bulk loading of data. For an operation in which the data is changed via large batch jobs that can run during off-hours and the normal workload is query only, Read Only is a good choice.

Even if your database is not Read Only, you might want to perform off-hour maintenance tasks and bulk loading operations with the Single User option enabled, as shown here:

```
EXEC sp_dboption 'dbname', 'single user', TRUE
```

This option also eliminates the need for locking, since only one connection can use the database at a time. Of course, you need locking to make a multiple-user system behave like a single-user system. But in this case, it *is* a single-user system, so locking is not required. If you need to do a big bulk load and index creation at night while no one else is using the system, you can eliminate the need to take locks during the bulk load.

Two other options are particularly useful if you are running the SQL Server Desktop Edition on a small machine and your resources are extremely limited: Auto-Close and Auto-Shrink. The Auto-Close option causes the database to shut down cleanly and free resources after the last user exits. By default, it is set to TRUE for all databases when SQL Server runs on Windows 95 or Windows 98. The database reopens automatically when a user tries to use the database. The Auto-Shrink option can be useful if your disk space resources are extremely limited, though there is a performance tradeoff. Shrinking a database is a CPU-intensive operation and takes a long time. Moreover, all indexes on heaps affected by the shrink must be adjusted because the row locators change.

Finally, two database options control the automatic gathering of statistics: Auto-Create Statistics and Auto-Update Statistics.

Buffer Manager Options

As you have seen previously, the Buffer Manager (also known as the Cache Manager) uses a queue of "favored pages," which you can think of as a *least-recently-used* (LRU) algorithm, but no queue list of buffers is maintained in the order of most recent access. You can use the Pintable option to directly influence the favoring behavior.

Pinning a Table in the Cache

You can permanently remove a table from the queue of pages examined by the lazywriter so that once the pages are read into the data cache, they are never forced from cache. (This favors them permanently, though it is really more than that: They are entirely exempted.) You can enable this option using the SP_TABLEOPTION stored procedure with the Pintable option.

This option is not appropriate for most sites. But if you get very random cache hits and you have some relatively small tables that are hot (that is, getting a substantial amount of traffic) compared to other larger tables, this option might be beneficial. If those small, hot tables keep getting forced out by the random access to larger tables and if you have plenty of memory, you can pin those small tables. By pinning, you override the Buffer Manager. But you take away the pages in cache used for that table, so you give the Buffer Manager less memory to work with. Pinning the table does not initially read it in; pinning just makes the table "sticky" so that once a page of the table is in the cache, it does not get forced out. If you want the table preloaded and sticky, you can enable the option and then do SELECT * FROM table to read all the pages into cache. (The table should not be so big that you eat up more memory than your system can afford to use.)

Monitoring Buffer Manager Performance

Two DBCC commands exist to monitor the performance of the Buffer Manager; they are known as SQLPERF(WAITSTATS) and SQLPERF(LRUSTATS). The DBCC SQLPERF(WAITSTATS) command not only provides an overview of the Buffer Manager, it also helps identify where a transaction is delayed. It shows the total milliseconds of wait time and how much of the time is due to waiting for reads, waiting for different types of locks, waiting to add a log record to the log buffer, and waiting for log buffers to be physically written. The command DBCC SQLPERF(LRUSTATS) gives details on the lazywriter and the state of the cache, such as the cache-hit ratio, the size of the cache, the average number of pages scanned to find an available buffer, and the number of free pages. Although this information is available through the Performance Monitor, the DBCC

SQLPERF command lets you capture the output to a table and save the data for analysis.

For example, to capture the DBCC SQLPERF(WAITSTATS) output, you can create a table with four columns and use the dynamic EXECUTE command to populate the table. The following script shows one way to define and populate such a table. It actually adds a fifth column to the table, which indicates the current date and time that the rows were inserted into the table.

```
CREATE TABLE waitstats
    (
        wait_type       varchar (20),
        requests        numeric(10,0),
        wait_time       numeric(12,2),
        signal_wait     numeric(12,0),
        recorded_time   datetime DEFAULT getdate()
    )
GO
INSERT INTO waitstats
(wait_type, requests, wait_time, signal_wait)
    EXEC ('DBCC SQLPERF(WAITSTATS)')
```

Startup Parameters on SQLSERVR.EXE

You can alter startup parameters used by the SQL Server process to tune performance by disabling the performance statistics collection or specifying trace flags.

Disabling the Performance Collection

Normally, SQL Server keeps performance statistics such as CPU usage and amount of I/O on a per-user basis. The values are materialized in the Sysprocesses table (really just memory) when queried. If you never query or monitor these values, the work to keep track of them is unnecessary. You can eliminate the calls that produce these performance statistics by passing the -*x* startup flag to SQLSERVR.EXE. Or, you can add -*x* as an additional parameter from the Setup program via the Set Server Options dialog box.

Specifying Trace Flags

We have discussed the use of trace flags several times, and we have seen how to enable them using DBCC TRACEON. You can also specify a trace flag at server startup; some trace flags make the most sense if they are specified server-wide rather than on a per-user basis. For example, trace flag 1204, which records information to the error log when a deadlock occurs, does not make sense for a specific connection because you probably have no idea ahead of time which connections will encounter deadlocks. To enable a trace flag server-wide, you add the flag as a parameter when you start SQL Server from the command line (for example, sqlservr.exe -c -t1204).

To support tracing on a per-user basis, a flag in the PSS must also be set to enable any of the trace flags that are tested with the original (non-user-specific) TRACE macro. Each place in the code that tests for these trace flags first determines whether the PSS flag is set before testing the trace-flag array. Many trace flags (such as 1081) do not make sense on a per-user basis. If you specify a lowercase *t*, SQL Server skips the per-user test to determine whether the trace flag is enabled. Using an uppercase *T* sets the PSS flag and requires per-user checking. A lowercase *t* flag is not enabled unless at least one uppercase *T* is also set or until some connection executes a DBCC TRACEON with -1 (which means that it is set for all connections).

System Maintenance

SQL Server requires much less regular system maintenance than most comparable products. (For example, because pages are automatically split, it maintains data clustering characteristics; most products that support data clustering make you do data reorganization to keep the data clustered.) However, you should perform a couple of regular maintenance tasks for performance reasons. You can easily schedule these tasks (such as updating statistics and rebuilding your clustered index) using SQL Executive or the Database Maintenance Plan Wizard.

When tuning queries, index distribution statistics are crucial. If you have not enabled automatic updating of statistics, you should update statistics frequently so that any significant changes in the volumes or distribution of data are reflected. Although it is not essential to dump and reload tables to keep clustering properties intact, it can be useful to rebuild tables to re-establish fill factors and avoid page splits. The simple way that you can do this is by rebuilding the clustered index on the table using the DROP_EXISTING option that we have discussed previously. Using this option, the existing nonclustered indexes will not have to be re-created, since the clustering key will stay the same. You can also use the DBCC DBREINDEX command to rebuild all the indexes on a table. Rebuilding the clustered index helps keep a table from becoming fragmented and makes read ahead more effective. You can use DBCC SHOWCONTIG to determine how contiguous a table is. Of course, you should also regularly do other tasks, such as performing backups and periodically checking the structural integrity of the database (for example, by using DBCC CHECKDB), but these are not performance-related tasks.

MONITORING SYSTEM BEHAVIOR

Throughout this book, we have looked at statements that are useful for monitoring some aspect of SQL Server's performance. These include procedures such as SP_WHO2, SP_LOCK, SET SHOWPLAN_TEXT ON, DBCC SQLPERF, and various trace flags for analyzing deadlock issues. SQL Server Enterprise Manager provides a graphical display that is a combination of SP_WHO2 and SP_LOCK, and you should make use of it. In addition, two other tools let you monitor the behavior of your SQL Server system: SQL Server Profiler and Performance Monitor.

SQL SERVER PROFILER

SQL Server Profiler was included with SQL Server 7.0. It looks similar to the SQL Trace tool in version 6.5, but it has far greater capabilities. SQL Trace was basically an "ODS sniffer," which itself was based on an earlier freeware product called SQLEye. SQLEye was essentially a filter that listened on the network using the ODS API for all the batches that were sent to a specified SQL Server. When SQLEye received an incoming batch, it could apply one of several filters to it and record in a file all batches that satisfied the filters' conditions. In version 6.5, the same developer who wrote SQLEye put a GUI wrapper around its configuration and specification commands and created the SQL Trace tool.

Because SQL Trace worked only at the ODS layer, it could capture only the commands that were actually being sent to SQL Server. Once SQL Server received the command, SQL Trace had no further knowledge of what SQL Server did with it. For example, if a client connection sent a batch to SQL Server that consisted of only a stored procedure call, that is all SQL Trace could capture and record. It could not record all the statements that were executed within the stored procedure, and it had no knowledge of other procedures that were called by the original stored procedure.

SQL Server Profiler belongs to a new generation of profiling tools. Not only can it keep track of every statement executed and every statement within every stored procedure, it can keep track of every time a table is accessed, every time a lock is acquired, and every time an error occurs. In fact, it can capture 68 predefined events, and you can configure five additional events of your own.

SQL Server Profiler relies on the concept of events. Event producers write to queues maintained by SQL Server. Event consumers read events off of the queues. (Event *producers* are server components such as the lock manager, Buffer Manager, and ODS, which generate the events recorded in the queue.)

SQL Server Profiler is more than just the user interface that is available through the SQL Server Profiler icon. You use the interface for defining traces from a client machine, watching the events recorded by those client-side traces, and replaying traces. SQL Server Profiler can also define server-side traces that run invisibly, using extended stored procedures. One of the advantages of server-side traces is that they can be configured to start automatically. We will see more on server-side traces later.

Defining a Trace

We will look at how to define a trace by using the SQL Server Profiler interface, but the details regarding the types of events, data elements available, and filters are equally applicable to server-side traces defined using the extended stored procedures. To start a new trace, choose New from SQL Server Profiler's File menu. You will see a dialog box with four tabs for defining the trace properties.

You can define a trace as either shared or private. A private trace is available only to the operating system user (as opposed to the SQL Server user) who created it. Private and shared traces defined in the SQL Server Profiler interface are available only on the client machine on which they were defined, but you can export the definition to another client machine. Import and Export options are available from the File menu. You can specify where you want the captured information to be saved. The captured events are always displayed in the SQL Server Profiler user interface, and when you define client-side traces, you cannot turn this off. In addition, you can save the events to either a file or a table within SQL Server. If you save to a table, the table is created automatically, with the appropriate columns defined to hold the data values that are being collected.

On the Events tab of the Trace Properties dialog box, you can select from the 68 available events, which are grouped into 12 categories. You can select an entire category or select events from within a category. The online documentation gives a complete description of each event.

On the Data Columns tab, you can specify which data items you want to record for each event. For example, you might want to keep track of only the SQL Server user, the application being used, and the text of the SQL statement being executed. Or, you might want to record performance information such as the duration of the event, the table or index accessed, the severity of an error, and the start and end times of the event. Three data elements—Binary Data, Integer Data, and Event Sub Class—have different meanings depending on what event is being captured. For example, if you are capturing the Execution Plan event, Binary Data reflects the estimated cost of the query and Integer Data reflects the estimate of the number of rows to be returned. If you are capturing the Server Memory event, Event Sub Class data can be 1, which means that the server memory was increased, or 2, which means it was decreased. The Integer Data column reflects the new memory size. Not all events have meaningful values for every possible data element. Again, full details are available in the online documentation.

TIP: By default, you do not see all 68 events and 13 data elements listed in the Trace Properties dialog box. You see only a subset of the events and data elements. To see the complete list, you must close the dialog box and choose Tools | Options. Select the All Event Classes and All Data Columns option buttons.

On the Filters tab of the Trace Properties dialog box, you can filter out events that are not of interest. Three types of filters are available—name filters, range filters, and ID filters. Each possible data element can be filtered in only one of the three ways.

You use a name filter to include or exclude specific values. Typically, values entered in the Include box override values entered in the Exclude box. For example, if you enter **MS SQL Query Analyzer** in the Include box, you capture only events that originate through the Query Analyzer. All other events are ignored, regardless of what you entered in the Exclude box. The exception is when you use wildcards. You can enter **%SQL Server%** in the Include box to include all applications whose name includes that string, and then you can exclude specific applications that include that string, such as SQL Server Profiler. By default, all traces exclude events originating from SQL Server Profiler, because typically you do not want to trace the events that are involved in the actual tracing.

A range filter takes a low value and a high value. Only events for which the filtered data element falls within the specified range are recorded. Probably the most common filter is for duration. If you are tracing your long-running queries, you are probably not interested in any queries that take less than a second to execute. You can enter 1000 (milliseconds) as the minimum duration and leave the maximum unspecified.

An ID filter lets you indicate specific values that you are interested in. For example, if you want to record only events that occur in a particular database, you can select one specific value for the Database ID filter. In the first release of SQL Server 2000, you can choose only one specific value. If you want to trace two different databases, you must set up two separate traces. One of the data elements that allows an ID filter is the Object ID that an event is affecting (that is, the table being updated). If you want to record Object ID information but are not interested in when system tables are accessed, you can select a special checkbox for that purpose. You can either record events dealing with one specific Object ID or you can select the checkbox to indicate that you want all objects except the system tables.

The SQL Server online documentation provides full details of all the filters and which data elements allow which of the three types of filters.

Information gathered by SQL Server Profiler can be extremely useful for tracking all kinds of performance problems. By saving the captured events to a table, you can analyze usage patterns and query behavior using Transact-SQL stored procedures. By saving your captured events to a file, you can copy that file to another machine or e-mail it to a central location (or even to your support provider).

Gathering Diagnostic Information

A lot of the information that SQL Server Profiler gathers can help you and your team of support providers troubleshoot system problems. However, this information is usually not enough by itself. Support providers need to ask a standard set of questions when the end users call. A special utility in SQL Server 2000 helps you gather this information with a single command: SQLDIAG. It can work with SQL Server Profiler if you have enabled automatic query recording, as shown here:

```
c xp_trace_setqueryhistory 1
```

This procedure tells SQL Server to automatically keep track of the most recent 100 queries in an internal ring buffer. When the 101st query is recorded, it overwrites the first, so there are never more than 100 queries in the buffer. Once enabled, it auto-starts every time SQL Server starts. The only way to stop the automatic recording of queries to the ring buffer is by running the XP_TRACE_SETQUERYHISTORY procedure with an argument of 0.

When you execute SQLDIAG from a command prompt while SQL Server is running, it gathers the following information:

▼ Text of all error logs

■ Registry information

■ DLL version information

■ The contents of MASTER.DBO.SYSPROCESSES

■ Output from the following SQL Server stored procedures: SP_CONFIGURE, SP_WHO, SP_LOCK, SP_HELPDB, XP_MSVER, and SP_HELPEXTENDEDPROC

■ Input buffer from all active processes

■ Any available deadlock information

▲ Microsoft Diagnostics Report for the server

The information is stored in a file called SQLDIAG.TXT; you can specify a different filename in the command line for SQLDIAG. Executing SQLDIAG also places the contents of the internal ring buffer containing the most recent 100 queries in the file called SQLDIAG.TRC. This is a normal SQL Server Profiler trace file that you can open and examine using SQL Server Profiler.

Obviously, if SQL Server is not running, some of the information in the above list will not be available. If SQL Server is down because of a severe system error, knowing the nature of the most recent queries could be of tremendous value. If you have enabled the ring buffer by using XP_TRACE_SETQUERYHISTORY, that information is available. Every time SQL Server encounters a system-generated error with a severity level greater than 17, it automatically dumps the contents of the ring buffer to a trace file called BLACKBOX.TRC. Thus, if the server has crashed with a severe error, you will have a record of the final moments of activity.

Note that BLACKBOX.TRC is created only if the error is system-generated. Also note that SQL Server always appends to the BLACKBOX.TRC file. If you encounter a situation in which frequent failures occur, this file will continue to grow. You must periodically delete this file or remove all its contents (perhaps after copying its contents to another location) to keep it from growing indefinitely.

If you use RAISERROR to generate an error of your own, even if you request a severity level greater than 17, BLACKBOX.TRC will not be created. However, you can use the command XP_TRACE_FLUSHQUERYHISTORY at any time to dump the ring buffer to a file of your choice. A complete description of this command is in the online documentation.

You can save and restart traces that you define by using SQL Server Profiler. You can also copy the definition to another machine and start it from the SQL Server Profiler user interface there. If you want to start a particular trace programmatically (or automatically) or to save the captured events someplace other than a SQL Server table or trace file, you must define a server-side trace using the XP_TRACE_* extended stored procedures. You can include the calls to these procedures in any SQL Server stored procedure or batch.

To define a server-side trace, client programs can use the SQL Server Profiler extended stored procedure XP_TRACE_ADDNEWQUEUE. They can use XP_TRACE_SETQUEUEDESTINATION to direct the output of the trace to one of four destinations: a file, the Windows NT application log, a table, or a forwarded server. The procedure XP_SQLTRACE is still available for backward compatibility, but the options for configuring traces using this procedure are much more limited, so you should use XP_TRACE_ADDNEWQUEUE to define a trace.

Here are the steps for defining a trace from a client application:

1. Execute XP_TRACE_ADDNEWQUEUE with the required parameters to create a trace queue and determine the columns to record. This is run once for each trace. An integer bit mask is used to specify all the data columns to be captured.

2. Execute XP_TRACE_SETEVENTCLASSREQUIRED with the required parameters to select the events to trace. This is run

once for each event class for each trace. All events in the specified event class will be captured.

3. You can optionally execute the applicable XP_TRACE_SET* extended stored procedures to set any, none, or a combination of filters.

4. Execute SP_SETQUEUEDESTINATION with the required parameters to select a consumer for the trace data. This is run once for each destination for each trace.

5. Optionally, you can execute XP_TRACE_ SAVEQUEUEDEFINITION to save the trace queue definition.

6. Execute XP_TRACE_STARTCONSUMER with the required parameters to start the consumer, which sends the trace queue information to its destination.

Here is an example that creates a queue that writes events to a file and optionally saves the trace and marks it for auto-start whenever SQL Server is restarted. (For full details on the arguments of all the extended procedure calls, see the online documentation.)

```
-- Declare variables.
declare @queue_handle int  -- queue handle to refer to this trace by
declare @column_value int  -- data column bit mask

-- Set the column mask for the data columns to capture.
SET @column_value = 1|16|32|128|512|4096|8192
-- 1 = Text data
-- 16 = Connection ID
-- 32 = Windows NT username
-- 128 = Host
-- 512 = Application name
-- 4096 = Duration
-- 8192 = Start time

-- Create a queue.
exec xp_trace_addnewqueue 1000, 5, 95, 90, @column_value,
    @queue_handle output
```

```
-- Specify the event classes to trace.
exec xp_trace_seteventclassrequired @queue_handle,
    10 ,1 -- RPC:Completed
exec xp_trace_seteventclassrequired @queue_handle,
    12 ,1 -- SQL:BatchCompleted
exec xp_trace_seteventclassrequired @queue_handle,
    14 ,1 -- Connect
exec xp_trace_seteventclassrequired @queue_handle,
    16 ,1 -- Disconnect
exec xp_trace_seteventclassrequired @queue_handle,
    17 ,1 -- ExistingConnection

-- Create a filter that omits events created by
-- SQL Server Profiler and this script from the trace.
EXEC xp_trace_setappfilter @queue_handle, NULL,
    'SQL Server Profiler%'
EXEC xp_trace_settextfilter @queue_handle, NULL,
    'EXEC xp_trace%;SET ANSI%'

-- Configure the queue to write to a file.
exec xp_trace_setqueuedestination @queue_handle, 2, 1, NULL,
    'c:\temp\test_trace1.trc'

-- Start the consumer that actually writes to the file.
exec xp_trace_startconsumer @queue_handle

-- Display the queue handle; will need it later to stop the queue.
select @queue_handle

-- Save the definition as TestTrace1.
-- exec xp_trace_savequeuedefinition @queue_handle, "TestTrace1" ,1

-- Mark it for autostart.
-- exec xp_trace_setqueueautostart "TestTrace1" ,1
```

You might find it useful to have certain traces running constantly, but be careful about the amount of information you capture. Trace files can grow quite large if they are left running the entire time SQL

Server is running. To address such problems, you might want to create a SQL batch that stops a trace if it is running and restarts it with a new filename. You can use SQL Server Agent to run the batch periodically—for example, every four hours—so that each file contains only four hours' worth of trace information.

Tuning SQL Server Profiler

SQL Server Profiler uses a "pay as you go" model. There is no overhead for events that are not captured. Most events need very few resources. SQL Server Profiler becomes expensive only if you trace all 68 event classes and capture all data from those events. Early testing shows an absolute maximum of 5 to 10 percent overhead if you capture everything. In addition, most of the performance hit is due to a longer code path; the actual resources needed to capture the event data are not particularly CPU-intensive.

You can tune the behavior and the resources required by SQL Server Profiler on the General tab of the Trace Properties dialog box. To the right of the server name is an icon of a server; if you click on that icon, you see the dialog box which shows four options. If you are defining a server-side trace using an extended procedure, these options are specified as parameters to the XP_TRACE_ADDNEWQUEUE procedure.

The Number of Rows to Buffer setting indicates the maximum number of events that can be buffered on the server queue to which the producers are writing. One consumer thread on the server consumes events to send back to whatever clients are collecting the events. The Server Timeout setting indicates when to auto-pause after a producer has been backed up.

The Boost Priority setting indicates how full (by percentage) the queue can be before a boost in priority takes place. If the queue exceeds the setting, the consumer thread priority is boosted to consume events faster. Because the consumer thread can read events faster after the priority is boosted, either the number of events in the queue decreases or the queue fills more slowly. The Reduce Priority setting is also expressed as a percentage. If the number of events drops below this level, the priority of the consuming thread will be reduced.

If the queue fills up, events back up on a producer-by-producer basis. When a producer is backed up for longer than the time-out setting, it is auto-paused and an event is written to the trace so that you know that the trace was auto-paused. Backed-up events and any events that occurred during the auto-pause are lost. When the queue opens up, producers begin producing events again. If the queue opens up before the time-out, backed-up events are written to the queue and no events are lost.

This discussion is just the tip of the iceberg as far as SQL Server Profiler is concerned. The online documentation offers much more information, but the best way to understand SQL Server Profiler's event tracing capabilities is to plunge in and start using the tool. The SQL Server Profiler user interface comes with six predefined traces, so you can run one of them while you work through examples in this book. Save the traces to files, and then reopen the files to see what kinds of replaying are possible and how you can reorganize the events to get different perspectives on your server's behavior.

PERFORMANCE MONITOR

You can use SQL Server Profiler to monitor the behavior of your server on a query-by-query or event-by-event basis. But if you want to monitor your server's performance as an entire system, the best tool is the Performance tool included with Windows 2000. This tool is extensible, which allows SQL Server to export its performance statistics so that you can monitor your entire system. That is crucial because such important statistics as CPU use must be monitored for the entire system, not just for SQL Server. In fact, many of the most important counters to watch while performance tuning SQL Server do not even belong to any of the SQL Server objects.

Traditionally, in mainframe and minicomputer systems, you had to buy a separate system monitor—at considerable expense—or use a hodgepodge of utilities, some to monitor the operating system and others to monitor the database. Then, if you worked on some other system, it lacked the same set of tools you were accustomed to using. The Windows 2000 Performance tool is based on the new Microsoft Management Console (MMC). It is simply a snap-in component.

In the SQL Server folder, click on the Performance Monitor icon to start the Performance tool with a saved PMC file that allows certain counters to be preloaded. There is no separate performance monitoring tool for use with SQL Server; the icon in the SQL Server folder calls the Windows 2000 Performance tool with a specific set of counters. You can also manually save your own settings in a PMC file and set up a shortcut in the same way.

Performance provides a huge set of counters. Probably no one understands all of them, so do not be intimidated. Peruse all the objects and counters and note which ones have separate instances. Use the Explain button for helpful information, or see the SQL Server and Windows 2000 documentation.

Performance Counters

In this section, we will look at several important counters. We will provide a brief explanation of how they can be useful and what actions you should consider based on the information they provide. Often, of course, the appropriate action is generic—for example, if CPU usage is high, you should try to reduce it.

The methods you can use to make such adjustments are varied and vast—from redesigning your application to reworking some queries, adding indexes, or getting faster or additional processors.

Processor Object's % Processor Time Counter

This counter monitors system-wide CPU usage. If you use multiple processors, you can set up an instance for each processor. Each processor's CPU usage count should be similar. If not, you should examine other processes on the system that have only one thread and are executing on a given CPU. Ideally, your system should not consistently run with CPU usage of 80 percent or more, though short spikes of up to 100 percent are normal, even for systems with plenty of spare CPU capacity. If your system runs consistently above 80 percent or will grow to that level soon, or if it frequently spikes above 90 percent and stays there for 10 seconds or longer, you should try to reduce CPU usage.

First, consider making your application more efficient. High CPU usage counts can result from just one or two problematic queries. The queries might get high cache-hit ratios but still require a large amount of logical I/O. Try to rework those queries or add indexes. If the CPU usage count continues to be high, you might consider getting a faster processor or adding processors to your system. If your system is running consistently with 100 percent CPU usage, look at specific processes to see which are consuming the CPUs. It is likely that the offending process is doing some polling or is stuck in a tight loop; if so, the application needs some work, such as adding a `sleep` invocation in some of the processes so that they release processor time on occasion.

You should also watch for excessively low CPU usage, which indicates that your system is stalled somewhere. If locking contention is occurring, your system might be running at close to 0 percent CPU usage when no productive work is happening! Very low CPU usage can be a much bigger problem than very high CPU usage. If you have poor overall throughput and low CPU usage, your application has a bottleneck somewhere and you must find and clear it.

TIP: The Task Manager (CTRL-ALT-DELETE) in Windows 2000 also provides a way to monitor CPU usage. The Task Manager is even easier to use than the Performance tool.

PhysicalDisk Object's Disk Transfers/sec Counter

This counter shows physical I/O rates for all activity on the machine. You can set up an instance for each physical disk in the system or watch it for the total of all disks. SQL Server does most I/O in 8K chunks, though read-ahead I/O is essentially done with an I/O size of 64K. Watch this counter to be sure that you are not maxing out the I/O capacity of your system or of a particular disk. The I/O capacity of disk drives and controllers varies considerably, depending on the hardware. But today's typical SCSI hard drive can do 80 to 90 random 8K reads per second, assuming that the controller can drive it that hard. If you see I/O rates approaching these rates *per drive,* you should verify that your specific hardware can sustain more.

If not, add more disks and controllers, add memory, or rework the database to try to get a higher cache-hit ratio and require less physical I/O (via better design, better indexes, possible denormalization, and so on).

To see any of the counters from the PhysicalDisk object, you must reboot your computer with the Diskperf service started. You do this from the Devices applet in the Control Panel. Find Diskperf and change its startup option to Boot; then reboot the machine. After you are done monitoring, disable Diskperf.

PhysicalDisk Object's Current Disk Queue Length Counter

This counter indicates the number of reads that are currently outstanding for a disk. Occasional spikes are OK, especially when asynchronous I/O such as a checkpoint kick in. But for the most part, the disks should not have a lot of queued I/O. Those operations, of course, must ultimately complete, so if more than one operation is queued consistently, the disk is probably overworked. You should either decrease physical I/O or add more I/O capacity.

Memory Counter Object's Pages/sec and Page Faults/sec Counter

This counter watches the amount of paging on the system. As the system settles into a steady state, you want these values to be 0—that is, no paging going on in the system. In fact, if you allow SQL Server to automatically adjust its memory usage, it will reduce its memory resources when paging occurs. You should find that any paging that does occur is not caused by SQL Server. If your system does experience regular paging, perhaps as a result of other applications running on the machine, you should consider adding more physical memory.

Process Object's % Processor Time Counter

Typically, you run this counter for the SQL Server process instance, but you might want to run it for other processes. It confirms that SQL Server (or some other process) is using a reasonable amount of CPU time. (It makes little sense to spend a lot of time reducing SQL Server's CPU usage if some other process on the machine is using the larger percentage of the CPU to drive the total CPU usage to near capacity.)

Process Object's Virtual Bytes Counter

Use this counter to see the total virtual memory being used by SQL Server, especially when a large number of threads and memory are being consumed. If this number gets too high, you might see Out of Virtual Memory errors.

Process Object's Private Bytes Counter

This counter shows the current number of bytes allocated to a process that cannot be shared with other processes. It is probably the best Performance Monitor counter for viewing the approximate amount of memory committed by any threads within the SQLSERVR.EXE process space.

Process Object's Working Set Counter

This counter shows the amount of memory recently used by a process. For the SQL Server process instance, this counter can actually be a valuable indicator of how much memory has been allocated within the SQL Server process space, especially for a dedicated server (because working-set trimming will likely not happen much). The value recorded by the working set should be very close to the value reported in the Task Manager, on the Processes tab, as the Mem Usage value for SQLSERVR.EXE. Working Set is the current memory that SQL Server (and any components loaded in it) is currently accessing. It might not reflect the total amount of memory that SQL Server (and any component loaded in its process space) has allocated. Here, we use the term "allocated" to mean memory that has been committed to SQL Server. As long as no trimming has occurred, Working Set is the best counter for seeing how much memory has been allocated within the SQL Server process space.

Private Bytes (described in the previous section) does not show all the memory committed, but the value can be more stable than Working Set if trimming occurs. You should consider monitoring both Private Bytes and Working Set. If you see Working Set dip below Private Bytes, you should look at Private Bytes. If Working Set dips below Private Bytes, the operating system must be trimming SQL Server's Working Set. This means other processes are competing for memory that SQL Server might need to get back, and you should evaluate what other processes are competing with SQL Server for memory resources.

SQLServer: Buffer Manager Object's Buffer Cache Hit Ratio Counter

There is no right value for the buffer cache-hit ratio since it is application-specific. If your system has settled into a steady state, ideally you want to achieve rates of 90 percent or higher, but this is not always possible if the I/O is random. Keep adding more physical memory as long as this value continues to rise or until you run out of money.

SQLServer: Memory Manager Object's Total Server Memory Counter

This counter can be useful, but it does not reflect all memory allocated within the SQL Server process space. It only reflects memory allocated in the SQL Server buffer pool. Note that the buffer pool is used much more extensively in version 7 and later than in previous versions. It is not just for data pages; it is also for other memory allocations within the server, including plans for stored procedures and for ad hoc queries. Certain components can get loaded into the SQL Server process space and allocate memory that is not under SQL Server's direct control. Examples of these are extended stored procedures, OLE Automation objects, and OLE DB provider DLLs. The memory space needed for these types of objects is included in SQL Server's Working Set, but not in the Total Server Memory counter.

SQLServer: Cache Manager Object

This object contains counters for monitoring how the cache is being used for various types of objects, including ad hoc query plans, procedure plans, trigger plans, and prepared SQL plans. A separate Cache Hit Ratio counter is available for each type of plan, as is a counter showing the number of such objects and the number of pages used by the objects.

SQLServer Buffer Manager Object's Page Reads/sec Counter

Watch this counter in combination with the counters from the PhysicalDisk object. If you see rates approaching the capacity of your hardware's I/O rates (use 80 to 90 I/Os per disk per second as a guide), you should reduce I/O rates by making your application more efficient (via better design, better indexes, denormalization, and so on). Or you can increase the hardware's I/O capacity. This statistic measures only read operations, not writes, and it does so only for SQL Server, so you do not see the whole picture. However, you will see enough to reach some general conclusions.

SQLServer Buffer Manager Object's Checkpoint Writes/sec Counter

Since the checkpoint process happens only at periodic intervals, you will see a 0 value for this counter much of the time. During the checkpoint process, you should sustain as high an I/O rate as possible (perhaps hundreds per second) to get the checkpoint to complete as quickly as possible. If you have multiple disks and a fast controller, consider changing the Max Async IO option using SP_CONFIGURE to try to sustain higher rates and shorter durations for the checkpoint. You can also use the Recovery Interval configuration option to affect the frequency of checkpointing.

SQLServer: Buffer Manager Object's Page Writes/sec Counter

This value keeps track of all physical writes done by SQL Server, for any reason. It includes checkpoint writes, lazywriter writes, and large block writes done during index creation or bulk copy operations. Separate counters are available for checkpoint writes and lazywriter writes; you are probably better off using these more specific counters.

SQLServer: Databases Object's Log Flushes/sec Counter

This value should be well below the capacity of the disk on which the Transaction Log resides. It is best to place the Transaction Log on a separate physical disk drive (or on a mirrored drive) so that the disk drive is always in place for the next write, since Transaction Log writes are sequential. There is a separate counter for each database, so make sure you are monitoring the right database instance.

SQLServer: Databases Object's Transactions/sec Counter

This counter measures actual transactions—either user-defined transactions surrounded by BEGIN TRAN and COMMIT TRAN or individual data modification statements if no BEGIN TRAN has been issued. For example, if you have a batch that contains two individual INSERT statements, this counter records two transactions. The counter has a separate instance for each database, and there is no way to keep track of total transactions for all of SQL Server. Use it only as a general indication of your system's throughput. There is obviously no "correct" value—just the higher, the better.

User-Defined Counters

SQL Server 2000 offers ten Performance Monitor counters for keeping track of any data or information that is useful to you. These counters come under the User Settable object. The only counter is called Query, and there are ten instances to choose from. Ten stored procedures are available for specifying a value that Performance Monitor will chart for a particular instance. For example, if you want to invoke User Counter 1 to keep track of how many rows are in the Invoices table, you can create triggers on the Invoices table so that every time a row is inserted or deleted, the stored procedure SP_USER_COUNTER1 is executed. You can include the following code in the triggers:

```
DECLARE @numrows int
SELECT @numrows = count(*) FROM invoices
EXEC sp_user_counter1 @numrows
```

Once it is assigned a value, the user counter maintains that value until a new value is assigned. User counters are much more passive in SQL Server 2000 than in earlier versions. In version 6.5, the stored procedures for defining user counters contained whatever calculations were needed to generate the counter's value, and Performance Monitor continually polled the server to determine the value for the counter. Polling meant actually executing the stored procedure for the counter. It took place at whatever polling interval Performance Monitor was configured to use. If your stored procedure was complex, it could take longer than the polling interval to generate the new value, and the cost of generating the values could be quite expensive. In SQL Server 2000, the stored procedure must be called explicitly to set a counter value.

Note that the value passed to the stored procedure must be a constant, a variable, or a parameterless system function starting with @@, and its datatype must be Integer.

Other Performance Monitor Counters

The counters mentioned in this chapter are just a few of the most commonly used. SQL Server has dozens of others for monitoring almost every aspect of SQL Server behavior discussed in this book. The best way to learn about them is to experiment with Performance Monitor. Look through the list of available objects and counters, select a few for viewing, and see what results you get. You will probably find a few that you will want to monitor all the time, and others that you will be interested in only occasionally. But do revisit the list of all available counters, because there are too many to remember. A month from now, you will rediscover a useful counter that you completely overlooked the first time. You should also revisit the available objects and counters after every service pack upgrade, because new ones might be added as the Microsoft SQL Server development team gets feedback.

Tables 8-1 through 8-5 show some of the counters with which you might want to experiment; the descriptions are adapted from the online documentation.

Counter	Description
Extents Allocated/sec	Number of extents allocated per second to database objects used for storing index or data records
Forwarded Records/sec	Number of records per second fetched through forwarded record pointers
Full Scans/sec	Number of unrestricted full scans per second; these can be either base-table or full-index scans
Index Searches/sec	Number of index searches per second; these are used to start range scans and single index record fetches and to reposition an index
Page Splits/sec	Number of page splits per second that occur as the result of overflowing index pages
Pages Allocated/sec	Number of pages allocated per second to database objects used for storing index or data records
Probe Scans/sec	Number of probe scans per second; these are used to find rows in an index or base table directly
Range Scans/sec	Number of qualified range scans through indexes per second
Skipped Ghosted Records/sec	Number of ghosted records per second skipped during scans
Table Lock Escalations/sec	Number of times that locks on a table were escalated
Worktables Created/sec	Number of worktables created per second

Table 8-1. Counters for the Access Methods Object

Counter *	Description
Active Transactions	Number of active transactions for the database
Bulk Copy Rows/sec	Number of rows bulk copied per second
Bulk Copy Throughput/sec	Amount (in kilobytes) of data bulk copied per second
Data File(s) Size (K)	Cumulative size (in kilobytes) of all the data files in the database, including any automatic growth; this counter is useful for determining the correct size of TEMPDB, for example
Log Cache Hit Ratio	Percentage of log cache reads satisfied from the log cache
Log File(s) Size (K)	Cumulative size (in kilobytes) of all the Transaction Log files in the database
Log Growths	Total number of times the Transaction Log for the database has been expanded
Log Shrinks	Total number of times the Transaction Log for the database has been shrunk
Log Truncations	Total number of times the Transaction Log for the database has been truncated
Percent Log Used	Percentage of space in the log that is in use
Shrink Data Movement Bytes/sec	Amount of data being moved per second by auto-shrink operations or by DBCC SHRINKDATABASE or DBCC SHRINKFILE statements
Transactions/sec	Number of transactions started for the database per second

*Separate instances of these counters exist for each database.

Table 8-2.   Counters for the Databases Object

Counter	Description
Average Wait Time (ms)	Average amount of wait time (in milliseconds) for each lock request that resulted in a wait
Lock Requests/sec	Number of new locks and lock conversions per second requested from the lock manager
Lock Timeouts/sec	Number of lock requests per second that timed out, including internal requests for NOWAIT locks
Lock Wait Time (ms)	Total wait time (in milliseconds) for locks in the last second
Lock Waits/sec	Number of lock requests per second that could not be satisfied immediately and required the caller to wait
Number of Deadlocks/sec	Number of lock requests per second that resulted in a deadlock

Table 8-3.   Counters for the Locks Object

Counter	Description
Connection Memory (K)	Total amount of dynamic memory the server is using for maintaining connections

Table 8-4.   Counters for the Memory Manager Object

Counter	Description
Lock Memory (K)	Total amount of dynamic memory the server is using for locks
Maximum Workspace Memory (K)	Maximum amount of memory available for executing processes such as hash, sort, bulk copy, and index creation operations
Memory Grants Outstanding	Total number of processes per second that have successfully acquired a workspace memory grant
Memory Grants Pending	Total number of processes per second waiting for a workspace memory grant
Optimizer Memory (K)	Total amount of dynamic memory the server is using for query optimization
SQL Cache Memory (K)	Total amount of dynamic memory the server is using for the dynamic SQL cache
Target Server Memory (K)	Total amount of dynamic memory the server is willing to consume
Total Server Memory (K)	Total amount (in kilobytes) of dynamic memory that the server is currently using

Table 8-4.   Counters for the Memory Manager Object *(continued)*

Counter	Description
Auto-Param Attempts/sec	Number of auto-parameterization attempts per second. Total should be the sum of the failed, safe, and unsafe auto-parameterizations. Auto-parameterization occurs when SQL Server attempts to reuse a cached plan for a previously executed query that is similar to, but not exactly the same as, the current query.
Batch Requests/sec	Number of Transact-SQL command batches received per second.
Failed Auto-Params/sec	Number of failed auto-parameterization attempts per second. This should be small.
Safe Auto-Params/sec	Number of safe auto-parameterization attempts per second.
SQL Compilations/sec	Number of SQL compilations per second. Indicates the number of times the compile code path is entered. Includes compiles due to recompiles. Once SQL Server user activity is stable, this value should reach a steady state.
Unsafe Auto-Params/sec	Number of unsafe auto-parameterization attempts per second. The table has characteristics that prevent the cached plan from being shared. These are designated as *unsafe*. The fewer of these that occur, the better.

Table 8-5. Counters for the SQL Statistics Object

Other Performance Monitoring Considerations

Anytime you monitor performance, you also slightly alter performance simply because of the overhead cost of monitoring. It can be helpful to run the Performance tool on a separate machine from SQL Server to reduce that overhead. The SQL Server-specific counters are obtained by querying SQL Server; thus they use connections to SQL Server. It is best to monitor only the counters in which you are interested, however.

OPTIMIZING BACKUP AND RESTORE PERFORMANCE

SQL Server 2000 offers several methods for increasing the speed of backup and restore operations. Using multiple backup devices allows backups to be written to all devices in parallel. Similarly, the backup can be restored from multiple devices in parallel. Backup device speed is one potential bottleneck in backup throughput. Using multiple devices can increase throughput in proportion to the number of devices used.

Alternately, use a combination of database backups, differential database backups, and Transaction Log backups to minimize the time necessary to recover from a failure. Differential database backups reduce the amount of Transaction Log entries that must be applied to recover the database. This is normally faster than creating a full database backup.

Optimizing Database, Differential Database, and File Backup Performance

As you have learned in previous chapters, creating a database backup comprises two steps:

1. Copying the data from the database files to the backup devices.

2. Copying the portion of the transaction log needed to roll forward the database to a consistent state and to the same backup devices.

Creating a differential database backup comprises the same two steps as creating a database backup, except that only the data that has changed is copied (though all database pages need to be read to determine this).

Backing up a database file comprises a single step:

- Copying the data from the database file to the backup devices.

The database files used to store the database are sorted by a disk device, and a reader thread is assigned to each device. The reader thread reads the data from the database files. A writer thread is also assigned to each backup device. The writer thread writes data to the backup device. Parallel read operations can be increased by spreading the database files among more logical drives. Similarly, parallel write operations can be increased by using more backup devices.

Generally, the bottleneck will be either the database files or the backup devices. If the total read throughput is greater than the total backup device throughput, then the bottleneck is on the backup device side. Adding more backup devices (and SCSI controllers, as necessary) can improve performance. However, if the total backup throughput is greater than the total read throughput, then increase the read throughput by adding more database files on devices or by using more disks in the RAID device, for example.

Optimizing Transaction Log Backup Performance

Creating a Transaction Log backup comprises only a single step:

- Copying the portion of the log not yet backed up to the backup devices.

Even though there might be multiple Transaction Log files, the Transaction Log is logically one stream read sequentially by one thread. A reader/writer thread is assigned to each backup device. Higher performance is achieved by adding more backup devices.

The bottleneck can be either the disk device containing the Transaction Log files or the backup device, depending on their relative speed and the number of backup devices used. Adding more backup devices will scale linearly until the capacity of the disk device containing the Transaction Log files is reached, whereupon no further gains are possible without increasing the speed of the disk devices containing the Transaction Log (for example, by using disk striping).

Optimizing Restore Performance

As you saw in Chapter 7, restoring a full database backup or differential database backup requires that the SQL Server complete four steps:

1. Create the database and Transaction Log files if they do not already exist.
2. Copy the data from the backup devices to the database files.
3. Copy the Transaction Log from the Transaction Log files.
4. Roll forward the Transaction Log and then restart recovery if necessary.

Restoring a Transaction Log backup requires the performance of two steps:

1. Copy data from the backup devices to the Transaction Log file.
2. Roll forward the Transaction Log.

Similarly, restoring a database file comprises two steps:

1. Create any missing database files.
2. Copy the data from the backup devices to the database files.

If the database and Transaction Log files do not already exist, they must be created before data can be restored to them. The database and Transaction Log files are created and the file contents initialized to zero. Separate worker threads create and initialize the files in parallel. The database and Transaction Log files are sorted by disk device, and a separate worker thread is assigned to each disk device. Because creating files and initializing them requires very high throughput, spreading the files evenly across the available logical drives yields the highest performance.

Copying the data and Transaction Log from the backup devices to the database and Transaction Log files is performed by reader/writer threads; one thread is assigned to each backup device. Performance is limited by either the ability of the backup devices to deliver the data or the ability of the database and Transaction Log files to accept the data. Therefore, performance increases linearly with the number of backup devices added, until the ability of the database or Transaction Log files to accept the data is reached.

NOTE: The performance of rolling forward a Transaction Log is fixed and cannot be further optimized, apart from using a faster computer.

Optimizing Tape Backup Device Performance

Three variables affect tape backup device performance and allow SQL Server backup and restore performance operations to roughly scale linearly as more tape devices are added: software data block size, the number of tape devices that share a small computer system interface (SCSI) bus, and the tape device type. The software data block size is computed for optimal performance by SQL Server and should not be altered.

TIP: For more information about settings that affect tape drive performance, see your tape drive vendor's documentation.

Many high-speed tape drives perform better if they have a dedicated SCSI bus for each tape drive used. Drives whose native transfer rate exceeds 50 percent of the SCSI bus speed must be on a dedicated SCSI bus.

CAUTION: Never place a tape drive on the same SCSI bus as disks or a CD-ROM drive. The error-handling actions for these devices are mutually incompatible.

Optimizing Disk Backup Device Performance

Raw I/O speed of the disk backup device affects disk backup device performance and allows SQL Server backup and restore performance operations to roughly scale linearly as multiple disk devices are added.

The use of RAID for a disk backup device needs to be carefully considered. For example, RAID 5 has low write performance, approximately the same speed as for a single disk (due to having to maintain parity information). Additionally, the raw speed of appending data to a file is significantly slower than the raw device write speed.

If the backup device is heavily striped, such that the maximum write speed to the backup device greatly exceeds the speed at which it can append data to a file, then it might be appropriate to place several logical backup devices on the same stripe set. In other words, backup performance can be increased by placing several backup media families on the same logical drive. However, an empirical approach is required to determine if this is a gain or a loss for each environment. Usually, it is better to place each backup device on a separate disk device.

Generally, on a SCSI bus, only a few disks can be operated at maximum speed, though Ultra-wide and Ultra-2 buses can handle more disks, and more of the disks can be operated at the maximum speed. However, careful configuration of the hardware is likely to be needed to obtain optimal performance.

TIP: For more information about settings that affect disk performance, see your disk vendor's documentation.

Optimizing Data Compression

Modern tape drives have built-in hardware data compression that can significantly increase the effective transfer rate of data to the drive. Data compression increases the effective transfer rate to the tape drives over what can be achieved with hardware compression disabled. The compressibility of the real data in the database depends both on the data itself and on the tape drives used. Typical data compression ratios range from 1.2:1 to 2:1 for a wide range of databases. This compression ratio is typical of data in a wide variety of business applications, though some databases can have higher or lower compression ratios. For example, a database consisting largely of images that are already compressed will not be compressed further by the tape drives.

TIP: For more information about data compression, see your tape drive vendor's documentation.

By default, SQL Server supports hardware compression, though this can be disabled by using the 3205 trace flag. Disabling hardware compression can, in rare circumstances, improve backup performance. For example, if the data is already fully compressed, disabling hardware compression prevents the tape device from wasting time trying to compress the data further.

Amount of Data Transferred to Tape

Creating a database backup captures only the portion of the database containing real data; unused space is not backed up. The result is faster backup operations. Although SQL Server version 7.5 databases can be configured to grow automatically as needed, you can continue to reserve space within the database to guarantee that this space is available. Reserving space within the database adversely affects neither backup throughput nor the overall time needed to back up the database.

SUMMARY

Configuration alone can rarely turn slow, plodding applications and databases into screamers. In fact, despite your best intentions, you are more likely to misconfigure your system by taking manual control of the options that SQL Server sets automatically. Knowing what each configuration option does can keep you from misconfiguring your system.

In this chapter, we looked at the configuration options and discussed some guidelines for their use. We also discussed how to monitor the effects on your system's performance, using SQL Server Profiler and Windows 2000's Performance tool. SQL Server Profiler lets you determine which queries, procedures, or users have the biggest performance impact. Performance Monitor gives you a scientific method of holding constant all but one variable within the system as a whole so that you can measure the effect on the single value as you vary the whole system.

In Chapter 9, we will consider the automation of tasks in SQL Server. We will look at the creation of jobs, operators, and the use of agents. Automation of SQL Server is one of the most important administrative tasks you can perform. Effective management is crucial—so we will look carefully at all the important issues surrounding automation.

CHAPTER 9

Automating
SQL Server

Any administrator who has been called into work at 3:00 A.M. to solve a relatively simple problem fully understands and appreciates the value of automation. Even in organizations that maintain a 24-hour support staff, the automation of certain tasks has become an important part of the support plan, because it frees up much of the time that an administrator would normally have to spend performing routine maintenance or responding to minor problems.

Automating the SQL Server begins as a simple task in which you configure the SQL Server to perform an operation you would normally have to perform yourself, and you schedule it to occur at a specific time. From there, automation grows into a planned response, where you configure the SQL Server to perform operations based on performance conditions or as a result of a specific error.

As an administrator, you will configure your SQL Server to carry out a wide variety of automated tasks that are performed based on times, errors, conditions, and more. When combined, the operations that you automate will add to the functionality of the server, making it a more complex design that is both customized to your environment and capable of handling most errors or conditions without input from you.

We recommend that you approach this chapter a little differently than the others: We suggest that you first read through the entire chapter before attempting any actual configurations. Once you have completely read the chapter, then go back through it again, this time practicing as you go.

The reason we suggest this is simply that the different aspects of automation work together to create a sound solution. Each piece will build on the others, at the end combining into a complete plan for automating your SQL Server.

From the Field

The automation tools in SQL Server 2000 are very valuable and can help you create a server that handles most situations automatically. You should be careful, though, not to let a well-designed automation set replace the involvement of a good administrator. Assuming that just because you have not had to take any action for a while means that you don't have to watch the server carefully anymore can be disastrous.

WHY YOU WANT TO AUTOMATE

One of the first things that you will want to know is *why* you should automate to begin with (besides cutting down on the amount of time you actually have to sit at the console and execute operations as part of day-to-day maintenance). Many reasons will probably occur to you, if you think about it for a moment. You will want to create automated tasks so that you can execute them easily from a distance, have them automatically execute at a specific time, and have them automatically execute as a response to a prespecified condition or alert. For example, one of the most common tasks (and frequently the first SQL Server task) that is automated is backup. Once the backup solution and procedures are designed, you can configure SQL Server to automatically back up databases at regular intervals in keeping with your backup plan. This means that you do not need an employee to be present at the server each time a backup is executed. Nor, significantly, does it mean that you can automate backups and then forget about them—because you should always check to ensure that your backups were actually performed. It simply means that SQL Server can initiate the backup process automatically.

As an example of automating tasks that execute based on performance conditions, assume that the Transaction Log for an important database is 75 percent full. You can configure SQL Server to watch the Transaction Logs and notify you when they reach a specific level. This in turn lets you know that you have to plan for the expansion or clearing of the Transaction Log, and it does so before any problems crop up that affect network users.

In the case of an error, you could, for example, reserve a smaller disk in the server, one that is present for emergencies only. By preparing a series of automated tasks set to trigger if a database runs out of space, you can create a scenario in which SQL Server will automatically create additional database files on the emergency disk for databases that run out of space. This way, even in situations where a database grew very quickly and ran out of room before you could catch up and install new drives, SQL Server can recover and continue to provide functionality, giving you time to implement a more permanent solution.

UNDERSTANDING THE SQLSERVERAGENT

As you learned in Chapter 2, the SQLServerAgent (we'll call it the Agent) is a Windows Service that controls the automation of SQL Server. The Agent is responsible for controlling and maintaining the different software components, which are responsible for all SQL Server automation. The Agent uses the MSDB database as the primary location for storing and reading data that pertains to automation tasks and operations.

While it is true that when the SQL Server service is running, the SQL Server is functional; without the SQLServerAgent service, SQL Server is incapable of automating tasks. You should, therefore, always verify that the SQLServerAgent service is set to automatically start when the operating system starts. This way, the software component that controls your automation will run even if the server is rebooted for any reason. After all, you do not want to spend a lot of time creating automated tasks, only to be called in to work at 3:00 A.M. just to start the service.

TIP: You can set the SQLServerAgent service to start automatically either from the Services dialog box within the Server Manager or from the SQL Service Manager.

In addition to making sure that the service is running, you should be aware of some other details when checking or setting up the Agent service. Chief among them is the ability for the service to connect to the SQL Server. You should always log in to Windows using the domain account that you assigned to the Agent service. This step is not necessary if you are using a local system account, but you will remember from Chapter 1 that we recommend you always use a domain user account for SQL Server services. To review, you should use a domain user account because it enables the service to access remote resources from across the network and also to send and receive e-mail. If you choose to use a local system or local user account, the Agent service will not be able to use e-mail or access remote resources. You should also remember to make certain that the account is in a Windows NT or 2000 group mapped to a SYSADMIN server role, within SQL Server.

CONFIGURING E-MAIL SERVICES

One of the more powerful features of SQL Server 7 is its ability to use e-mail. SQL Server is capable of using e-mail to send you notifications of events and errors and can also actually process queries that you send into the server or return result sets to you via e-mail. This functionality is produced by two separate internal components, each of which handles a different set of e-mail services.

SQLAgentMail is the e-mail service responsible for sending notifications when an alert is triggered or scheduled jobs succeed or fail. The Agent uses this service as one of the primary means of notifying administrators of conditions within SQL Server.

SQL Mail is the service that processes incoming e-mail messages and also handles the sending of e-mail from within a database application. The Agent uses this service to process queries through e-mail as well as to deal with application-driven messages. Later in this chapter you will learn more about sending mail from within a database application.

Configuring mail services is a relatively simple process so long as you meet all the prerequisites and complete all the required tasks. When configuring mail services, keep the following points in mind:

▼ You must have an e-mail client installed on the machine that is running SQL Server.

■ You must use an e-mail server that is Messaging Application Programming Interface (MAPI) version 1–compliant. Moreover, you must ensure that you have a MAPI version 1–compliant e-mail client on the SQL Server itself. The easiest way to install such a client is to add Windows Messaging services from the CD-ROM for Windows 2000.

TIP: Note that installing IE 4.01 before SQL Server installation is not sufficient for the purpose of installing the client. To take advantage of SQL mail services, you must ensure that a MAPI version 1 client is installed on the SQL Server.

▲ You must use a Windows NT or 2000 domain user logon account for each of the services.

One aspect of configuring mail services that many administrators overlook is giving each user account that is responsible for a mail service its own mail profile. When using some of the newer e-mail clients, having a separate profile for each service is very important.

Technically, you could use the same account and mail profile for each service. We do not recommend that you do, however, because there might come a time when you will want to grant user access to some mail services, while restricting others. If you use a different user account for each mail service, separating access to the services is a much easier task.

You should always name the mail profile for the mail service with a specific name that describes its use. This will prevent the accidental deletion of the profile, and ensures that there is no MAPI conflict between the mail profile and the administrator's live e-mail account.

We have seen administrators use the e-mail client on the server. While this is generally not a good idea, we think you should know what to look out for because so many administrators do it.

Actually configuring the mail services within SQL Server can be confusing if you do not know where to look. When you are ready to configure mail, first create the domain user accounts that SQL Server will use for mail services. Next, log off Windows and log on as each of the user accounts. Once logged in, create a mail profile for the account and send mail to the administrative account as a test. While it is true that you can configure mail profiles for others when logged in as the administrator, we recommend that you do it this way because it removes the potential for profile error. The steps for creating a mail profile will vary, depending on the mail client that you use. Remember to give each mail profile a specific and descriptive name. Once done, you are ready to begin the configuration of the mail services in SQL Server. To configure the SQLAgentMail service, you will need to access the properties page for the SQLServerAgent. To do this, simply connect to SQL Server using Enterprise Manager and perform the following steps:

1. Expand the object list so that you can see the objects contained in your server.

2. Right-click on the SQL Server Agent object and choose the Properties option.

When you complete the steps, SQL Server will display the SQL Server Agent Properties page. You should see the Mail Profile field in the center of the dialog box as shown in Figure 9-1.

TIP: While you could change mail profiles within the SQL Server from Transact-SQL code (by writing a custom batch file and then invoking it from the code itself), this is generally not a recommended practice and can even cause substantial performance errors on your SQL Server.

Once you have located the Mail Profile field, simply click on the drop-down list button found to its right. This will display a list of available profiles on the server. Choose the name of the profile that

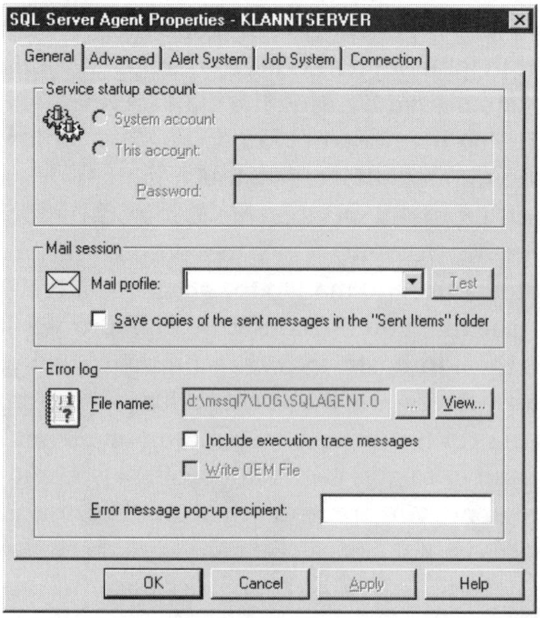

Figure 9-1. The Agent Properties dialog box

you created for SQLAgentMail. You will notice that a checkbox
below the field lets you specify whether SQL Server should save
a copy of sent messages in the Sent Items folder. If you want to
keep a record of all messages that have been sent, you should place a
checkmark in this box. If you are not worried about keeping a record
or think that too much space will be taken by this profile, do not
place a mark in the checkbox. As a final step, you should click on
the Test button. SQL Server will attempt to establish communication
between the server and the profile and will return a confirmation if
all is well, or an error if a problem exists.

Configuring SQL Mail services is performed almost identically.
You will find the dialog box for this configuration by expanding
the Support Services folder in the SQL Server object list and then
right-clicking on the SQL Mail object and choosing Properties.
You can see the folder and object in Figure 9-2.

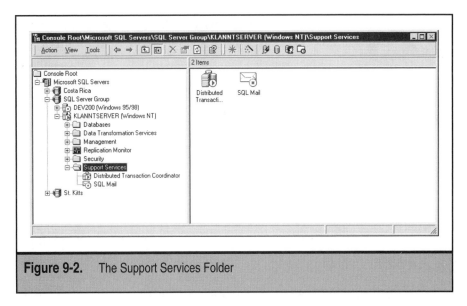

Figure 9-2. The Support Services Folder

Once you have right-clicked on the SQL Mail Object, a smaller dialog box is displayed that lets you configure and test the mail profile. You will perform the same operation here that you did when configuring SQLAgentMail, but you will not have additional options to configure. The SQL Mail Configuration dialog box is shown in Figure 9-3.

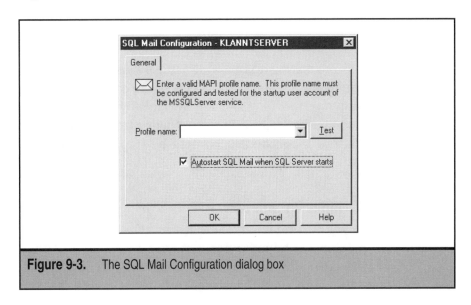

Figure 9-3. The SQL Mail Configuration dialog box

Just click on the drop-down list box and choose the name of the profile that you created for this mail service. Remember to click the Test button so that you can be sure the profile is working.

WORKING WITH OPERATORS

Now that you have configured mail services, the next step is to create *operators*. Operators are basically the people who get notified when jobs complete or if alerts are fired. You will create operators so that an administrator or administrative assistant is notified when things happen in SQL Server.

You will remember from Chapter 2 that operator information is stored in the Sysoperators table, within the MSDB Database. As always, we do not recommend that you alter the system table directly, but rather that you create and manage operators using the tools that SQL Server provides you. You can create an operator using either Transact-SQL or Enterprise Manager. Although you will probably create and manage operators using Enterprise Manager most of the time, we believe it is important for you to know how to do it using Transact-SQL, because you might have SQL Server installations without Enterprise Manager installed.

Creating an Operator

The task of creating an operator using Transact-SQL is one that you perform using a system-stored procedure called SP_ADD_OPERATOR. This stored procedure has a few variables that let you control the way the operator works. In the following text, we will explore each of the optional parameters in a step-by-step process so that you learn the syntax in a logical way.

The @Name Parameter

The first thing you will want to learn is the minimum requirements for this statement and how you can get it to function right away. As with other stored procedures, if it is the only line of code in the execution window, the statement might begin with the name of the stored procedure. However, if you are including the execution of this stored procedure in the middle of other Transact-SQL statements, you must preface the name of the procedure with the word `exec`. For example, if you wanted to execute the `SP_ADD_OPERATOR` stored procedure to create an operator named `Testoperator`, and it was the only line of code in the window, you could do so by connecting to SQL Server using Query Analyzer and executing the following statement:

```
sp_add_operator @name = 'Testoperator'
```

The statement in the example will work only if it is the sole line of code in the execution window. If it is not, you would add the word `exec` as seen below:

```
exec sp_add_operator @name = 'Testoperator'
```

In the second example, the statement will run no matter whether it is the only line of code in the execution window. We recommend that you always include the `exec` specification, because if you get into the habit of including it, your statements will always work and you will not have to go back and look for errors that occur merely because of statement structure. With that in mind, all remaining examples in this section will include the `exec` specification.

Before we consider the parameters available for the `SP_ADD_OPERATOR` stored procedure, it is worthwhile to briefly consider *why* we use operators. Basically, operators are simply a notification target—that is, they are some token defined within SQL Server that corresponds to an address of one type or another. Typically, people whom you denote as operators will also be given rights on the server—so they can solve whatever problems might arise—but this is not necessary. In fact, operators might not have any other roles on the SQL Server in question at all.

Operators are server objects; a single operator can receive notifications from every table in every database on the server. As you will see later, operator access is an important and valuable tool in administration, as a page from a SQL Server followed by an e-mail to your home address can be a big time-saver, allowing you to determine (before you ever get dressed) whether a problem requires that you go into the office.

Managing operators is a relatively straightforward process; most of the control comes from parameters to the SP_ADD_OPERATOR stored procedure. The following sections discuss some of these parameters, starting with the @enabled parameter.

Understanding the @enabled Parameter

Of the variable parameters available for this procedure, the @enabled parameter is perhaps the most commonly ignored or forgotten. Frequently, administrators will have a memory lapse about using this variable when using Transact-SQL because they have no little checkbox to remind them.

Operators can be stored in a condition of enabled or disabled. When enabled, the operator is active and can receive notifications from SQL Server; when disabled, the reverse conditions apply.

The syntax for this variable is relatively simple. If you include the @enabled parameter, it must additionally have a numeric value of either enabled (1) or disabled (0). This value is always specified after the equal (=) sign and tells SQL Server to activate or deactivate the operator. For example, if you want to create the Testoperator in an enabled condition, you will connect to SQL Server using Query Analyzer and execute the following statement:

```
exec sp_add_operator @name = 'Testoperator', @enabled = 1
```

Such a statement creates an operator named Testoperator and specifies that it be enabled. You should know that the default specification for this parameter is enabled and that you could have left off the specification and achieved the same results. This statement actually does nothing more than the example at the beginning of the section. It is included only as a tool to help you learn the syntax.

So, you might be asking yourself at this point, what is the purpose of creating an operator with notifications disabled? Well, several answers come to mind. Although you will generally not *create* an operator with disabled notifications, you will often disable operators later on. Disabling an operator lets you perform some management on the nature of the operator's actions—for example, by disabling a given operator, you might make the fail-safe operator the active operator for a given database. Similarly, if someone goes on leave or gets fired, you might want to disable that person as an operator.

The ability to enable and disable operators lets you track operator information without loss in the event of a disabled action. Moreover, effective use of the operator-based stored procedures in conjunction with jobs can force a notification to a different operator than the normal one in the event that the error is especially critical, for example. Notifying the operator is obviously a crucial part of its usefulness. The following sections discuss some of the different ways in which operators can be notified.

Understanding the @e-mail_address Parameter

If an operator is going to receive notifications via e-mail, he or she must have an e-mail address stored so that SQL Server can reference the MSDB Database, obtain the address, and then send the notification. To specify an e-mail address for an operator using Transact-SQL, you use the @e-mail_address parameter. The syntax is straightforward and you must enclose the actual address within single quotation marks. For example, to specify an e-mail address of TestOperator@organization.com for the Testoperator operator, you will connect to SQL Server using Query Analyzer and execute the following statement:

```
exec sp_add_operator @name = 'Testoperator',
    @e-mail_address = 'TestOperator@organization.com'
```

The example assumes that you are using an Internet address and does so because it is the most widely understood form of e-mail addressing. If you were using an internal messaging server with another addressing method, the address might look different. No matter what the address format is, if you enclose the address within single quotation marks and have installed the SQL mail services correctly, the statement should be valid for all but a few rare systems.

Understanding the @pager_address Parameter

In the same way that an operator who is receiving notifications via e-mail must have an e-mail address, operators who are receiving notifications via pager must have a pager address specified and stored in SQL Server. In addition, to use this function you must have a messaging system capable of supporting pagers.

Assuming that you have a compatible messaging system, to specify the pager address for an operator you will use the `@pager_address` parameter. Like the `@e-mail_address` parameter, this specification requires that you place the actual address inside single quotation marks. An example of the syntax can be found below:

```
exec sp_add_operator @name = 'Testoperator',
    @pager_address = 'pageraddress'
```

In the example, we substitute the word `pageraddress` for an actual address. Depending on the messaging system that you are using, the actual address might take many different forms. You should be able to obtain the addressing scheme for your system from its reference materials.

TIP: In many of the latest paging systems, the `pageraddress` will actually be another e-mail address in the form of `AdminName@pager-company.com`. Sending e-mail to this address will result in a page being forwarded to the operator in question.

Understanding the @weekday_pager_start_time and @weekday_pager_end_time Parameters

When you are using pagers as a means of notification, you will want to take some additional considerations into account. First off, pagers are typically assigned to an individual for the entire term of his or her employment and are not passed around between employees. Since employees rarely work 24 hours every day (including, with any luck, you!), we can safely assume that there will be different people you want to notify of certain events on different work shifts. This means that an employee whose pager address is a valid point of contact for notification at 8:00 A.M. will not necessarily be a valid contact at 4:00 A.M.

The developers at Microsoft also took this into account and created a scheme in which you can specify certain hours that a pager is valid, and hours when it is not. When specifying valid pager hours for an operator using Transact-SQL, you will use the `@pager_start_time` and `@pager_end_time` variables. These variables come in three different sets, each of which covers a specific type of day. There is a single set that covers all weekdays, and one set each for Saturday and Sunday, respectively.

To specify a start and end time for a weekday, you will use the `@weekday_pager_start_time` and `@weekday_pager_end_time` parameters. These options use as a value a numeric sequence that maps to a 24-hour clock. For example, if you want to specify 9:00 A.M., you would use 090000 as a value. If you wanted to specify 9:00 P.M., you would use 210000 as a value. So, if you wanted to create an operator named `Testoperator` who has a pager start time of 8:00 A.M. and a pager end time of 5:00 P.M. Monday through Friday, you would connect to SQL Server using Query Analyzer and execute the following statement:

```
exec sp_add_operator
    @name = 'Testoperator',
    @pager_address = 'pageraddress',
    @pager_days = 62,
    @weekday_pager_start_time = 080000,
    @weekday_pager_end_time = 170000
```

You should note that to specify pager start and end times, you must also specify the `@pager_days` parameter, as seen in the example. To specify the time that a pager is available and not specify the days that a pager is available would make little sense, but would be easy to overlook when using Transact-SQL as a control tool. You will learn how to control the days that a pager is valid in the following subsection.

Understanding the @pager_days Parameter

As you have seen in the previous subsection, the nature of using pagers as a means of notification adds to the complexity of configuring operators. In addition to specifying times that a pager is valid, you must specify the days of the week that the pager is valid. When using Transact-SQL to configure an operator, you will use the

@pager_days parameter to specify the days of the week that
are valid.

The syntax of this parameter can be difficult to understand. To
further complicate the situation, many of the instructional texts and
syntactical guides available fail to fully explain how this parameter
works—so we do that here. To begin with, you should understand
how SQL Server stores the days of the week. Each day is assigned a
number, as seen here:

Sunday	1
Monday	2
Tuesday	4
Wednesday	8
Thursday	16
Friday	32
Saturday	64

With each day of the week mapped to a different number, SQL
Server can combine days to create a single number that specifies which
days are valid. For example, if you wanted a pager to be active on each
Monday, Wednesday, and Friday throughout an entire year, you would
add the numbers 2, 8, and 32 together to create 42. The value 42, then,
becomes the specified parameter for the @pager_days specification. If
you wanted to specify that the Testoperator pager would be active
Monday through Friday, you would add 2, 4, 8, 16, and 32 to create 62.
Once you have obtained the correct number, you would connect to SQL
Server using Query Analyzer and execute the following statement:

```
exec sp_add_operator
    @name = 'Testoperator',
    @pager_address = 'pageraddress',
    @pager_days = 62
```

This statement would create the Testoperator operator and
would additionally specify that the operator had a pager available
Monday through Friday. This statement, however, does not specify
the *times* that the pager is valid and therefore is technically an

incomplete statement. An example of a complete statement is listed in the next subsection.

Understanding the @saturday and @sunday Start and Stop Time Variables

Now that you understand the @pager_days specification and the weekday_pager start and end time variables, we will complete the picture with the Saturday and Sunday pager variables. In this area, we will give you a more complete example of the syntax you are likely to use when configuring operators.

Since many environments use the SQL Server seven days a week, and even in those installations where no work is performed on the weekend, the server is left running so that it can perform backups or other maintenance, the pager schedule must be able to accommodate Saturdays and Sundays as well. To create a complete configuration of an operator, you will in many cases have to include all the pager variables within a single statement. The Saturday and Sunday variables are specified using the same syntax as the weekday specifications but must be listed separately. In the following example, we create an operator named Testoperator with an active status, who uses a pager that has an address of pageraddress. The pager is available Monday through Friday from 8:00 A.M. to 5:00 P.M. and on Saturday from 9:00 A.M. to 2:00 P.M. The pager is also active on Sunday from 8:00 P.M. to 11:30 P.M. The statement to create the account is as follows:

```
exec sp_add_operator
    @name = 'Testoperator',
    @active = 1,
    @pager_address = 'pageraddress',
    @pagerdays = 127,
    @weekday_pager_start_time = 080000,
    @weekday_pager_end_time = 170000,
    @saturday_pager_start_time = 090000,
    @saturday_pager_end_time = 140000,
    @sunday_pager_start_time = 200000,
    @sunday_pager_end_time = 233000
```

The statement is this complex only when you are using pagers as a means of notification. If you are using e-mail addresses or sending notifications directly over the network through the net send method, the configurations are less complex. You will learn how to configure net send addressing in the following text.

Understanding the @netsend_address Parameter

Administrators who have been using Windows NT or 2000 for a while are likely to already be familiar with the net send command. Just in case you do not already know about it, be advised that Windows, when operating in a domain, has the ability to send a message directly to any registered NetBIOS name. This means that if you know the name of a machine on the network or the name of a logged-on user on the network, you can send a message directly to that machine or user by typing **net send** followed by the name you wish to send to, followed by the actual message, all entered directly into the command prompt.

SQL Server can make use of the net send command when sending notifications. To configure an operator to use a net send, you must simply specify the name of the computer or user to whom you want the notification sent. We recommend that if you are using net send as a means of notification, you configure multiple recipients for the message at all times. This way, if a user is not logged in, or if the machine you are sending to is rebooting or offline, the message will still be delivered to someone.

TIP: Generally, as you might expect, we find that most people who use net send in their network do so as a convenience and as a backup to e-mail. We therefore strongly recommend that you not use net send as your primary communication tool for your network.

To configure a net send address using Transact-SQL, you will use the @net_send parameter. The syntax for this specification is similar to that of the e-mail_address parameter. You simply insert the parameter and enclose the actual address within single quotation marks. For example, if you want to send a notification to the administrator, no matter at what location in the network he or she is logged on, you will connect to SQL Server using Query Analyzer and execute the following statement:

```
exec sp_add_operator
    @name = 'Testoperator',
    @netsend_address = 'administrator'
```

As you can see in the example, the syntax for this parameter is simple and easy to follow: We create the operator, specify a name, and then specify the net address to which SQL Server should send the notification.

Managing Operators Using Enterprise Manager

Now that you have a firm understanding of the techniques for creating and controlling operators using Transact-SQL, you will probably want to know how to do it the *easy* way. The easy way is, of course, by using Enterprise Manager.

As you know, Enterprise Manager contains many tools that help you graphically control SQL Server by converting your clicks and specifications into Transact-SQL in a sort of behind-the-scenes type of interface that has become standard in Windows environments. In this section, you will learn how to create and control operators using the tools provided with Enterprise Manager.

All tasks and controls relating to the automation of SQL Server are handled from within the SQL Server Agent object in Enterprise Manager. To access the tools, you must first expand the object so that you can see the different child objects. To expand the SQL Server Agent object, simply locate it in the Enterprise Manager object list and click on the plus sign next to it, as seen in Figure 9-4.

Once you have expanded the list, you can see the child-objects both in the objects list and in the right-hand pane of the operating window. The child-objects each represent a different aspect of the SQL Server automation process and are named accordingly. As you can see in Figure 9-4, the objects are named Alerts, Operators, and Jobs. Later in this chapter, we will discuss Jobs and Alerts, but for now we will restrict ourselves to talking about Operators.

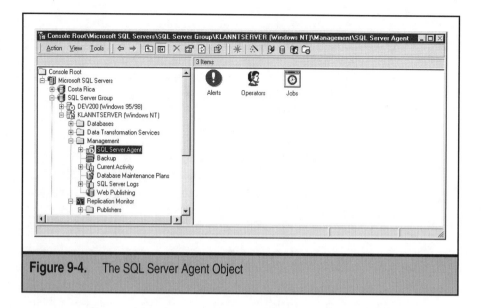

Figure 9-4. The SQL Server Agent Object

To create an operator in Enterprise Manager, simply right-click on the Operators object and choose New Operator from the menu that appears. SQL Server, in turn, will display the New Operator Properties dialog box as seen in Figure 9-5.

Once you have the dialog box open, the first thing you should do is type a name for the operator. The name should be a descriptive one that will make it easy to distinguish in a list that might contain many different operators. Now that you have named the operator, you must designate the method of notification. You have three choices here, just like when creating an operator using Transact SQL. If you want to notify the operator via e-mail, you will use the E-mail field, either typing in an acceptable e-mail address or choosing from a list using the ellipsis (…) button to the right of the field.

If you want to notify the operator using a pager, you will use the Pager field to insert a valid address. If you choose to notify the operator using a pager, the choices that let you control the hours and days that the pager is valid will become enabled when you place an address in the Pager field. Once the options are available, you can specify the desired settings by clicking in the checkboxes and changing the times listed in the Workday Begin and Workday End fields.

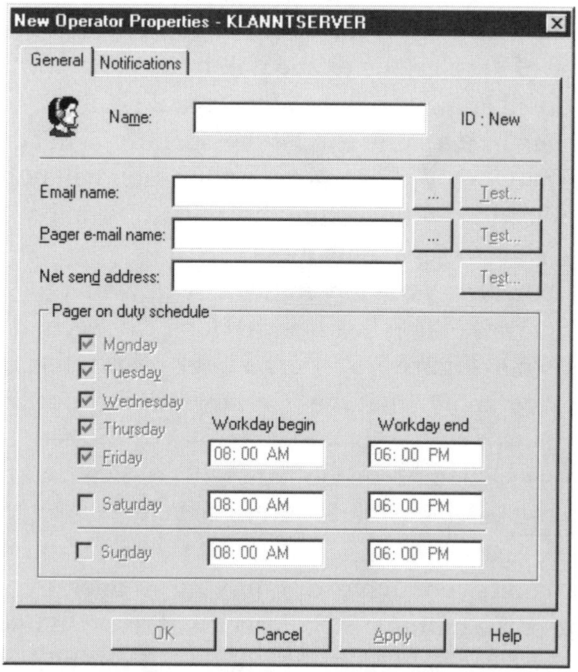

Figure 9-5.   The New Operator Properties dialog box

The final option for notification is Net Send Address. As with the other choices, you need only insert a valid address to activate the net send notification type. The only difference in the Net Send field is that there is no ellipsis button present and you are required to manually type the address into the field.

When you choose a notification method, no matter what type, you should always click on the Test button to ensure that the notification type works. The Test button will send the operator a test notification via the option that you have chosen. If the notification is not received, you will know that there is a problem and can respond accordingly. You should also know that you could configure the operator to be notified by two or more methods. This way, the operator can be notified as quickly as possible. For example, if you wanted to notify an operator when a certain alert was detected, you could configure the operator so that he or she is notified both via e-mail and net send. This way, if the operator is connected to the network at the time of the alert, he or she will receive the notification via net send and will know about the alert even if he or she is not currently reading e-mail. In the same way, if the operator is not currently logged in to the network, the net send notification will not work, but an e-mail notification will be left in the operator's mail reader the next time he or she looks at new messages.

You have probably noticed by now that the New Operator Properties dialog box has two tabs. The second tab, Notifications, shown in Figure 9-6, offers a few options that are helpful if you already know what the operator will be notified for, and also contains the checkbox that enables or disables the operator. In the upper section of the tab, you will see two radio buttons that let you choose between Alerts and Jobs. While we have not yet talked about these tasks, it is sufficient at this point for you to know that these are the choices you have for notifying an operator. When you click on one of the buttons, SQL Server will respond by changing the list in the large field below the radio buttons to display the option you selected. For example, if you choose Alerts, the default selection, a list of defined alerts is displayed. You can select any of these alerts by clicking in the checkboxes to the right of the description. Doing so will cause SQL Server to add this operator to the list of operators that will be notified if this alert is detected. If you had chosen the Jobs radio button, a list of defined jobs would be displayed and you could also choose the jobs that this operator will be added to for notification. You can configure an operator to receive notifications from both Jobs and Alerts by using multiple means of notification.

To summarize some of the issues involved in automation of SQL Server, the big objects involved in automation are *operators*, *jobs*, *alerts*, and *schedules*. Operators receive notifications. Jobs perform activities. Alerts perform notifications. Schedules specify when notifications or activities occur. In the following sections, we will consider jobs, alerts, and schedules.

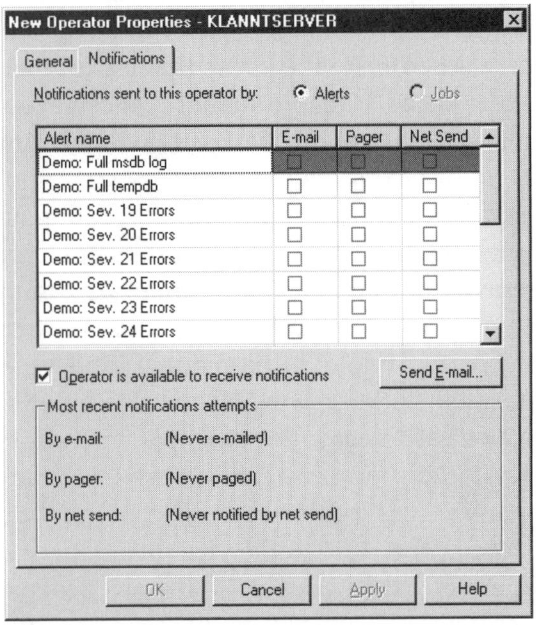

Figure 9-6.   The Notifications tab

CREATING AND MANAGING JOBS

Now that you have created your operators, the next step in automating SQL Server is to create the jobs that will perform tasks on the server. Jobs are special configurations in SQL Server that are capable of performing tasks on the system as if they were a user. You create jobs so that certain tasks might be executed either at an assigned time or as a result of a condition in SQL Server.

Creating and managing jobs is basically a process that is broken into multiple steps. The first thing that you must do is create the job. Then you can add *job steps,* the actual commands or tasks that the job will perform, broken down into pieces so that you can control the way that the job executes. You will learn more about controlling job steps later in this chapter. After you have created job steps, you can assign a schedule to the job so that it executes at a specific time, or leave the job as available so that you can execute it manually, or execute the job from an alert. You will learn how to configure alerts in the next section.

As a SQL Server administrator, creating and managing jobs is something that you should learn—and learn *well*—as it is a time-saving task that actually can make your job easier. As mentioned, most administrators commonly create jobs initially for the performing of backup activities. However, as you get more comfortable with the way jobs work, you will often find other jobs you can easily create—for example, you might create a job that runs a stored procedure that generates a result set comprising your company's sales for the week. The job might then send the results of the stored procedure to the vice president of sales via e-mail, as well as other department heads, so that everyone can review the sales figures before a regular weekly meeting. You might commonly schedule such a job to run every Sunday night at midnight. In previous versions of SQL Server, you could create and manage jobs using a variety of stored procedures such as SP_ADD_JOB or SP_UPDATE_JOB. In SQL Server 7, however, these stored procedures have been removed and you must create and manage jobs using Enterprise Manager, using the much simpler graphic interface of the Manager, rather than the textual interface that writing jobs in Transact-SQL requires you to use.

Managing Jobs Using Enterprise Manager

Creating a job using Enterprise Manager can be a little confusing at first but becomes easy after you have done it a few times. To begin with, you must create the actual job. Like operators, jobs are created using the Jobs child-object in the Enterprise Manager object list. To display the object, connect to SQL Server using Enterprise Manager and expand the object list so that the SQL Server Agent object is visible, as seen in Figure 9-7.

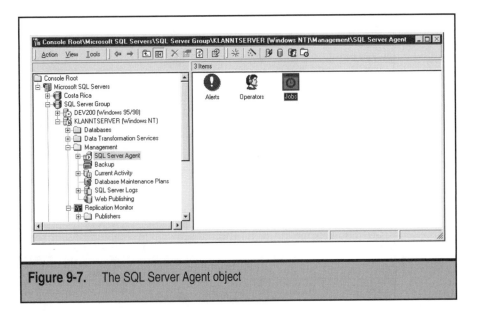

Figure 9-7.   The SQL Server Agent object

Creating a Job

To create a new job, right-click on the Jobs object and choose the
Properties option from the pop-up menu that appears. SQL Server,
in turn, will display the New Job Properties dialog box as seen in
Figure 9-8.

Now that the dialog box is open, the first thing you will need to
do is type in a name for the job. Like most other things that you must
name in SQL Server, the name should be descriptive so that you can
easily differentiate between this job and others. When the dialog box
opens, the Name field is selected by default and you should only
have to begin typing to enter a name. If, however, you clicked your
mouse somewhere or pressed the TAB key by mistake, you can
return to the Name field simply by clicking in the field one time.

Once you have named the job, you can specify additional
information that will help describe and categorize it for managerial
purposes. Using the Category drop-down field, you can choose a
category for this job. Categorizing jobs will help you manage the jobs
because you can choose to list only the jobs in a certain category. The

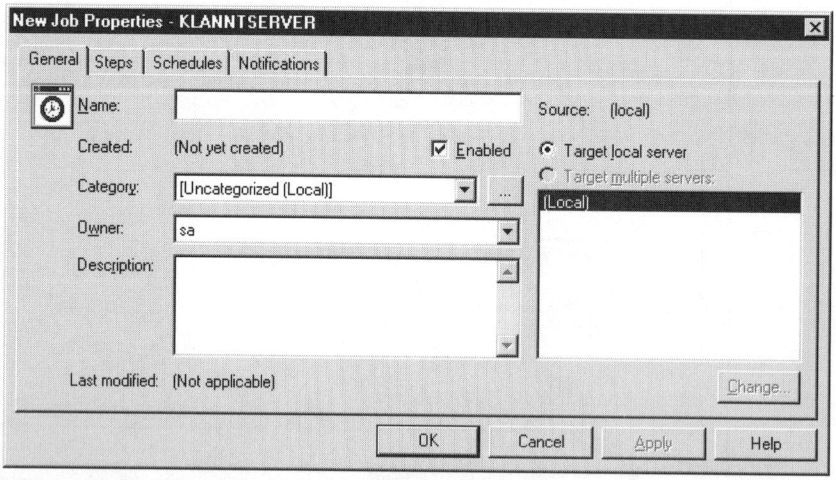

Figure 9-8. The New Job Properties dialog box

following list contains the choices that are available to you in the Category field:

- ▼ Database Maintenance
- ■ Full-text
- ■ REPL-Alert Response
- ■ REPL-Checkup
- ■ REPL-Distribution
- ■ REPL-Distribution Cleanup
- ■ REPL-History Cleanup
- ■ REPL-Log Reader
- ■ REPL-Merge
- ■ REPL-Snapshot
- ■ REPL-Subscription Cleanup
- ■ Web Assistant
- ▲ Uncategorized

Remember that these are just categories and are there only to help you manage the jobs. ("REPL," by the way, stands for replication, to be discussed later.) Placing a job in the incorrect category will not adversely affect the job.

The next thing that you should specify, or at least verify, is the Job Owner. Job Owner is actually a very helpful specification because it lets the administrator create a job for another user. Only a System Administrator can assign a job to another user.

In some deployments, the Job Owner is a valuable designation because you can configure SQL Server to restrict the actions of users who are not System Administrators. For example, if you wanted to enable certain jobs that process standard SQL statements for all users while restricting jobs that contain operating system commands or active scripting language steps, you can do so by making changes to the SQL Server Agent properties.

You can even use a job to enable a user to perform actions that he or she would otherwise not have the permissions to perform. This is because users who are not members of the SYSADMIN role actually run job steps as the SQLAgentCmdExec user account. You will remember from the first chapter that this account is automatically created when you install SQL Server and that the SQL Server Agent reserves it for use. This means that you can create jobs that perform actions that would normally require the rights of a System Administrator, and assign the permission to run the job to any user. When the user runs the job, the job is executed by the SQL Server Agent, and runs under the security context of the SQLAgentCmdExec account. If the SQLAgentCmdExec account has been granted administrative rights, as it should be, the job runs as if it were a System Administrator and can therefore perform actions that the user who initiated the job could not.

Because jobs can run as a System Administrator, you should also be careful about which users you grant permission to run the job. The most common way to make a security error in SQL Server 7 is in tasks that have been automated through jobs. One simple tip, for example, would be to never create a job that deletes databases.

TIP: Be careful about what tasks you automate, because a job runs at a higher level of permission than the user who initiates it.

Although not necessary, you can also type in a detailed description of the job in the Description field. We have seen many deployments of SQL Server in which the Description field is not used at all, and have also seen deployments where it was used extensively because many jobs were so similar that without the description you would be unable to tell them apart easily.

You probably noticed that there is a checkbox on the General tab that lets you enable or disable the job. As you have learned, jobs can exist in a condition of enabled or disabled, which tells SQL Server if the job is available for use or is merely saving the configuration for later. When using Enterprise Manager, you control the availability of a job by checking or unchecking this checkbox.

The final area in the General tab of the New Job Properties dialog box is the Target Server area. Composed of two radio buttons and a selection field, this area lets you choose which servers the job will be created on. If your SQL Server is a standard installation, the Multiple Servers option and the selection field are unavailable. However, if you have enabled multiserver administration, both of these options will become active and you will be able to create and execute the job on multiple servers simultaneously. Later in this chapter, you will learn more about configuring multiserver administration.

As you have probably noted, the New Job Properties dialog box is actually made up of four different tabs. Each tab has a specific function and plays its own part in controlling the operation of a job. Now that you have learned all the options on the first tab, it is time to move on to the second tab, which controls the job steps.

Managing Job Steps

Even though it must have a name and other identifying information, a job is actually composed of the steps that it performs during execution. Each job contains at least one step in which some type of action takes place. To control the steps of a job, you must access the Steps tab by clicking on it. SQL Server, in turn, will respond by altering the display of the dialog box to reflect the new options, as seen in Figure 9-9.

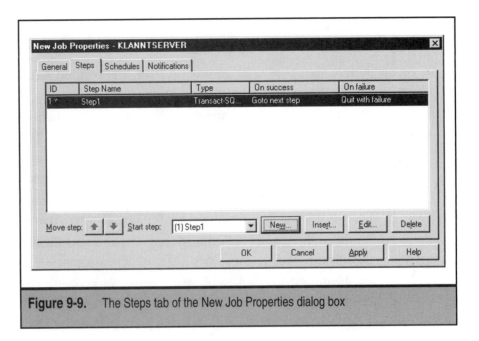

Figure 9-9.   The Steps tab of the New Job Properties dialog box

The first time this tab is displayed, the only option available to you is the New button. You must click on this button to create a new step. When you do so, SQL Server will open another new dialog box called the New Job Step dialog box. In this dialog box, you must specify the four main parts of a job step:

▼ The step name

■ The type of command

■ The database on which to operate

▲ The actual command

Take a look at each part of the step. The name is there, of course, so that you can identify this step in the job and differentiate it from other steps. The type of command lets you determine what kind of command this step will contain. You can choose a command type from the drop-down list activated when you click on the field. Table 9-1 describes the choices available.

Command	Description
Active Script	A command from an installed Active Scripting Language
Operating System Command	A command line executable such as `cls` or `dir`
Replication Distributor	A Replication command specifically designed for the Distribution Agent
Replication Distributor	A Replication command specifically designed for the Log Reader Agent
Replication Distributor	A Replication command specifically designed for the Merge Agent
Replication Distributor	A Replication command specifically designed for the Snapshot Agent
T-SQL	A standard set of Transact-SQL statements just like you would write in Query Analyzer

Table 9-1.   Types of Commands

Depending on the type of command you are issuing, you might or might not have additional choices to configure. For example, if you choose an Active Script command type, the dialog box will display choices for Visual Basic Script, JavaScript, or Other Script. If you choose Operating System Command, the dialog box will provide an area for you to specify an exit code that SQL Server can identify if the command is successful. If you choose T-SQL (for Transact-SQL), the dialog box will let you choose the database on which the step will operate. The Replication command types have no additional parameters and so none are displayed.

If you have chosen either Active Script or T-SQL as a command type, the dialog box will also enable the Open and Parse buttons. The Open button will let you open a file as a source for the code that you want to run. For example, if you want the step to execute a query that you have already written and saved, you will choose the T-SQL command type, click the Open button, and choose your query as the file to open. The Parse button lets you invoke the syntax checker for either SQL Server or the installed active scripting language as a means of checking your work. If, for example, you want to verify that your query has no syntactical errors, load or write the query in the command field and then click the Parse button. If errors are detected, you will receive a message describing where the problem is, and if there are no errors, SQL Server will display a message telling you all is well. As an administrator, you are likely to find many instances where, even though the syntax checker fails to find a problem, the query does not function correctly. You should, therefore, always run a query in Query Analyzer to make sure that it functions correctly prior to trusting it as a job step.

TIP: Create a new connection in Query Analyzer and log in as the user who will be running the job. This will ensure that the job executes correctly, particularly if you have tied the job's security permissions to the user in question.

Once the command for the step has been defined, click on the Advanced tab (not shown here) to control the behavior of this step. The tab lets you tell SQL Server what to do when the job completes, and has some additional options for T-SQL commands. On this tab you will specify what SQL Server should do when the step completes successfully, how many times to try the step before halting it as a failure, and also what to do if the step fails. By specifying conditions, you can exercise a great deal of control over the job. For example, if you specify that SQL Server should quit the job and report a failure if the job fails, and if you have additionally configured an alert for such a failure, you can actually define backup jobs, which fire only if the current job fails. Additionally, you can create a job where certain steps will execute only if previous steps were successfully accomplished. This type of control will prevent the job's performing actions that would have no benefit or that could even do harm to the server because they depended on other operations.

At the bottom of the Advanced tab, you can specify an output file that records the results of SQL statements, choose between appending to or overwriting this file, and designate a database user that the job step will run as. To specify to which file it should be appended, simply place a checkmark in the Append To field. Remember that while the job runs either as the System Administrator or the SQL Server Agent account, you still need to have a database user identified to perform many operations inside a database. The Run As User field lets you choose what user to run the step as. If you choose Self, the step will run as whatever user executed the job. While this is an easy choice to make for most jobs, there might be some jobs for which you want to designate a specific user. Any user already defined in the database of choice will be listed as part of the choices for this field.

There will often be times, however, when you want a job to be able to take advantage of advanced access (that is, at a higher security level) than the user executing the job—that is, you might want to grant rights to the job itself that you do not also grant to the user. In such cases, you should specify an actual user account in the Run As User field, rather than choosing the Self option.

Creating and Managing Schedules

The third tab in the New Job Properties dialog box lets you create and manage schedules. SQL Server stores the schedules independently from the job and job steps so that you can apply one schedule to multiple jobs. SQL Server uses schedules to tell jobs when to run. The schedules, along with alerts, are the configuration components that actually let you automate a server. Configuring a schedule has very few choices, and the dialog box is simplicity itself to navigate.

To create a new schedule, merely change to the Schedules tab and click the New Schedule button. SQL Server, in turn, will display the New Job Schedule dialog box, as shown in Figure 9-10.

Once the dialog box is open, the first thing to do is give the schedule a name. As always, the name should be descriptive so that you can differentiate it from other schedules. The next step is to

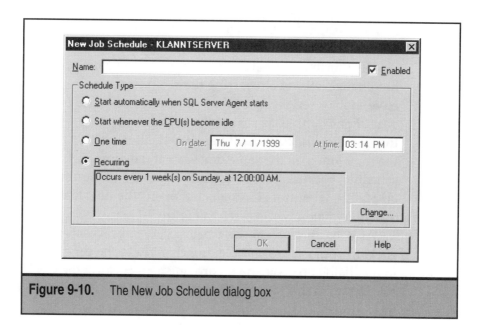

Figure 9-10.   The New Job Schedule dialog box

choose when and how often the job controlled by this schedule will run. To do this, SQL Server provides you with a series of four radio buttons, each of which configures the schedule to perform a different way.

The first radio button from the top configures the schedule to start its job each time that SQL Server starts. You would use this button if the schedule controls a job that must run when the server is rebooted, such as a job that configures database parameters or checks the validity of data.

The second button down configures the schedule so that it will initialize its job or jobs whenever the CPU becomes idle. You use this option when the job is one that performs general maintenance or generates statistical information, but is a job that you do not want to run when the server is being actively used by a large number of users.

The third button configures the schedule to start its jobs one time only, at a time and date that you specify. If you have a job or a series of jobs that you want to execute, but just not at the time you are creating them, you can use this option to schedule the operation for a later date and time. An additional advantage to scheduling tasks in this way is that the tasks will be stored and can easily be retrieved and re-executed whenever you wish.

The fourth and final radio button lets you configure the schedule to initialize jobs on a recurring basis. You use this option when you have a job or series of jobs that you want to execute on a regular basis. For example, as part of the backup plan, you will create jobs that perform the backups and schedule them so that they happen at the same time, on the same day each and every week. A recurring schedule, because it demands more specific configuration, also has an additional button, Change, that opens the Edit Recurring Job Schedule dialog box, as seen in Figure 9-11.

As you can see, you can create a very specific schedule simply by clicking your mouse and making changes to the time and date areas in the dialog box. When you are finished, clicking the OK button will return you to the New Job Schedule dialog box on the Schedules tab.

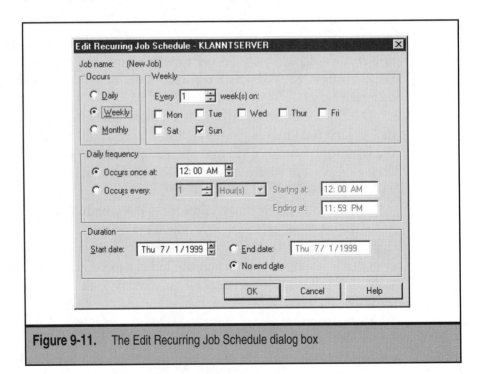

Figure 9-11.   The Edit Recurring Job Schedule dialog box

NOTE: Creating a schedule within the New Job Schedule and supporting dialog boxes is an intuitive process—just like using a calendar. For that reason, in this chapter we do not go any further into the exact steps necessary to create a schedule.

You probably noticed a button on the Schedules tab that lets you create new Alerts. This button will in fact open the correct dialog boxes to create an alert, but we will ignore it here since we have not yet discussed alerts. You will learn how to create and manage alerts later in this chapter.

Managing Notifications

The last tab in the New Job Properties dialog box is the Notifications tab. You use this tab to control whom SQL Server will notify when the job is complete. As you have learned, operators can be notified using e-mail, pagers, or net send operations so that they are informed whenever conditions change within SQL Server. Within the context of a job, you can specify an operator who will be notified when the job completes.

The Notifications tab grants you a high level of control because you can specify different operators to notify if the job is successful, if the job fails, or whenever the job completes no matter what the status. For example, you can configure the job to notify the operator on staff at that time if the job completes, but will notify you if the job fails. This way, someone is always aware that the job completed, and you are notified automatically if there is a problem.

You have a total of five options on the Notifications tab that let you control SQL Server actions. The first three options let you choose between an e-mail, pager, and net send operation, and when to notify each operator. The fourth option tells the job that it should write an error to the Windows application log whenever the job completes with the condition you specify. The fifth option is a job control option that tells SQL Server that it should delete the job if it completes under the specified conditions.

All the options on this tab have an additional drop-down list box that lets you specify conditions. The boxes are all the same and contain the following conditions:

▼   When the job succeeds

■   When the job fails

▲   When the job completes

As you configure each option, you will choose one of these conditions for that option. Since the job must complete as either a success or a failure, you will use these conditions most of the time. You can additionally configure a general operator who is always notified of all events in SQL Server. If this is the case, you will use the option that sends a notification whenever the job completes.

EXAMPLE: AUTOMATING THE BACKUP OF TESTDB

Now let's put all that together and run through the creation of a job. If you have a test server to practice on, we recommend that you follow the steps on your server so that you gain practical, hands-on experience and can easily recognize the dialog boxes and fields that you will be working with. For this example, we will be creating a job that automatically backs up the TESTDB database.

As you know, the first thing to do when automating backups is to create a permanent dump device to which you will send the backups. Since not all servers have a tape device or utilize named pipes, we will create the device on disk. You will remember from Chapter 6 that you create a permanent device using either Enterprise Manager or Transact-SQL (SP_ADDUMPDEVICE). For the purpose of the example, assume that the TestdbBack dump device has already been created. To automate the backup of the TESTDB database, perform the following steps:

1.   Connect to SQL Server using Enterprise Manager.

2.   Expand the object list so that you can see the Jobs object.

3.   Right-click on the Jobs object and choose New Job from the menu.

4. Type **Normal Backup - Testdb** in the Name field for the job.

5. Choose Database Maintenance as the Job category.

6. Leave the Job Owner field set to sa, for System Administrator.

7. In the Description field, type in the following: **This job backs up the Testdb database every day at midnight**.

8. Click on the Steps tab. SQL Server will change the display to reflect the new choices.

9. Click the New button. SQL Server, in turn, will open the New Step dialog box.

10. Type **Backup Testdb** in the Name field.

11. Choose T-SQL from the Type drop-down list.

12. Choose Master from the Database drop-down list.

13. Type the following statement into the command window: **Backup database Testdb to TestdbBack**.

14. Click on the Advanced tab. SQL Server will change the display.

15. Change the On Success option to Quit the Job Reporting Success.

16. Click OK. SQL Server will return to the Steps tab.

17. Click the Schedules tab. SQL Server, in turn, will change the display to reflect the new choices.

18. Type **Occurs every day at midnight** in the Name field.

19. Click the Change button. SQL Server will open the Edit Recurring Schedule dialog box.

20. Click the Daily radio button and then click OK.

21. Click OK.

22. Click the Notifications tab. SQL Server, in turn, will change the display to reflect the new choices.

23. Verify that the Notifications tab is set so that an error is written to the Windows application log if the job fails.

24. Click OK.

At the end of these somewhat lengthy instructions, you have created a job that performs a normal backup on the TESTDB database every day at midnight. If the job fails, an error is written to the Windows application log. The job is stored within SQL Server, and can be changed any time you want.

To create jobs appropriate to your own environment, you can use these same steps—just in a different order, and with objects specific to the environment. As noted previously, the most difficult part of creating jobs is to create your first one. Once you do that, the rest of them become relatively simple.

Now that you know how to create and edit jobs, you will need to learn how to complement and combine jobs with alerts. In the following section, you will learn how to create, configure, and manage alerts.

UNDERSTANDING ALERTS

Simply put, alerts are events or conditions for which you have specified a response. Said another way, alerts are notifications held in SQL Server waiting for a specific server error or a specific change in the operating status of the server, at which time they will execute. As an administrator, you will configure alerts for all sorts of reasons, ranging from a simple notification that a database has reached a certain size, to alerts that trigger jobs as a response to errors detected within SQL Server.

The requirement for an alert to function is that the error be written to the Windows application log. This is because SQL Server monitors the application log and is capable of responding in a predefined manner to specified errors that it detects therein.

Some errors are automatically logged in the application log and as a result must merely have the responses defined. Other errors or conditions will require you to write Transact-SQL statements, which include the RAISERROR command in order to be written into the log. For example, if the error is configured at a severity level between 19 and 25, the error will automatically be entered into the application log. However, if the errors are configured at a severity level outside this range, then you will have to manually program the database application to raise the error and log it in the application log. An example of the RAISERROR command is included in the following Transact-SQL statement:

```
CREATE PROCEDURE Customer_Remove
    @vEmail varchar(30),
    @vCount int OUTPUT
AS
DECLARE @vCustomerID int
SELECT @vCustomerID = CustomerID FROM Customers
    WHERE Email = @vEmail
IF @vCustomerID IS NULL
    RAISERROR ('No customers exist for deletion.', 4, 1)
ELSE
    begin
    DELETE FROM Customers
    WHERE CustomerID = @vCustomerID
    SELECT @vCount = COUNT(*) FROM Customers
    return (1)
    end
```

In the example, the RAISERROR command is invoked only if the vCustomerID field is empty. While the statement is running, if it encounters a field with a null value, it executes the RAISERROR command as an error-handling method. By doing so, the statement writes an error in the application log, which is then detected by SQL Server. Depending on how you have configured SQL Server, the error might simply result in a notification or might cause a job to execute.

Now that you understand how an error gets written to the application log, let's take a look at how SQL Server processes the error so that it can respond. As you have learned, SQL Server monitors the application log for errors. When an error enters the log, SQL Server is made aware of the error and compares it against the alerts that have been defined. Defined alerts are stored in the MSDB Database. If the error matches a predefined alert, SQL Server will respond by performing whatever action you defined in the alert process. In the following section, you will learn how to define and control an alert.

Creating and Managing Alerts

Alerts, like jobs and operators, are controlled by the SQL Server Agent and are therefore configured as child-objects under the SQL Server Agent Object. To create new alerts, you simply expand the Enterprise Manager object list until you can see the Alerts object. To begin the creation process, right-click on the Alerts object and choose New Alert from the menu. SQL Server, in turn, will open the New Alert Properties dialog box.

The big benefit to creating an alert—particularly for administrators who are not as comfortable with Transact-SQL—is that it allows you to create complex application logic on your servers with a simple user interface. For example, you might create an alert that responds to the size of the Transaction Log—for example, when it reaches 75 percent of capacity. That alert might send an information message to the administrator and then execute a job you have created that runs a backup process to back up the Transaction Log. Even more interesting, you might have a second alert that, on failure of the Transaction Log backup (because a tape is full, for instance), sends a notation to the administrator of *that* fact, and then backs up the Transaction Log to a local file. Alerts, then, when used in conjunction with jobs, allow you to automate not only simple tasks but a series of fail-safe tasks as well, all designed to protect against unexpected errors.

Once the New Alert Properties dialog box is open, the first thing to do is give the alert a name. As you have learned, each alert should have a descriptive name, which makes it easy to differentiate from other alerts. After naming the alert, the next step is to choose the type of alert that this will be. You have two choices in the Type drop-down list box: a SQL Server Event Alert and a SQL Server Performance Condition Alert. The first choice is an alert that fires as a result of an error that has been detected in the application log. When you have selected this option, the remaining fields in the dialog box reflect the configuration choices that let you specify what error will fire this alert. Choices for this option are contained in an area named Event Alert Definition, as seen in Figure 9-12.

As you can see, the choices in this area of the dialog box are four basic configurable options: Error Number, Severity, Database Name, and Error Message contents.

From the Field

We have found an alarming number of instances where the servers alert responses are rendered useless because the Application Log for the server is full. Remember to manage your server logs so that your server can continue to handle alerts and problems.

The Error Number field lets you specify the number for this alert. SQL Server allows you to choose from a list of predefined alert numbers, which carry with them predefined error messages, or will let you specify a custom alert number and message. To choose one of

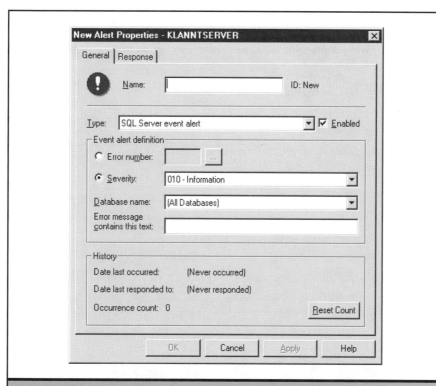

Figure 9-12.   The New Alert Properties dialog box set for event alert definition

the predefined error numbers, simply click the Error Number radio button and then click on the ellipsis (…) button. SQL Server will then open the Manage SQL Server Messages dialog box. This dialog box lets you search for predefined error numbers either by number or by text contained in the message. You should always search for a predefined error before attempting to create new errors. You would not, after all, want to re-create errors that are already defined in SQL Server. You can see the Manage SQL Server Messages dialog box in Figure 9-13.

If you type anything into the Message Text Contains box, or type a number into the Error Number field, and then click the Find button, SQL Server will search through the MSDB Database for a predefined message that matches what you typed. You can further restrict the search criteria at the bottom of the dialog box using the Only Include Logged Messages checkbox, which will restrict the results of the

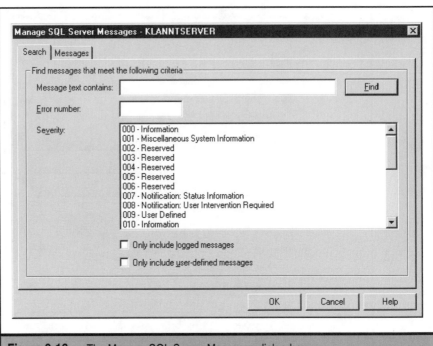

Figure 9-13. The Manage SQL Server Messages dialog box

search to messages programmed to register an error in the Windows application log. You can also use the Only Include User-Defined messages, which restricts the search results to messages that meet the criteria and that also have an error number above 50,000.

When you search for a message, or when you simply click on the Messages tab, you are taken to the Messages tab, and the dialog box changes to display the new choices. The dialog box will now have a large area in the middle that either displays error messages matching the criteria specified in your search or stands empty. Three buttons across the bottom let you create new messages, edit existing messages, or delete messages. If you want to create a new message, for example, click the New button. SQL Server, in turn, will display the New SQL Server Message dialog box, as seen in Figure 9-14.

As its name indicates, this dialog box lets you create new messages. You can specify the Error Number, Severity, Language, or a custom message, and you can even select whether the message should be logged in the application log.

TIP: All custom messages must be numbered over 50,000. SQL Server reserves numbers below 50,000 for predefined messages.

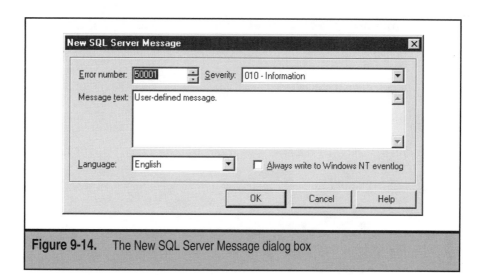

Figure 9-14.   The New SQL Server Message dialog box

When you have either selected or created a message, clicking the OK button will return you to the New Alert Properties dialog box. You will notice that when you choose a defined message number, the Severity field is disabled. This is because the severity is already specified at the message level and unnecessary here. You *do,* however, have the option of specifying all or certain databases for this alert using the Database Name field, and also adding additional text to the alert message in the final customized field.

The second choice fires the alert as a result of a condition such as the size of a database. You can configure the alert to monitor various conditions in SQL Server and to inform you if the conditions rise above or fall below your specified boundaries. If you choose this option, the dialog box will change, giving you new fields for configuration. These fields are Alert, Counter, Instance, Alert If Counter, and Value. In the previous chapter, you learned about Performance Monitor and how to use it when monitoring SQL Server. Here, you will use the same counters to define an alert that is performance-based. To set the alert, simply choose the object that you want to monitor, the appropriate counter for the object, and the instance (if there are instances), and then specify that the alert should fire if the condition rises above, falls below, or becomes equal to the value that you specify in the alert. You do not have to run Performance Monitor for these alerts to work. SQL Server will monitor the server at all times, and will tell you if a defined conditional alert is detected.

TIP: SQL Server will execute a maximum of one alert for any defined error number or defined conditional alert. The most specific alert will always be the one that fires. For example, if you have an alert that monitors the size of all databases and is set to tell you when any database reaches 10GB, plus you have an alert defined that notifies you if the `TESTDB` database specifically reaches 10GB, if a time comes that the `TESTDB` database reaches 10GB, only the alert specified for that database is fired. That is, if the specific alert was not present, then the general alert covering all databases would have fired. SQL Server makes this determination automatically, which prevents multiple alerts from being sent as a result of the same error or condition.

Configuring Event Forwarding

You can configure SQL Server Agent to forward unhandled event messages, or all event messages, to another SQL Server. You can specify that only events above a certain severity level be forwarded. The other SQL Server handles the events, based on its own alert definitions. The name of the server on which the error occurred will be reported in the alert notification.

In a multiserver environment, this means that you need to define alerts on only one server. You might want to forward events to a server that has less traffic than other servers.

For example, you can configure errors with severity levels of 18 or above to be forwarded to the Accounting server, as shown in

Figure 9-15. If an error occurs on your server with severity level 19, the event is automatically forwarded to the Accounting server to address the problem.

NOTE: Event forwarding is available only when SQL Server is installed on Windows NT or 2000, not Windows 95 or Windows 98.

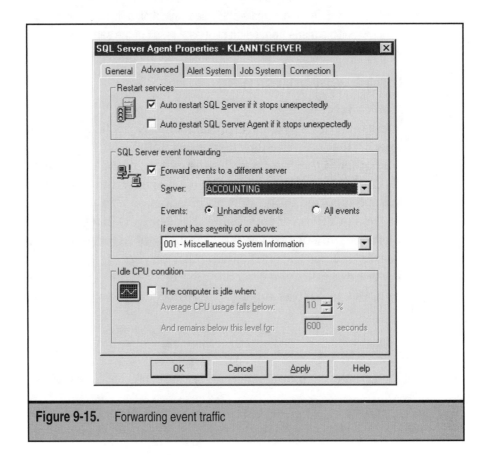

Figure 9-15. Forwarding event traffic

AUTOMATING JOBS
IN A MULTISERVER ENVIRONMENT

One of the more powerful aspects of Microsoft SQL Server's management capabilities is the ability to manage multiple SQL Servers from a single location. This functionality has been extended in version 7 so that you can actually create and schedule a job on multiple servers simultaneously. Multiserver administration involves first configuring the SQL Servers in the enterprise so that one server is a Master server, and then configuring all other servers that you want to administer to be Target servers that can accept control actions from the Master server.

Configuring the Master Server

You configure a Master server using the SQL Server Agent object in Enterprise Manager. When you right-click on the agent object, one of the choices in the pop-up menu is Multiserver Administration. When you move your mouse to this option, a submenu is displayed that contains the choices Make This a Master and Make This a Target. To configure your server as a Master server, simply choose the Make This a Master option. While most administrators will configure multiserver administration using Enterprise Manager, you can, if you want, also designate a server as Master by executing the SP_MSX_ENLIST system stored procedure.

TIP: You learned how to configure Master and Target servers in Chapter 5.

When you specify that a server should be a Master, you should do so with the thought in mind that this server will be acting as a control point for multiple servers. This means that the server must be in the same Windows domain as all Target servers, that you must be using a domain user account for the SQLServerAgent service, and that you should choose a server that has a lower level of use than other servers, because the server will now be handling jobs, alerts, and messages for and from Target servers.

When a server is defined as Master, a special operator called the MSXOperator is created on the server. This special operator is the only operator who can receive notifications from Target servers.

Configuring Target Servers

Using either Enterprise Manager or the SP_MSX_ENLIST system stored procedure, you can configure a server to be a Target server to an existing Master server. From within Enterprise Manager, you simply right-click on the SQL Server Agent object, choose the Multi-Server Administration option from the pop-up menu, and then choose Make This a Target from the submenu.

Target servers must be assigned to a Master server and can only be assigned to one Master server at any one time. Additionally, a Target server must reside in the same Windows domain of which the Master server is a member. If you want to change the Master server assignment for a Target server, you must first have the server defect from its current Master—that is, make it no longer a Target server to that Master—and then reconfigure the server so that it is now a Target server to the new Master.

Once a Master and at least one Target server have been defined, you create jobs just like you would in a single-server environment. Now that multiserver administration has been enabled, the Target server option in the New Job Properties dialog box is also enabled and you can define multiple servers on which the job will execute. For example, if you want to create a backup routine that backs up the Master database on all servers, you can write the Transact-SQL statement one time, designate all servers as Target servers, and save the job. The job will then be created on all servers and, as long as the backup location is the same and available on all servers, the job will run at the appointed time, on all specified servers.

SUMMARY

In this chapter, you learned about the different aspects of SQL Server automation. You learned about operators, jobs, alerts, and how to configure and manage them. You learned about combining jobs and alerts to create error-handling tasks that help your deployment run smoothly. You learned about multiserver automation and how to configure both Master and Target servers. Now that you have the pieces, you will need to practice creating and managing the different parts so that you can gain insight on how to most effectively combine them in your deployment. In the next chapter, you will learn about replication. You will discover that replication is a widely used tool for spreading data across the enterprise.

CHAPTER 10

Replication

Simply put, replication is the act of distributing additional copies (replicas) of data to different servers throughout the enterprise. Depending on the organization, the reasons for distributing data might vary. For example, replication is often a tool for load-balancing solutions, by which the replication process provides multiple servers with the same information so that users can access different servers to achieve the same goal. In organizations that have a great many users, distributing the workload caused by user access across multiple servers is a method that provides higher functionality to each user, and also gives you (as administrator) the ability to grow the SQL Server deployment as the organization itself grows. When the number of users reaches a point where the number of servers is no longer adequate to handle the workload, you merely install additional servers and replicate necessary data to them.

Another common reason for distributing data is to provide functionality to users who are separated geographically and who must otherwise connect to the SQL Server over slow Wide Area Network (WAN) links. Installing additional SQL Servers at remote locations is frequently a solution that increases the productivity of the organization while it reduces the workload on the primary SQL Server.

THE METAPHOR

So that understanding replication would be easier, Microsoft, as it was developing SQL Server, early on chose a metaphor to help explain the replication process it would enable. The concept of replication, it concluded, is based on the distribution of data in much the same way that a newspaper or magazine is distributed to the public to share information contained in it. The organization that distributes magazines and newspapers has three basic parts that must be present for the process to work. These parts are commonly called the publisher, the distributor, and the subscriber. In the text that follows, we will draw comparisons between each part so that you can easily distinguish between the components, and so that you will understand the job of each as it relates to replication in SQL Server.

The Publisher

It is the publisher's job to produce the material that will be distributed. When applied to newspapers, magazines, or books, it is the written work that is produced by the publisher. When applied to SQL Server replication, the original database or subset of data from an original database is considered to be the publication, or the material that the publisher produces. In SQL Server replication, the publisher is the server that holds the original database.

The Distributor

When discussing the distributor of a book, magazine, or newspaper, you are basically talking about the person or organization that takes material developed by a publisher and distributes it to the reader/ subscriber. The distributor's job is really just moving the books, magazines, or newspapers from the publisher to the reader.

In SQL Server replication, the distributor is responsible for moving the data from the publisher (the server containing the original database) to the subscriber (the server receiving the copied data).

The Subscriber

For a magazine or newspaper, the subscriber is the person who actually reads the publication. When you pick up the Sunday paper on your driveway, or a magazine from your mailbox, and take it inside to read, you are the subscriber for that periodical.

In SQL Server replication, the subscriber is the server receiving the copied data. The subscriber is, in effect, the end recipient of the data. It is the subscriber that most people get confused about, because the subscribing server usually makes the copied data available to users, and many people therefore think that the *user* should then be thought of as the subscriber. However, the SQL Server replication metaphor does not take users into account and deals only with the servers involved. The server that receives the replicated data is thus the subscriber.

The Process

When you combine each part of the replication metaphor, you create a scenario that is fairly easy to understand. Let's take a look first at the distribution of a magazine and then at how it relates to the distribution of data in SQL Server.

The publisher of a magazine produces the periodical. The job of the publisher is then to produce the material and make it accessible to a distributor, without which it would never be read. In some cases the publisher has a distribution department and so is actually one company. Nevertheless, the publisher and its distributor are considered separate entities that play their own part in the distribution of the periodical. The distributor's job is to obtain the magazine and move it from the publisher to the subscriber or the reader. The distributor maintains a list of customers who will receive the magazine and sends it to them at a specified time, over an acceptable means of transport such as the mail or private delivery. In some cases, the distributor might also place the magazine in a location where anyone can buy it without having to have their name maintained by the distributor.

In SQL Server replication, the job of the distributor is very similar. The distributor is responsible for moving the data from the publisher to the subscriber. Like the magazine distributor, the distributor can be part of the same server that is the publisher, or a different server entirely. In both cases the distributor is technically separate from the publisher and plays its own part in the process. The distributor maintains a list of subscribing servers and transfers the copied data to those servers. Just like a magazine, the distributor can send data to only listed servers, or can make the data available for anonymous subscribers that can obtain the copied data without being maintained in a list of acceptable servers. The subscriber obtains the data from the distributor. Since obtaining the data is the last step, and the subscriber is the final player, the process stops here.

When configuring replication, you will use terms from this master metaphor to describe what you are working with at the time. To replicate, for example, you will need to configure five components: a publisher, a distributor, a subscriber, publications, and articles. The following table provides an easy-to-follow description of each of these terms:

Component	Description
Publisher	The server that maintains the original database
Distributor	The server that performs the transfer of data from publisher to subscriber
Subscriber	The server that receives the copied data
Publication	The basis for all subscriptions; a collection of articles made available for replication
Article	A single table or subset of table data made available for replication

The SQL Server replication process is divided into these five parts. As the administrator, you will configure each of these parts separately. Once all the parts have been configured, SQL Server combines the parts into a replication solution.

THE REALITY OF REPLICATION

Replication is probably one of the more complex configurations that an administrator has to perform. This is so because there are so many different parts that must work together for the solution to function. As you proceed, remember to take things one step at a time. As with almost everything else that relates to SQL Server, replication solutions seem to work better if you spend more time planning and less time configuring. In the following text, you will learn about the different components and concepts that make up a replication solution. Once you have combined these, you will be able to plan and design a replication solution that best fits your deployment.

One basic concept that you will need to grasp in order to proceed is that, for all types of replication, subscriptions can take one of two forms. A subscription can either be a *push subscription* or a *pull subscription*. Many people get confused as to what determines if a subscription is push or pull, because sometimes you set up a push subscription from the subscriber and a pull subscription from the publisher. The actual determining factor is the location of the Distribution agent. As you will learn in the sections that follow, each type of replication makes use of SQL Server components called *agents*. Each agent has its own responsibility and might or might not be used for a specific type of replication, though all replication types use the Distribution agent. As it relates to subscriptions, if the Distribution agent is running on the distributor, the subscription is considered to be push; if the Distribution agent is running on the subscriber, the subscription is considered to be pull. You will learn more about the functionality of each agent as the different types of replication are explored in later sections.

As you have learned, SQL Server's functionality and configuration are maintained by system databases that store all the information that SQL Server requires to perform its internal functions. When you configure replication, a new system database called DISTRIBUTION is created. The DISTRIBUTION Database functions differently depending on the type of replication that you are using; you will learn more about replication types later in this chapter. In addition to the DISTRIBUTION Database, replication uses a special folder called the *working folder* to manage replication. This folder is always on the distributor and contains various types of data, once again depending on the replication method that you choose. In the following sections, we will take you through the different aspects of replication design. At the end of this chapter, you will be able to choose the most appropriate replication type and model for your organization and configure replication for that design.

Understanding Replication Models

The very first thing you will want to understand are the different physical models on which you base a replicated scenario. The models are simply ways of describing the physical implementation and have little to do with the actual replication methods.

Central Publisher/Distributor

The first model is called a central publisher/distributor. In this model, a single server or group of clustered servers is configured as the publisher/distributor. This model might have one or more subscribers that receive data. You can see the physical design of this model in Figure 10-1.

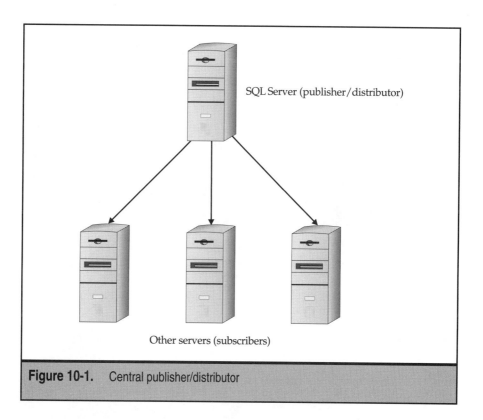

Figure 10-1.   Central publisher/distributor

Central Publisher/Remote Distributor

A derivative of the central publisher/distributor model, this model
is almost identical to the first, the only difference being that a separate
server acts as a distributor. This is a common variance of the standard
model designed to reduce the amount of data that must be transferred
over a wide geographical area. For example, if your main server
was located in Las Vegas and you had three satellite offices in Paris,
Stockholm, and London, the standard replication model would
represent three long-distance connections, each of which has a
significant cost associated with it. If, however, you placed a
distributing server in Las Vegas, and used local connections for
the other offices, you could reduce the cost required to implement
replication by a substantial amount. Figure 10-2 shows the
separation of publisher and distributor.

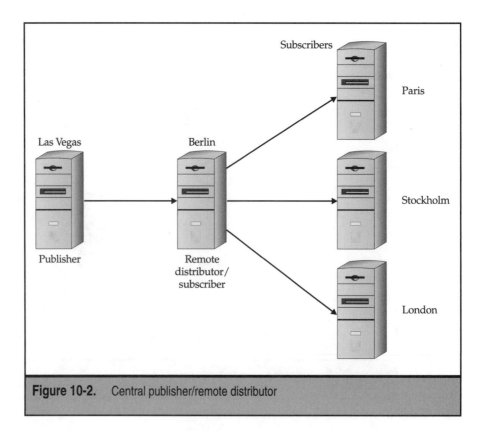

Figure 10-2. Central publisher/remote distributor

Central Subscriber/Multiple Publishers

This model is one that retail establishments frequently use because it lets changes made in multiple locations be updated into a single database. For example, a retail shoe store that does purchasing for an entire district might implement this replication model so that the retail outlets can update their sales to a central office. Once the central office has collated the information from the multiple outlets, it can ascertain what products need to be ordered for the district and finally can place the order for the products. The model is shown graphically in Figure 10-3.

Multiple Publishers/Multiple Subscribers

In organizations where multiple locations must be able to share information with all other locations, the answer is the multiple

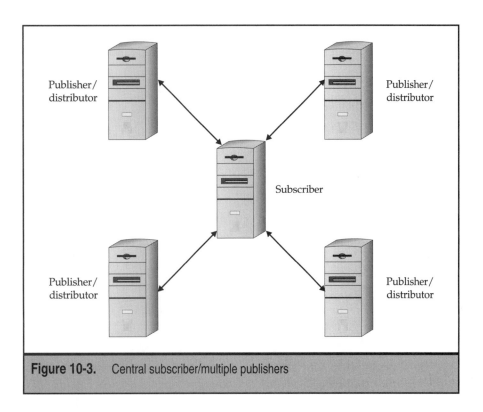

Figure 10-3.   Central subscriber/multiple publishers

publishers/multiple subscribers model. This model lets all publishers communicate with all subscribers. Each server acts as both a publisher/ distributor and a subscriber at the same time, as seen in Figure 10-4.

Again, we stress that the physical models are simply a way of looking at the geographical layout of the implementation. Replication can function in a variety of ways, but the functionality is determined by the replication method. You will learn more about the different methods of replication in the following section.

Understanding the Role of Agents

Because at times it can be difficult to understand the role of agents, we will pause here to define the different agents that SQL Server uses to produce replication. SQL Server has four agents, called Snapshot, Distribution, Log Reader, and Merge. These agents each perform a function that might or might not be used, depending on the type of

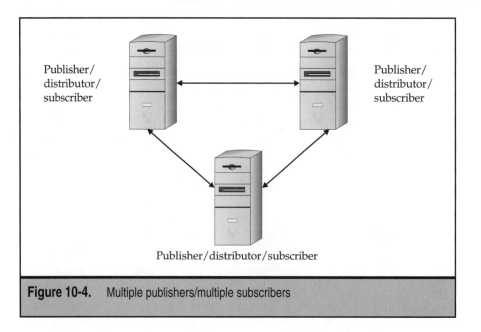

Figure 10-4. Multiple publishers/multiple subscribers

replication that you use. The following is a description of each agent and its duties.

Snapshot

SQL Server uses the Snapshot agent at least once in all types of replication as a means to set up the initial copy of the data to be replicated. The Snapshot agent prepares published databases for replication and stores files on the distributor.

Distribution

SQL Server uses the Distribution agent to apply Snapshot files from the distributor's working folder to subscribers, as well as to apply transactions from the DISTRIBUTION Database to subscribers. The Distribution agent is active at some point in all forms of replication. You can think of the Distribution agent as the transport agent, because it is responsible for actually moving replicated data or transactions from distributor to subscriber.

Log Reader

SQL Server uses the Log Reader agent to monitor the transaction log of each database that has been set up for replication. The Log Reader agent looks for transactions that will be replicated using transactional replication and stores them in the DISTRIBUTION Database. Once the transactions have been stored, the Distribution agent can apply the transactions to subscribers.

Merge

SQL Server uses the Merge agent to meld the changes from different sites that have changed since the last snapshot was made. In some cases, there is only an initial snapshot, after which the Merge agent updates all changes that have been made since. In other cases, a snapshot is performed on a regular basis to ensure consistency, and the Merge agent merely updates changes between snapshots.

Each of the preceding descriptions is a simple description of the job for each agent. In the following sections, you will learn about the different methods that you will use for replication. As you read the methods, take note of the different agents that are used. You will also further consider the agents and their work later in our discussion of replication.

From the Field

Agents are the core of replication; in order to ensure that your replicated environment is functioning well, you need to monitor the replication agents often. You can start Performance Monitor with all four replication agent counters already in it by right-clicking on the Replication Monitor object.

Understanding Replication Methods

A replication method or replication type is a way of describing the actual replication process. Three basic methods for replication exist, and in some instances they can be combined to create custom solutions. At the heart of all replication schemes, you will find one of the basic three: snapshot replication, transactional replication, and merge replication. Each method of replication has a component inside SQL Server called an agent. The agent is responsible for managing and controlling the replication process and is designed to handle that type of replication specifically. As you will find, sometimes a replication design uses more than one agent, but all types use at least one. In the following text, you will learn the process, the advantages and disadvantages, and some tips on when to use each replication method.

Snapshot Replication

The simplest method to set up, and perhaps the easiest to understand, the snapshot replication method functions by periodically sending data in bulk format. You will use this method when the subscribing servers can function in a read-only environment, and also when the subscribing server can function for some time without updated data.

Functioning without updated data for a period of time is referred to as *latency*. For example, in the case of the retail shoe store used in a previous example, the store uses replication as a means of maintaining an accurate inventory throughout the district. Since the inventory can be managed on a weekly or even monthly basis, the retail stores can function without updating the central server for days at a time. This scenario has a high degree of latency and is a perfect candidate for snapshot replication.

Additional reasons to use this type of replication include scenarios with low-bandwidth connections. Snapshot replication will take a long time, but can be scheduled for a time when other activity on the network is low. Since the subscriber can last for a while without an update, this provides a solution that is lower in cost than other methods while still handling the requirements.

Snapshot replication occurs once in almost all replication scenarios, because SQL Server uses snapshot replication to establish the first copy of data on a subscriber. Later in the chapter, you will learn more about how SQL Server initiates replication. Snapshot replication also has the added benefit of being the only replication type in which the replicated tables are not required to have a primary key.

Snapshot replication works by reading the published database and creating files in the working folder on the distributor. These files are called snapshot files and contain the data from the published database as well as some additional information that will help create the initial copy on the subscription server. SQL Server stores configuration and status information in the DISTRIBUTION Database, but stores all actual data in the snapshot files.

In the case of a push subscription, the Distribution agent runs on the distributor and sends the snapshot files to the subscriber. If you are using a pull subscription, the Distribution agent runs on the subscriber and obtains the snapshot files from the working folder on the distributor. The difference is important to understand. The computer that is running the Distribution agent has the higher workload. If you are using a push subscription, the distributor machine carries the majority of the workload. If you are using a pull subscription, the subscribing machine carries the majority of the workload. Depending on the machines in your deployment, you will often choose what type of subscription to use based on the number of users and the total overhead of the servers. In most cases, you will want to place the Distribution agent on the machine with the lower workload.

From the Field

Snapshot replication is the most common implementation for small organizations who connect using modems, but do not have to merge data. If your organization uses a modem to connect, and only needs to send the data one way, you will most likely use snapshot replication.

Transactional Replication

In what could be considered the opposite of snapshot replication, transactional replication works by sending changes to the subscriber as they happen. As you know, SQL Server processes all actions within the database using Transact-SQL statements. Each completed statement is called a *transaction*. In transactional replication, each committed transaction is replicated to the subscriber *as it occurs*. You can control the replication process so that it will accumulate transactions and send them at timed intervals, or transmit all changes as they occur. You use this type of replication in environments having a lower degree of latency and higher bandwidth connections. Transactional replication requires a continuous and reliable connection, because the Transaction Log will grow quickly if the server is unable to connect for replication and might become unmanageable.

Transactional replication begins with a snapshot that sets up the initial copy. That copy is then later updated by the copied transactions. You can choose how often to update the snapshot, or choose not to update the snapshot after the first copy. Once the initial snapshot has been copied, transactional replication uses the Log Reader agent to read the Transaction Log of the published database and stores new transactions in the DISTRIBUTION Database. The Distribution agent then transfers the transactions from the publisher to the subscriber.

Transactional Replication with Updating Subscribers

An offshoot of standard transactional replication, this method of replication basically works the same way, but adds to subscribers the ability to update data. When a subscriber makes a change to data locally, SQL Server uses the Microsoft Distributed Transaction Coordinator (MSDTC), a component included with SQL Server 2000, to execute the same transaction on the publisher. This process allows for replication scenarios in which the published data is considered read-only most of the time, but can be changed at the subscriber on occasion if needed. Transactional replication with updating subscribers requires a permanent and reliable connection of medium to high bandwidth.

From the Field

Though the distributed transactions required by updating subscribers work best in high bandwidth, reliable network connections, you can adjust the replication agent profiles to tolerate a higher level of packet loss or general network error. Don't think that you cannot use this method if the first installations fail.

Merge Replication

In situations where two or more servers must share all information equally, and where all sites must be able to update data, merge replication is the answer. In merge replication, each server accepts changes from the local users, and changes are later merged at defined intervals or when manually initiated. This method of replication has the potential for conflicts and transactional inconsistencies, which makes it the most difficult type to design and manage. Additionally, merge replication requires changes to be made to the database schema. A few system tables are added and unique columns are required to identify each server's database from the others.

Just like transactional replication, merge replication begins with a snapshot; however, merge replication is thereafter maintained by the Merge agent. The Merge agent is the active SQL Server component in this type of replication and is responsible for the replication workload. In pull subscriptions, the Merge agent runs on the subscribing computer. For push subscriptions, the Merge agent runs on the distributor.

Because this type of replication moves data both ways, the Merge agent will first copy changes from the publisher and apply them to the subscriber, and then take changes from the subscriber and apply them to the publisher. Once the changes have been applied both ways, the Merge agent will look at and resolve any conflicts. Prior to being applied, changes for each server are stored in the DISTRIBUTION Database.

> ### From the Field
>
> Merge replication is subject to conflicts, though most organizations find these to be infrequent. You would do well to watch the replication carefully for the first few months to determine if a full-time administrator is required to watch and control the result of conflicts.

You should use merge replication in situations that require independent updates to data at more than one server location. Conflict handling is a matter of design; the typical method of conflict resolution is to use the Merge agent, which resolves conflicts based on preassigned priorities. You can, however, take greater control over the process and create custom triggers that handle conflict resolution.

PLANNING REPLICATION

Designing a replicated environment can be difficult. A lot of variables must be considered to produce the most effective solution. The first thing that you will have to do is gather as much information as you can. Even a small amount of information could alter the way you design your implementation. In the following text, we will take you through some common questions that we have asked ourselves repeatedly when planning for replication. We recommend that you try to approach the task as if you were a consultant who does not know much about the network. Ask the questions even if you know the answers, and write everything down. At the end, you will have a good idea what direction you should follow for replication, and will have a quantity of information about your deployment that might surprise you.

Why Replicate?

The very first question that we ask is, "Why replicate?" This question is a probing one, with much more complex answers than you might expect. Reasons to replicate typically involve a need to have data more readily accessible to users in multiple locations. You should use replication if the organization needs multiple copies of the same data. Keep in mind that the reason to replicate should always have to do with functionality, not data protection. Many administrators make the mistake of thinking that replication makes an ideal backup solution, when in fact it does not. You should *not* use replication as a primary backup solution, because the components that make up replication are not designed to protect data and cannot be relied on to perform such a task. Always use the right tools for the right job: Use backup tools for backup solutions.

What Data Needs to Be Replicated?

You need to know exactly what data needs to be replicated. Sometimes you will be replicating an entire table or even multiple tables, but many times only a small subset of data is required at the subscriber. As a general rule, never replicate more data than you have to because it needlessly adds to the workload of both servers.

You should be thinking about how to organize the data if you are replicating more than one article. This is especially true if the replicated data comes from multiple tables. Knowing what data is going to be involved in replication will lead you to organizational thoughts that you might otherwise miss, such as descriptively naming the articles and publications.

Who Are the Subscribers?

You must know as much about the subscribers as possible. In some cases, they will be anonymous and you will configure the publication so that it will accept anonymous subscribers. At other times, you will know a great deal about subscribers and will be able to use that information to determine how to best use the subscribing machine in the overall picture.

You should take into account the hardware level of the machine, the number of users it serves, the connection to the machine, its bandwidth, and its reliability. You need to know how many subscribers exist, because your design might change if there are more than one, or more than five. If you are designing a solution that requires merge replication or updating subscribers, you must determine how conflicts will be addressed and handled.

How Often Must You Replicate?

Knowing how long the subscribing site can function efficiently without an update from the publisher is vital knowledge that determines many of the choices involved in your design. For example, if your site cannot function more than a few minutes without an update from the publisher, snapshot replication will not be a viable choice because it takes too long to copy the snapshot to the subscriber. However, if the data on the subscriber does not need to be updated more frequently than say, once a month, week, or day, you might be able to reduce the resource cost of replicating by choosing a method that replicates only on demand, or at widely spread, predetermined intervals. Additionally, you might be able to reduce costs by using a connection method that is not available 24 hours a day—for example, you might be able to use snapshot replication with some type of dial-up networking, rather than maintaining an expensive ISDN or fractional-T1 connection that is unnecessary for a given location's needs.

What Will You Use for the Remote Connection?

All through this chapter we talk about the connection and how important it is when designing a replicated SQL Server deployment. When you are designing a replicated SQL Server deployment and want to determine the most appropriate model and method for replication, you must know all you can about the type of connection that you either have or plan to have. For example, you should not design a replication scenario that includes the use of distributed transactions if the connection is subject to frequent failures. Some of the things that you will want to be aware of when designing the replication model for your environment(s) are the speed of the connection, the reliability of the connection, and the cost of transmitting data. In some cases, Internet service providers (ISPs) charge different rates for transmission during certain hours. If you can plan replication so that the data is copied during these hours, the organization might benefit from a significant cost reduction.

What Replication Method?

Since replication can function in a variety of ways, knowing what method or type of replication you want to use is an important part of the planning process. You might decide to change the replication method based on other requirements or pre-existing conditions, or you might choose to maintain the replication type and instead make other changes, like installing a new server to act as a distributor, or increasing the abilities of an existing server. Knowing what the planned replication type is will add complexity to the plan and might reveal potential problems that might have otherwise been missed until you began to configure the servers.

What Replication Model?

As you have learned, a variety of physical models are available to provide a way of looking at the geographical layout of the design. As part of the initial plan, you should decide on a physical model and include the model in your discussions. In the same way that knowing the replication method can add to the discovery of potential problems, knowing the model as you plan will help you identify potential problems and might reveal conditions that affect the overall design.

Where Is the Distribution Agent?

As part of your design, you should try to ascertain the most efficient location for the Distribution agent. As you know, depending on the type of subscription you choose, the Distribution agent will run on

> ### From the Field
> The push or pull choice is probably one of the most overlooked factors in replication. Give careful consideration as to where the active agent will run because it will impact the performance of that server.

either the distributor or the subscriber. Knowing where the agent will run during the planning stage will help you determine hardware requirements for the servers involved.

Is the DISTRIBUTION Database Shared?

One of the many choices you have when designing replication is to share or not share the DISTRIBUTION Database. In some replication models, such as central subscriber/multiple publishers designs, multiple publishers share a single distributor. When that is the case, you can choose for each publisher to maintain and use its own DISTRIBUTION Database, or you can choose to have all publishers use the same DISTRIBUTION Database. If you choose to use independent databases, the replication scheme will be able to maintain separate and independent backups for each publisher. If you choose to share the database, separation of publishers is not possible, but management and care of the distributor is easier. There might also be some advantages or disadvantages to either choice depending on the design of the published database, which you would obtain from the database developer.

Push or Pull?

To properly design a replication scenario, you must, of course, know whether you will use a push or a pull subscription. In addition to affecting the location of the distributor, the subscription choice will determine who initiates the action during replication and, in some cases, will even dictate the physical location where you must perform configuration settings.

What Hardware Will You Use?

Replication adds complexity to the operation of SQL Server. In addition to the increased workload that the servers will endure, there are increased space requirements for storage of the newly replicated data, the snapshot files, and the DISTRIBUTION Database. When you are designing replication, be sure to take into account the need for additional hardware such as memory, processor speed, and disk space.

Information that might help you make such decisions includes the amount of replicated data, how many publications will be present, how many articles are contained by the publications, how frequently replicated data will be sent (plus how long replicated data might have to be stored prior to transmission), and the normal workload of both the publisher and subscriber.

TIP: We have observed that many administrators tend to gloss over the importance of hardware improvements when adding replication to a SQL Server environment. Many times, we have found that there will be a substantial impact on the performance of the SQL Servers from the addition of replication. When building your replication solution, do not underestimate the value of additional memory, additional hard drive space, and other hardware improvements.

Completing the Replication Planning

Once you have asked all the questions and gathered the information, you can create an outline of sorts that describes the process you will use to set up replication. As with any planning process, you should write everything down and have a written plan before you begin to configure. The most effective administrators typically have a peer or consultant check the plan and attempt to find errors or problems. Even if the plan appears to be sound, having someone play devil's advocate can often bring issues to light that you might otherwise have missed. In the following section, you will begin to learn how to actually configure replication. Remember as you proceed, that although the wizards and other configuration interfaces are simple

---

From the Field

One planning tool that seems to help a great deal is a network drawing. If you have nothing else, create a crude drawing of the servers involved in replication and mark what role you have assigned to each one. This visual aid may help to identify potential problems early, when you may otherwise have missed them.

---

and easy to follow, replication itself is a complex process—and the more planning you put into the process, the better off you will be.

SETTING UP REPLICATION

To set up replication is to follow a truly step-by-step process. For one step to work properly, you must have first completed the previous step. Understanding the process is really just a matter of breaking apart the pieces involved and looking at what is required to replicate.

The first thing that you will need to do is configure a distributor. You must have a distributor configured before you can configure a publisher. The reason for this is simply that not all publishers are also the distributor, and for a publisher to use a remote distributor the distributor must have already been configured.

Once the distributor is configured, the next logical step is to configure the publisher. The publisher, after all, is the foundation of replication and you cannot configure a subscriber without a publisher. You will, therefore, configure a publisher along with its publications and articles at this point.

The final step is configuring the subscriber. No matter whether you configure the subscriber from the subscribing machine or remotely from another machine, it will always be the last step that you will complete.

Now that you understand the steps, let's jump right into configuration. The following sections will teach you how to configure a distributor, publisher, and subscriber, in that exact order, because that is the order in which you must perform the configuration, as you have seen previously.

Configuring a Distributor

The initial configuration of a distributor in Microsoft SQL Server 2000 is performed using a wizard. Using Enterprise Manager, you will activate the wizard either by choosing the correct option from the Wizard list, or by choosing the correct option from the Replication submenu. You will find replication choices under the Tools menu in Enterprise Manager. To open the wizard, perform the following steps:

1. Connect to SQL Server using Enterprise Manager and click on the name of your server.

2. From the Tools menu, choose Replication. SQL Server, in turn, will display the options in the Replication submenu.

3. Choose the Configure Publishing and Subscribers option. SQL Server will open the Configure Publisher and Distribution Wizard.

The wizard begins by displaying a splash screen that has no configuration choices and that is merely there so that you can be sure that you are in the right wizard. To move onto the actual configuration, click the Next button. SQL Server will change the display to reflect your first choice.

The first choice that you have in this wizard is whether or not to use this server as the distributor. If you have already configured a distributor elsewhere and wish to use that server as a distributor, you can choose that server by selecting the lower radio button. There is also a Register Server button available, in case you wish to use a server that is not registered in Enterprise Manager. If this is the first server you are configuring, or even if it is not but you still want to use this server as a distributor, you will select the upper radio button (selected by default) and click the Next button. You can see the first dialog box for this wizard in Figure 10-5.

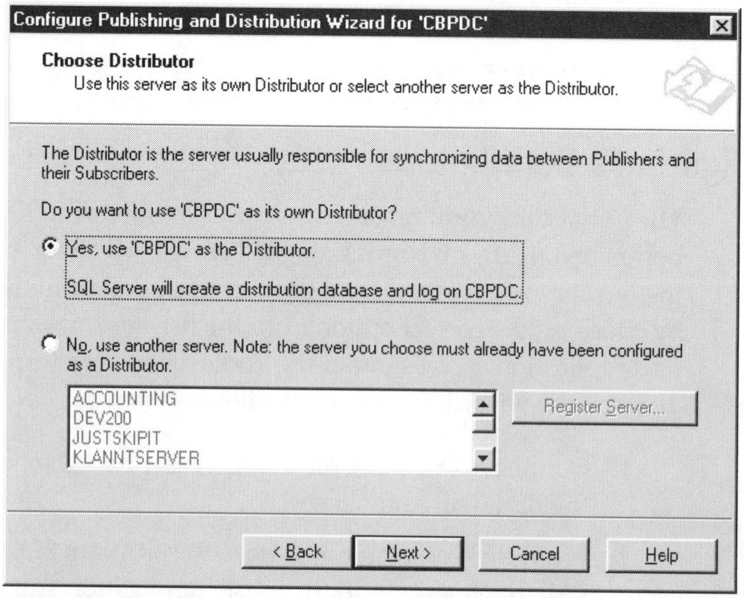

Figure 10-5. The Configuring Publishing and Distribution Wizard

When you click the Next button, the wizard will change to display the second choice. This choice is whether to use the default settings for the DISTRIBUTION Database. By default, the wizard will configure your server to act as the distributor, and will enable only your server to act as a publisher or subscriber. If you choose the default selection, this is the last choice you have and clicking the Next button will take you to the end of the wizard. If, however, you choose to make changes to the default configuration, click the upper radio button and then click the Next button. You can see the dialog box showing the second choice in Figure 10-6.

If you chose to accept the default settings, the wizard will be at an ending screen with only Back or Finish as options. If, however, you chose to make changes to the configuration, the wizard will now display configuration choices for the DISTRIBUTION Database. You can control

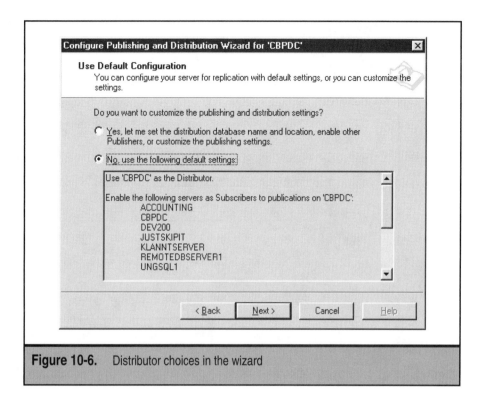

Figure 10-6.   Distributor choices in the wizard

the name of the database and the location of the database files. If you plan to use only one DISTRIBUTION Database, we recommend that you leave the name of the database as DISTRIBUTION because it will be easy to identify and will help remind you to manage it. If you plan to have multiple DISTRIBUTION Databases, we recommend that you change the name to be descriptive. A name that identifies which publisher this database will be for is ideal.

The other two fields available in the wizard at this stage let you control the database files. The upper of the two lets you control the primary database file, while the lower of the two lets you control the Transaction Log file for the database. To change the default locations, simply type a complete path for each into the fields provided and then click the Next button. You can see the wizard showing the third choice in Figure 10-7.

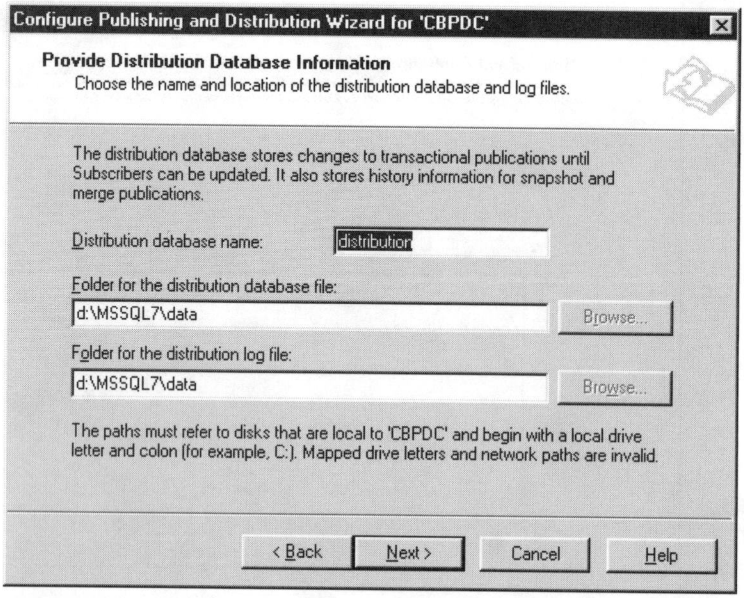

Figure 10-7. Controlling the DISTRIBUTION Database

The fourth choice in the wizard lets you specify which servers are to be enabled as publishers for this distributor. The dialog box has a large window in which you will find all servers that are registered in Enterprise Manager. Additionally, there are buttons that let you enable all servers, enable none of the servers, and register additional servers. You can see the wizard showing the fourth choice in Figure 10-8.

You can also specify additional parameters for any server by clicking on the ellipsis (...) button found inside the Register Server window. If you click this button, you can configure the DISTRIBUTION Database (if multiple databases are present), the Snapshot folder, and the account with which replication agents will connect to the server for the specified server, as seen in Figure 10-9.

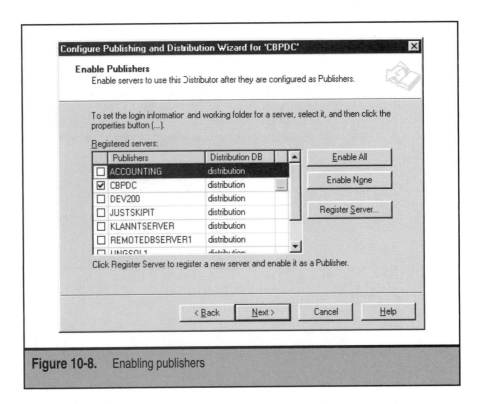

Figure 10-8. Enabling publishers

Once you have configured the servers that you want to enable as publishers for this distributor, clicking the Next button will change the display in the wizard to show you the fifth choice. This lets you enable databases for transactional or merge publication. There is no option to enable databases for snapshot replication, because snapshot replication does not require any changes to be made to the databases. The dialog box includes a list of databases in which you can enable one database at a time, as well as buttons to enable all or none of the databases for both replication types, as shown in Figure 10-10.

Although technically it makes little difference as to the order in which publishers and subscribers are enabled for a specific distributor,

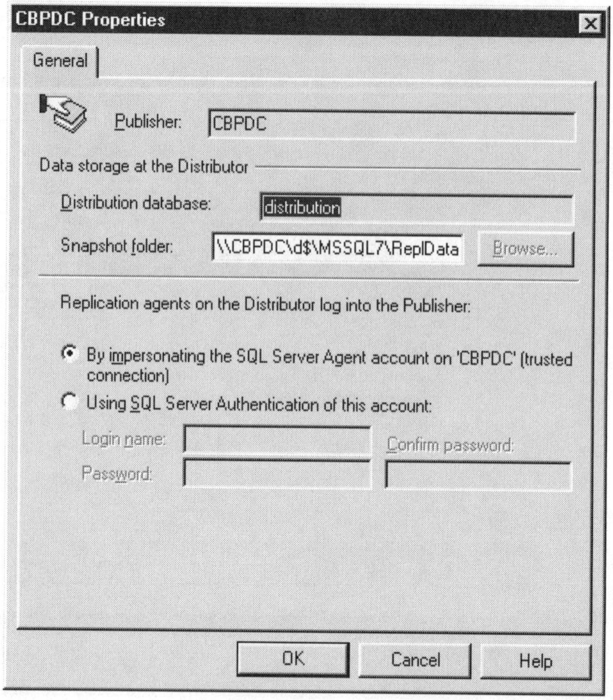

Figure 10-9. Controlling the replication agents' connection type

the Configuration Wizard presents the choice to enable subscribers after publishers. The sixth choice in the wizard will let you enable subscribers for this distributor. The dialog box is almost identical to the one that lets you enable publishers, and has the same options.

Once the subscribers have been configured, the wizard takes you to a completion screen that has only Back and Finish options available. If you are sure of your choices and do not want to check anything, click on the Finish button and the wizard will complete the process, performing your specified configurations. If you want to go back and check any of your settings, click the Back button to return to previous screens.

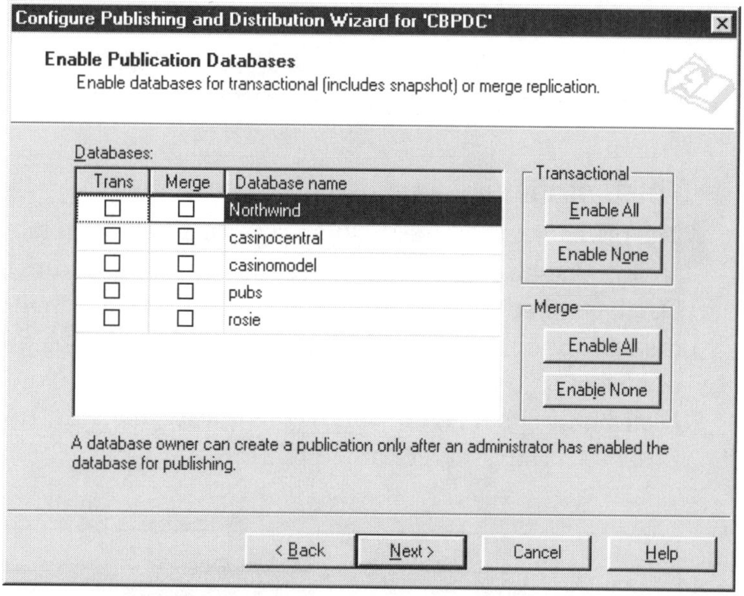

Figure 10-10.   Enabling databases for publishing

Modifying the Publisher and Distributor

If you chose to take the default settings when you were setting up the
distributor, or if you want to change publisher or distributor settings
after initial setup, you will need to access the distributor properties
dialog box. After the initial setup, you can access the Publisher and
Distributor Properties dialog box using the same menu option that
let you set up the distributor to begin with. Using Enterprise
Manager, if you choose Replication from the Tools menu, a submenu
is displayed. If you choose the Configure Publishing, Subscribers,
and Distribution option, the dialog box will be displayed.

The Publisher and Distributor Properties dialog box has four tabs
that let you change the appearance of the dialog box so that you can
configure the appropriate settings. The tabs are Distributor, Publishers,

Publication Databases, and Subscribers. Each tab has configurable options that relate specifically to the replication component for which it is named. In the following sections, you will learn how to use each tab to configure a specific replication component.

The Distributor Tab

The primary tab for the dialog box is the Distributor tab, which is always displayed by default. On this tab you configure DISTRIBUTION Databases, access a configuration screen that lets you make changes to the replication agents, and specify the distribution password that publishers use when connecting to this distributor. You can see the Distributor tab in Figure 10-11. (In this case, the DISTRIBUTION Database is on a server named JUSTSKIPIT.)

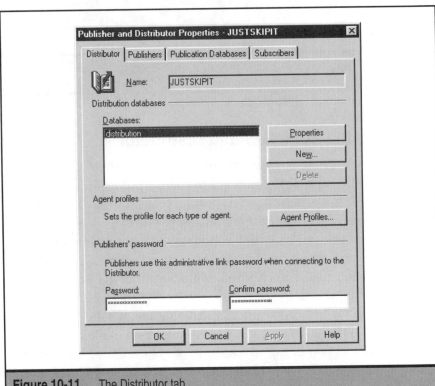

Figure 10-11. The Distributor tab

The upper portion of the tab contains a small window that lists the DISTRIBUTION Databases currently configured on this server. You can make changes to any listed database by selecting it and clicking on the Properties button, create new databases by clicking on the New button, or delete existing databases using the Delete button. If you choose to create a new database, SQL Server will display the Distribution Database Properties dialog box as shown in Figure 10-12.

Using this dialog box, you can specify the name of the database, the location of the database files, and how long the database should store transactions and performance history. If you choose to affect the properties of an existing database, you will not be able to change the name of the database or the location of the files, but

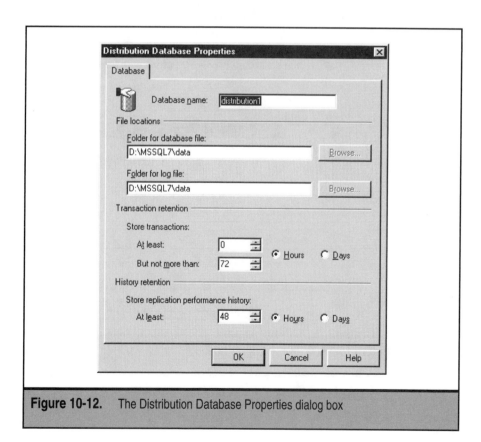

Figure 10-12.   The Distribution Database Properties dialog box

you *will* be able to control the storage options for transactions and performance history.

In the middle of the Distributor tab there is a button named Agent Profiles. When clicked, this button opens the Agent Profiles dialog box, as seen in Figure 10-13.

This dialog box lets you fine-tune the replication agents to perform exactly the way you want. You will learn more about advanced tuning of replication agents in the next chapter.

At the very bottom of the Distributor tab, there are two fields that let you specify the Distributor password. Publishers use this password when connecting to a distributor. Here you can change

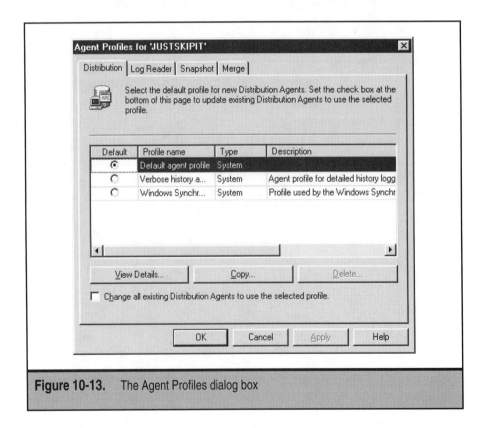

Figure 10-13. The Agent Profiles dialog box

the password so that when you configure other publishers, you can specify the correct password. The distributor password ensures that unauthorized users cannot connect to the distributor.

The Publishers Tab

The second tab in the Publisher and Distributor Properties dialog box, the Publishers tab, contains a window that displays all registered servers. Here you can enable or disable servers to be publishers for this distributor. You can also access the properties for a specific server from within this window. If you click on the ellipsis (…) button, the Server Properties dialog box will be displayed. Just as in the initial setup wizard, you can use this dialog box to affect both the location of the snapshot files and the account that the replication agents on the distributor use when logging in to the publisher. To the right of the window you will find three buttons that let you enable all listed servers, enable none of the listed servers (which has the effect of turning all enlistments off), or register a new server so that you can then enable it. Enabling a server to be a publisher does not automatically configure publishing on that server, but merely configures the distributor so that it will accept publications from that server when you *do* configure it. Figure 10-14 shows the Publishers tab.

The Publication Databases Tab

The third tab in the Publisher and Distributors Properties dialog box, the Publication Databases tab, lets you enable or disable databases on the server for publication. The only databases listed are those that are on the server that you selected when you opened the dialog box from Enterprise Manager. The list will let you enable transactional or merge replication. To enable a database, simply click in the checkbox that represents the database for transactional or merge replication. To the right of the window, a series of four buttons will let you enable all databases or none of them for both replication types. The buttons

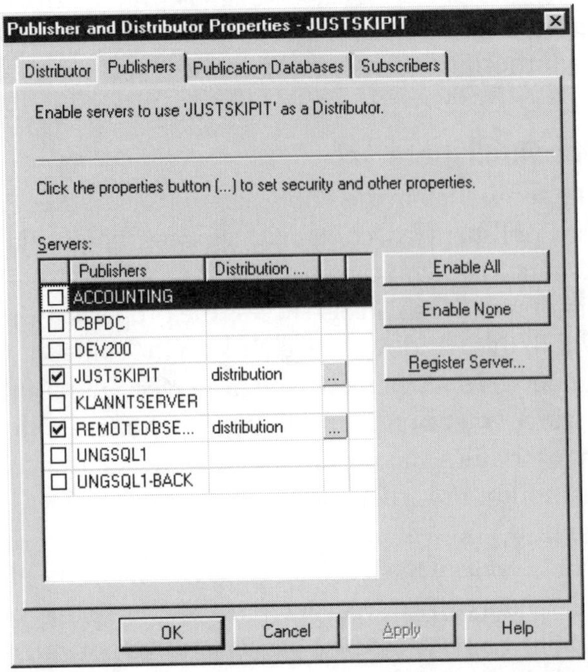

Figure 10-14. The Publishers tab

permit you to easily enable or disable all databases at the same time. You can see the Publication Databases tab in Figure 10-15.

The Subscribers Tab

The fourth tab, the Subscribers tab, lets you enable servers to be subscribers for this distributor. The dialog box it summons looks quite similar to the Publishers tab and has a window that displays registered servers in it, along with buttons that let you enable all servers, enable no servers, and register new servers so that you

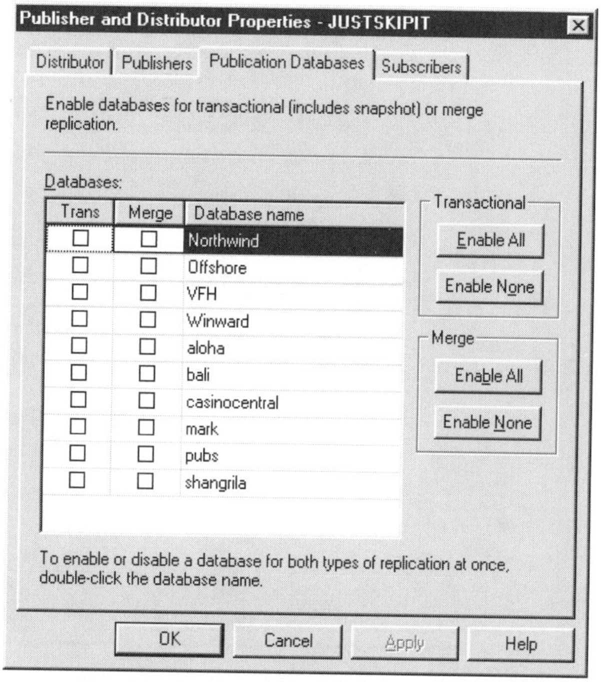

Figure 10-15.   The Publication Databases tab

can then enable them. Enabling a subscriber does not configure a subscription, but merely configures the distributor so that it will accept a subscription from that server. Figure 10-16 shows the Subscribers tab.

The four tabs together let you configure all the options for the distributor, publisher, and subscriber at a server level. To actually produce publications, or to create subscriptions, you must use other dialog boxes. In the following sections, you will learn how to create a publication, and later how to subscribe to it.

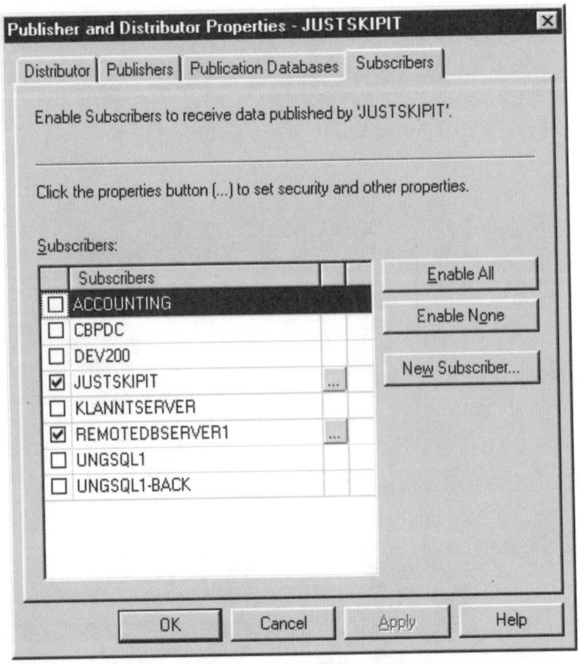

Figure 10-16. The Subscribers tab

CREATING A PUBLICATION

Once a distributor has been configured, a publisher has been enabled for that distributor, and a database has been enabled for publication, the next step is to create a publication. Creating a publication in SQL Server 2000 is performed using a wizard. You can activate the wizard from the list of available wizards, or you can choose Tools | Replication | Create and Manage Publications in Enterprise Manager.

No matter which method you choose to start the wizard, the first dialog box displayed does not at first appear to be a wizard at all. The first dialog box is the Create and Manage Publications dialog box shown in Figure 10-17.

This dialog box contains a list of available databases on the server, and identifies databases that are enabled for publication by placing a

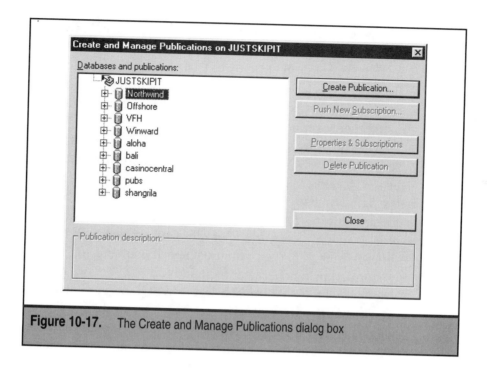

Figure 10-17. The Create and Manage Publications dialog box

cupped hand under the image for the database, which is similar to the hand that indicates a shared folder in Windows. To the right of the window, you will find buttons that let you create publications, push new subscriptions, affect the properties of existing subscriptions, and delete publications. To create a new publication, click on the Create Publication button. SQL Server in turn will start the Create Publication Wizard.

Navigating the Create Publication Wizard

As usual, the first screen of the wizard is just a splash screen that will let you cancel or continue and is there only to let you verify that you are using the right wizard. Clicking the Next button will take you to the first choice of the wizard.

The first choice in the Create Publication Wizard lets you choose what kind of replication this publication will be. You can choose from snapshot, transactional, or merge replication by clicking the appropriate radio button and then clicking the Next button.

The second choice in the wizard lets you decide whether to allow immediate updating subscribers. To use this feature, both servers must be running the Microsoft Distributed Transaction Coordinator (MSDTC). Click the appropriate radio button for your choice and then click the Next button. This option is not available if you are using merge replication.

The third choice lets you specify whether all the subscribing servers will be SQL Servers or if one or more subscribers will not be a SQL Server. If all the subscribing servers will be SQL Servers, the data will be replicated in a format native to SQL Server. This format requires fewer bytes than standard characters and takes less workload to process. If one or more subscribers will be on a system other than SQL Server, you must specify so here so that replication is performed using character format. Non-SQL Server systems will not understand the data transfer if it is in SQL Server native format.

The fourth choice lets you create articles for the publication. As you know, articles are the smaller portions of a publication. An article represents the actual data that is being replicated to the subscriber. The dialog box lists the tables and stored procedures that are available on the server from which you started the wizard. Using the radio buttons on the right side of the dialog box, you can choose to list all the tables and stored procedures, or only those that have already been configured for replication. Another set of radio buttons will let you restrict the view so that only the stored procedures or only the tables on the server are displayed. In addition to the radio buttons that you find in the dialog box, two buttons let you publish all the objects in the list or none of them (which has the effect of disabling any objects in the list that have already been published).

The fifth choice lets you name and describe the publication. You should give the publication a name that easily identifies it from the other publications and place a detailed description into the appropriate field. Creating a detailed description now will save you or another administrator a great deal of time later, when you are trying to troubleshoot or simply need to understand what publications have which articles and data published.

The sixth choice presented to you lets you decide whether to affect the default properties of the publication. By default, the publication will publish all data in the tables and stored procedures that were specified. As you know, you can filter data in an article so that only a subset of the data is replicated to the subscriber. To filter data in any way, you will have to change the properties of the publication. You will learn how to filter data later in this chapter. For now, assume that you do not want to filter data and proceed to the next screen.

NOTE: You can only replicate data—you cannot replicate things like views or schema changes. If you change the design of a published database, you will need to set up replication again for that database.

The final choice presented by the wizard is the ending splash screen. This screen lets you back out to make changes to any of the specifications that you have made, or click the Finish button to end the wizard and create the publication.

After the publication is created, from time to time you will likely want to make changes to the configuration, or simply check to ensure that all is well. You should have noticed at the end of the wizard that you were returned to the original dialog box that lets you manage publications and articles. Now that a publication has been created, the image of a book will appear under the database on which the publication is based. To affect the properties of this publication, simply select it and then click the Properties & Subscriptions button. SQL Server, in turn, will display the Publication Properties dialog box.

Exploring the Publication Properties Dialog Box

This dialog box is divided into nine tabs that let you configure the different aspects of a publication. In the following text, you will learn about each tab and how you will use it to configure a publication.

The General Tab

The default tab is called General. The General tab will automatically be displayed each time you access this dialog box. You use the General tab to change the description of the publication. Further, you can specify a transfer format and also set a time when the publication will expire if it has not yet been synchronized. Expiration is an important specification because it ensures that the publication will not continue to try to synchronize data if for some reason the publisher/distributor is unable to connect to the subscriber.

The Articles Tab

You use the Articles tab to make changes to the published articles in the publication. The dialog box is the same one you saw in the wizard when you first created the publication. Using this tab, you can publish (or choose to no longer publish) articles based on tables and stored procedures on the server you are configuring.

The Filter Columns Tab

This tab is where you will go if you want to filter a table by column to produce a subset of information for replication. Depending on your environment, you might not have to replicate all the columns in the table. For example, if your table includes a column of information that is present only to differentiate it from tables in other servers, you will not need to replicate that information and so will filter that column out.

The Filter Rows Tab

Just as with the Filter Columns tab, you use this tab to filter a table by row so that it produces only a subset of data for replication. If you want to replicate only rows that meet certain criteria, use this tab to create a filter that lists the criteria. If you click on the ellipsis (...) button found next to each article, a query builder is launched that will help you create the restrictions.

The Subscriptions Tab

You will go to the Subscriptions tab when you want to push a new subscription to a subscriber. Remember that push subscriptions are initiated by the distributor and that in push subscriptions, the

From the Field

Many organizations new to replication forget to think about and then create filters in their early models. As the organization grows, the amount of data being needlessly replicated can begin to impact the network as a whole, and certainly the servers involved in replication. Remember to only replicate the data that is needed at the remote server. If you do it correctly the first time, you will save yourself a lot of work and stress later.

Distribution agent runs on the distributor as well. If you want to pull a new subscription, you must do so from the subscriber. You will learn more about pulling a subscription later in this chapter.

The Subscription Options Tab

You use the Subscription Options tab to make some advanced specifications to the subscription properties. In the uppermost portion of the tab, you will find options to configure the creation and synchronization parameters for the subscription. For example, if you are setting up a publication that will support anonymous subscribers, and you have other publications that do not support anonymous subscribers on the same server, you must have a separate Distribution agent for that publication.

To configure this, click on the checkbox that creates a separate agent for the publication, as well as the two checkboxes that are subsequently made available. If you have no specific reason to use a separate agent, you should always use the same agent because it is more efficient and represents less of a workload than multiple agents would. Another special case that would require you to make changes on this tab would be if you wanted to allow snapshot files to be downloaded using the File Transfer Protocol (FTP). To have this functionality, you must enable it in the appropriate checkbox on this tab.

The Publication Access List Tab

You use this tab only when you have configured pull subscriptions or when you are using the Immediate Updating Subscribers option. This tab lets you configure a special access list that subscribers use when accessing the distributor. The replication agents must connect in the context of an approved account listed on this tab or they will be rejected. This prevents unauthorized or accidental access to the published data, which in turn prevents data corruption.

The Status Tab

This tab is present mostly as a means of providing you with status information about the Snapshot agent. You will go to this tab when you want to see the last time the agent was run, or to make configuration changes to the agent itself. The dialog box includes a window that provides information about the SQLServerService on the server, as well as two fields that tell you when the agent was last run and when it is scheduled to run next. Additionally, there are four buttons that let you run the Snapshot agent now, configure the properties of the Snapshot agent, start the SQLServerService on the server if it is not already started, and refresh the window so that it displays current information.

The Scripts Tab

Probably the least-used tab in all of replication is the Scripts tab. At the same time, it is one of the most important tabs available to you. You use this tab when you want to create Transact-SQL statements that are capable of re-creating the current configuration simply by running the scripted statements against the server. You should always script configurations, because scripts will save you a great deal of time if you have to rebuild the server or create an identical configuration on another server for some reason.

Scripts also guarantee that the configuration will be exactly as it was before and will save you from running the risk of forgetting a step or missing an option. The dialog box will let you create a script that creates the publication or deletes the publication, and will let you specify the file format and whether to append the script to an existing file or create a new one.

Although many administrators favor using a single script file that performs all the actions that might be required, we recommend that you maintain a separate file for *each* configurable object, and then name the files descriptively so that you can quickly tell one script from another. You never know when you will have to re-create just a single piece of the larger puzzle, and having multiple scripts will lend itself to that scenario while still providing you with the ability to combine them and produce the whole. Two buttons at the bottom of the screen will let you either preview the script before saving or save the script.

TIP: You will learn more about replication scripts in Chapter 11.

Once the publication has been created and configured, the next step is to send it to a subscriber. As you know, subscriptions can either be pushed or pulled to the subscriber. If you push the subscription, you are initiating the connection from the distributor. If you pull the subscription, you are initiating the connection from the subscriber.

When pushing a subscription, you can perform the configuration selections and create the subscription at the publisher/distributor level. When pulling a subscription, you must perform the operation from the subscriber. This is not to say that you must be physically sitting at the console of the subscriber, but rather that you must have the subscriber registered in Enterprise Manager and must have that server selected when you begin to pull the subscription. In the following text, you will learn how to pull a subscription to a server. You will remember from earlier in this chapter that you can push a subscription using one of the tabs in the Publication Properties dialog box.

CREATING A SUBSCRIPTION

As with most of the other configurable options in SQL Server 2000, you create a subscription using a wizard. You can choose the wizard from the Wizard list in Enterprise Manager, or you can choose Tools | Replication | Pull New Subscription To. SQL Server will then display the Pull Subscription dialog box.

The initial dialog box lets you pull new subscriptions, modify the properties of existing subscriptions, delete subscriptions, and reinitialize subscriptions that have fallen out of sync. To pull a new subscription, click on the Pull New Subscription button. SQL Server will start the Pull Subscription Wizard. The first screen shown in the dialog box is a splash screen that lets you know you are in the right wizard. The sole option you have here is to cancel or proceed using the Next button.

The first actual choice in the wizard lets you choose the publication to which you want to subscribe. The dialog box has a window that displays a list of registered servers. When you expand the servers, a list of available publications will appear. To choose a publication, simply select the publication and click the Next button.

The next screen lets you specify the Synchronization agent login. The dialog box simply has three fields that provide a location for the Username, a Password, and Password verification.

The third screen lets you choose a database in which the subscription will be created. A list of available databases for the server is shown in the large window, and a button in the lower-right corner will let you create a new database for the subscription. To choose existing databases, simply select one and then click the Next button.

The fourth screen lets you specify whether or not to initialize the database schema, which creates any special configurations required at the subscriber site and then performs the initial snapshot. If you have already created the database through another method, you might choose not to perform this step.

The fifth screen lets you specify how often the Distribution agent should update this subscription. You can choose continuous updates, a scheduled update, or no updates. Your selection will depend on your replication design.

The sixth screen lets you start services that might be required for replication to function. The screen includes a large window, which displays a list of services. At a minimum you will have to ensure that the SQLServerAgent service is started.

The final screen is another splash screen, which only provides you with the option to go back and check or alter configuration choices you have made, or to click the Finish button to end the wizard and create the subscription.

At this point, the subscription is created and replication is enabled. Depending on your configuration choices, replication might begin immediately, begin at a scheduled time, or merely stand in readiness for you to manually initiate the process. All the components have been configured and replication is ready to be functional even if it has not already begun.

SUMMARY

In this chapter, you have delved into the basics of replication. You learned the concepts, the metaphor, various configuration methods, and useful tools for replicating. You are now able to plan and configure replication for most common SQL Server deployments. In the following chapter, you will learn how to monitor and troubleshoot replication so that you can be sure that all is operating the way you intended. You will additionally pick up some tricks for managing complex replication scenarios, as well as the details that you will need for planning replication in complicated environments.

CHAPTER 11

Advanced Replication

In the last chapter, you learned how to plan and set up replication for most common environments. In this chapter, we expand on your knowledge of replication so you can configure and troubleshoot environments that use replication in less common and, sometimes, more advanced ways. You begin by learning some of the additional considerations involved in merge replication or when using updating subscribers. Then you learn how to configure replication agents and the DISTRIBUTION Database. Also included in this chapter are some tips and additional information you need to perform replication to and from host computers that are not running SQL Server.

DESIGNING MERGE REPLICATION

As we mentioned in Chapter 10, the major problem with merge replication is that SQL Server must understand where the data was changed originally. Part of the reason for this is so a method of resolution can be implemented when a conflict occurs. Another reason SQL Server must be able to distinguish between data originators is to protect against data being replicated back and forth between servers in an unending circle.

Ideally, the developers who design and install SQL Server deployments that will use merge replication have replication in mind when the database is developed. The developers will have planned for most of the considerations involved. This is not always the case, however, and the administrator must, at a minimum, understand what is needed so he or she can solve issues or explain what is required to the developer. Then the developer can resolve any potential problems and ensure the replication will function properly. The primary issue in merge replication is data definition, as described in the following section.

Data Definition

Simply put, *data definition* is the act of separating the data from similar tables on multiple servers using a special column that is unique. SQL Server actually creates this column if it is not already present when you set up a table for publication using merge replication. SQL Server will know you have a unique identifier column because the column will have the ROWGUID property set, which specifies that row as the unique identifier. If no column exists that has the ROWGUID property set, SQL Server creates a column named ROWGUID, which has the ROWGUID property set.

TIP: The GUID that SQL Server replication places into the ROWGUID column is a 128-bit number generated by an operating system application, known as GUIDGEN.EXE. This same type of number is used for many different purposes, but in the case of merge replication, it is necessary because *unique* indexes alone are not sufficient to ensure that merge replication will know which values are which when merging.

At the same time, SQL Server also creates triggers on both the publisher and the subscriber that track the changes made to data and store the changes in the system tables created by SQL Server specifically for that purpose. The system tables are added to both publisher and subscriber databases when you set up merge replication. The triggers fire when data changes in the replicated table. Their execution stores information about the change in the new system tables as well as information that tells SQL Server a specific row has been changed. New rows are appropriately marked as additions.

Because the special system tables track data and changes to data, the potential conflicts possible in merge replication can be handled logically. Conflicts occur when the same row is changed on more than one server between replication cycles. When SQL Server attempts to merge changes, the system tables from each server recognize that a row has been changed on more than one server. At this time, SQL Server resolves any conflicts that are detected. Books Online tells us conflicts can be resolved in a variety of ways.

The first method uses a predefined priority system wherein you specify the table from one server has a higher priority than the same table on other servers and that table's data will "win"—that is, its data will always be replicated—if a conflict occurs.

Another method simply picks the server that made the change first and chooses that server as the winner when a conflict occurs. Note, this second method does not use time stamping by default, but rather relies on where the change is stored in the list of changes. The first change processed is the winner for conflicts. If you want to use time stamping as a means of conflict resolution, a custom method must be defined. SQL Server does support the TIMESTAMP property as a means of tracking row changes.

Lastly, we learn from Books Online that you can create custom conflict resolution systems using system stored procedures, triggers, or Component Object Model (COM) program objects. We recommend you consult a programmer with experience in COM programming and Transact-SQL programming to develop a conflict-resolution system specific to your needs.

Merge replication is not the only issue in which you must deal with the possibility of conflicts. Any form of replication may suffer from potential conflicts if you allow the use of the Immediate Updating Subscribers option. Subscribers that can make changes to their own databases have the potential to cause conflicts, though it is less common because of the way that the option functions.

The Immediate Updating Subscribers option makes use of the Distributed Transaction Coordinator (DTC) component that ships with SQL Server 2000. This component is actually part of Microsoft Transaction Server, which has been separated and somewhat customized specifically for the purpose of enabling subscribers to update tables without using merge replication. Chapter 5 discussed distributed transaction processing in some detail.

Basically, DTC works by causing the same transaction that modified the table on the subscription server to also run on the publishing server. This means the data is not replicated back to the publishing server, but rather that the publisher runs the same transaction and modifies its own database as if the transaction were originally run on the publisher.

Conflicts can occur only if the row in the subscriber database is changed in close proximity to the time it is also being changed in the publisher database. To resolve the issue of potential conflicts, you must implement the use of a Timestamp column. A *Timestamp column* records the time a row is changed, at the time it is changed. By including this column into the database schema, you create a scenario wherein the only time a true conflict could occur is if the row were changed at the same time, down to the second, on both servers. When you attempt to update a row in the subscriber database, SQL Server uses the Timestamp column to determine if any changes have been made in the publisher's database, and it rejects changes at that time. Users who encounter a rejection are forced to refresh the row they are viewing before a change is permitted.

Using the Immediate Updating Subscribers option carries with it some restrictions that you should be aware of. For example, subscribers are unable to update the Timestamp column or identity, text, or image datatypes. They cannot update primary key fields or unique indexes, and, in addition, they must have a unique index to insert new rows into tables with Timestamp or Identity columns. These restrictions are usually not a problem because they apply only to the subscriber. We include them here, however, so you do not suffer from surprises when selecting this option.

Now that you understand some of the difficulties associated with some types of replication, the next thing is to familiarize yourself with the details of replication agents and to determine how to configure them best for your deployment.

CONFIGURING REPLICATION AGENTS

As you learned in the previous chapter, certain configurable options for replication agents enable you to take control of the process at an advanced level. You can configure these properties by accessing the Agent Properties dialog box. To open the dialog box, you must first access the Publisher and Distributor Properties dialog box by right-clicking on the Replication Monitor object and selecting properties. Remember, you must have already specified the server on which you are performing the configuration as a distributor or a publisher. You learned how to open this dialog box in the last chapter as well.

Once you have opened the Distributor and Publisher Properties dialog box, you find a button on the first tab named Agent Profiles. If you click on the Agent Profiles button, SQL Server responds by opening the Agent Profiles dialog box, as shown in Figure 11-1.

As you can see, the dialog box is divided into four tabs: Distribution, Log Reader, Snapshot, and Merge. Each tab represents a series of profiles for the agent for which it is named. Each profile can be viewed as a container of configuration options for the agent. When you select a profile, you are choosing a defined set of configuration choices. You can also choose to create a new profile, to make specific choices yourself, and to store them as a profile.

For example, notice that on the Distribution tab, which is the default tab, three preconfigured profile choices are available from which to choose. The first choice is named Default Agent Profile and contains the most common configuration choices for the Distribution

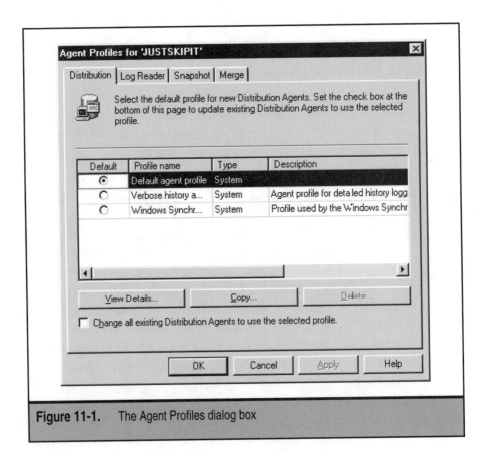

Figure 11-1.   The Agent Profiles dialog box

agent. In most deployments, you will not change the agent properties and this profile will be sufficient for your needs. Now, suppose you want the Distribution agent to keep better track of what is going on and to keep a more detailed record of what happens during the replication process. To accomplish this, choose the second profile for the agent, which is named Verbose History Agent Profile. The configurable options in this profile are designed to keep a more accurate and detailed history of the replication process and to store it, so you can access the file and obtain valuable information about the replication process. You will learn more about the actual configuration choices later in this chapter. To complete the discussion of the Distribution agent profile choices, the third choice is named Windows Synchronization Manager and represents a series of configuration choices that must be assigned to use the Windows Synchronization Manager, an add-on application that enables you to control a replicated environment from a single interface.

Examining the Configuration Choices for Replication Agents

Notice as you move from tab to tab that each profile has a basic description that tells you what the profile is used for. Because this is the case, we won't describe each profile here; instead, we describe the configuration choices common to all agents and those specific to a single agent. In the following text, we examine each of the configurable options available for the replication agents and how these choices affect SQL Server Replication.

BcpBatchSsize

This parameter controls the amount of rows copied as a single transaction to the server during a BCP IN operation. As you know, the bcp utility moves data in volume into and out of SQL Server. The replication process uses the bcp utility in the background to perform the same operations by bulk copying data from the published database and into the subscription database. This functionality is not present in transactional or merge replication except during the initial snapshot, but is the actual method used for all transfers in snapshot replication.

The BCPBatchSize parameter determines the number of rows to be transferred during a single transaction when the operation is moving data into a database. When transferring data out of a database, a default parameter of 1,000 is always used. You would take control of this parameter if you wanted to reduce the number of rows copied during a single transaction to decrease the number of transactions that fail due to loss of packets. In short, you would reduce the number of rows copied during a transaction if your network connection lacked reliability or suffered from excessive transmission errors. If unchanged, this parameter is set to a default setting of 1,000.

CommitBatchSize

The CommitBatchSize parameter controls the amount of transactions sent to a subscribing computer before a COMMIT statement is issued. As you learned in previous chapters, SQL Server processes all actions using Transact-SQL statements that can be either explicit or implicit transactions. When you perform replication using transactional replication, the transactions are sent as explicit transactions. Because the transactions are explicit, both a BEGIN TRAN and a COMMIT statement must be issued so SQL Server knows where to end the transaction.

The CommitBatchSize parameter controls how many replicated transactions are sent to the subscribing computer before a COMMIT statement is issued. Once the COMMIT statement is issued, the replicated transactions can be applied to the subscribing database during a checkpoint. You would take control of this parameter in cases where data security was an issue of higher than normal importance. The default setting for this parameter is 100. The more important the data security, the lower the parameter—though extremely low settings can have substantial negative impact on system performance.

CommitBatchThreshhold

Like the CommitBatchSize parameter, CommitBatchThreshhold controls the amount of replication commands sent to a subscribing computer before a COMMIT statement is issued. This parameter differs from the CommitBatchSize parameter because it deals with commands that have to do with the replication process and the setup of the subscribing database, instead of the replicated transactions from the published database. The default setting for this parameter is 1,000.

HistoryVerboseLevel

During replication, the various agents are sent status information in the form of notifications. This process is automatic and internal to the replication process. While you cannot control the actual sending of the messages that notify replication agents, you can control the number of messages stored in the DISTRIBUTION Database, which affects the amount of information stored that has to do with the history of a distribution operation. The HistoryVerboseLevel parameter specifically controls the amount of stored notifications sent to the Distribution agent.

Three possible settings are possible for this parameter; they are defined as numeric values of 1, 2, or 3. A setting of 1 sets the agent so new notifications always replace existing notifications that are the same. If no existing notification is stored in the database, a new row is created to store the new notification. A setting of 2 sets the agent so new notifications will always be stored and do not replace existing messages of the same type, with the exception of idle messages that are repeated for long-running transactions. A setting of 3 sets the agent so new notifications will always be stored and do not replace existing messages of the same type. In the case of setting 3, idle messages for long-running transactions are also stored.

You will take control of this parameter if you want a more detailed or less detailed history for the actions of the agent. The default setting is 2. If you want a more detailed listing, set the parameter to 3; if you want a less detailed listing, specify a setting of 1. Depending on the space requirements of your deployment and the amount of replication you are performing, you may or may not choose to make changes to this setting. Remember, the more detailed the history you keep, the more space is taken up by the information.

More detailed histories could result in a substantially oversized DISTRIBUTION Database.

LoginTimeout

As you learned in the previous section, the Distribution agent must be logged into by the subscribing machine and the publishing machine at different times to perform replication. The agent logs in as if it were a network user and uses information stored in the replication parameters to perform the login. The LoginTimeout setting determines the amount of time the Distribution agent waits to process login information, before the login times out and is rejected. If your network suffered from high-packet loss or other communication problems, you would increase this setting to accommodate those issues.

MaxBcpThreads

Because SQL Server and its associated utilities run on Windows platforms, which are multitasking operating systems, SQL Server utilities such as bcp are capable of running in multiple instances. This simply means you can actually run two or more copies of bcp at the same time, each of which is moving a different set of information from the other. The MaxBcpThreads setting determines the amount of bcp instances that may run at the same time when called by the Distribution agent. If you had an exceptionally powerful server with a low workload running the Distribution agent, you could increase this setting from a default of 1, thereby increasing the efficiency of the agent.

MaxDeliveredTransactions

During transactional or merge replication, subscribers are updated using transactions, whether or not the subscription is set up as push or pull. The MaxDeliveredTransactions parameter specifies the amount of transactions that may be delivered to the subscriber in a single synchronization. This parameter can be a bit deceptive because the default setting is 0. For this parameter, a setting of 0 means no limitation is placed on the agent and the number of permitted transactions is infinite. Change this setting only if your subscription servers have a sufficient workload to warrant the reduction of transmitted transactions during replication. We recommend that whenever possible, you increase the capacity of the server rather than change this setting.

PollingInterval

During transactional replication, the `DISTRIBUTION` Database is queried at regular intervals to see if transactions are waiting to be delivered. The default setting for this function is three seconds. This means if no problems exist, no more than three seconds worth of transactions will ever be waiting to be delivered to a subscriber. The `PollingInterval` parameter enables you to change the amount of time the agent must wait before checking the database for changes. You should increase the wait period in busy installations that have so many transactions running that the agent never stops sending updates.

QueryTimeout

As mentioned in the previous section, transactional replication is maintained by polling the `DISTRIBUTION` Database for transactions waiting to be replicated to subscribers. The polling is done in the form of a query that checks the contents of the `DISTRIBUTION` Database.

The `QueryTimeout` setting controls the amount of time the Distribution agent will wait before assuming the query has halted and re-sent a query. Increase this number from a default of 300 in deployments where the server has a workload that is too high, which results in longer wait times for queries. We recommend you increase the capabilities of the server rather than change this setting.

SkipFailureLevel

This option is almost always set to a numeric value of 1 because it determines the amount of times the Distribution agent will retry a transmission following a failure, without generating an error. Setting this value to 0 causes the agent to generate an error on the first failure; setting the option above 1 causes the agent to retry more than once each time a transmission error occurs. We recommend you change this setting only if transmission errors are common in your network and you have determined the errors are acceptable.

TransactionsPerHistory

As you know, part of the replication process is to notify the replication agents of status as operations are in progress. The `TransactionsPerHistory` parameter controls how many transactions are processed before a notification is entered into the history store. This means the agent looks at the history to see when the last notification was entered, checks this parameter for instructions, and, based on information found in this setting, enters a new notification into the history store at the appropriate time. The default setting is 100, and an entry of 0 represents no restrictions, which means the number of transactions between notifications can be infinite. While you may find a reason to change this parameter from its defaults, we have never found a reason to do so.

ReadBatchSize

As you learned in Chapter 10, the job of the Log Reader agent is to monitor the Transaction Log of published databases for changes that must be stored in the `DISTRIBUTION` Database. The job of the Distribution agent is to apply changes to the subscribers.

The `ReadBatchSize` parameter applies specifically to the Log Reader agent and the Distribution agent. In the case of the Log Reader agent, the parameter controls the amount of transactions that may be read out of the Transaction Log. In the case of the Distribution agent, the parameter controls the amount of transactions that may be read out of the `DISTRIBUTION` Database. No matter where the information is read from, it is always read into memory, where it is then processed and sent to the destination.

ReadBatchThreshhold

Applying only to the Log Reader agent, this parameter specifies the number of replication commands that may be read from the

Transaction Log and then applied to a subscriber at any one time by the Distribution agent. The default setting for this parameter is 100.

ChangesPerHistory

This parameter controls the amount of changes that may be affected during a single merge operation when using merge replication. Each merge operation is recorded by a notification that is saved in the DISTRIBUTION Database. The Merge agent can process a specific number of transactions, which you specify here, during a single merge operation, or can be set to process all transactions waiting to be processed by entering a value of 0.

DownloadGenerationsPerBatch

A *generation* is defined as a logical group of changes for a single article. The DownloadGenerationsPerBatch parameter controls the number of generations that may be processed in a single-batch operation when downloading information from the publisher to a subscriber. The default setting for this parameter is 100, which assumes you have a reliable network connection. If you have an unreliable network connection (such as a slow WAN connection), you should set the parameter to 10 or some other similarly low value.

DownloadReadChangesPerBatch

This parameter specifies the number of changes that should be read as a single batch operation when downloading changes from the publisher to a subscriber. The default setting for this parameter is 100 and should only be changed if your server has an unusually high amount of available memory.

DownloadWriteChangesPerBatch

The counterpart to the DownloadReadChangesPerBatch parameter, this setting specifies the amount of changes that should be written as a single-batch operation when downloading changes from the publisher to a subscriber. The default setting for this parameter is

100 and should only be changed if you have already changed the `DownloadReadChangesPerBatch` parameter.

FastRowCount

This parameter actually controls the way SQL Server counts the rows that will be moved during a single replication operation. A setting of 1 causes SQL Server to use a fast row-counting method that simply checks the row identifier and matches it against information stored in previous operations. A mathematical calculation produces the row count. A setting of 0 specifies that a full row-counting method should be used. The full row-counting method is more accurate, but requires more resources than a fast row-counting method.

UploadGenerationsPerBatch

In the same way that changes may be downloaded from a publisher to a subscriber, some replication schemes such as merge involve uploading changes from a subscriber to the publisher. The `UploadGenerationsPerBatch` setting specifies how many generations may be processed as a single-batch operation when uploading changes from a subscriber to the publisher.

UploadReadChangesPerBatch

This parameter specifies the amount of changes that may be read as a single-batch operation when uploading changes from a subscriber to the publisher. Remember, changes are read into memory. We recommend you do not change this setting unless you have a server with an unusually high amount of available memory.

UploadWriteChangesPerBatch

This parameter specifies the amount of changes that may be written as a single batch operation when uploading changes from a subscriber to the publisher. As with downloading, we recommend you do not change this setting unless you have already changed the `UploadReadChangesPerBatch` parameter.

Validate

This parameter specifies whether validation should be done at the end of a merge operation. If you enter a value of 0, no validation will take place. If you enter a value of 1, a rowcount-only validation method will be used to verify the number of rows that changed on both servers. If you enter a value of 2, a rowcount and checksum validation method will be invoked.

ValidateInterval

This parameter specifies how often validation is performed. Applying to continuous replication environments, the default setting for this parameter is 60 minutes. You should reduce this number in environments where conflicts and network problems are common, and validation should be performed more frequently.

UNDERSTANDING THE DISTRIBUTION DATABASE

As you know, the DISTRIBUTION Database is a system database produced when you configure SQL Server for replication. Depending on the type or method of replication you choose to use, the DISTRIBUTION Database will store different kinds of information. In some replication types, the database stores configuration information that SQL Server uses to set up databases on subscribers, status information that SQL Server uses as a guideline for when it should replicate, and transactions waiting to be replicated to subscribers. Other times, the database will not store transactions, just pointers that identify the location of snapshot files, which, in turn, hold the transactions waiting to be replicated.

In addition to the standard system tables present in all databases, the DISTRIBUTION Database has a variety of tables that store replication information for SQL Server. The following is a list of tables present in the DISTRIBUTION Database.

Msarticles	Msdistribution_agents	Msdistribution_history
Mslogreader_agents	Mslogreader_history	Msmerge_agents
Msmerge_history	Msmerge_subscriptions	Mspublication_access
MS_publications	Mspublisher_databases	Msrepl_commands
Msrepl_errors	Msrepl_originators	Msrepl_transactions
Msrepl_version	Mssnapshot_agents	Mssnapshot_history
MSsubscriber_info	Mssubscriber_schedule	Mssubscriptions

All the replication tables are always present in the database, even though all types of replication do not use them. For example, transaction replication first uses snapshot replication to establish the initial database copy on the subscriber. It then uses transactional replication to maintain that copy. This means when you configure and initiate transaction replication, the DISTRIBUTION Database makes use of the snapshot and transaction tables, but does not use the merge tables, even though they exist in the database.

While we do not recommend that you manually change any of the information stored in the DISTRIBUTION Database directly, we do recommend you become familiar with the layout of the database and the data contained in the tables. You should do this because you can create and run queries against the database that will provide large amounts of information in a single result set. Information about replication that is presented in a single result set is often more helpful in troubleshooting and optimization than the same information can be when gathered from different sources. For example, you can learn a great deal about what is happening in your system by reading the replication commands stored in the DISTRIBUTION Database. To list the commands currently listed, connect to SQL Server using Query Analyzer and execute the following statement:

```
use distribution
    Select * From Msrepl_commands
```

This statement provides you with a list of commands that have been stored. These commands tell SQL Server how to set up databases and agents on servers that are involved in replication. You can run similar queries against all the tables in the DISTRIBUTION

Database. We recommend you take the time to run a standard SELECT query against each of the system tables in the database that begins with "MS," if for no other reason than the education about what SQL Server is doing. Once you understand which tables are being used for your deployment, you can better determine which tables to use in queries.

Using Stored Procedures to Obtain Replication Information

In addition to the special tables stored in the DISTRIBUTION Database, a number of stored procedures also exist, which the replication process uses to set up and maintain replication. Stored procedures of particular use include those described in the following sections.

SP_HELPREMOTELOGIN

This procedure lists login information that remote servers will use, when logging in to the server upon which the procedure is run. An example of running this procedure is as follows:

```
use master
    exec sp_helpremotelogin TESTSERVER
```

In this example, you specify the name TESTSERVER as the SQL Server about which you want information. If you are running the procedure on the only distributor in the deployment, you may leave off the name of the server.

SP_HELPDISTRIBUTOR

Providing information about the distributor, this procedure can help you understand the dynamics of a deployment about which you are unfamiliar. You use this procedure to find out information quickly about how the distributor runs, as shown in the following statements:

```
use master
    exec sp_helpdistributor
```

SP_HELPPUBLICATION

This procedure provides statistical information about the specified publication. You use this procedure to discover the options with which a specific publication runs in context. For example, if you were a consultant who needed to find out how a specific publication is configured, you would use this procedure to obtain all the needed information quickly:

```
use master
    exec sp_helppublication @publication = 'TESTPUBLICATION'
```

SP_HELPSUBSCRIPTION

In the same way that you would use SP_HELPPUBLICATION to obtain information about a publication, you use this procedure to find out information about a specific article, subscriber, or destination database, as shown here:

```
use master
    exec sp_helpsubscription @article = 'TESTARTICLE'
```

SP_HELPSUBSCRIBERINFO

This procedure lists a large amount of data about the subscriber, including the current settings for the replication agents. An example of this procedure is as follows:

```
use master
    exec sp_helpsubscriberinfo @subscriber = 'TESTSUBSCRIBER'
```

SP_REPLCMDS

This procedure works using the Log Reader agent and provides you with a list of transactions that have not yet been replicated to the subscriber. This option includes the Transact-SQL commands that cause the transaction to be replicated. You use this option to view the status of replication, as shown in the following example:

```
use master
    exec sp_replcmds @maxtrans = '5'
```

The statement in the example produces the last five transactions waiting to be replicated. If you had left off the `maxtrans` parameter, the default number of transactions returned would be 1.

SP_REPLTRANS

This procedure is similar to the SP_REPLCMDS procedure and lists the transactions waiting at a publisher to be transferred. This procedure differs because the commands to replicate are not included in the result set. The following is an example:

```
use master
    exec sp_repltrans
```

SP_REPLCOUNTERS

The SP_REPLCOUNTERS stored procedure is a helpful procedure that lists statistics about latency and throughput for a published database. You use this procedure to verify a publication is functioning properly. The following example shows you standard syntax:

```
use master
    exec sp_replcounters
```

The preceding is not an all-inclusive list of helpful stored procedures, but is merely some of the more common ones we have used in the past. Please refer to the stored procedure reference at the end of this book for a complete listing of all stored procedures and the syntax for each of them.

While knowing and querying the DISTRIBUTION Database can provide you with lots of information that can help you keep replication up and running, it is also cumbersome and requires detailed knowledge of the database and of Transact-SQL. Because not all administrators have this knowledge, SQL Server ships with a variety of tools to help you monitor and maintain replication. In the following section, you learn how to use these tools to keep your replicated environment running as smoothly as possible.

MONITORING REPLICATION

Replication is probably one of the more complicated tasks a SQL Server can perform. While widely used, replication involves many different components and is a process that requires observation. You should monitor the aspects of replication to ensure the process runs smoothly and transactional consistency is maintained on all involved servers.

Microsoft recognizes the complexity of replication and provides you with tools to assist you in the monitoring of replication. Primary among these tools are the Performance Monitor and the Replication Monitor. You learned how to use the Performance Monitor in an earlier chapter. Using the Performance Monitor for replication merely involves choosing counters that are for replication. In the following section, you learn how to use the Replication Monitor for daily monitoring and configuration.

Using the Replication Monitor

The Replication Monitor is on servers that have been configured as a distributor. The tool is absent from servers that are only publishers and from subscribers because the Replication Monitor deals primarily with the DISTRIBUTION Database and replication agents.

If you expand the object list for a Distribution server in Enterprise Manager, you will find a new object called Replication Monitor. You will notice immediately the object has a plus (+) sign next to it, indicating child objects are below it. If you click on the plus sign, the object list expands to include three parent objects called publishers, agents, and replication alerts. Expanding these objects reveals any configured publishers and a list of folders that represent the different replication agents, as seen in Figure 11-2.

Depending on what you want to do, you will use different areas of the Replication Monitor. For example, if you want to configure the properties of the Distribution agent, you access the dialog box by right-clicking on the Replication Monitor object and choosing Distributor Properties from the submenu that appears.

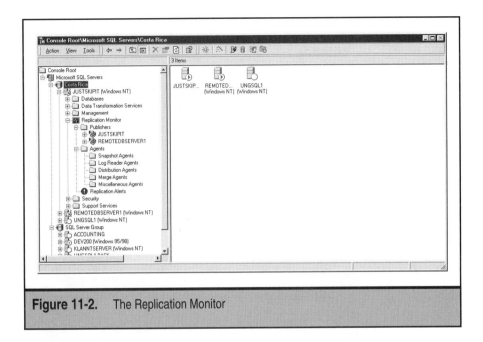

Figure 11-2. The Replication Monitor

You will recognize the Publisher and Distributor Properties dialog box from the last chapter because it is the same dialog box you accessed from the Configure Distributors and Publishers Wizard. You use this dialog box to configure the distributor, publisher, publication databases, and subscribers, as well as to access configuration screens that enable you to choose or create new Agent Profiles. You learned about Agent Profiles earlier in this chapter. You can see the Publisher and Distributor Properties dialog box in Figure 11-3.

The first time you try to expand the Replication Monitor, you are prompted to specify refresh rates for it. This dialog box enables you to configure how often to refresh the information gathered by the Replication Monitor, how often to refresh items in the object tree beneath the Replication Monitor, and how much time should pass before an agent with no listed activity is considered suspect. On the second tab of the dialog box, you can specify a path to store information that you can then access using the Performance Monitor. You can see this dialog box in Figure 11-4.

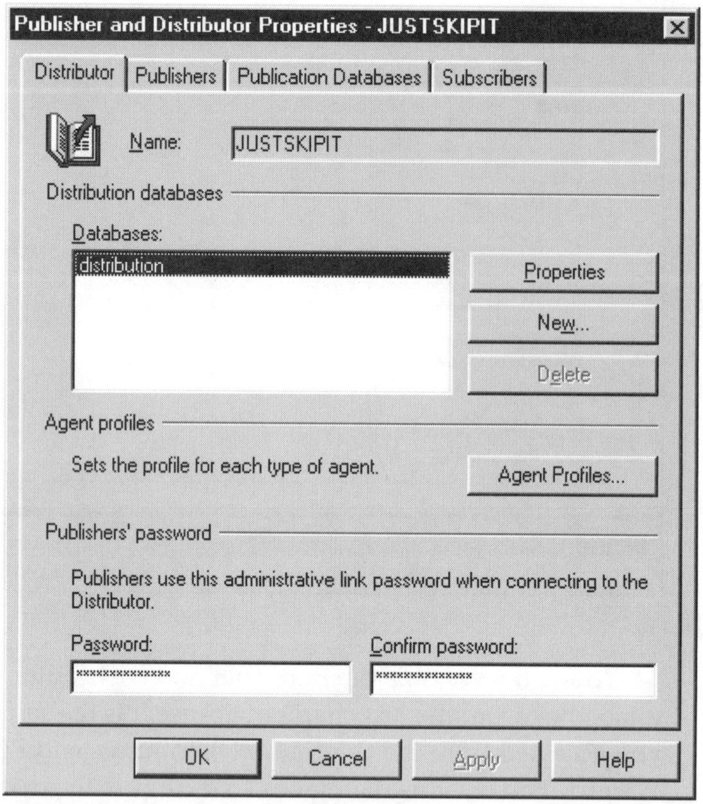

Figure 11-3.   The Publisher and Distributor Properties dialog box

Once you have configured the refresh rate for the Replication Monitor, the object can be expanded to list the child objects, which, in turn, enables you to view information about publishers and agents directly. To alter the refresh rate settings after the first configuration, right-click on the Replication Monitor object and choose the Refresh Rates and Settings option from the submenu that appears.

Select Columns is the final option you will find on the submenu that you get when you right-click on the Replication Monitor object. If you choose this option, a dialog box is displayed that enables you to specify which columns of information to display when you view the properties of any agent. By default, the Replication Monitor is set

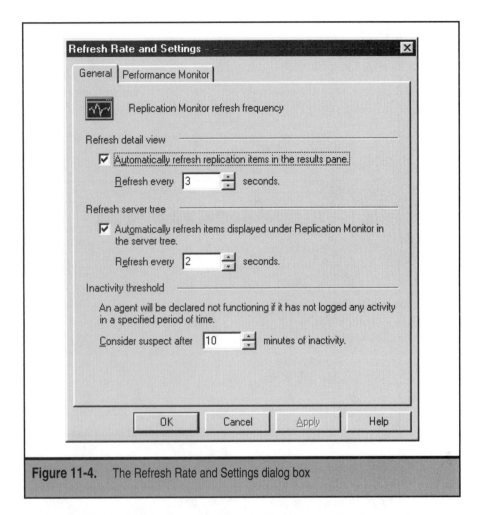

Figure 11-4.   The Refresh Rate and Settings dialog box

to display all columns. If you reduce this number by deselecting a column, less information is available to you in the Agent view, but the Replication Monitor has a lower impact on the workload of the distributor. We recommend you leave all columns selected until you know which columns from which agents you never use, and then you can deselect those columns. You can see the Select Columns dialog box in Figure 11-5.

Viewing and Configuring Agents

Once you have the default settings for the Distribution agents configured, the next thing you will want to do is familiarize yourself with the different views you have for each agent.

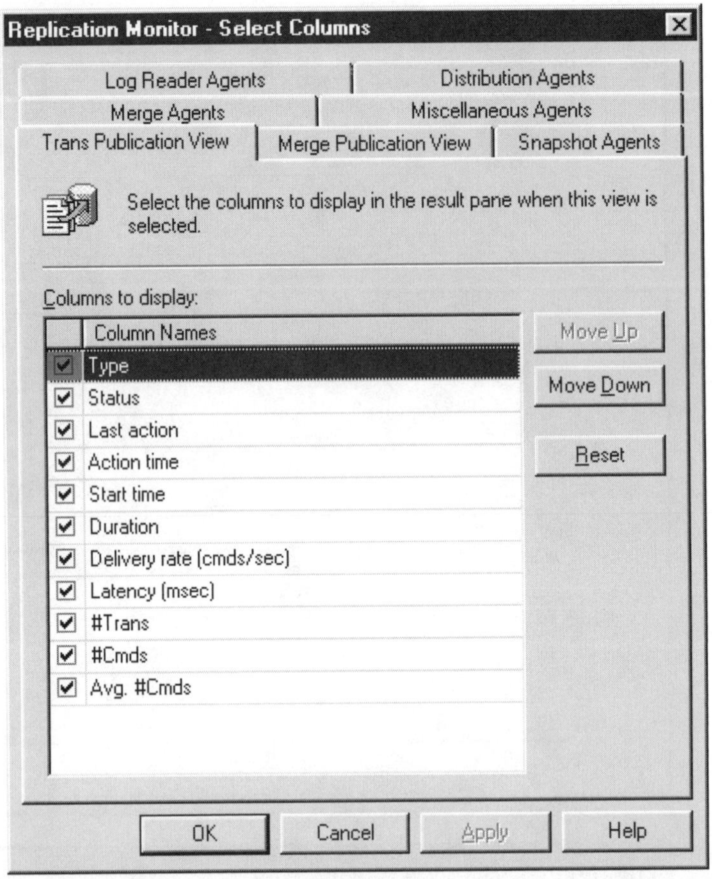

Figure 11-5. The Select Columns dialog box

If you select any folder listed under agents with your mouse, a list of agents will appear in the work window on the right side of the screen. If you then right-click on any listed agent, a menu appears that gives you three important choices: Agent History, Agent Properties, and Agent Profiles. Each of these options gives you a different view, which, in turn, enables you to view details of, or make changes to, the configuration of the agent.

Agent History   The Agent History option displays a dialog box that enables you to view what the agent has done so far and enables you to change options in the Agent Profile. Depending on the agent you have chosen to look at, the Agent History dialog box will look different. We encourage you to look at the history of all agents frequently.

Agent Properties   The Agent Properties option displays the configurable choices for that agent. Agents are actually implemented as jobs on SQL Server and the dialog boxes that appear are simply the Job Property dialog box for that agent. You learned about jobs and configuring jobs in Chapter 9.

Agent Profiles   The Agent Profiles option displays a dialog box that enables you to choose from or create a new agent profile for that agent. You can choose to configure the agent profile from here, as well as from the Agent Profiles dialog box, which you learned about earlier in this chapter.

Publishers

As you have learned, this object lists the configured publishers for this distributor. Options for publishers listed are accessed by right-clicking on the object and include the capability to choose refresh rates for that publisher.

Replication Alerts

This object lists alerts specifically configured for replication. While the alerts are listed in a separate area, they are alerts like any other and are configured the same as the other alerts you learned about in Chapter 9. In addition to custom alerts that you create for your deployment, eight predefined alerts exist for replication, which are present by default. These alerts represent the eight most common errors that affect replication. Rather than define them here, we recommend you take the time to look at each alert so you do not define new ones that serve the same purpose. Remember, alerts are your primary means of identifying problems, and they provide you with invaluable assistance when problems occur. In the following section, you will learn more about troubleshooting replication.

TROUBLESHOOTING REPLICATION

As with any complex system configuration, replication is subject to problems and errors that cause replication either to fail completely or to function at a reduced capacity. When problems do occur, you can follow some general steps to identify and solve the problem.

The first thing to do, of course, is to see if any alerts have fired. Sometimes a problem can be located and solved quickly, simply by taking the time to check your e-mail for alerts.

Once you have eliminated alert messages as a source of information, the next step is to check the error logs. Frequently, an error occurs for which no defined alert exists. Errors are still logged in either the SQL Server Error Log or the SQL Server Agent Error Log, both of which can be found in the MSSQL7 root folder. If you open and read the error log starting at the bottom and working your way up, you can often locate the cause of a problem.

Many times, the problem is produced as a result of services that are not running, logon errors, or design flaws in deployments that span multiple domains. Be sure all SQL Server services are running, the domain user accounts can log on to each server, and required trust relationships are in place.

Many difficulties in replication processing involve connectivity and security. Before these can be addressed, you must determine which servers are involved in a replication problem by observing the processing order of the replication agents. Troubleshooting and resolution should focus on the access to each of the servers and to the databases involved in the replication scenario.

Checking the Error Logs

Several error logs can assist you in troubleshooting replication problems: SQL Server Error Log, SQL Server Agent Error Log, and

Windows Event Viewer. You also can use SQL Server Profiler to troubleshoot replication.

Configuring and Monitoring Replication Alerts

Replication alerts are standard SQL Server alerts, configured to respond to conditions caused by the replication process. In SQL Server Enterprise Manager, you can configure all the replication alerts under Alerts in SQL Server Agent or under Replication Alerts in the Replication Monitor. You must add new replication alerts under Replication Alerts in the Replication Monitor; otherwise, they will show up only in SQL Server Agent. If you use the SP_ADD_ALERT system stored procedure to add a replication alert, you must specify the category "Replication" with the @category_name argument if you want the new alert to be listed under Replication Alerts in the Replication Monitor.

A number of predefined replication alerts are created when you enable publishing and distribution. To use any of these alerts, you must enable each alert and add one or more operators to be notified when the alert fires. As for standard SQL Server Agent alerts, you can specify a job to be executed when the alert fires. The following predefined replication alerts are created for you:

▼ Replication: Agent custom shutdown

■ Replication: Agent failure

■ Replication: Agent retry

■ Replication: Agent success

■ Replication: Expired subscription dropped

■ Replication: Subscriber has failed data validation

■ Replication: Subscriber has passed data validation

▲ Replication: Subscriber reinitialized after validation failure

Verifying SQL Server Services

Replication agents run under the user context of the SQLServerAgent service. If you have difficulty with the

MSSQLServer service or the SQLServerAgent service, verify
MSSQLServer and SQLServerAgent services are running and
ensure the following:

▼ The service account and password are properly configured for
the SQLServerAgent service. We recommend all
participants in the replication process use the same Windows
domain account for the SQLServerAgent service.

▲ Multidomain environments have service accounts that are
trusted across domains.

Testing the Connectivity

By default, SQL Server replication uses the same Windows domain
user account that SQLServerAgent uses. If you experience a
problem with connectivity, test the connectivity as follows:

▼ For a push subscription, log on to the distributor with the
same Windows account the SQLServerAgent service uses
on the distributor. From the distributor, use SQL Server
Query Analyzer, choose Windows NT/2000 Authentication
Mode, and connect to the subscriber.

▲ For a pull subscription, log on to the subscriber with the
same Windows account SQL Server Agent uses on the
subscriber. From the subscriber, use SQL Server Query
Analyzer, choose Windows NT/2000 Authentication Mode,
and connect to the distributor.

If you cannot connect using either of these methods, the problem
is with security rather than replication.

Connectivity to Windows 95 and Windows 98 Servers

On Windows NT/2000-based SQL Servers that need to replicate data
from a Microsoft Windows 95-based or Windows 98-based SQL
Server, use the SQL Server Client Network Utility to define an alias
for the Windows 95 or Windows 98 server that uses the TCP/IP or
Multiprotocol network library. This is necessary because Windows

NT/2000-based SQL Servers use the Named Pipes client network library by default, and Windows 95-based and Windows 98-based SQL Servers do not support incoming Named Pipes connections.

Checking the Replication Agent Schedules

If replication is not occurring as you expected, you may either have to wait for the agents to start as scheduled or you can manually start the agents to initiate the replication process.

Consider the following transactional replication scenario: After creating a publication and a subscription, the tables corresponding to the publication articles are not being created and populated on the subscriber. You have checked the security and the connectivity between the publisher, the distributor, and the subscriber, and they are working correctly.

In this case, the most likely cause for the replication not occurring is that the initial synchronization has not taken place. This is probably because the Snapshot agent has not run to generate the initial snapshot the Distribution agent needs to perform the initial synchronization. Depending on how the initial snapshot was scheduled when the publication was created, the initial snapshot may be created later or on demand. You need to either wait for the snapshot to be created or start the Snapshot agent for the publication manually before the initial synchronization occurs. After the initial synchronization is complete, regular transactional replication will begin.

If you fail to find the problem in any of these areas, refer to standard troubleshooting techniques, which are discussed in Chapter 12. Another good idea is to be prepared to remove and to reinstall replication—using scripts. In the following section, you learn how to create and manage replication scripts.

USING REPLICATION SCRIPTS

As you learned in Chapter 10, SQL Server is capable of automatically creating replication scripts, which you can then use to set up replication on a server where it failed or on new servers that must have the same setup.

Replication scripts can be created from a variety of locations, the easiest of which to reach is the menu choice found in the Replication submenu. To reach the dialog box, choose Tools | Replication | Generate Replication Scripts. SQL Server responds by opening the Generate SQL Scripts dialog box. This is the same dialog box you reach from within other areas. The dialog box enables you to choose from configured publications and to specify the options by which you want to store the script. The actual steps are described in Chapter 10. An example script that has been generated by the script creation process follows:

```
use master
GO
exec sp_adddistributor  @distributor = N'SQLPUBLISHER', @password = N''
GO
-- Adding the Distribution database
exec sp_adddistributiondb  @database = N'distribution',
@data_folder = N'e:\MSSQL7\data', @data_file = N'distribution.MDF',
@data_file_size = 4, @log_folder = N'e:\MSSQL7\data',
@log_file = N'distribution.LDF', @log_file_size = 2,
@min_distretention = 0, @max_distretention = 72,
@history_retention = 48, @security_mode = 0, @login = N'sa',
@password = N''
GO
-- Adding the distribution publisher
exec sp_adddistpublisher  @publisher = N'SQLPUBLISHER',
@distribution_db = N'distribution', @security_mode = 0,
@login = N'sa', @password = N'',
@working_directory = N'e:\MSSQL7\ReplData',
@trusted = N'false', @thirdparty_flag = 0
GO
-- Adding the registered subscriber
exec sp_addsubscriber @subscriber = N'SQLSUBSCRIBER',
@type = 0, @login = N'sa', @password = N'',
@security_mode = 0, @frequency_type = 64, @frequency_interval = 1,
@frequency_relative_interval = 2, @frequency_recurrence_factor = 0,
@frequency_subday = 8, @frequency_subday_interval = 1,
@active_start_date = 0, @active_end_date = 0,
```

```
@active_start_time_of_day = 0,
@active_end_time_of_day = 235900, @description = N''
exec sp_changesubscriber_schedule @subscriber = N'SQLSUBSCRIBER',
@agent_type = 1, @active_end_date = 0
GO
-- Adding the registered subscriber
exec sp_addsubscriber @subscriber = N'SQLPUBLISHER',
@type = 0, @login = N'sa', @password = N'', @security_mode = 0,
@frequency_type = 64, @frequency_interval = 1,
@frequency_relative_interval = 2, @frequency_recurrence_factor = 0,
@frequency_subday = 8, @frequency_subday_interval = 1,
@active_start_date = 0, @active_end_date = 0,
@active_start_time_of_day = 0, @active_end_time_of_day = 235900,
@description = N''
exec sp_changesubscriber_schedule @subscriber = N'SQLPUBLISHER',
@agent_type = 1, @active_end_date = 0
GO
-- Enabling the replication database
use master
GO
exec sp_replicationdboption N'test', N'publish', N'true'
GO
use [test]
GO
-- Adding the transactional publication
exec sp_addpublication @publication = N'test',
@restricted = N'false', @sync_method = N'native',
@repl_freq = N'snapshot',
@description = N'Snapshot publication of test database from
Publisher SQLPUBLISHER.',
@status = N'active', @allow_push = N'true',
@allow_pull = N'true', @allow_anonymous = N'false',
@enabled_for_internet = N'false', @independent_agent = N'false',
@immediate_sync = N'false', @allow_sync_tran = N'false',
@autogen_sync_procs = N'false', @retention = 72
exec sp_addpublication_snapshot @publication = N'test',
@frequency_type = 4, @frequency_interval = 1,
```

```
@frequency_relative_interval = 1, @frequency_recurrence_factor = 0,
@frequency_subday = 8, @frequency_subday_interval = 1,
@active_start_date = 0, @active_end_date = 0,
@active_start_time_of_day = 0, @active_end_time_of_day = 235959
GO
exec sp_grant_publication_access @publication = N'test',
@login = N'distributor_admin'

GO
exec sp_grant_publication_access @publication = N'test', @login = N'sa'
GO
-- Adding the transactional articles
exec sp_addarticle @publication = N'test',
@article = N'TABLE1', @source_owner = N'dbo',
@source_object = N'TABLE1', @destination_table = N'TABLE1',
@type = N'logbased', @creation_script = null,
@description = null, @pre_creation_cmd = N'drop',
@schema_option = 0x0000000000000071, @status = 0,
@vertical_partition = N'false', @ins_cmd = N'SQL',
@del_cmd = N'SQL', @upd_cmd = N'SQL', @filter = null,
@sync_object = null
GO
-- Enabling the replication database
use master
GO
exec sp_replicationdboption N'testdb', N'publish', N'true'
GO
```

The example script configures transactional replication between the publisher named SQLPUBLISHER and the subscriber named SQLSUBSCRIBER. The script defines the setup options, the type of replication, and the properties of the articles contained in the publication. This script is designed to create replication. The dialog box that produces such scripts also gives you the option of creating scripts that can remove the replication setup.

TIP: As stated in the last chapter, we recommend you always create and store replication scripts in a safe location because they can be invaluable if you have to reconfigure replication for any reason.

At this point, you know how to plan, configure, and optimize standard forms of replication for most environments. In the following text, you will learn about replicating to and from foreign hosts. This type of replication is more difficult, but it is also substantially less common. The chances of running into this are low.

REPLICATING TO FOREIGN HOSTS

When you are configuring replication, sometimes the system you want to replicate to or from is not a SQL Server. When this is the case, you must take additional information and considerations into account. In this section, you will learn what SQL Server components provide functionality for replication to and from foreign hosts.

Just as you can copy data to heterogeneous sources, SQL Server 2000 can replicate to and from databases—such as Microsoft Access and Oracle—naturally because these systems use Open Database Connectivity (ODBC) drivers that are compliant with SQL Server. Other systems that use ODBC drivers that are SQL Server-compliant can also replicate with relative ease. In short, SQL Server comes with ODBC drivers that can connect to Microsoft Access, Oracle, and IBM DRDA databases. Because the drivers ship with SQL Server, implementing replication is easy.

You can establish replication with other systems with generic ODBC drivers, so long as they are ODBC level 1-compliant. Microsoft states that the driver must allow updates; support transactions, Transact-SQL, and Data Definition Language (DDL) statements; and be a 32-bit thread-safe driver. While many of the texts you may encounter lead you to believe replication with a foreign host is easy if the ODBC driver is ODBC level 1-compliant, a closer look at the SQL Server replication specifics reveals some additional complexity that may cause you problems when configuring replication. For example, simply searching through Books Online thoroughly teaches you that common replication functions such as batched statements are not supported when replicating to a foreign host because the `CommitBatchSize` parameter you learned about earlier is ignored by many ODBC level 1 drivers. In addition, options such as Truncate Before Synchronization will not function if the ODBC DSN is not a SQL Server DSN. As a result, you will be unable to subscribe from foreign hosts to publications with this option set. Another restriction to an ODBC DSN is that it must conform to the SQL Server naming conventions because of the way SQL Server stores the DSN.

As you have learned, SQL Server can move data either in native SQL Server format or in character format. You must be careful to choose character format when replicating to foreign systems because they will not understand SQL Server's native format. Subscriptions from foreign hosts will also be unable to include new articles dynamically, which have been added to the publication, like SQL Server can. Each time you add a new article, you must re-establish the subscription.

These restrictions and tips are, unfortunately, not all-encompassing and you will have to do your own detailed research to configure and be sure of replication to foreign systems. In the following section, we discuss some of the considerations you should take into account when doing your research and when planning replication for use in a heterogeneous environment.

Replicating to a Foreign Subscriber

Replicating *to* a foreign system is somewhat easier than replicating *from* one because the original data comes from SQL Server. The first thing to do is ensure the ODBC drivers will communicate. You can obtain valuable information about the ODBC drivers on SQL Server and about the stored ODBC DSN using system stored procedures, such as `SP_ENUMDSN` or `SP_DSNINFO`.

Once you are sure the systems will talk to each other, you need to look at the characteristics of replication itself. When replicating to a foreign host, you must use a push subscription. Foreign systems cannot create a pull subscription to SQL Server. Issues to watch for include the mapping of datatypes and the format of moved data. For example, SQL Server uses a variety of datatypes for storage that the foreign system may not use. In such cases as these, the data automatically is mapped to the foreign system's closest matching datatype, unless a custom written program is used to map data. As you learned before, you must also be sure to use character format for data movement instead of SQL Server native format.

Replicating from a Foreign Publisher

SQL Server does not naturally act as a subscriber to foreign systems. In cases where you must subscribe to a foreign host, you must develop a special program capable of communicating with both the foreign host and SQL Server. This program takes the place of the SQL Server Agent. Microsoft states that the program must be developed using Visual Basic, C, or C++, and the program must use SQL-DMO (Data Manipulation Objects). Using SQL-DMO, the program will seem as if it were just another SQL Server to SQL Server and all replication functions may be used, including the use of Enterprise Manager as a tool for administration. Because the idea here is to create a program that will speak to a database system for which no established SQL Server driver exists, we can provide you with no further instructions. We recommend you consult a developer with experience in the listed languages if you need to subscribe to a foreign system.

USING SQL SERVER REPLICATION MONITOR

SQL Server Replication Monitor is a component of SQL Server Enterprise Manager that is added to the console tree on the distributor when the distributor is enabled. It is designed for viewing the status of replication agents and for troubleshooting potential replication problems.

You can use SQL Server Replication Monitor to perform the following monitoring activities:

▼ View a list of publishers, publications, and subscriptions to the publications supported by the distributor.

■ View the real-time status of scheduled replication agents.

■ Display current execution data for a replication agent to obtain a running total of transactions, statements, inserts, and updates that have been processed.

■ Configure replication agent profiles and properties.

■ Set up and monitor alerts related to replication events.

▲ View replication agent histories.

TIP: Although the Distribution and Merge agents run on the subscriber for pull subscriptions, the Replication Monitor is unavailable on the subscriber. The status of the agents running on the subscriber is monitored in the Replication Monitor running on the distributor to which the subscriber agents connect.

MAINTAINING REPLICATION

When you manage replication, you need to address certain maintenance issues, including space management and backup strategies. The following sections consider some of these important issues.

Space Management

In a replicated environment, space management is important because a lack of space on either the publisher or the subscriber can cause replication to fail. Space management requires you to perform the following activities:

▼ Monitor the size of the DISTRIBUTION Database to ensure enough space exists to store the replication jobs. This involves both determining the retention period for the replication history and replicated transactions, and setting up Distributor Properties to control the retention period.

▲ Monitor miscellaneous agents.

History tables and replicated transactions consume database storage space. Several replication agents clear these tables periodically. Ensure the agents listed in the following table are running.

Miscellaneous Agent	Description
Agent History clean up: distribution	Removes replication Agent History records from the DISTRIBUTION Database
Distribution clean up: distribution	Removes replicated transactions from the DISTRIBUTION Database
Expired subscription clean up	Detects and removes inactive subscriptions from published databases
Reinitialize subscriptions having data validation failures	Reinitializes (performs another initial synchronization of) all subscriptions that have failed due to data validation failure
Replication agents checkup	Detects replication agents not actively logging history

Backup Strategies

Backing up the DISTRIBUTION Database is important because if it is lost you must re-create all publications and subscriptions. By default, the Trunc. Log on Chkpt. option is enabled when the DISTRIBUTION

Database is created. If you choose to perform Transaction Log backups on the DISTRIBUTION Database, you must first disable this option. Plan and implement backup strategies by:

▼ Monitoring any issues with the DISTRIBUTION Database that will affect the publisher. For example, if the DISTRIBUTION Database runs out of space, transactions waiting to be published cannot be removed from the Transaction Log on the publisher.

▲ Preparing recovery and resynchronization plans in the event that a publisher, distributor, or subscriber fails.

Because of the large number of different possible replication configurations, detailed backup and restore strategies are not presented in this book. Books Online has matrixes that present strategies for each possible configuration.

MONITORING SQL SERVER REPLICATION PERFORMANCE

You can use the Replication Monitor in SQL Server Enterprise Manager, Microsoft Windows Performance Monitor, and system stored procedures to monitor replication performance. You can obtain information on delivered transactions, undelivered transactions, rates of delivery, and latency.

Using Windows 2000 Performance Monitor

Replication counters that graphically display replication details are useful for retrieving information about replication. You can use the counters described in this section in Windows 2000 Performance Monitor.

SQLServer:Replication Agents

The counter for the SQLServer:Replication Agents object has an instance for each type of replication agent.

Counter	Description
Running	The number of replication agents, of the specified type, currently running

SQLServer:Replication Dist.

The `SQLServer:Replication Dist.` object has counters for monitoring instances of the Distribution agent. The following table lists the three defined counters.

Counter	Description
Dist:Delivery Latency	The current amount of time, in milliseconds, that elapses between when transactions are delivered to the distributor and when they are applied at the subscriber
Dist:Delivered Commands/sec	The number of commands per second delivered to the subscriber
Dist:Delivered Transactions/sec	The number of transactions per second delivered to the subscriber

SQLServer:Replication Logreader

The `SQLServer:Replication Logreader` object has counters for monitoring instances of the Log Reader agent. The following table lists the three defined counters.

Counter	Description
Logreader:Delivery Latency	The current amount of time, in milliseconds, that elapses between when transactions are applied at the publisher and when they are delivered to the distributor

Counter	Description
Logreader:Delivered Commands/sec	The number of commands per second delivered to the distributor
Logreader:Delivered Transactions/sec	The number of transactions per second delivered to the distributor

SQLServer:Replication Merge

The SQLServer:Replication Merge object has counters for monitoring instances of the Merge agent. The following table lists the three defined counters.

Counter	Description
Uploaded Changes/sec	The number of rows per second merged from the subscriber to the publisher
Downloaded Changes/sec	The number of rows per second merged from the publisher to the subscriber
Conflicts/sec	The number of conflicts per second occurring during the merge process

SQLServer:Replication Snapshot

The SQLServer:Replication Snapshot object has counters for monitoring instances of the Snapshot agent. The following table lists the two defined counters:

Counter	Description
Snapshot:Delivered Commands/sec	The number of commands per second delivered to the distributor

Counter	Description
`Snapshot:Delivered Transactions/sec`	The number of transactions per second delivered to the distributor

Using System Stored Procedures

You can retrieve information about replication using system stored procedures. This method enables you to reference replication information that may be used in triggers, user-defined stored procedures, or scripts. Some of these system stored procedures are listed in the following table.

To Retrieve Information On . . .	Use . . .
Servers	`SP_HELPSERVER`
	`SP_HELPREMOTELOGIN`
Databases	`SP_HELPDB`
	`SP_HELPDISTRIBUTOR`
	`SP_HELPPUBLICATION`
	`SP_HELPSUBSCRIPTION`
	`SP_HELPSUBSCRIBERINFO`
Replication activity	`SP_REPLCMDS`
	`SP_REPLTRANS`
	`SP_REPLCOUNTERS`

Viewing Replication Agent Histories

History tables contain information for all replication agents. You should regularly view replication histories to identify any tasks that fail and the reasons for the failures. Message detail provides an indicator of the issues; for example, connectivity problems, permission restrictions, and log-full errors.

Viewing Selected Replication Agent Histories

With the Agent History in SQL Server Replication Monitor, you can view replication information from the history tables for one or more sessions of a selected agent. Agent History enables you to filter the list of sessions to show one of three possible types of filters:

▼ All sessions

■ Sessions in a specified time frame, such as the last 24 hours, the last two days, or the last seven days

▲ Sessions with errors

Using System Tables

The history tables in the DISTRIBUTION Database track replication job activity for all replication agents. Instead of viewing the agent histories in the Replication Monitor, you can query the tables directly in the DISTRIBUTION Database. These history tables (one for each agent) are as listed in the following:

▼ MSsnapshot_history

■ MSlogreader_history

■ MSdistribution_history

▲ MSmerge_history

SUMMARY

In this chapter, we focused on advanced replication techniques, as well as the necessary tools for monitoring and optimizing replication, and some consideration of the basic troubleshooting steps involved in solving replication problems.

In the next chapter of the book, we move on to a more generalized consideration of troubleshooting and the issues you should take into account when you begin to encounter problems with your SQL Server installation.

CHAPTER 12

Planning, Maintaining, and Troubleshooting with SQL Server

Throughout this book, we have discussed many of the issues relating to the successful administration of your SQL Server installations. While much of SQL Server runs itself—the product, after all, is designed to be extremely robust—from time to time you will likely encounter certain problems, to which you must be able to respond. Many of these problems are handled using administrative alerts, but some require more serious action.

Additionally, many typical problems can be avoided through the use of effective planning of the database and servers during the initial setup and installation of the server. This chapter, then, is something of a potluck collection of many of the different issues that you might encounter during the administration of the SQL Server, and offers suggestions for how to address those issues.

One of the most common problems that new—and even experienced—administrators encounter is the continued growth of databases that reside on the server. *Capacity planning*, or preparing for the effective handling of database growth, is therefore an extremely important part of effective administration. We will consider the issues surrounding capacity planning in the next section.

CAPACITY PLANNING

One of the main functions of a system administrator is to allocate, manage, and monitor the space and storage requirements for a database. Estimating the space that a database requires can help you plan your storage layout and determine hardware requirements. In the following sections, we will consider some of the most common issues that you must evaluate when making size determinations.

Estimating the Minimum Size of a Database

Figure 12-1 displays a number of factors that you should consider when attempting to determine the space requirements of your database.

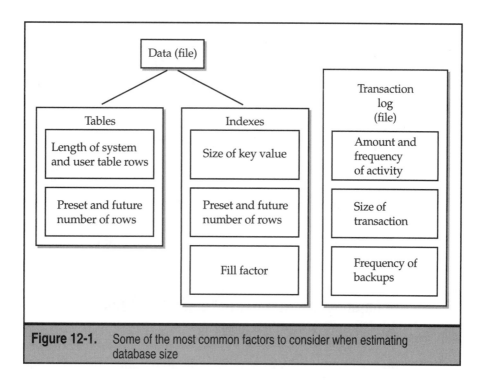

Figure 12-1.   Some of the most common factors to consider when estimating database size

Consider the following when you estimate the amount of space that your database will occupy:

▼   The size of the MODEL Database and the system tables (include projected growth). This is typically not a large percentage of the database size.

■   The amount of data in your tables (include projected growth).

■   The number of indexes and the size of each, especially the size of the key value, the number of rows, and the fill factor setting.

▲   The size of the Transaction Log. Your estimate should take into account factors such as the amount and frequency of modification activity, the size of each transaction, and how often you back up (dump) the log.

TIP: As a starting point, you should allocate 25 percent of the database size to the Transaction Log for online transaction processing (OLTP) environments. You can allocate a smaller percentage for databases that are used primarily for queries.

Estimating the Amount of Data in Tables

After you consider the amount of space that is allocated to the MODEL Database, you should estimate the minimum amount of data in each table, including projected growth. This can be calculated by determining the total number of rows, the row size, the number of rows that fit on a page, and the total number of pages required for each table in the database.

Estimating the Number of Pages in a Table

To estimate the minimum number of pages required for a table, find out the number of characters for each row and the approximate number of rows that the table will have. Calculate the number of pages using the following method:

1. Calculate the number of bytes in a row by totaling the number of bytes that each column contains. If one or more columns are defined as variable length—such as a column for names—you can add the column average to the total. Add 9 bytes to the total, as each row has an overhead of 9 bytes.

2. Determine the maximum number of rows contained in each data page. To do this, divide 8,094 by the number of bytes in a row. Round the result down to the nearest whole number because SQL Server does not allow a row to cross pages. In practice, it is unlikely that this many rows will actually be stored on a page. SQL Server keeps some free space on each page to allow for a small amount of individual row growth per page when variable-length data is updated to a larger size.

3. Divide the approximate number of rows in the table by the number of rows contained in each data page. The result equals the minimum number of pages needed to store your table.

For example, suppose that you have a table that has four `int` columns, three `char(30)` columns, and one `datetime` column. The table will have 250,000 rows. Calculate the number of pages as follows:

▼ Total row size: 4 × 4 bytes (the `int` columns) + 3 × 30 bytes (the `char` columns) + 1 × 8 bytes (the `datetime` column) + 9 bytes (row overhead) = 123 bytes

■ Number of rows per page: 8,094 / 123 = 65 rows per page

■ Number of pages in the table: 250,000 / 65 = 3,847 pages

▲ Size of the table: 3,847 × 8K = 30,776K or about 30MB

Therefore, SQL Server stored 65 rows per page for this table. The total number of pages is 2,842, and the table size is 30,776K.

Estimating the Amount of Data in Indexes

It becomes more difficult to estimate index space when indexes have two types of pages. The first type, called *leaf pages,* holds the indexed key values. The second type forms the binary search tree that speeds indexed search and retrieval.

Index pages can intentionally be left unfilled by specifying a fill factor of less than 100 (percent) when building the index. This increases the number of pages in the index but makes table row inserts and updates faster because fewer new index pages need to be allocated during these operations.

Considering Clustered Versus Nonclustered Indexes

A *clustered index* stores the data rows of a table in the indexed order of the key values of the index. As you have learned, a table can have only one clustered index. A *nonclustered index* is a separate structure that stores a copy of the key values from the table in indexed order plus a pointer to each corresponding data row in the table.

Extra space for a clustered index is taken up only by the B-tree (that is, balanced-tree) index pages because the data rows in the table are the index leaf pages. Also, if a fill factor is specified when building a clustered index, the data pages of the table are filled only to the level specified by the fill factor, making the table larger.

A nonclustered index consists of the B-tree index pages as well as the leaf pages of the index. The leaf pages hold a pointer to and an indexed copy of the key value of each row in the table. If the table has a clustered index, the pointer in a nonclustered index is the clustered index key value. For this reason, you should use small key values for the clustered index of a table that will have nonclustered indexes, otherwise, the nonclustered indexes can become very large.

Considering Index Sizes in More Depth

Table 12-1 shows some examples of the sizes of various indexes added to the table for which the size was calculated in the previous example.

The table first gives the size of an index based on a char(30) key column when there is no clustered index on the table. The size of the same index is then given when there is a clustered index on the table. Finally, the size of the index is given when the index has a fill factor of 50 percent and there is a clustered index on the table. Note that this index is larger than the table! The clustered index uses a char(30) key column—this is not recommended and illustrates the dramatic increase in size over nonclustered indexes if you do use such a large key column for a clustered index.

Key	Clustered on Table	Fill Factor	Pages	Size
One char(30) column	No	100	1,360	10,880K
One char(30) column	Yes	100	2,296	18,368K
One char(30) column	Yes	50	4,548	36,384K
One int column	No	100	560	4,480K
One int column	Yes	100	1,492	11,936K
One int column	Yes	50	2,944	23,552K

Table 12-1.   Sample Index Sizes

The same figures are then repeated for an index based on an `int` key column instead of a `char(30)` key column.

TIP: Remember, the table has 250,000 rows and is 3,847 pages (or 30,776K) in size.

Many factors are involved in estimating space required for a database, including the size of the rows in your tables, the estimated growth of the tables, the number and size of the indexes, and the fill factor for the indexes. Once you have estimated the size requirements of a database and made your determinations about allocations appropriately, you can build the databases as necessary. After databases are created on your server, you have to maintain those databases—and the server itself. In the next section, we consider some of the most important issues involved in the successful care and maintenance of a SQL Server.

MAINTAINING SQL SERVER

To maintain your database, you should perform several tasks, either manually or automatically. These tasks form the core of a database maintenance plan. They include:

▼ Updating information about data optimization

■ Verifying the integrity of data

■ Performing backups

▲ Creating reports and a maintenance history of the database

If you choose to have these tasks performed automatically, you can set up and schedule your database maintenance plan with the Database Maintenance Plan Wizard. However, in the following subsections, we will consider the details on each task you should consider for your database maintenance plan. We will also consider the process of automating your plan.

Developing a Database Maintenance Plan

Several tasks can help you maintain your database. The most important tasks, which should be performed for all SQL Server databases, are updating data optimization information, verifying data integrity, performing backups, and keeping a history of maintenance activities. These tasks should be performed on a regular basis. How often you run these tasks depends on the level of database activity and the size of your database. As you have learned in previous chapters, you can create scheduled SQL Server jobs to perform these tasks automatically.

Updating Information About Data Optimization

As data and index pages fill up, updating requires more time and pages can become fragmented. Reorganizing your data and index pages can greatly improve performance. You can do this in several different ways, all of which were discussed in Chapter 3. However, the following sections also discuss some of the related options.

Maintaining Indexes Using the fillfactor Option

You can specify the percentage of available free space (`fillfactor`) in your index and data pages. This enhances performance: If space is available in existing pages when performing inserts and updates, SQL Server does not have to split pages or allocate new pages. The `fillfactor` percentage is used when the index is first created and whenever the index is rebuilt. You can specify a percentage or allow SQL Server to automatically select the optimal value. You learned about the `fillfactor` specification in detail in Chapter 3.

Updating Statistics That Are Used by the Query Optimizer

You should run `UPDATE STATISTICS` on tables that are being modified. This updates the information about the key value distribution for one or more indexes in a table, which the query optimizer will then use to generate optimal query plans. Updating the statistics will result in highly optimized query plans—meaning that queries will execute substantially faster.

Removing Unused Space from the Database Files

You can execute DBCC SHRINKDATABASE to recover any unused disk space in the database tables. You can also enable the auto-shrink option on databases. Both these techniques are important because, while SQL Server will grow to fill needs and will allocate space as necessary, it will *not* recover unused disk space automatically (unless you set auto-shrink to TRUE).

Verifying the Integrity of Data

Data integrity tests detect inconsistencies in the database caused by hardware or software errors. This is partially your responsibility and partially that of the database developer. You need to make sure, however, that your system maintains information accurately—for relational errors and the like not only can cause the database to perform incorrectly, they can also cause the database (and in some very rare cases even the server) to stop working entirely.

Performing Internal Data Integrity Tests

Execute DBCC CHECKALLOC to check the allocation of data and index pages for each table within the extent structures of the database. It is not necessary to execute DBCC CHECKALLOC if DBCC CHECKDB has already been executed. DBCC CHECKDB is a superset of DBCC CHECKALLOC and includes allocation checks in addition to checks of index structure and data integrity.

DBCC CHECKDB is the safest repair statement because it catches and repairs the widest possible range of errors. If only allocation errors are reported for a database, execute DBCC CHECKALLOC with a repair option to correct them. However, to ensure that all errors (including allocation errors) are repaired properly, execute DBCC CHECKDB with a repair option. DBCC CHECKALLOC messages are sorted by object ID, except for those messages generated from TEMPDB. DBCC CHECKALLOC validates the allocation of all data pages in the database, while DBCC CHECKDB validates the page information used in the storage of data in addition to validating the allocation information.

DBCC CHECKALLOC acquires a schema lock to prevent schema modifications while DBCC CHECKALLOC is in progress. DBCC CHECKALLOC might report errors for TEMPDB work tables that are created or dropped for user queries while the DBCC CHECKALLOC is running; these can safely be ignored.

Performing Database Integrity Tests

Execute DBCC CHECKDB to check the allocation and structural integrity of the objects in the database. Execute DBCC CHECKTABLE to check the integrity of the data, index, text, and index pages for a table. If DBCC finds an error, you can specify that it repair the error automatically.

DBCC CHECKDB performs all the checks performed by DBCC CHECKALLOC and DBCC CHECKTABLE on each table in the database. If you run DBCC CHECKDB regularly, it is not necessary to run DBCC CHECKALLOC and DBCC CHECKTABLE as well. If time is limited, you can use DBCC CHECKALLOC and DBCC CHECKTABLE to perform smaller checks at different times rather than running a full DBCC CHECKDB at one time. If DBCC CHECKDB reports only allocation errors, you can use DBCC CHECKALLOC to repair the errors. The safest option is to run DBCC CHECKDB with the repair option; this fixes all errors, including allocation errors. While DBCC CHECKDB is running, it is not possible to create, alter, or drop tables.

Performing Backups

You should perform backups on a regular basis to protect against data loss and back up the Transaction Log to capture changes to the database between full database backups. You learned all about the steps involved in designing an effective backup sequence in Chapter 6, and in Chapter 7 you learned how to recover data after a failure.

Maintaining a Maintenance History

Keep a history of the maintenance tasks you (or the system on your behalf) perform. This history should include what actions were performed, as well as the results of any corrective actions. Keeping a history of maintenance actions can be particularly helpful in determining what corrupted a database, particularly if you are able to identify the exact point at which the error occurred— allowing you to determine which task was performed precipitously to cause the error.

Automating the Database Maintenance Plan Tasks

You can use either the Database Maintenance Plan Wizard or the `sqlmaint` utility to automate your database maintenance plan so that it runs on a regularly scheduled basis. The following sections discuss some of the issues surrounding the creation of a maintenance plan.

Using the Database Maintenance Plan Wizard

You can use the Database Maintenance Plan Wizard to set up the core maintenance tasks necessary to ensure that your database performs well, is regularly backed up in the event of a system failure, and is checked for inconsistencies. When you run the wizard, you will specify the following.

Databases That the Plan Maintains   You can define a single maintenance plan for all databases or plans for one or more databases. Typically, in more complex environments, you will create separate plans for each database or group of databases, which provide both fault tolerance and easier management.

Data Optimization Information   You can have the wizard reorganize data and index pages, update the index statistics to ensure that the query optimizer has current information regarding the spread of data in the tables, and compress data files by removing empty database pages. Having your regular maintenance plan perform this processing helps to ensure that you do not have to remember to perform such tasks regularly.

Data Verification Tests   You can have the wizard perform internal consistency checks of the data and data pages within the database to ensure that a system or rare software problem has not damaged data.

You can specify whether indexes should be included in the checks and whether the wizard should attempt to repair minor problems that it finds. The wizard will typically use DBCC statements to perform consistency checks on your behalf.

Frequency and Destination of Backups   You can schedule both database and Transaction Log backups and can keep backup files for a specified time. Issues surrounding the methods and techniques of performing backups were discussed in Chapter 6.

Location of History Files   The results that the maintenance tasks generate can be written as a report to a text file, saved in history tables, or sent in an e-mail message to an operator. This particular issue is an important one—after all, history maintenance does not do you any good if it is not accessed and reviewed regularly.

Using the sqlmaint Utility

Use the sqlmaint utility to execute DBCC statements, dump a database and Transaction Logs, update statistics, and rebuild indexes. The sqlmaint utility is a command-prompt utility that performs functions similar to those handled by the Database Maintenance Plan Wizard.

Using the Database Maintenance Plan Wizard to Create a Database Maintenance Plan

To create a database maintenance plan that consists of multiple jobs using the Database Maintenance Plan Wizard, perform the following steps:

1. Switch to SQL Server Enterprise Manager.

2. On the Tools menu, click on Wizards.

3. Expand Management, click on Database Maintenance Plan Wizard, and then click OK to run the wizard. Click Next on the first screen of the wizard.

4. Click on These Databases and then check only Nwind in the Databases list. Click Next.

5. Check the Update Statistics Used by Query Optimizer option. Set the value of the Sample option to 10 percent of the database.

6. Check the Remove Unused Space from Database Files option. Set the value of the When It Grows Beyond option to 5MB. Set the value of the Amount of Free Space to Remain After Shrink option to 15 percent of free space.

7. Click Change to open the Edit Recurring Job Schedule dialog box. In Occurs, click on Monthly. In Monthly, set the value to Day 1 of Every 3 Month(s).

8. Click OK to close the Edit Recurring Job Schedule dialog box. Click Next.

9. Check the Check Database Integrity option.

10. Click Change to open the Edit Recurring Job Schedule dialog box. In Occurs, click on Monthly. In Monthly, set the value to The 1st Saturday of Every 1 Month(s).

11. Click OK to close the Edit Recurring Job Schedule dialog box. Click Next.

12. Check the Back Up the Database As Part of the Database Plan option.

13. Click Change to open the Edit Recurring Job Schedule dialog box. In Occurs, click on Weekly. In Weekly, set the value to Every 1 Week(s) on Sunday. In Daily Frequency, set the value to Occurs Once at 11:00 PM.

14. Click OK to close the Edit Recurring Job Schedule dialog box. Click Next.

15. Check and set the Remove Files Older Than 2 Week(s) option.

16. Click Next.

17. Check the option Backup the Transaction Log as Part of the Maintenance Plan.

18. Click Change to open the Edit Recurring Job Schedule dialog box. In Occurs, click on Weekly. In Weekly, set the value to Every 1 Week(s) on Monday, Wednesday, and Friday. In Daily Frequency, set the value to Occurs Once at 11:00 PM.

19. Click OK to close the Edit Recurring Job Schedule dialog box. Click Next.

20. Check and set the option Remove Files Older Than 1 Week(s).

21. Click Next.

22. Check the option Write Report to a Text File in Directory.

23. Click Next.

24. Check Write History to the `msdb.dbo.sysdbmaintplan_history` Table on the Local Server.

25. Check the option Limit Rows in the Table To. Set the value to 1,000 rows for this plan.

26. Click Next.

27. In the Plan Name, type **Nwind Maintenance Plan**.

28. Click Finish to create the new plan. Click OK to close the confirmation that your maintenance plan has been created.

29. In the console tree, expand Management and then click the Database Maintenance Plans icon.

30. In the details pane, right-click Nwind Maintenance Plan and then click Properties. Review your new plan, noting that the wizard has created a plan with all the settings that you selected.

31. Click Cancel to close the Database Maintenance Plan dialog box. If you are prompted to save changes, click No.

32. In the console tree, expand SQL Server Agent and then click the Jobs icon. Verify that four jobs were created successfully for Nwind Maintenance Plan.

33. In the details pane, right-click on Integrity Checks Job for DB Maintenance Plan 'Nwind Maintenance Plan' and click Start to manually start the Integrity Check Job.

It is important to regularly perform various maintenance tasks on your databases. Regular maintenance includes keeping table and index statistics up to date, performing database consistency checks, making backups, and organizing database space allocation. You can automate maintenance by creating your own jobs or by creating a database maintenance plan using the Database Maintenance Plan Wizard.

One of the most common situations we encounter in the field is individuals upgrading from SQL Server 6.5 or 7 to SQL Server 2000. You should be aware of certain specific issues surrounding such an upgrade. The following section discusses these issues.

TROUBLESHOOTING ISSUES THAT ARISE AFTER USING THE SQL SERVER UPGRADE WIZARD

Because of the significant improvements and changes made in Microsoft SQL Server 2000, it is possible that some of the objects in an upgraded database will not be correctly created in SQL Server 2000. You should therefore be aware of the changes in SQL Server 2000 and should plan to change your databases to use fully supported SQL Server 2000 options. You will have to troubleshoot any number of issues, and in the following sections we discuss not only such troubleshooting issues but also standard maintenance issues.

Removing SQL Server 7

After upgrading the SQL Server 7 databases to SQL Server 2000, you might want to leave SQL Server 7 on your computer until you are sure you no longer need it. When ready, you can remove SQL Server 7 by using the SQL Server 7 Setup Utility.

Troubleshooting the Upgrade

If you encounter difficulties in upgrading, identify the problem and view the upgrade log files. However, some of the most common problems with upgrading occur *after* the upgrade completes—so you should watch out for both types of errors. The following sections consider some of the most common problems that you will encounter.

Identifying Common Upgrade Problems

You cannot upgrade some objects and settings to SQL Server 2000 without modification. If you encounter problems during the upgrade process, check the following.

Objects with Inaccurate or Missing Entries in syscomments   To upgrade objects, the text description stored in the syscomments table in SQL Server 7 must be intact. Objects will not upgrade if any of the following conditions are met:

▼ Text in syscomments has been deleted.

■ They were renamed using SP_RENAME. This system stored procedure does not alter the entry in syscomments for an object.

▲ They are stored procedures that were created within other stored procedures. There is no entry in syscomments for these stored procedures.

TIP: Objects created with encrypted text in the syscomments table are upgraded.

A Server Name That Does Not Match the Computer Name   The computer name on which SQL Server runs must match the server name returned by @@SERVERNAME. If the names do not match, the SQL Server Upgrade Wizard might fail. To correct this problem, change the server name returned by @@SERVERNAME to match the computer name, using the SP_DROPSERVER and SP_ADDSERVER system stored procedures.

Stored Procedures That Modify and Reference System Tables   Stored procedures that do the following will not upgrade automatically:

▼ Modify system tables

▲ Reference system tables or columns that do not exist in SQL Server 2000

Instead, you should take the text that you used to originally create the stored procedures and re-execute it on the SQL Server, ensuring the creation of new stored procedures.

Noting Restrictions on Creating Tables

During the upgrade process, you might encounter the following problems in upgrading tables and views:

▼ Tables and views with NULL column names will not upgrade because the wizard cannot script these objects.

▲ Tables created by the system administrator on behalf of another user who does not have create-table permissions will not upgrade. Because the object owner does not have CREATE permissions, the script to create the object fails.

Should you encounter such problems, you might end up backing up the version 7 database, re-creating the schema on the version 2000 server, and restoring the backup manually. However, be careful when doing so—if you fail to solve the problems before creating the backups, the restorations will not work either.

Viewing the Upgrade Log Files

The SQL Server Upgrade Wizard creates a subfolder in the C:\Program Files\Mssql\Upgrade folder each time it runs. The folder name consists of the server name and the current date and time to distinguish multiple runs of the SQL Server Upgrade Wizard. For example, the name SQLCONV1_092199_151900 indicates that the wizard was run on a SQL Server called SQLCONV1 on 9/21/99 at 15:19 hours.

This folder contains a number of descriptively named log files describing each upgrade step. It contains subfolders for each upgraded database, including the MASTER Database. These subfolders contain log files indicating the success or failure of creating objects in the database.

Files with an .OK extension indicate that all instances of that type of object were created successfully. Files with an .ERR extension indicate that at least one instance of that type of object was *not* created successfully. The error files list each failed object creation statement and the reason the object was not created successfully.

Any log files that indicate a problem are listed at the end of the upgrade, in the SQL Server Upgrade Wizard, for easy access.

Specifying Compatibility Levels

If you are upgrading databases to SQL Server 2000, you will probably have objects in the upgraded database attempting to use features that have changed. SQL Server 2000 supports different compatibility levels to make the transition from previous versions as easy as possible.

Understanding Compatibility Levels

When run with default settings, most SQL Server 6.*x* applications work unchanged after an upgrade to SQL Server 2000 made by the SQL Server Upgrade Wizard.

The compatibility level can be set for any SQL Server 2000 database, using the SP_DBCMPTLEVEL system stored procedure. The level can be set to 60, 65, 70, or 2000 (version number), according to the version of SQL Server with which you require compatibility; it defaults to 2000 for new databases.

When you upgrade existing systems with existing applications, you can use the database compatibility level settings to retain earlier behaviors if your existing applications depend on those behaviors. Setting a compatibility level gives you time to upgrade applications in a planned, orderly manner, though it is recommended that you update all your scripts to full SQL Server 2000 compatibility when possible. Future versions of SQL Server will not necessarily offer compatibility with versions earlier than SQL Server 2000. Many applications are not affected by the changes in behavior.

The effects of the compatibility level settings are generally limited to the behaviors of a small number of Transact-SQL statements that also exist in earlier versions of SQL Server. When the database compatibility level is set to 60 or 65, applications still gain almost all the benefits of the new performance enhancements of SQL Server 7 or 2000.

Selecting Initial Settings

You can select initial compatibility level settings for user, MODEL, and MASTER databases. The following sections consider some specific issues about each.

User Databases   The SQL Server Upgrade Wizard sets the compatibility level of upgraded databases to the version number of the export server.

For example, if your server was SQL Server 6.5 and you upgrade to SQL Server 2000, the compatibility level for all existing user-defined databases is set to 65. This setting enables existing applications to run with a minimum number of changes after an upgrade.

The MODEL Database   The compatibility level of an upgraded MODEL Database is set to 2000. If you change this setting, it will propagate to new databases. Note, however, that changing the MODEL Database setting will result in *every* new database that you create having the compatibility level of the MODEL Database.

The MASTER Database   The compatibility level of an upgraded MASTER Database is set to 2000. You should not change this setting. If an upgraded stored procedure in the MASTER Database requires an earlier SQL Server compatibility level, you must move it out of the MASTER Database.

Understanding Backward Compatibility Details

If you have been using a previous version of SQL Server, you should be aware of the major feature changes that affect the operation of SQL Server 2000. These changes are grouped into four levels:

▼ **Level 1**   Statements, stored procedures, or other items that have been removed in SQL Server 2000. Code or scripts that use these items must be changed before they are used with SQL Server 2000. The DISK REINIT and DISK REFIT commands have Level 1 compatibility.

■ **Level 2**   Changes that cause significantly different behavior in SQL Server 2000. Code or scripts that use these items probably need to be changed; new behavior must at least be well understood so that you are not taken by surprise. For example, when restoring multiple Transaction Logs, the last RESTORE statement must specify the WITH RECOVERY option; all other RESTORE statements must specify the WITH NORECOVERY option.

■ **Level 3**   Items that are fully supported in SQL Server 2000, but for backward compatibility only. Future versions of SQL Server might not support these items, and you should begin using the SQL Server 2000 replacement when possible. For example, DBCC ROWLOCK enabled Insert Row Locking in previous versions of SQL Server. Row locking is now automatic and DBCC ROWLOCK is not required.

▲ **Level 4**   Changes that produce slightly different behavior in SQL Server 2000. For example, the ANSI SQL-92 syntax for outer joins (LEFT OUTER JOIN and RIGHT OUTER JOIN should be used instead of the older *= and =* indicators).

Your upgrade planning should include checking your existing databases and scripts for items that fall into any of these levels and replacing them before or after the upgrade, as necessary.

Registering a SQL Server 7 Server Using Enterprise Manager

You can register a version 7 server in SQL Server Enterprise Manager. The version 7 server can be started and stopped, and selecting the version 7 server launches the version 7 SQL Server Enterprise Manager. The version 7 SQL Server Enterprise Manager must be installed on the computer. Both versions of Enterprise Manager and the other SQL Server client utilities can be installed on the computer where SQL Server 2000 is installed or on any Microsoft Windows 95, Windows 98, or Windows NT or 2000 computer residing on a network.

One of the most important issues in performing an upgrade is testing the upgrade and reviewing the upgrade log files to ensure that the upgrade correctly transferred your databases. It is possible that you will have to create some objects manually after changing the old scripts for these objects to use new SQL Server 2000 syntax. After upgrading, you should begin updating all your scripts to use SQL Server 2000 syntax, even if the objects transfer correctly with the Upgrade Wizard.

You can use the compatibility level to force SQL Server 2000 to use SQL Server 6.x or 7 functionality for certain Transact-SQL statements. The four levels of changes described previously have been defined to help you prioritize the modifications you need to make to your code and scripts.

In previous chapters, you have learned about your ability to perform automated SQL Server administration tasks. Doing so greatly simplifies complex management issues and makes your life easier. In the following section, we will discuss some of the issues surrounding the troubleshooting of automated administration practices.

TROUBLESHOOTING SQL SERVER AUTOMATED ADMINISTRATION

You must perform six major tasks to troubleshoot an automated installation. Each of the following items is discussed in turn in the subsequent paragraphs:

- ▼ Verifying that SQL Server Agent has been started
- ■ Verifying that the job, schedule, alert, or operator is enabled

■ Ensuring that the SQLAgentCmdExec account is correctly configured

■ Reviewing error logs

■ Reviewing job history

▲ Verifying that the mail client is working properly

Verifying That SQL Server Agent Has Been Started

If SQL Server Agent has stopped for any reason, the server will be unable to execute jobs or fire alerts. You should consider having the SQLServerAgent service start automatically whenever the Windows Server is started to help avoid such problems.

The SQLServerAgent Monitor provides self-checking for SQL Server Agent. If the SQLServerAgent service stops unexpectedly, SQLServerAgent Monitor can attempt to restart the service. Enable SQLServerAgent Monitor through SQL Server Enterprise Manager as shown in Figure 12-2, or by running the XP_SQLAGENT_MONITOR extended stored procedure. When SQL Server Agent Monitor restarts the SQL Server service, an error is written to the Windows application log, making it possible to configure an alert to fire when the service is restarted.

Verifying That the Job, Schedule, Alert, or Operator Is Enabled

If jobs are not executing as scheduled, alerts are not being fired, or operators are not receiving notifications, verify that the job, schedule, alert, or operator is enabled.

The fact that a job, schedule, alert, or operator is disabled is *not* recorded in the SQL Server Agent error log or the job history.

Ensuring That the SQLAgentCmdExec Account Is Correctly Configured

An operating system command or Active Scripting job step in a job owned by a user who is not a member of the SYSADMIN role cannot execute under the following conditions:

▼ If the SQLAgentCmdExec account has been improperly installed

■ If the SQLAgentCmdExec account has been removed

■ If changes to the SQLAgentCmdExec account password have been made outside of the SQL Server Agent Properties dialog box

▲ If SQL Server Agent has been set to allow only members of SYSADMIN to execute CmdExec and Active Scripting job steps

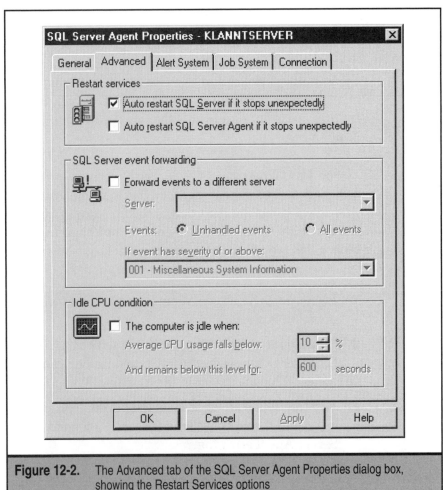

Figure 12-2. The Advanced tab of the SQL Server Agent Properties dialog box, showing the Restart Services options

TIP: If a job step fails for this reason, you will probably not see an entry in the SQL Server Agent Error Log. The error will, however, be recorded in the job step history.

Reviewing Error Logs

By reviewing error messages in the Windows application log and the SQL Server Agent and SQL Server error logs, you might be able to more easily troubleshoot the source of your problem.

Windows Application Log   If the maximum size of the Windows application log is too small or is defined to be overwritten frequently, events might not exist for SQL Server to process. To avoid losing event information about SQL Server, increase the maximum log size for the Windows application log. Use Windows Event Viewer to check that events are being recorded for SQL Server. SQL Server Agent fires alerts only for events that are recorded in the Windows application log.

SQL Server Agent Error Log   SQL Server Agent errors are recorded in the SQL Server Agent error log. By default, all SQL Server Agent errors and warnings are recorded in the error log. You can also record execution trace messages when troubleshooting specific problems; this can cause the log to become large, however, so it should not be enabled during normal operation. Note the following:

▼ Each time SQL Server Agent is stopped and restarted, a new error log is created.

■ You can view the current error log with SQL Server Enterprise Manager or any text editor. Up to nine previous versions of the error log are saved in the C:\Mssql7\Log folder.

▲ You can define an error message pop-up recipient to be sent a NET SEND command when errors are logged in to the SQL Server Agent error log.

SQL Server Error Log   You should also review the SQL Server error log. By comparing the dates and times for events in the SQL Server error log, the SQL Server Agent error log, and the Windows application log, you can narrow down the list of probable causes of problems.

Reviewing Job History

After you review the SQL Server Agent error log, you also might want to review history information on an alert, an operator, or a job. The date and time of the single most recent action is recorded for alerts and operators. Full job history is captured in the MSDB Database.

The maximum amount of job history information can be resized. Having a full sysjobhistory system table can cause both alerts and jobs to fail. If you must keep large amounts of job history information, you should expand the MSDB Database to a size that is sufficient to accommodate the growth.

TIP: Some job errors are not written in the SQL Server Agent error log but do get written in the job history, so you should check the job history even if the SQL Server Agent error log shows no error.

Verifying That the Mail Client Is Working Properly

If e-mail or pager notifications are not working, verify that the mail client is working properly. To do so, log on to the mail client, using the SQL Server Agent domain user account, and send an e-mail or pager notification to an operator.

Troubleshooting Alerts

Because SQL Server Agent both depends on and monitors SQL Server events, it can become caught in an endless loop, firing the same alert repeatedly. This generally occurs when SQL Server runs out of an essential global resource and an alert has been defined on this event.

A looping condition occurs when SQL Server Agent fires an alert that attempts to execute a job. Executing the job, in turn, causes the same error that originally fired the alert. This causes the job to be executed again, and so on.

Signs that looping alerts might be occurring are that the Windows application log rapidly fills with the same error, the CPU use is unusually high, or the number of alert responses is high.

Under these conditions, the delay increases between when the event appears in the Windows application log and when SQL Server Agent responds to that event. This causes a backlog of alerts.

Resolving Looping Alerts

When looping alerts occur, resolve the error condition and clear the backlog of events from the Windows application log. You can do this in one of the following ways:

▼ Use Windows Event Viewer to clear the Windows application log. If you do this, all events, including those not generated by SQL Server, are cleared. You should try to resolve the alert backlog by other means if you do not want to lose your current Windows application log.

▲ SQL Server Agent processes an alert only once within a defined period of time. This time defaults to one minute, so SQL Server Agent will process the same alert only once every minute, no matter how many times the error on which the alert is based occurs. Use the Delay Between Responses option for each alert to set this time. A longer delay reduces the number of alerts that can fire as a result of any one condition and will decrease the number of alerts fired when looping alerts are occurring.

TIP: The default delay between responses is 0 for alerts added with the Create Alert Wizard or the SP_ADD_ALERT system stored procedure. In most cases, it is recommended that you change this to 1 minute after using the wizard to create alerts.

To prevent recurring alerts on specific error numbers from consuming all your resources, you can define them as non-alert-generating. To create an error that is non-alert-generating, you must modify the Windows registry. The result of this modification is that SQL Server Agent will not fire the alert when the error occurs. However, you should use this solution as a *last resort only*. Refer to Books Online for information on how to configure non-alert-generating errors.

Most problems with automated administration are caused by accounts or services that are configured incorrectly or by services that are not running. When errors occur, you can check the SQL Server and SQL Server Agent error logs as well as the job histories to determine the source of the problem. Planning your alerts carefully will prevent looping alerts from occurring.

In addition to the errors that can result from automated administration tasks, one of the other common areas where administrators run into problems is with replication. In the following section, we will discuss some of the steps you should take to troubleshoot replication problems in your environment.

TROUBLESHOOTING REPLICATION

Many difficulties in replication processing involve connectivity and security. Before these can be addressed, you must determine which servers are involved in a replication problem by observing the processing order of the replication agents. Troubleshooting and resolution should focus on the access to each of the servers and to the databases that are involved in the replication scenario.

Items to Check for Resolving Replication Problems

As with automated administration issues, you should check a series of locations to ensure that everything is configuring and processing correctly in your replicated environment. The following sections discuss those locations.

Checking the Error Logs

Several error logs can assist you in troubleshooting replication problems: SQL Server Error Log, SQL Server Agent Error Log, and

Windows Event Viewer. You also can use SQL Server Profiler to troubleshoot replication.

Configuring and Monitor Replication Alerts

Replication alerts are standard SQL Server alerts, configured to respond to conditions caused by the replication process. In SQL Server Enterprise Manager, you can configure all the replication alerts under Alerts in SQL Server Agent or under Replication Alerts in the Replication Monitor. You must add new replication alerts under Replication Alerts in the Replication Monitor; otherwise, they will show up only in SQL Server Agent. If you use the SP_ADD_ALERT system stored procedure to add a replication alert, you must specify the category 'Replication' with the @category_name argument if you want the new alert to be listed under Replication Alerts in the Replication Monitor.

A number of predefined replication alerts are created when you enable publishing and distribution. To use any of these alerts, you must enable it and add one or more operators to be notified when it fires. As for standard SQL Server Agent alerts, you can specify a job to be executed when the alert fires. The following predefined replication alerts are created for you:

- ▼ Replication: Agent custom shutdown
- ■ Replication: Agent failure
- ■ Replication: Agent retry
- ■ Replication: Agent success
- ■ Replication: Expired subscription dropped
- ■ Replication: Subscriber has failed data validation
- ■ Replication: Subscriber has passed data validation
- ▲ Replication: Subscriber reinitialized after validation failure

Verifying SQL Server Services

Replication agents run under the user context of the SQLServerAgent service. If you have difficulty with the MSSQLServer service or the SQLServerAgent service, verify that:

▼   MSSQLServer and SQLServerAgent services are running.

■   The service account and password are properly configured for the SQLServerAgent service. It is recommended that all participants in the replication process use the same Windows domain account for the SQLServerAgent service.

▲   Multidomain environments have service accounts that are trusted across domains.

Testing the Connectivity

By default, SQL Server replication uses the same Windows domain user account that SQL Server Agent uses. If you experience a problem with connectivity, test the connectivity. You will do this slightly differently for push subscriptions versus pull subscriptions:

For a push subscription, perform the following steps:

1.   Log on to the distributor with the same Windows account that the SQLServerAgent service uses on the distributor.

2.   From the distributor, use SQL Server Query Analyzer, choose Windows NT/2000 Authentication Mode, and connect to the subscriber.

For a pull subscription, perform the following steps:

1.   Log on to the subscriber with the same Windows account that SQL Server Agent uses on the subscriber.

2.   From the subscriber, use SQL Server Query Analyzer, choose Windows NT/2000 Authentication Mode, and connect to the distributor.

If you cannot connect using either of these methods, the problem is with security rather than replication.

Understanding Connectivity Issues with Windows 95 and Windows 98 Servers

On Windows NT/2000-based SQL Servers that need to replicate data from a Microsoft Windows 95-based or Windows 98-based SQL Server, use the SQL Server Client Network Utility to define an alias for the Windows 95 or Windows 98 server that uses the TCP/IP or Multiprotocol network library. This is necessary because Windows NT/2000-based SQL Servers use the Named Pipes client network library by default, and Windows 95-based and Windows 98-based SQL Servers do not support incoming Named Pipes connections.

Checking the Replication Agent Schedules

If replication is not occurring as expected, you might simply have to wait for the agents to start as scheduled, or you can manually start the agents to initiate the replication process.

Consider the following transactional replication scenario:

After creating a publication and a subscription, the tables corresponding to the publication articles are not being created and populated on the subscriber. You have checked the security and the connectivity between the publisher, the distributor, and the subscriber, and they are working correctly.

The most likely cause for the replication not occurring in this case is that the initial synchronization has not taken place. This is probably because the Snapshot agent has not run to generate the initial snapshot that the Distribution agent needs to perform the initial synchronization. Depending on how the initial snapshot was scheduled when the publication was created, the initial snapshot might be created later or on demand. You need either to wait for the snapshot to be created or to manually start the Snapshot agent for the publication before the initial synchronization will occur. After the initial synchronization is complete, regular transactional replication will begin.

The last big issue to consider for the effective maintenance and management of your SQL Server is the maintenance and implementation of stored procedures and triggers. The following section explores some of the debugging issues that you will encounter.

DEBUGGING STORED PROCEDURES AND TRIGGERS

By now, it should be obvious that stored procedures and triggers can represent a significant portion of an application's code—as well as a significant portion of the installed objects on the SQL Server. Even so, for a long time, no decent debugger support existed for stored procedures. (The typical debugging tool was the liberal use of PRINT statements—a solution that seems almost comical now.) Some independent service vendors (ISVs) jumped in and helped by adding some "pseudo-debugging" products—but these products lacked access to the actual SQL Server execution environment. They typically added debugging support by doing tricks behind the scenes, such as adding additional PRINT statements or adding SELECT statements to get the current values of variables. Although some of these products were helpful, they had significant limitations. Typically, they could not step into nested stored procedures or into triggers. A Transact-SQL debugger was always prominent on the wish list of SQL Server customers. Anybody who has done any serious coding in Transact-SQL will know firsthand how frustrating it is not to have a proper debugger and probably has spent many late nights putting PRINT statements into stored procedures.

Still, it did not make sense for the SQL Server developers to write a new SQL Server-specific debugger because there were already too many debuggers on the market. If you are anything like most programmers, you want to do your work in one development environment. For example, if you are a C programmer, you probably want to use the same debugger on your SQL code that you use on your C code. Or if you program in Visual Basic, you probably will want to use the Visual Basic development environment for debugging. Fortunately, this environment-specific debugging capability now exists, and its availability is rapidly expanding. If you are a developer in Microsoft Visual C++, Microsoft Visual J++, or Visual Basic, you can now debug Transact-SQL using the *same debugger* you use in those environments.

To accomplish this, the SQL Server developers defined a DLL and a set of callbacks that SQL Server would load and call at the beginning of each SQL statement. In essence, they defined a set of debug events that would allow them to control the execution on a statement-by-statement basis within SQL Server. This has come to be known as the SQL Server Debug Interface, or SDI. The interface that originally shipped with the version 6.5 release was a work in progress. SDI's first customer was Visual C++ version 4.2. SQL Server 6.5 shipped several months before Visual C++ 4.2, and, of course, the developers did not get the interface quite right. Specs are never perfect, and they nearly always get tweaked—at a minimum—during implementation. This was certainly true for SDI, so to use it with Visual C++ version 4.2 or later you need SQL Server version 6.5 with Service Pack 1 or later. The developers debugged the debugging interface using the Visual C++ team as guinea pigs, and now other development tools are adding support for SDI. Today, SDI is available with Visual C++, Visual Basic, Visual J++, and other development tools from Microsoft. (The exact packaging is always subject to change, but in general, the debugger support for Transact-SQL is available only in each product's Enterprise Edition.)

Although the interface is quite likely to change in future releases, it is also made available via a technical note to ISVs that want to add SQL Server debugger support. SDI is a specialized interface of interest only to those writing debuggers, so it is not considered a general feature of SQL Server.

With the existence of SDI, you now have a true debugging environment for Transact-SQL if you are using Microsoft Visual Studio. For example, as a C/C++ developer using Visual Studio, you can do the following:

▼ Perform line-by-line debugging of all your Transact-SQL code.

■ Step directly from the C/C++ code executing on your client machine into the Transact-SQL code executing remotely at the SQL Server machine.

■ Remotely debug your procedures, with the actual execution of the procedures happening at the SQL Server machine and your debugging environment happening locally. (Or, if you prefer, you can do it all from one machine.)

■ Set breakpoints anywhere in your SQL code.

■ Watch the contents of SQL Server local variables and certain system functions. You can even examine function values that are not used in your SQL code; for example, you can watch current status codes using @@ERROR or the number of rows selected using @@ROWCOUNT.

■ Modify the values of most variables in a watch window, testing conditional logic in your code more easily. (Note that variables with datatypes for which there is no direct mapping in C cannot be edited in a watch window.)

■ Examine the values of parameters passed to stored procedures.

■ Step into or over nested procedures. And if a statement causes a trigger to fire, you can even step into the trigger.

■ Use Visual Studio to edit your procedures and save them to the server. This makes it easy to fix bugs on the fly. SQL keywords and comments in your code are color-coded, as they would be in C, to make them easier to spot.

▲ Optionally send results of your SQL statements to the result window directly in Visual Studio.

The SDI is implemented via the pseudo-extended stored procedure SP_SDIDEBUG. (The SP_ convention was used so that the procedure could be called from any database without being fully qualified.) By "pseudo" we mean that, as with a normal extended stored procedure, you will see an entry in the sysobjects table of type X for SP_SDIDEBUG. But unlike a normal extended stored procedure, the code for SP_SDIDEBUG is internal to SQL Server and does *not* reside in a separate DLL. This is true for a few other procedures as well, such as the remote cursor calls made by ODBC and DB-Library cursor functions. This was done so that new capabilities could be added to the server without having to change the tabular data stream (TDS) protocol that describes result sets back to the client application. It also eliminates the need for new keywords (potentially breaking a few applications) when the commands are of the sort that would not be executed directly by an application anyway.

You should never call SP_SDIDEBUG directly. Procedures exist to load a DLL that the provider of the debugger would write and to toggle debugging on and off for the specific SQL Server connection being debugged. When debugging is enabled, the DLL is given access to internal state information for the SQL Server connection being debugged. All the APIs defined in the interface are synchronous calls, and they are called in the context of the thread associated with the connection, which allows for callbacks to SQL Server to occur in the context of the client's thread. The internal Process Status Structure (PSS) in SQL Server holds status information for the connection being debugged, and the DLL is then able to read this structure to determine local variable, parameter, system function, and symbol information.

The debugging support of the Enterprise Editions of the programming tools seems pretty normal if you are already familiar with the environment. Typically, the biggest problem users have with debugging Transact-SQL is getting it configured in the first place. Here are some tips that might help you in debugging Transact-SQL from Visual Studio:

▼ You must use the Enterprise Edition, not the Professional or Standard Edition.

■ Run SQL Server under a user account, not as a Local System. You can change this in the Services applet of the Windows NT Control Panel. If SQL Server is running under the local account, breakpoints are ignored. While you are running the Services applet, also make sure that the RPC Service and the RPC Locator Service are running. You might consider setting them to start automatically. Make sure that the user account doing the debugging has access to the SP_SDIDEBUG stored procedure. By default, only a System Administrator has permission to run this procedure.

▲ SQL Server Debugging must be enabled in each of the Visual Studio components from which you want to allow debugging. Check the documentation for the particular programming environment for details. For example, in Visual Basic 6 (Enterprise Edition) select Add Ins and then Add In Manager. Toward the bottom, there will be a selection for the VB tsql debugger; select it and then click on the Loaded/Unloaded box. This will add the debugger to the Add In list. Do not debug on a production server; because of the added overhead and break-in nature of the debugging product, you could adversely affect other users.

For simple debugging, you might find yourself still using the PRINT statement; for tougher problems, you might come to regard the new debugging capability as a lifesaver.

ENVIRONMENTAL CONCERNS

To finish this discussion of Transact-SQL programming and administration, we will look briefly at some of the environmental concerns that you need to be aware of for effective database administration—for example, case sensitivity, which can greatly affect your applications. We will also look at nullability issues and ANSI compatibility.

Case Sensitivity

Various options and settings affect the semantics and thus the executability of your Transact-SQL statements. You must be sure that your Transact-SQL code can work regardless of the setting, or you must at least control the environment so that you know what the setting is.

Case sensitivity is by far the most common environmental problem, and it is simple to avoid. You should seriously consider doing most of your development in a case-sensitive environment, even if you will deploy your application mostly in a case-*in*sensitive environment. The reason is simple: Nearly all operations that work in a case-sensitive environment will also work in a case-insensitive environment, but the converse is not true. For example, if we write the statement select * from authors in the PUBS database of a case-sensitive environment, it will work equally well in a case-insensitive environment. On the other hand, the statement SELECT * FROM AUTHORS will work fine in a case-insensitive environment but will fail in a case-sensitive environment. The table in PUBS is actually named authors, which is lowercase. The only statement that would work in a case-sensitive environment but fail in a case-insensitive environment is the declaration of an object name, a column name, or a variable name. For example, with the statement declare @myvar int, another statement declaring @MYVAR *int* would work fine in a case-sensitive environment because the two names are distinct, but it would fail in a case-insensitive environment because the names would be considered duplicates.

The easiest way to determine whether your environment is case-sensitive is to perform a SELECT statement with a WHERE clause that compares a lowercase letter with its uppercase counterpart—you would not need to access a table to do this. The following simple SELECT statement returns 1 if the server is case-sensitive and 0 if the server is case-insensitive:

```
SELECT CASE
   WHEN ('A'='a') THEN 0
   ELSE 1
END
```

Case sensitivity is just one of the issues surrounding the character set used by SQL Server. The character set choice will affect both the rows selected and their ordering in the result set for a query such as this:

```
SELECT au_lname, au_fname FROM authors
   WHERE au_lname='Réné'
   ORDER BY au_lname, au_fname
```

If you never use characters that are not in the standard ASCII character set, case sensitivity is really your primary issue. But if your data has special characters like the "é" in this example, be sure that you understand character set issues.

Nullability and ANSI Compliance Settings

To pass the National Institute of Standards and Technology (NIST) test suite for ANSI SQL-92 compliance, various options had to be enabled in SQL Server because of subtle differences in semantics between the traditional SQL Server behavior and what is mandated by ANSI. We already covered the majority of these issues in earlier chapters. To preserve backward compatibility, the prior behavior could not simply be changed. So options were added (or, in a few cases, previous options were toggled on) to change the semantics to comply with the ANSI SQL requirements. These options are summarized below, along with the statement used to change the behavior:

▼   Disable SQL Server's = NULL extension (set ansi_nulls on).

■   Automatically display a warning if a truncation would occur because the target column is too small to accept a value. By default, SQL Server truncates without any warning (set ansi_warnings on).

■   Always right-pad *char* columns and do not trim trailing blanks that were entered in *varchar* columns, as SQL Server would do by default (set ansi_padding on).

■   Make statements implicitly part of a transaction, requiring a subsequent COMMIT or ROLLBACK (set implicit transactions on).

■   Terminate a query if an overflow or divide-by-zero error occurs (set arithabort on). By default, SQL Server returns NULL for these operators, issues a warning message, and proceeds.

■   Close any open cursors on COMMIT of a transaction. By default, SQL Server keeps the cursor open so that it can be reused without incurring the overhead of reopening it (set cursor_close_on_commit on).

■   Allow identifier names to include SQL Server keywords if the identifier is included in double quotation marks, which by default is not allowed. This causes single and double quotation marks to be treated differently (set quoted_identifier on).

▲   By default, create as NOT NULL a column in a CREATE TABLE statement that is not specified as NULL or NOT NULL. set ansi_null_dflt_on on toggles this so that the column can be created with NULL. (We recommend that you always specify NULL or NOT NULL so that this setting option is irrelevant.) The nullability of a column not explicitly declared is determined by the setting at the time the table was created, which could be different from the current setting.

All the previous options can be set individually, but you might want to avoid doing that because there are 256 (2^8) permutations to consider. You might want to set a few of the options individually, such as set arithabort or set arithignore. But by and large, you should either leave them all at their default settings or change them as a group to the ANSI SQL-92 behavior. These options can be enabled as a group by setting set ansi_defaults on.

The ability to set these options on a per-connection basis makes life interesting for you as a SQL Server application programmer. Your challenge is to recognize and deal with the fact that these settings will change the behavior of your code. Basically, that means you need to adopt some form of the following four strategies:

▼ **The Optimistic Approach**   Hope that none of your users or the person doing database administration will change such a setting. Augment your optimism by educating users not to change these settings.

■ **The Flexible Approach**   Try to write all your procedures to accommodate all permutations of the settings of all the various options (usually not practical).

■ **The Hard-Line Approach**   Explicitly set your preferences at startup and periodically recheck them to determine whether they have been subsequently altered. Simply refuse to run if the settings are not exactly what you expect.

▲ **The Clean Room Approach**   Have a "sealed" system that prevents anyone but you or a trusted aide from having direct access to change such a setting.

Whichever of these approaches you take is your choice, but recognize that if you do not think about the issue at all, you have basically settled for the Optimistic Approach. This approach is certainly adequate for many applications for which it is pretty clear that the user community would have neither the desire nor the ability to make environmental changes. But if you are deploying an application and the machine running SQL Server will be accessed by applications that you do not control, it is probably an overly simplistic approach. Philosophically, the Flexible Approach is nice, but it probably is not realistic unless the application is quite simple.

You can change the SQL Server default values for the server as a whole by using SP_CONFIGURE 'user options'. A specific user connection can then further refine the environment by issuing one of the specific SET statements we just discussed. The system value @@OPTIONS can then be examined by any connection to see the current settings for that connection. The @@OPTIONS value and the value to be set using SP_CONFIGURE 'user options' are a bit mask with the values depicted in Table 12-2.

Decimal Value	Hexadecimal Value	Option and Description
2	0x0002	IMPLICIT_TRANSACTIONS. Controls whether a transaction is started implicitly when a statement is executed.
4	0x0004	CURSOR_CLOSE_ON_COMMIT. Controls behavior of cursors once a commit has been performed.
8	0x0008	ANSI_WARNINGS. Controls truncation and NULLs in aggregate warnings.
16	0x0010	ANSI_PADDING. Controls padding of variables.
32	0x0020	ANSI_NULLS. Controls NULL handling by using equality operators.
64	0x0040	ARITHABORT. Terminates a query when an overflow or divide-by-zero error occurs during query execution.
128	0x0080	ARITHIGNORE. Returns NULL when an overflow or divide-by-zero error occurs during a query.

Table 12-2.   Bit Mask Values for SQL Server Options

Decimal Value	Hexadecimal Value	Option and Description
256	0x0100	QUOTED_IDENTIFIER. Differentiates between single and double quotation marks when evaluating an expression, allowing object names to include characters that would otherwise not conform to naming rules or would collide with a reserved word or a keyword.
512	0x0200	NOCOUNT. Turns off the message returned at the end of each statement that states how many rows were affected by the statement.
1024	0x0400	ANSI_NULL_DFLT_ON. Alters the session's behavior to use ANSI compatibility for nullability. New columns defined without explicit nullability will be defined to allow NULLs.
2048	0x0800	ANSI_NULL_DFLT_OFF. Alters the session's behavior to not use ANSI compatibility for nullability. New columns defined without explicit nullability will be defined to prohibit NULLs.

Table 12-2.   Bit Mask Values for SQL Server Options (continued)

By default, none of these options is enabled for SQL Server itself. Therefore, in a brand-new installation, the run value for SP_CONFIGURE 'user options' will be 0. A System Administrator can set this so that all connections have the same initial default settings. If you query the value of @@OPTIONS from an application that has not modified the environment, the value will also be 0.

However, be aware that many applications, or even the SQL Server ODBC or OLE DB drivers that the application uses, might have changed the environment. Note that this includes the SQL Server Query Analyzer, which uses ODBC. To change the default behavior, simply set the corresponding bit by doing a bitwise OR with the previous value. For example, suppose that your run value is 512, which indicates that NOCOUNT is the only option turned on. You want to leave NOCOUNT enabled, but you also want to enable option value 32, which controls how NULLs are handled when using equality comparisons. You would simply pass the decimal value 544 (or 0×220) to SP_CONFIGURE 'user options', which is the result of doing a bitwise OR between the two options (for example, SELECT 32|512).

You can examine current options that have been set using DBCC USER OPTIONS. The output is similar to the code below.

```
Set Option      Value
----------      ----------
textsize        64512
language        us_english
dateformat      mdy
datefirst       7
arithabort      SET
nocount         SET
```

This DBCC command shows only options that have been set—it does not show all the current settings for SP_CONFIGURE 'user options'. But you can also decode your current connection settings fairly easily from @@OPTIONS using something like this:

```
SELECT "IMPLICIT TRANSACTIONS", CASE WHEN
    (@@OPTIONS & 0x0002 >> 0) THEN 'ON' ELSE 'OFF' END
UNION
SELECT "CURSOR_CLOSE_ON_COMMIT", CASE WHEN
    (@@OPTIONS & 0x0004 >> 0) THEN 'ON' ELSE 'OFF' END
UNION
SELECT "ANSI_WARNINGS",CASE WHEN (@@OPTIONS & 0x0008 >> 0) THEN
    'ON' ELSE 'OFF' END
UNION
```

```
SELECT "ANSI_PADDINGS", CASE WHEN (@@OPTIONS & 0x0010 >> 0) THEN
    'ON' ELSE 'OFF' END
UNION
SELECT "ANSI_NULLS", CASE WHEN (@@OPTIONS & 0x0020 >> 0) THEN 'ON'
    ELSE 'OFF' END
UNION
SELECT "ARITHABORT", CASE WHEN (@@OPTIONS & 0x0040 >> 0) THEN 'ON'
    ELSE 'OFF' END
UNION
SELECT "ARITHIGNORE", CASE WHEN (@@OPTIONS & 0x0080 >> 0)
    THEN 'ON' ELSE 'OFF' END
UNION
SELECT "QUOTED_IDENTIFIER", CASE WHEN (@@OPTIONS & 0x0100 >> 0)
    THEN 'ON' ELSE 'OFF' END
UNION
SELECT "NOCOUNT", CASE WHEN (@@OPTIONS & 0x0200 >> 0) THEN 'ON'
    ELSE 'OFF' END
UNION
SELECT "ANSI_NULL_DFLT_ON", CASE WHEN (@@OPTIONS & 0x0400 >> 0)
    THEN 'ON' ELSE 'OFF' END
UNION
SELECT "ANSI_NULL_DFLT_OFF", CASE WHEN (@@OPTIONS & 0x0800 >> 0)
    THEN 'ON' ELSE 'OFF' END
ORDER BY "OPTION"
```

Here is the result:

```
OPTION                    SETTING
----------------------    -------

ANSI_NULL_DFLT_OFF        OFF
ANSI_NULL_DFLT_ON         OFF
ANSI_NULLS                OFF
ANSI_PADDINGS             OFF
ANSI_WARNINGS             OFF
ARITHABORT                OFF
ARITHIGNORE               OFF
CURSOR_CLOSE_ON_COMMIT    OFF
IMPLICIT_TRANSACTIONS     OFF
NOCOUNT                   ON
QUOTED_IDENTIFIER         OFF
```

Unfortunately, running the previous SELECT statement will not give you a complete picture. As you have seen previously, many of the options, especially those involving NULL handling, can also be changed at the database level by using SP_DBOPTION. To really get the full picture, you must examine @@OPTIONS for your current session in addition to SP_DBOPTION for your current database.

Locale-Specific SET Options

Beware of the locale-specific SET options! SET DATEFORMAT and SET DATEFIRST change the recognized default date format. If DATEFORMAT is changed to *dmy* instead of the (United States) default *mdy*, a date such as '12/10/98' will be interpreted as October 12, 1998. A good strategy for dates is to always use the International Standards Organization (ISO) format *yyyymmdd*, which is recognized no matter what the setting of DATEFORMAT is.

DATEFIRST affects what is considered the first day of the week. By default (in the United States), it has the value 7 (Sunday). Date functions that work with the day-of-week as a value between 1 and 7 will be affected by this setting. These day-of-week values can be confusing, since their numbering depends on the DATEFIRST value; but the values for DATEFIRST do not change. For example, as far as DATEFIRST is considered, Sunday's value is always 7. But having then designated Sunday (7) as DATEFIRST, if you executed the statement SELECT DATEPART(dw,GETDATE()) and your date falls on a Sunday, the statement will return 1. You just defined Sunday to be the first day of the week, so 1 is correct.

SUMMARY

Throughout this book, we have discussed nearly every substantial issue that you are likely to encounter during the administration of your SQL Server. We have examined closely each of the common—and many of the uncommon—parts of the SQL Server installation to help expose the areas you must be aware of to ensure that your SQL Server is as healthy and happy as possible. In other words, we have tried to provide you with the tools you need to ensure that you have maximized the Mean Time Between Server Failures (MTBSF).

Moreover, we have focused on many of the specific techniques, objects, and management tools that you will need to take advantage of to ensure that your SQL Server is not just stable, but also performs at the best possible levels. In this chapter, in specific, we have focused on the majority of the troubleshooting issues that you are likely to encounter during the ongoing administration of your SQL Server. We have provided you with the tools and information you need to address those issues.

Throughout this book, our goal has been to provide you with the best information—and where appropriate, direction—to help ensure that you have the best possible SQL Server environment. In some cases, this focus has resulted in our *not* giving you specific suggestions about how to implement a solution (for example, replication), but rather direction on what types of solutions work best for different types of environments.

In closing this book, we would just like to emphasize that, while there are any number of important players in the deployment of database solutions for your company—from the application developers who build the front-end to the Web developers who build your Internet applications to yourself—the database administrator is the most important player in the ongoing performance of your server. We hope that you will take the tools that we have provided you and use them to the best possible advantage for your environment.

CHAPTER 13

Understanding Transact-SQL

No matter how much you learn about the various graphical tools that are included with SQL Server, at some point in time you are probably going to want to accomplish something that simply cannot be done with a graphical tool, and you will be forced to deal with Transact-SQL. Additionally, many administrators find that once they get familiar with the language and practice a bit, they actually prefer to manage and manipulate SQL Server using its natural language through the Query Analyzer, or a similar tool that will let you write Transact-SQL statements and run them directly against the server.

This chapter will teach you the basics of Transact-SQL. In the following pages, you will learn about the different types of statements that make up the language, and how to best use them to your advantage. Once you have the basic statements down, you can then take some of the modifying elements in the language and combine them with basic statement types to create powerful and creative scripts for your SQL Servers.

UNDERSTANDING STATEMENT TYPES

At its core, Transact-SQL is divided into three types of statements or language components that make up the most common tasks that a SQL server must perform. These statement types are Data Definition, Data Manipulation, and Data Control Language statements. Simply put, you use Data Definition Language (DDL) statements to create a database and database objects, Data Manipulation Language (DML) statements to manipulate data and obtain result sets, and Data Control Language (DCL) statements to effect security by controlling which users can see or modify the data.

There are some additional modifying elements in Transact-SQL that are an integral part of the language, but we will begin by defining the basic statement types and then expand on them later in the chapter.

Data Definition Language (DDL) Statements

The three basic words that make up the heart of any DDL statement are "Create," "Alter," and "Drop." To create a complete statement, you must modify each of the words by adding the type of object and the variable attributes that make up the object class. For example, if you wanted to create a new table in the TEST database which stored contact information, you would first connect to the serer using Query Analyzer, and ensure that the TEST database was selected as the active database. Once you have connected to the server and attached to the correct database, you can create a new table by executing the following statement.

```
Create Table Contacts
    (FirstName varchar(20), LastName varchar(30), Phone char(12))
```

You can see in this statement that the keyword "Create" is the primary function of the statement. The statement will create a new table called Contacts in the TEST database. The additional elements in the lower portion of the statement are the column names and datatypes that will make up the columns, or fields, of the table. In the example, the Contacts tables will have three columns: FirstName, LastName, and Phone. These columns are character-based datatypes with sizes also specified. Varchar(20), for example, defines a column that is variable character, 20 characters wide.

NOTE: It is important at this point for you to focus on the first part of the statement. We include modifying elements in the example only so that the statement will be accurate. Don't worry too much if you don't understand the datatypes yet.

In the same way that you created the Contacts table, you can remove the table or change its structure using the Drop and Alter statements respectively. Where the Drop Table command needs only the name of the table as a variable in order to operate, the Alter Table statement requires you to apply just as many or perhaps more variables than the Create Table statement did.

Data Control Language (DCL) Statements

You are actually already familiar with most of the DCL statements from the chapter on security. You learned what statements would let you Grant, Deny, or Revoke permissions for objects and statements to database users. So that this chapter is complete, the following example should remind you of how you would assign permission to user Cathy to enable her to select information from the Contacts table.

```
Grant Select on Contacts to Cathy
```

As you can see, since the DCL keyword "Grant" is the beginning of the statement, you can infer that you are assigning a positive permission to Cathy from the use of this word. The next important element in the statement is the word "on," which tells SQL Server that an object is about to be referenced, whereupon the Contacts table is listed. The final part of the statement tells SQL server that the permission will be granted to the user Cathy.

Data Manipulation Language (DML) Statements

DML statements are by far the most common statement type that new users will become familiar with initially. This is because the first thing that users usually want to do is read, insert, and change data in the database. Manipulating the data that is stored in the tables is what DML statements are all about. For example, the following statement is a classic simple query.

```
Select * from Contacts
```

This example simply obtains a result set that includes all information from the Contacts table. Said another way, this statement will ask SQL Server for a list of all the records in the Contacts table and display the results. Other examples of DML statements include Insert, Update, and Delete. One way to keep this type of statement separate from the other types is to remember that DML statements affect data instead of data structures.

Elements of Control

Statements alone cannot create a well-written Transact-SQL script. To complete the picture, you need to have a variety of words, phrases, and variable object identifiers that make the script complete. For example, if you were to try and select data without using a word like FROM or the object identifier Contacts, as listed in the preceding example, the statement as a whole would be incomplete and fail. These additionally added elements of control within the Transact-SQL language are what fill in the spaces between statement types and make the scripts whole.

There is a wide variety of additional control words and methods for referencing objects and statement types within any single script. While a complete discussion on all of these words is well beyond the scope of this book, as we look at some of the more common scripts that you will write as an administrator, you will learn how to use and place some of these words and, by the end of this chapter, will have a sound foundation for learning Transact-SQL.

UNDERSTANDING THE DIVISION OF TASKS

The first thing you need to understand when learning to write in Transact-SQL is that there is a distinct division of tasks. Said another way, in any single batch of statements, you will be trying to accomplish a specific goal. When you look at the goal and compare it to the types of Transact-SQL statements that are available, you will quickly see that each type of statement lends itself to a specific type of goal. In the following sections, we will take you through a series of tasks in what we think is a logical order for an administrator.

> ### From the Field
>
> In this chapter, you are going to write quite a few statements in Transact-SQL. We recommend that you save each statement as you write it so that you can easily open and run them again. This practice is invaluable in the real world, and if you get into the habit now, you are likely to avoid a lot of retyping of statements later.

Creating Objects

Among the first things that you will want to do with Transact-SQL will be to create databases and database objects. Looking back at the types of available statements, you will find that DDL statement types, combined with some additional elements of control, will let you create scripts that create a database and the objects that it contains. For example, if you want to create a database called TEST, you will begin the statement with the DDL keyword CREATE. To define what is being created, you will add the keyword DATABASE, which is simply an object class identifier. You will have to give the new database a name and any special parameters that you want the database to have, including things like file size or location. You are not, however, required to include anything but the CREATE DATABASE statement and a database name. The complete script would look like this:

```
Create Database Test
```

This statement tells SQL Server that you want to create a new database, with the name TEST. SQL Server will then use the MODEL database as a template for the creation of the new database and will create your new database. If you issue this statement from within Query Analyzer and then switch back to Enterprise Manager, you can compare the MODEL and TEST databases. You will find that they are duplicates in every way but name.

Since all data in SQL Server is stored in tables, your next task is likely to be the creation of a table in the database test. There is really very little difference in the way this statement is written because we are still using the DDL keyword CREATE. This time, however, we will use the object identifier TABLE to tell SQL Server that you want to create a new table.

The first step is to tell SQL Server what database you want to work in. This action requires the use of an additional control element known as the USE keyword. USE is a Transact-SQL statement all by itself; it lets you specify the database upon which your statement will perform. You could accomplish the same goal by setting the current database to TEST in Query Analyzer, but we feel that it is a good idea to include a USE statement in all scripts because it prevents errors from happening if you should forget to set the current database. The script will begin then with this text:

```
Use Test
```

Using the ENTER key, line down from the USE statement so that the script is easier to read. You should note here that we also like to indent parts of a script to separate the tasks it performs. To indent text, simply hit the TAB key. Now you will enter the CREATE TABLE statement, along with the name of the new table, and the columns that will make up the table. Let's use the earlier example and create the Contacts table here. At this point, your CREATE TABLE script will look like this:

```
Use Test
    Create Table Contacts
    (FirstName varchar(20), LastName varchar(30), Phone char(12))
```

Notice that the CREATE TABLE statement is one line below the USE statement, and that the column names and types are one line below the CREATE TABLE statement. Writing the script this way makes it easier to read, easier to troubleshoot, and can actually prevent some errors from happening when you start using more advanced scripting techniques. So get into the habit now and save yourself a lot of stress later!

Creating objects of any kind within a database follows the same logic. Each type of object will have different parameters and will require a slightly different set of syntax. However, since they will all make use of the CREATE keyword, you can easily find the exact syntax for any object by searching Books Online. For example, if you wanted the complete syntax for creating a stored procedure, you would search for "Create Stored Procedure" in Books Online. From the resulting page, you will find links that will show you how to create a stored procedure both in Enterprise Manager and using Transact-SQL.

Controlling Data

Okay, so you have a database with a bunch of objects in it, storing a whole bunch of data. The first thing that usually pops into your mind is "How do I get to the data?" From a Transact-SQL perspective, controlling data is performed using DML statements, combined with some additional control elements that let you specify what data to affect, and where. The most basic of these types of statements is the SELECT statement. SELECT is a keyword that lets you read information from a database object. It tells SQL Server that you want to retrieve information from an object like a Table or a View.

Remember, the first thing that you will want to do is tell SQL Server what database you would like to work in. So this script will also begin with a USE statement. After that, you will use the SELECT statement to obtain the data that you want from the listed object. For example, if you wanted to obtain and review all of the data that has been stored in the Contacts Table that we created earlier, you would use the SELECT statement, followed by the name of the table, and any criteria that restricted the amount of information that is to be returned. If you want to return all of the information from the table, your script will look like this:

```
Use Test
    Select * from Contacts
```

In the example, you use the asterisk (*) as a wildcard that means "everything." If you type this statement into Query Analyzer, the resulting information displayed will be all data, from all columns, in the Contacts Table.

Now let's assume that you only want to obtain a list of contacts whose last name is Smith. This time we will create the statement with some specific criteria that tells SQL Server to restrict the result set. The primary keyword used for such restrictions is WHERE. Let's look at the following script:

```
Use Test
    Select * from Contacts where LastName = 'Smith'
```

NOTE: Table names are case-sensitive in scripts.

In this example, we have written the script the same way, but added the keyword WHERE, chosen a restricting column of LastName, and specified the restrictive criteria to be Smith. Because we are actually specifying stored information and want an exact match, we must enclose the criteria word Smith in single quotes. If you were trying to get the same information from a person, you would probably say something like "Show me all the contact records for anyone named Smith." In the example, you are saying the same thing, but using Transact-SQL because SQL Server does not understand English.

NOTE: Using English Query, you can create applications that understand English.

Now, let's suppose that your Contacts table is really big and has thousands of names in it; if that were the case, even restricting the statement to return only those people with a last name of Smith might return hundreds of records. If you were searching for a person whose name was Sally Smith, the statement would need to be altered a little bit more. In addition to the WHERE clause, you will need to include the keyword AND, which tells SQL Server that more than one set of criteria is being applied. Look at the following example:

```
Use Test
    Select * from Contacts where LastName = 'Smith' and FirstName = 'Sally'
```

In this example, you are telling SQL Server that you are looking for a record in the Contacts Table of the TEST database, where the column LastName contains the word "Smith," and for the same record, the column FirstName contains the word "Sally." Take note here that we do not repeat the word "WHERE," because the keyword is only required once in the statement.

NOTE: If you have been following along exactly and creating the database and objects as we go, you will likely be disappointed because there is no result set returned for the query. This is simply because there is no data in the Contacts table unless you put it there! To get a result set that actually shows you something, try this statement from Query Analyzer:

```
Use Northwind
    Select * from Categories
```

So now you can look into the tables of a database and see what data is there, either in a full list or by restricting information so that you only see what you want. Now let's take a look at the next most common database task, which is placing data into the tables. As an administrator, you are typically not the individual who will actually place data into tables one record at a time; that task is typically the responsibility of end users. It is, however, important for you to understand how this task is accomplished using Transact-SQL so that you can better understand what the users are actually doing, no matter what kind of application is actually displayed to them at the desktop.

Data is placed into tables using the INSERT keyword. INSERT tells SQL Server that you want to place a record into a specific table. The simple form of the INSERT statement lets you insert a single row into a given table as a single line of Transact-SQL. Let's look at the following example:

```
Use test
    INSERT INTO contacts VALUES('Sally', 'Smith', '555-1212',)
```

The exemplified statement is pretty easy to understand up until we get to the VALUES keyword. VALUES tells SQL Server that the information that follows are data values that should be inserted into the table. The values are then listed in the same order that the columns of the Table were created. If you were to look back at the example where we created the Contacts table, you would see that the table was created with three columns, which were (in order from left to right) FirstName, LastName, and Phone. It is important to know and understand the structure of the table in order to use the INSERT statement properly.

NOTE: Applications that end users work with typically have fields for the insertion of data. The application then uses these fields to create a properly formatted T-SQL statement so that the end user does not have to learn a language or understand the structure of the table.

Knowing what we do about the table when we look at the INSERT statement, it is logical that the words "INSERT INTO Contacts" tells SQL Server where to insert the data. After that, the VALUES keyword tells SQL Server that the next bit of information will be the data. If we then read the values from left to right, the word "Sally" is placed into the FirstName column, the word "Smith" is placed into the LastName column, and "555-1212" is placed into the Phone column.

Following logic, if you add another line with different values below the first entry, more values would be inserted into the table. Take, for example, the following statement:

```
Use test
INSERT INTO contacts VALUES('Mark', 'Linsenbardt', '446-8242',)
INSERT INTO contacts VALUES('Shane', 'Stigler', '432-8585',)
```

This example would insert two more rows into the Contacts table. There are, of course, more advanced methods of inserting data with Transact-SQL, but since this is just an overview of basic query techniques, such advanced topics are beyond the scope of our discussion.

If you used the examples in this chapter to create the Contacts table, and then populated it using the examples we have given here, when you execute a select statement against the table, requesting all records, you will receive a result set containing three records. As a review, let's try it. Connect to SQL Server using Query Analyzer and execute the following statement:

```
Use Test
    Select * from contacts
```

When finished, you should see a result set like this:

```
Sally Smith 555-1212
Mark Linsenbardt 446-8242
Shane Stigler 432-8585
```

Now let's throw a little control into the statement and organize this list in alphabetical order. To control the sort of result set, you will use the ORDER BY statement at the end of your script and specify the column that you want to sort the list by. The new statement will look like this:

```
Use Test
    Select * from contacts
    Order by FirstName
```

When executed, the result set will change to display the same information, which is now sorted in ascending order according to the values found in the FirstName column like this:

```
Mark Linsenbardt 446-8242
Sally Smith 555-1212
Shane Stigler 432-8585
```

The ORDER BY statement defaults to using an ascending order when it sorts; you need to include nothing else to achieve this sorted list. If, however, you want to create a list that is sorted in descending

order, you must include the optional modifier DESC at the end of the
ORDER BY statement. So if you want the list to be displayed in
reverse order, modify the statement to look like this:

```
Use Test
    Select * from contacts
    Order by FirstName DESC
```

When you execute the statement this way, the list returned will
now look like this:

```
Shane Stigler 432-8585
Sally Smith 555-1212
Mark Linsenbardt 446-8242
```

To review, you now know how to create a database, create a table,
insert records into the table, and select records from the table either
in their entirety or by restricting information, and while controlling
the sort order of the resulting data. The next logical step in
controlling data is modifying information in a table.

Modifying records is really just a matter of changing keywords
when you write a statement. To accomplish this, you will use the
UPDATE and SET keywords. The UPDATE statement tells SQL
Server that you want to change an entry in an existing record or
records, and the SET keyword tells SQL Server which columns you
want to change, and what you want to change them to. We will say
right up front that this is a potentially harmful statement if you are
not careful, because the UPDATE statement can modify a single
record, or all of the records in a table, depending on how you write
the statement.

Let's look at an example that changes all the records in a table:

```
Use Test
    UPDATE contacts
    SET FirstName = 'Bob'
```

This example is quite literally the terror of most administrators
because it does not specify a record. When executed, this statement
will change all of the first names in the table to Bob. Let's try this just so
you can see what happens. First, execute the statement in the example

above. When finished, the columns will have changed and you will receive a message that says three rows have been updated. Now let's look at the data. Run the following statement against the table:

```
Use test
    Select * from contacts.
```

When this statement is executed, you will receive a result set that looks like this:

```
Bob Smith 555-1212
Bob Linsenbardt 446-8242
Bob Stigler 432-8585
```

As you can see, the UPDATE statement destroyed the validity of the data in our table because it changed all of the records. The problem that we have is because the UPDATE statement did not have a WHERE clause to identify which records should change. Imagine the impact of this kind of statement in a table that had thousands of records and you will begin to understand why administrators typically do not want end users to have the rights to run their own handwritten statements against any data store.

In order to learn how to properly write an UPDATE statement, we are going to use individual statements using the WHERE clause to fix each record in our table. Of course, if you had a backup of the database, or if you have saved the scripts that we have written in this chapter, you could fix the problem by restoring or by re-creating the database and table from scratch using saved scripts.

Since the first record in the table used to be Sally Smith, we will fix that one first. Take a look at the following statement:

```
Use Test
    UPDATE contacts
     SET FirstName = 'Sally'
    Where LastName = 'Smith'
    And Phone = '555-1212'
```

In this example, we have used the WHERE clause (keyword) and also the AND clause to specify a specific record upon which the

UPDATE statement should work. When you have executed this statement, the data in one record changes and you will receive a notification that data in one record was updated. If you run the select statement again, the result set will now look like this:

```
Sally Smith 555-1212
Bob Linsenbardt 446-8242
Bob Stigler 432-8585
```

Obviously, you can use the same technique to fix the other two records. Said another way, to return the table to the condition that it was in prior to the evil UPDATE statement that had no WHERE clause, execute the following statement:

```
Use test
UPDATE contacts
     SET FirstName = 'Mark'
     Where LastName = 'Linsenbardt'
     And Phone = '446-8242'
Go
UPDATE contacts
     SET FirstName = 'Shane'
     Where LastName = 'Stigler'
     And Phone = '432-8585'
```

If you are paying attention, you will notice that we included another element of control here in the form of the word "GO." GO is a keyword that tells SQL Server to execute this part of the transaction and to begin again at the next line. We must use this word here in order to separate the two UPDATE statements. While we could run a single UPDATE statement for each record, we cannot include them both in the same script without separating them. This is a restriction built into certain types of statements that cannot be grouped together in Transact-SQL. Each set of scripted language found between GO statements is called a *batch*. Learning which statements can be grouped together in a single batch, and which cannot, is a matter of time, practice, and patience. As you write more and more T-SQL, you will get a feel for which statements can or cannot be grouped in a batch.

When you have finished executing the statement, the date will have been changed back to its original condition and will look like this:

```
Sally Smith 555-1212
Mark Linsenbardt 446-8242
Shane Stigler 432-8585
```

Let's pause for a second and review again. You now know how to create databases and tables, how to insert information into tables, how to select information from tables, and how to change information in tables. You additionally know how to restrict information for SELECT and UPDATE statements using the WHERE clause, and you know how to order a result set using the ORDER BY statement. Logically speaking, the next task you will want to know about is how to remove information from a table.

Removing information from a table involves the use of the DELETE keyword. The DELETE statement represents the same potential for damage that the UPDATE statement does, because without the use of a WHERE clause, the DELETE statement can remove all records from a table in a single execution. For example, execute the following statement:

```
Use Test
    DELETE FROM contacts
```

When finished, if you run a SELECT statement against the Contacts table, you will receive no result set because all of the records have been deleted. Now let's repopulate the table so that we can write a more accurate DELETE statement. Run the following script to place the three records back into the table.

```
Use test
INSERT INTO contacts VALUES('Sally', 'Smith', '555-1212',)
INSERT INTO contacts VALUES('Mark', 'Linsenbardt', '446-8242',)
INSERT INTO contacts VALUES('Shane', 'Stigler', '432-8585',)
```

This script uses techniques that you already know to re-create the information stored in the Contacts table. When finished, the table will have all three records.

Now let's suppose that your goal is to delete the record for Shane Stigler only. To create a properly formatted script that removes this record, execute the following statement:

```
Use test
     DELETE FROM contacts
     WHERE LastName = 'Stigler'
```

If you have been playing along with all of these scripts, you should have noticed that this statement would remove all entries in the table that have a last name of Stigler. If you had a listing for Shane, Sue, Don, Debbie, and Sharon, all who had the last name of Stigler, the script would have removed all five records with a single execution.

As a general rule, you should always write scripts that do exactly what you want, even if you believe that a more general script would accomplish the same goal. It is, after all, better to be safe than sorry. Keeping that in mind, if our goal was to remove the record for Shane Stigler, then we should have written the script like this:

```
Use test
DELETE FROM contacts
     WHERE LastName = 'Stigler
     AND FirstName = 'Shane'
```

Written this way, the script will remove only records that have a first name of Shane and a last name of Stigler. You should understand that if the table contained more than one Shane Stigler, the statement would remove them all. So let's make sure that we are removing only the Shane Stigler that we want to by including the AND word twice. Take a look at the new script:

```
Use test
     DELETE FROM contacts
     WHERE LastName = 'Stigler'
     AND FirstName = 'Shane'
     AND Phone = '432-8585'
```

Of course, if you were in a very rare scenario where there were two people with the same name who had the same phone number, but were actually different people, this statement would still remove them all. In such cases, you would have to use another field as a restriction, but we think that you probably understand the concept by now.

At this point you have a basic understanding of how to manipulate data. You can insert new records, select and view them, update records that need changing, and delete records that are no longer required. If you really want to take this information to new levels, we recommend that you obtain one of the database development titles from this series.

Controlling Objects

In order for the chapter to make sense, we had to show you how to create objects like databases and tables before we started working with data. Now that you have worked with data a little bit, we will expand on your control of objects.

In the same way that you can change existing data in a table using the UPDATE keyword, you can change the properties of a database object like a Table, a View, or even a Database using the keyword ALTER. ALTER is a statement unto itself that tells SQL Server that you want to change the properties of an existing database or database object.

Let's take, for example, the Contacts table. When we first created this table, it consisted of three columns: FirstName, LastName, and Phone. If we now want to modify this table to have a fourth column called Email, we would connect to SQL Server using Query Analyzer and execute the following script:

```
Use Test
    ALTER TABLE contacts
    ADD Email CHAR(30) NULL
```

This script will add the Email column to the table at the end of the existing columns, and additionally specifies that the column can contain null values. This is important because the new column will have no data in it, and you or another user will have to update the information in the table to contain the email addresses.

You can also use the ALTER statement to change the properties of an entire database, a view, a stored procedure, or anything that can be classified as a database object. The changing of any item requires only that you understand the particular properties of the object type. You can obtain this information directly from Books Online, but we again recommend that if you want to truly learn how to control SQL Server using its native language, you should obtain a database design or Transact-SQL dedicated title.

Like anything else, a database object that can be created and changed can also be removed. You can remove database objects using the DROP keyword. DROP tells SQL Server that you want the specified object to be removed. If, for example, you want to remove the Contacts table from the TEST database, you will connect to SQL Server using Query Analyzer and execute the following statement:

```
Use test
   Drop table Contacts
```

This statement will remove the table from the database. You should note there that SQL Server stores database information in the system catalog in case-sensitive format. In order to drop a table, you must specify its name using the proper case that was used when it was created.

You could also use the DROP command to remove an entire database. If, for example, you wanted to remove the TEST database entirely, you would execute this statement:

```
Use master
   Drop database Test
```

Again, upon completion of the statement, the TEST database will have been removed from SQL Server. Note that you cannot drop a database while a user is connected to it, while it is being loaded with data, or when it is configured as a publisher for replication.

Applying Security

Though at this point you already know how to apply security using Enterprise Manager, we thought it would be a good idea to include the method for doing so using Transact-SQL here so that your understanding of basic query writing would be complete.

As you have learned, there are different types of permissions such as SELECT, UPDATE, INSERT, and DELETE, each of which can exist in one of three conditional states called GRANT, DENY, and REVOKE. You already know that these permissive states determine what permissions a user has for any database object; what you may not know yet is that they get their names directly from the Transact-SQL keywords that you use to enforce security by directly applying T-SQL scripts.

To control the permissions of an object, you need to know what the security model is. Before using any of these statements, you should review the chapter on security and make a solid plan to determine the roles that will affect database security. Once you have a plan, however, applying security is really just a matter of using one of the DCL keywords, and then identifying the database object and the user. For example, if you wanted to apply the SELECT permission to the Contacts table to a database user named Sally, you would connect to SQL Server using Query Analyzer and execute the following script:

```
Use Test
    Grant select on contacts to sally
```

This statement tells SQL Server that you want to allow permissions on the Contacts table to user Sally. The statement will only work if there is a database object such as a table or view named Contacts (you cannot have two objects with the same name), and if there is a database user named Sally.

In the same way that you can grant permissions for an object, the statements to deny access to or revoke access from a user are similar. Look at the following statement:

```
Use Test
    Deny select on contacts to sally
```

This time the statement applies the deny permission to Sally, which, if you will recall, means that Sally does not have permission and cannot inherit permission from role membership.

Now look at this statement:

```
Use Test
    Revoke select on contacts to sally
```

In this example, we are removing SELECT permissions for the Contacts table from Sally, but are allowing that the SELECT permission could be inherited, if Sally is a member of a database role that has the SELECT permission. Notice that we have still used the word "TO" instead of the optional word "FROM." If you prefer, you can use the word "FROM" in place of the word "TO" and obtain the same results as seen in the following example:

```
Use Test
    Revoke select on contacts from sally
```

The two statements meet the same goal, and which word you use is really just a matter of choice.

Using the same logic, you can control higher levels of permissions so that you can control the permissions required to affect the properties of objects. Though SQL Server does not grant statement permissions to individual users by default, you will likely want to assign users the right to create views, tables, or other database objects within a specific database. You will use the same keywords to affect these permissions, changing only the latter parts of the script to reflect the desired goal. For example, if you wanted to let Sally create her own tables in the TEST database, you would execute a script like this:

```
Use Test
    Grant Create Table to Sally
```

You could also DENY or REVOKE permissions using the appropriate keywords.

Combining Techniques

Now that you have a functional foundation of basic techniques and keywords in Transact-SQL, let's take a look at how you can combine these different techniques into new, more powerful statements.

From the Field

Two words that you may find in scripts that are given to you are ALL and PRIVILEGES. These words are part of the ANSI standard, and are supported in the Microsoft versions of Transact-SQL for compatibility reasons. In the case of the ALL word, it is an acceptable value for granting all object permissions to a database user. You could, for example, write a script that looks like this:

```
Use Test
    Grant All on contacts to sally
```

This script would grant all of the available object permissions to Sally for the Contacts table. Sally would then have the SELECT, INSERT, UPDATE, DELETE, EXEC, and DRI permissions for the Contacts table. (You should remember reading about these permissions in the security chapter.) Optionally, you could include the word PRIVILEGES, though it would not affect the statement in any way. Look at this script:

```
Use Test
    Grant all privileges on contacts to sally
```

Note here that although the new statement includes another word, it is merely an option to you, and it performs the same way that the previous example did.

There is simply no way we could get into all the different ways to write a statement in Transact-SQL without filling another book with information. This example, however, will show you how you can combine certain elements into statements, and will hopefully help you decipher the statements written by others so that you can evaluate what is happening on your server.

For the purpose of this example, assume that once again your goal is to populate a table with information. This time, however, the data is already stored in another table, and you simply want to take the information from one table and place it into another.

For our example, we will use the Contacts table as a source for data and will create another table, which we will then populate. The first thing we need to do is create the new table. The following statement will create a new table that will be used as a mailing list:

```
Use Test
Create Table Mailing
    (FirstName varchar(20), LastName varchar(30))
```

Now that we have a new table, we populate it using data from the Contacts table like this:

```
Use Test
INSERT INTO mailing (FirstName, LastName)
    SELECT FirstName, LastName
    FROM Contacts
```

Look at the script carefully and you will see that we have combined the INSERT and SELECT statements to create a script that takes information from one table and places it in another. This script would be even more useful if we added some restrictions that limited the rows that get copied. For example, if we wanted to produce a list that contained only Mark and Shane and placed this information into the new table, our script would look like this:

```
Use Test
    INSERT INTO mailing (FirstName, LastName)
        SELECT FirstName, LastName
        FROM Contacts
        Where LastName = 'Linsenbardt' or 'Stigler'
```

As you can see, restricting this statement is no more difficult than restricting the simple SELECT or INSERT statements that you learned earlier. Most of Transact-SQL is like that, using a consistent set of rules throughout the language.

Another example of combining techniques would be selecting information from one table, using restrictions that are applied to a different table. This technique is especially useful when the information that you are searching for is divided amongst different tables. For this example, we will use the Contacts and Mailing tables. Take a look at this statement:

```
Use Test
    Select * from Contacts
    Where LastName in
        Select LastName from mailing where Phone = 446-4282
```

This statement tells SQL Server that it is looking for a specific name but that you cannot remember the name. You can remember the phone number, so you look for the phone number in another table, using that criteria to obtain the last name. It's true that in our example, you could have simply searched for the phone number in the Contacts table, but our tables are not normalized the way you would normally find them in a real database. So this technique will be very useful when applied to searches in live data environments. The example also uses the new keyword IN, which tells SQL Server to apply the criteria found in the following list to the beginning part of the statement. Said another way, SQL Server understands that it is going to perform a SELECT, that the SELECT will be restricted using a WHERE clause, and that the variables for the WHERE clause will be obtained using the SELECT statement that follows. Most professional database administrators would call this a simple example of a subquery, because the statement is a query in itself, which depends on a smaller query inside of itself to function.

Fully Qualified Object Names

Up until now, we have used simple names with the intention of making things easy to understand. There is a way, however, to reference objects in SQL Server that involves the use of a multipart name. This naming convention is very useful in many situations because it can reference an object by its server, its database, its owner, and finally, by the name of the object itself. In simple queries, it is usually enough to reference just the object name, but as your queries become more complex, referencing an object by its fully qualified name can be very helpful. If, for example, you were writing a query that spanned multiple servers, the use of a fully qualified name would be almost mandatory. Another example of where using fully qualified names is important would be in complex queries that involve selecting information from more than one database.

The structure of a fully qualified name is simple and uses the following format:

```
Server.Database.Owner.Object
```

So, for example, if the name of your server was SQLServer, then the fully qualified name of the Contacts table would be this:

```
SQLServer.Test.DBO.Contacts
```

The owner of the Contacts table is DBO based on the examples in this chapter, because we have been logged into SQL Server as SA, and the SA account is mapped directly to the database user DBO by default.

It is important for you to understand that SQL Server expects you to use this naming convention, and that it makes assumptions when you do not. The following list will tell you what SQL Server will think if you omit a particular part of the fully qualified name:

▼ **Server**   SQL Server will default to using the local server, even if there are linked servers attached.

■ **Database**   SQL Server will use the current database.

▲ **Owner**   SQL Server will assume the context of the currently connected user.

Of course, you cannot leave off the object name, since the statement contains at least a basic name for the objects upon which to act.

Using these names is simply a matter of changing the way you type. If, for example, you wanted to perform a standard complete SELECT on the Contacts table, the statement would look like this:

```
Select * from SQLServer.Test.DBO.Contacts
```

In this example, you will notice that there is no USE statement. This is because we no longer need to be in the correct database to execute the statement. The use of a fully qualified name ensures that we are running the statement against the correct database and object.

> ## From the Field
> The use of fully qualified names in stored scripts must be evaluated. If the database is copied to a new server, the stored scripts will need to be altered. Likewise, if the object is likely to ever be copied to another database, the stored scripts would no longer function unless changed to meet the new conditions.

Introducing Joins

If we had to pick just one thing that most people do not understand when it comes to relational databases of any kind, it would be the concept of joins. We will, therefore, close our introduction to Transact-SQL with a discussion on joins.

Joins are a way for you to tell SQL Server that the information in two tables is related to each other. Once upon a time, when databases were young, we stored all of the information in the database in large tables that included everything. For example, if we wanted to store information about classes and students, we would have created a table that contained fields (columns) like FirstName, LastName, SSN, ClassName, ClassDate, and perhaps some other fields for addresses and such, but you get the idea. The problem with this design is that it represents the loss of storage space because each time a student takes a class, information about the class, including the date and name of the class, is duplicated. Likewise, each time a class is held, information about students may be duplicated. Said another way, a student who has attended four classes has his name, address, and SSN recorded four times. This structure is not really a problem for small environments, but for larger organizations or for data that is stored for long periods of time, the duplication amounts to lots and lots of disk space.

Thanks to the efforts of a shining few, we no longer store information this way. Nowadays we store information in multiple tables. For example, to store the same information about students and classes we might now use two tables, one that stores student information and one that stores class information. Truthfully, a better design would be three tables, but we have found that people best learn joins by using only two tables, so we will restrict our discussion and examples to that number.

In order for the information between the tables to make sense when we retrieve it in both tables, we need to store one piece of information that establishes a link to the other. At this point in the design process, you need to decide which table will be the primary table and which will be the secondary table. With only two tables, the decision is easy; you simply pick the table that contains the least amount of records to be the primary table. In our example, we have chosen to use two tables named Students and Classes. Students will be the primary table because we will only enter a student one time in that table, while we will enter more than one class into the Classes table because more than one student may take the same class. The following script will create the Classes and Student tables and will populate them with some records:

```
use test
create table Classes
        (SSN char(11), ClassName Char(40), ClassDate Char(30))
GO
Create table Students
        (FirstName Char(10), LastName char(20), SSN char(11))
Go
INSERT INTO Students VALUES('Mark', 'Linsenbardt', '111-11-1111')
INSERT INTO Students VALUES('Shane', 'Stigler', '222-22-2222')
INSERT INTO Students VALUES('Sally', 'Smith', '333-33-3333')
INSERT INTO Students VALUES('Jerry', 'Raymond', '444-44-4444')
INSERT INTO Classes VALUES('111-11-1111' , 'Basic SQL' , 'January 1
000')
INSERT INTO Classes VALUES('111-11-1111' , 'Loving Math' , 'May 21 1999')
INSERT INTO Classes VALUES('222-22-2222' , 'English 101' , 'June 10
999')
INSERT INTO Classes VALUES('333-33-3333' , 'Loving Math' , 'May 21 1999')
```

When executed, your TEST database will now contain two new tables, each of which contains four records. Note here that there are actually only three classes being stored but that student Mark has taken two classes and has two records in the Classes table. Note also that although Jerry has been entered as a student, he has attended no classes yet.

Let's run a couple of SELECT statements to see what data is in the two tables. To check what is in the Students table, the following script will do:

```
Use Test
Select * from Students
```

This script will return the following result set:

```
FirstName   LastName              SSN
----------  --------------------  ----------
Mark        Linsenbardt           111-11-1111
Shane       Stigler               222-22-2222
Sally       Smith                 333-33-3333
Jerry       Raymond               444-44-4444
```

As you can see, there are in fact four records in the Students table. Now let's examine the Classes table:

```
Use Test
Select * from Classes
```

The following result set is returned:

```
SSN           ClassName                       ClassDate
------------  ------------------------------  --------------
111-11-1111   Basic SQL                       January 1 2000
222-22-2222   English 101                     June 10 1999
333-33-3333   Loving Math                     May 21 1999
111-11-1111   Loving Math                     May 21 1999
```

We have constructed this set of tables so that we can show you how information selected from tables can be incorrect when the join is absent, or if the wrong join type has been used. To begin with, let's try and select information from the tables without a join. Take a look at the following script:

```
SELECT Students.FirstName, Students.LastName, Students.SSN,
    Classes.ClassName, Classes.ClassDate
    FROM Students, Classes
```

This script uses fully qualified names to obtain the first and last names, the SSN, the class names, and the class dates from the two tables. This script will produce the following result set:

```
ClassName              ClassDate                FirstName   LastName
-----------------      --------------------     ----------  ----------

Basic SQL              January 1 2000           Mark        Linsenbardt
English 101            June 10 1999             Mark        Linsenbardt
Loving Math            May 21 1999              Mark        Linsenbardt
Loving Math            May 21 1999              Mark        Linsenbardt
Basic SQL              January 1 2000           Shane       Stigler
English 101            June 10 1999             Shane       Stigler
Loving Math            May 21 1999              Shane       Stigler
Loving Math            May 21 1999              Shane       Stigler
Basic SQL              January 1 2000           Sally       Smith
English 101            June 10 1999             Sally       Smith
Loving Math            May 21 1999              Sally       Smith
Loving Math            May 21 1999              Sally       Smith
Basic SQL              January 1 2000           Jerry       Raymond
English 101            June 10 1999             Jerry       Raymond
Loving Math            May 21 1999              Jerry       Raymond
Loving Math            May 21 1999              Jerry       Raymond
```

As you can see, this result set is completely wrong. There are 16 resulting records which came from two tables that do not contain 16 rows combined. This happened because SQL Server did not know how to return the results, and so returned a complete list of each table. Because there are two tables involved, SQL Server combined the answers, making single row answers for the two tables, even though no relationship was established. The end result is that SQL Server returns a row for each record in *both* tables. For each record in the Students table, SQL Server returns four records from the classes table. For each record in the Classes table, SQL Server returns four records from the Students table. Said another way, SQL Server produces a result set that is the number of rows in the left table multiplied by the number of rows in the table on the right. In our example, the contents of both tables is four, so SQL Server produces 4 × 4 rows, which is, of course, 16.

Since we obviously cannot use the information from this result set, we need to establish a join that will relate the two tables together. There are basically only three types of joins: inner joins, outer joins, and self joins. Outer joins are then divided into full outer joins, left outer joins, and right outer joins.

The first type of join we will look at is the inner join. Due to differences in many database application types, and various methods of learning, you will sometimes hear other database professionals use the term *equi-join* to describe an inner join. An inner join returns all rows from both tables that contain a matching entry for the field or column that the join is built on. The following script is an example of how an inner join would impact our query:

```
Use Test
SELECT Students.FirstName, Students.LastName, Students.SSN,
    Classes.ClassName, Classes.ClassDate
FROM Students INNER JOIN
    Classes ON Students.SSN = Classes.SSN
```

This script will produce a result set like this:

FirstName	LastName	SSN	ClassName	ClassDate
Mark	Linsenbardt	111-11-1111	Basic SQL	January 1 2000
Shane	Stigler	222-22-2222	English 101	June 10 1999
Sally	Smith	333-33-3333	Loving Math	May 21 1999
Mark	Linsenbardt	111-11-1111	Loving Math	May 21 1999

As you can see, this result is much more accurate. The use of the inner join creates a result set that is accurate. This join works because the information in the SSN field is the same in both tables. Since it is the common field, it is the field that we base the relationship, or the join, on. If you have been paying close attention, you will notice that the result set does not contain a record for Jerry Raymond, who is a student.

The reason for this is that Jerry has no record in the Classes table, since the specification for inner join is to return only those records with matching values. SQL Server finds no matching record for Jerry in the Classes table, and so omits information about Jerry from the result set.

Now suppose that what you wanted to obtain from your query was a list of all students and classes that they have attended. You want this list so that you can monitor the progress of your students and assign them to the next class. In the case of students like Jerry, you will want to assign him to his first class, so you want the result set to return ALL rows from the Students table, and matching rows from the Classes table.

To accomplish this goal, you must use an inner join. An inner join tells SQL Server that you want ALL of the rows from one table and matching rows from the related table. How the inner join does this depends on how you write the statement. Take a look at this script:

```
Use Test
SELECT Students.FirstName, Students.LastName, Students.SSN,
    Classes.ClassName, Classes.ClassDate
FROM Students LEFT OUTER JOIN
    Classes ON Students.SSN = Classes.SSN
```

This script uses a left outer join technique. The reason is simply that we have referenced the Students table first in the script. If you look again, you will notice that the columns from the Students table are referenced first. If you were doing this using a query builder like the one included with Enterprise Manager, or even the one included with Access, there would be a list of tables at the top of the screen, and the Students table would be the first listed on the left-hand side. Since the

Students table is referenced first, it is logically on the left because we read from left to right. So, if we want all records from the Students table, we use a left outer join. The result set will look like this:

```
FirstName   LastName      SSN           ClassName     ClassDate
---------   -----------   -----------   -----------   --------------

Mark        Linsenbardt   111-11-1111   Basic SQL     January 1 2000
Mark        Linsenbardt   111-11-1111   Loving Math   May 21 1999
Shane       Stigler       222-22-2222   English 101   June 10 1999
Sally       Smith         333-33-3333   Loving Math   May 21 1999
Jerry       Raymond       444-44-4444   NULL          NULL
```

As you can see, this script returns ALL of the rows from the Students table, matching rows from the Classes table, and inserts the word NULL for those entries in Students that have no match in Classes.

If we had written the script so that the Classes table was on the right, we would have to use a right outer join to accomplish the same goal. The script would look like this:

```
SELECT Classes.ClassName, Classes.ClassDate,
    Students.FirstName, Students.LastName, Students.SSN
FROM Classes RIGHT OUTER JOIN
    Students ON Classes.SSN = Students.SSN
```

And the result set, while containing the same information, is changed in order and looks like this:

```
ClassName     ClassDate        FirstName   LastName      SSN
-----------   --------------   ---------   -----------   -----------

Basic SQL     January 1 2000   Mark        Linsenbardt   111-11-1111
Loving Math   May 21 1999      Mark        Linsenbardt   111-11-1111
English 101   June 10 1999     Shane       Stigler       222-22-2222
Loving Math   May 21 1999      Sally       Smith         333-33-3333
NULL          NULL             Jerry       Raymond       444-44-4444
```

The difference between a left and right outer join is not really that hard to grasp once you see how it works. The only thing that remains is to understand the full outer join and the self join. These two types do not really require any further examples now that you understand the first two. A full outer join is a join that returns all rows from *both* tables, but does not multiply them, creating a false result set. A self join is actually a somewhat rare type of join that joins a column in one table to another column in the same table. You would use a self join in a scenario such as an employee table, where all employees are listed. Suppose you wanted to get a list of all employees and their supervisors. Since all supervisors are also employees, you may need to construct a self join to ensure that the result set performs correctly, returning all employees and the employees that are also their supervisors in the same row.

In summary, you have learned in this chapter about the different kinds of statements in Transact-SQL. You have learned how to create objects, populate objects, work with data, combine basic techniques together to create powerful queries, and how to create joins. This basic knowledge will give you a great head start into the world of Transact-SQL, and will provide a solid foundation should you decide to learn more about the language from a work dedicated to that subject.

INDEX

D

E

F

G

H

S

▼ T

ABOUT THE CD

The enclosed CD-ROM includes SQL Server™ 2000 120-Day Enterprise Evaluation Edition.

Environment

Microsoft Windows®

Difference from Retail Product

Product expires 120 days after installation. Restricted license rights.

System Requirements

▼ PC with an Intel or compatible Pentium 166 MHz or higher processor

■ Microsoft Windows NT Sever 4.0 with Service Pack 5 or later; Windows NT Server 4.0 Enterprise Edition with Service Pack 5 or later; Windows 2000 Server, Windows 2000 Advanced Server, or Windows 2000 Datacenter Server operation system

■ Minimum of 64MB of RAM (128MB or more recommended)

■ Hard-disk space required

■ 95–270MB for database server; approximately 250MB for typical installation

■ 50MB minimum for Analysis Services; 130MB for typical installation

■ 80MB for Microsoft English Query (supported on Windows 2000 operating system but not logo certified)

■ Microsoft Internet Explorer 5.0 or later

■ CD-ROM drive

■ VGA or higher resolution monitor

▲ Microsoft Mouse or compatible pointing device

WARNING: BEFORE OPENING THE DISC PACKAGE, CAREFULLY READ THE TERMS AND CONDITIONS OF THE FOLLOWING COPYRIGHT STATEMENT AND LIMITED CD-ROM WARRANTY.

Copyright Statement

This software is protected by both United States copyright law and international copyright treaty provision. Except as noted in the contents of the CD-ROM, you must treat this software just like a book. However, you may copy it into a computer to be used and you may make archival copies of the software for the sole purpose of backing up the software and protecting your investment from loss. By saying, "just like a book," The McGraw-Hill Companies, Inc. ("Osborne/McGraw-Hill") means, for example, that this software may be used by any number of people and may be freely moved from one computer location to another, so long as there is no possibility of its being used at one location or on one computer while it is being used at another. Just as a book cannot be read by two different people in two different places at the same time, neither can the software be used by two different people in two different places at the same time.

Limited Warranty

Osborne/McGraw-Hill warrants the physical compact disc enclosed herein to be free of defects in materials and workmanship for a period of sixty days from the purchase date. If the CD included in your book has defects in materials or workmanship, please call McGraw-Hill at 1–800-217-0059, 9am to 5pm, Monday through Friday, Eastern Standard Time, and McGraw-Hill will replace the defective disc.

The entire and exclusive liability and remedy for breach of this Limited Warranty shall be limited to replacement of the defective disc, and shall not include or extend to any claim for or right to cover any other damages, including but not limited to, loss of profit, data, or use of the software, or special incidental, or consequential damages or other similar claims, even if Osborne/McGraw-Hill has been specifically advised of the possibility of such damages. In no event will Osborne/McGraw-Hill's liability for any damages to you or any other person ever exceed the lower of the suggested list price or actual price paid for the license to use the software, regardless of any form of the claim.

OSBORNE/McGRAW-HILL SPECIFICALLY DISCLAIMS ALL OTHER WARRANTIES, EXPRESS OR IMPLIED, INCLUDING BUT NOT LIMITED TO, ANY IMPLIED WARRANTY OF MERCHANT-ABILITY OR FITNESS FOR A PARTICULAR PURPOSE. Specifically, Osborne/McGraw-Hill makes no representation or warranty that the software is fit for any particular purpose, and any implied warranty of merchantability is limited to the sixty-day duration of the Limited Warranty covering the physical disc only (and not the software), and is otherwise expressly and specifically disclaimed.

This limited warranty gives you specific legal rights; you may have others which may vary from state to state. Some states do not allow the exclusion of incidental or consequential damages, or the limitation on how long an implied warranty lasts, so some of the above may not apply to you.

This agreement constitutes the entire agreement between the parties relating to use of the Product. The terms of any purchase order shall have no effect on the terms of this Agreement. Failure of Osborne/McGraw-Hill to insist at any time on strict compliance with this Agreement shall not constitute a waiver of any rights under this Agreement. This Agreement shall be construed and governed in accordance with the laws of New York. If any provision of this Agreement is held to be contrary to law, that provision will be enforced to the maximum extent permissible, and the remaining provisions will remain in force and effect.

NO TECHNICAL SUPPORT IS PROVIDED WITH THIS CD-ROM.